STRANGE CODE

STRANGE CODE

14 Esoteric Programming Languages to Make You Think

by Ronald T. Kneusel

no starch press

San Francisco

Printed in the United States of America

First printing

26 25 24 23 22   1 2 3 4 5

ISBN-13: 978-1-7185-0240-6 (print)
ISBN-13: 978-1-7185-0241-3 (ebook)

Publisher: William Pollock
Managing Editor: Jill Franklin
Production Manager: Rachel Monaghan
Production Editor: Miles Bond
Developmental Editor: Alex Freed
Cover Illustrator: Gina Redman
Interior Design: Octopod Studios
Technical Reviewer: Robert Kneusel
Copyeditor: George Hale
Proofreader: Scout Festa

For information on distribution, bulk sales, corporate sales, or translations, please contact No Starch Press, Inc. directly at info@nostarch.com or:

No Starch Press, Inc.
245 8th Street, San Francisco, CA 94103
phone: 1.415.863.9900
www.nostarch.com

Library of Congress Cataloging-in-Publication Data

```
Names: Kneusel, Ronald T., author.
Title: Strange code / by Ronald T. Kneusel.
Description: San Francisco, CA : No Starch Press, [2022] | Includes
    bibliographical references and index.
Identifiers: LCCN 2022011375 (print) | LCCN 2022011376 (ebook) | ISBN
    9781718502406 (print) | ISBN 9781718502413 (ebook)
Subjects: LCSH: Programming languages (Electronic computers)--Popular
    works. | Microcomputers--Programming--Popular works. | Programming
    languages (Electronic computers)--History.
Classification: LCC QA76.7 .K59 2022  (print) | LCC QA76.7  (ebook) | DDC
    005.13--dc23/eng/20220429
LC record available at https://lccn.loc.gov/2022011375
LC ebook record available at https://lccn.loc.gov/2022011376
```

[S]

To all the souls whose beautiful obsession gifted us with such wonderful esolangs.
The late nights were worth it.

About the Author

A programming language enthusiast, Ron Kneusel had his first experience with programming languages circa 1980 when he first encountered an Apple II computer. Decades later, he completed a PhD in machine learning from the University of Colorado, Boulder, and now works in the industry developing deep learning systems. He is the author of *Practical Deep Learning: A Python-Based Introduction* (No Starch Press, 2021), *Math for Deep Learning: What You Need to Know to Understand Neural Networks* (No Starch Press, 2021), *Numbers and Computers* (Springer, 2017), and *Random Numbers and Computers* (Springer, 2018).

About the Technical Reviewer

Bob Kneusel has worked as a lead software developer and manager in the telecommunications field for more than 20 years. He has diverse experience in mobile application development, device control, and business process automation technology. In this time he has worked with a myriad of programming languages, including BASIC, 6502 machine code, Fortran, Pascal, ADA, Prolog, Lisp, Clipper, C/C++, Progress4GL, Java, HTML/CSS/JavaScript, jQuery[M], Python, and scripting (AOS/VS CLI, DCL, ksh, bash). He holds a bachelor's degree in computer science and an MSc in computer information systems.

BRIEF CONTENTS

Foreword xix

Acknowledgments xxiii

Introduction xxv

PART I: ON PROGRAMMING LANGUAGES

Chapter 1: A Cherry-Picked Review of Programming Languages 3

Chapter 2: The Essentials of Programming Languages 43

Chapter 3: Turing Machines and Turing Completeness 77

PART II: ATYPICAL PROGRAMMING LANGUAGES

Chapter 4: Forth 97

Chapter 5: SNOBOL 123

Chapter 6: CLIPS 163

PART III: ESOTERIC PROGRAMMING LANGUAGES

Chapter 7: The ABCs of ABCs 195

Chapter 8: FRACTRAN 217

Chapter 9: Piet 243

Chapter 10: Brainfuck 271

Chapter 11: Befunge 297

PART IV: HOMEGROWN ESOLANGS

Chapter 12: Filska 319

Chapter 13: Using Filska 341

Chapter 14: Firefly 373

Chapter 15: Using Firefly 391

Chapter 16: Going Further 415

Appendix: Genetic Programming with Firefly 433

Index 455

CONTENTS IN DETAIL

FOREWORD xix

ACKNOWLEDGMENTS xxiii

INTRODUCTION xxv

PART I
ON PROGRAMMING LANGUAGES

1
A CHERRY-PICKED REVIEW OF PROGRAMMING LANGUAGES 3

Programming Language Paleontology 4
The First Programming Languages 6
    Programming Before Computers 6
    The First Modern Programming Languages 8
ALGOL 9
APL 11
BASIC 13
PL/I 14
Logo 15
Simula 16
Pascal 19
Prolog 21
    Modeling Family Relationships 21
    Implementing the Fibonacci Sequence 24
Smalltalk 27
    Basic Smalltalk Features 29
    Going to the Races 33
Standard ML 36
Summary 41

2
THE ESSENTIALS OF PROGRAMMING LANGUAGES 43

Defining Programming Language 44
Syntax and Semantics 44

Implementing Programming Languages 45
    Tokens, Lexers, and Parsers 46
    Interpreters 47
    Compilers 49
    Bytecode Compilers 52
Data Types 53
    Primitive Data Types... 55
    Records 55
Data Structures 57
    Arrays 58
    Linked Lists 58
    Trees 59
    Hash Tables 59
Variables and Scope 59
    Lexical Scope.. 60
    Dynamic Scope 61
    Python 61
    C... 62
    SNOBOL.. 62
    Perl 63
Controlling Program Flow 64
    Unstructured Languages 64
    Structured Languages... 65
Programming Paradigms 68
    Imperative... 68
    Object-Oriented 68
    Declarative 70
    Array Processing 72
Summary 76

3
TURING MACHINES AND TURING COMPLETENESS   **77**

The Halting Problem 78
Turing Machines 79
Universal Turing Machine 81
Turing Completeness... 83
Let's Build a Turing Machine 84
    The Simulator 85
    The Examples... 88
Summary 93

PART II
ATYPICAL PROGRAMMING LANGUAGES

4
FORTH
97

Installation 98
Origins and Philosophy 98
The Language 99
    Understanding the Stack 99
    Using the Stack 100
    Words and Loops 103
    What Is Truth? 106
    Other Control Structures 109
    How Forth Uses Memory 111
    Input and Output 116
Square Root Redux 118
Discussion 121
Summary 122

5
SNOBOL
123

Installation 124
Origins and Philosophy 124
The Language 125
    Running SNOBOL 125
    Variables and Data Types 128
    Arrays and Tables 134
    A Blizzard of Patterns 139
    Functions 146
    Input and Output 149
Machine Learning with SNOBOL 151
    Machine Learning 101 151
    Implementing the Classifier 154
    Using the Classifier 158
Discussion 160
Summary 162

6
CLIPS
163

Installation 164
Origins and Philosophy 164

The Language 166
    Working with CLIPS 166
    Implementing Hello World 168
    Facts and Rules 169
CLIPS in Action 173
    An Elementary Calculator 173
    Family Redux 177
    At the Factory 181
    An Iris Expert System 184
Discussion 190
Summary 191

PART III
ESOTERIC PROGRAMMING LANGUAGES

7
THE ABCS OF ABCS   195

ABC 196
    The Language 196
    An ABC Implementation 196
    Testing ABC 197
ABC2 199
    The Extensions 199
    An ABC2 Implementation 200
ABC2 in Action 203
    HELLO WORLD! 204
    A Slice of Pi 205
    The Electromechanical Arithmometer 210
Discussion 214
Summary 215

8
FRACTRAN   217

The FRACTRAN Specification 218
A Tale of Two Implementations 218
    A Scheme Implementation 219
    A Python Implementation 220
Using FRACTRAN 221
Understanding FRACTRAN 222
More FRACTRAN Examples 226
    Subtraction 226
    Maximum of Two Integers 227
    Copying a Register 230
    Multiplication 232

Conway's PRIMEGAME 234
The Collatz Conjecture 236
A FRACTRAN Greeting 238
Discussion 239
Is FRACTRAN Turing Complete? 239
FRACTRAN and the Collatz Conjecture............................... 240
Final Thoughts on FRACTRAN 241
Summary 242

9
PIET   243

Installation 244
Understanding Piet 245
Piet Colors 245
Representing Numbers 245
Representing Programs 246
Piet Commands 246
Program Flow 249
Piet in Action... 251
Proving 2 + 2 = 4 251
Saying Hi 252
Countdown... 254
A Pseudorandom Number Generator 257
A Tribute to Piet Mondrian 261
The Piet Universe 266
About Piet.. 266
Code 267
Implementations and Tools 267
Discussion 268
Summary 269

10
BRAINFUCK   271

WTF Is BF? 271
The Two Implementations.. 273
The Original.. 273
SNOBOL Meets BF 275
BF in Action... 280
Baby Steps 281
Bunches O'Bits 283
Multiplicative Multiplicity 288
The BF Multiverse 292
Examples 292
Tutorials.. 293
Implementations 293

    Inspirations 294
    Academic BF 294
Discussion 295
Summary 296

11
BEFUNGE
297

Befunge-93 World Tour 297
    Building Befunge-93 298
    Printing Text 299
    Using BEdit 301
    Befunge Says Hello 302
Befunge in Action 303
    Going with the Flow 304
    Building Bridges 307
    Fun with Dice 308
    Wandering Around 310
    Updating the Playfield on the Fly 311
Discussion 314
Summary 315

PART IV
HOMEGROWN ESOLANGS

12
FILSKA
319

Philosophy and Design 319
    Program Structure and Syntax 321
    Flow Control 323
    Memory 325
    Arithmetic 327
    Comparisons 327
    Mathematical Functions 329
    Input and Output 330
Implementating Filska 331
    Overall Structure and Operation 332
    Parsing 333
    The Execution Loop 334
    Instructions Without Arguments 336
    Instructions with Arguments 337
    Flow Control Instructions 338
Summary 340

13
USING FILSKA　　　　　　　　　　　　　　　　341

Hello, World! 341
　　　Hello, Math! 342
　　　Hello, Poly! 343
　　　Hello, Poly Implementation! 345
Fibonacci, Anyone? 348
Random Numbers 352
　　　Implementing MINSTD 353
　　　Evaluating MINSTD 354
A Simple Fractal... 356
Getting to the Roots of the Problem 359
Linear Least-Squares Fit to a Line 365
Discussion 370
Summary 371

14
FIREFLY　　　　　　　　　　　　　　　　　　　　373

Philosophy and Design 374
　　　Movement 376
　　　Display 377
　　　Music 378
　　　What's Left 379
Implementation 380
　　　Interpreter Structure and Main Loop 380
　　　Movement 383
　　　Display 384
　　　Music 386
Configuring the Micro:bit 386
　　　Micro:bit Hardware Overview............................... 386
　　　Using an External Speaker 388
Summary 389

15
USING FIREFLY　　　　　　　　　　　　　　　　391

The Process 392
　　　Writing Firefly Code 393
　　　Using the Console Interpreter 394
　　　Packing a Bundle 395
Fly Time 397
Space Trek 400
Beethoven in Lights 402

Dance Dance 405
    The Stances 406
    The Dance 407
    The Music 408
Tea Time 409
Discussion 412
Summary 412

16
GOING FURTHER   415

The Runners-Up... 415
    Malbolge 415
    INTERCAL 416
    Whitespace 419
    Shakespeare 421
    Whirl 423
    Taxi 425
    Dathanna 428
Programming Language Resources 428
    Programming Languages 429
    Data Structures 430
    Compilers and Interpreters 430
Postlude 431

APPENDIX: GENETIC PROGRAMMING WITH FIREFLY   433

Introduction to Genetic Programming 433
How Genetic Programming Works 434
Defining Displays.. 435
A Tiny Firefly Interpreter 435
The Genetic Algorithm 437
Putting It All Together 439
Evolving Firefly Programs.. 440
    Warning Sign 440
    Radar Sweep 443
    Bouncing Ball... 444
Discussion 446
    Population Effects 446
    Final Program Diversity 449
    Can Genetic Programming Find the Shortest Program? 450
Final Thoughts 452

INDEX   455

FOREWORD

Consider the following program:

```
({ω,+/¯2↑ω} ⍣ 7) (1 1)
```

Many who are used to modern programming languages will find this mystifying, yet it was not written in a deceptive style or an esoteric language. Some might recognize the funny w as a lowercase omega and place this as APL, a mathematical programming language created in the 1960s. This program calculates the first nine Fibonacci numbers (seven after the provided 1 1) using the power operator, drawn as a star with a diaeresis, a composite mark that has likely never found use—in programming or natural language—outside of APL.

It's also a glimpse of how different "ordinary code" might have looked had language design taken a different path. Imagine an alternative computer history in which APL's style dominates. There, computer science is still a subdiscipline of math and this seemingly arcane mathematical lexicon is the norm. APL, after all, has its advantages. Its array-based approach is natural to engineering and scientific computing. Its single-character signifiers are concise next to let or Console.WriteLine. And these symbols are truly international, unlike the English keywords that dominate programming and are increasingly questioned by programmers from other linguistic backgrounds. Perhaps, in a world where APL is dominant, lexemes drawn from a single spoken language like English would seem strange.

In *Strange Code*, Ron Kneusel asks us to consider unusual languages in depth: those intended for practical programming (the atypicals) or for pure creative joy (the esolangs). Both expand our idea of what code might look like and bring new light to dominant programming styles that we might have accepted unquestioningly.

The atypicals were designed with the same goal as mainstream languages: to shorten the cognitive distance between what a programmer writes and what that code will perform. Only they have found more daring paths to that goal, or simply paths that have not been adopted into the prevailing style of commercial code. Take Forth, a beloved oddball language. Forth does its computation in the stack: it is a language where one must be aware of the state of the stack to understand just how an algorithm will unfold. Learning Forth leads to a different mindset than other languages, yet sometimes provides strategies that are useful in them.

Esolangs use the cognitive distance between programmer and machine as a place of play; many choose to eschew clarity in the pursuit of other objectives. Some early esolangers, who had few or no previous esoteric languages to look at, drew from the atypical languages as inspiration. In his interview with *esoteric.codes*, Chris Pressey, the creator of Befunge, says his toying with language design began with building a Forth interpreter. He was driven by "a certain technical curiosity that is probably shared by every programmer who has reached a certain point in programming—the one where you start to wonder just exactly *how* the computer is turning the programs you're writing into actions." Before creating Befunge, he built and abandoned a more directly Forth-inspired esolang called Maentwrog. This experimentation paid off when the idea for Befunge struck. In Befunge, code flows in multiple directions, scratching back and forth across the field of text, from right to left and vice versa, from bottom to top, in a labyrinth whose turns are determined by the code itself. Getting this to work as a language required commands that can be read in multiple directions, meaning most need to be expressed as single letters. This is much simpler when you put values in the stack instead of in, say, named variables. Forth's stack-based model gave him the tool to manifest his creative vision.

Befunge would have been but a curiosity if it hadn't created a community of programmers over the following years. As Scott Feeney, founder of the esolangs wiki, described to *esoteric.codes*: "When you build a new esoteric language with a weird set of constraints, you get people thinking: I wonder if I can do *X* in this language? I wonder if there's a way to do *Y*?" The esolanger poses a challenge through the language. A language is a system of thought, an abstraction, a virtual machine that hides or reveals aspects of the underlying physical machine to fit its own model of computation. But the esoprogrammers who use it give it life; composing their own algorithms for it, they discover its possibilities, its absurdities, its boundaries, its aesthetic, its character. Esolanging is thus a collaborative art: the designer of a language understands what they've made when others bring to it their own ideas, their own approach to coding. Befunge, one of the first, casts a long shadow, with interpreters and online debuggers by many other developers, along with dozens of derivative languages that expand on its ideas.

Designing a language or even writing an interpreter can seem intimidating at first. Esolangs tend to be far simpler, so offer a better entry point.

There's a reason it's a cliché that esolangers start by designing their own Brainfuck variant: BF's interpreter can be written in a few lines of code, making it an easy place to try out new ideas, augmenting the command list with new features to see how it affects the cadence of Brainfuck code. Kneusel shows us several Brainfuck interpreters but also interpreters for more complex esolangs, including John Conway's FRACTRAN, a masterpiece of bizarre elegance, coded here in Scheme. In the later chapters, he walks us through two esolangs designed for the book, which show how conceptual design decisions lead to implementation decisions and ultimately shape how code is constructed in the new languages. It is invaluable for programmers to better understand "how the computer is turning the programs you're writing into actions," as Pressey put it, and how to shape that process, whether for practical or creative ends.

Those inspired might take the next step and design their own language from scratch. Perhaps they want to break from bland, bloated multiparadigm languages with imperative roots that seem to add the same trendy features in near unison year after year. Perhaps they will create an esolang to see if some preposterous form of computation is possible. A language where all code uses three levels of indirection? It's Three Star Programmer, and turns out to be Turing complete. A language with only one command? SUBLEQ, also TC. A language where code is written by dancing in front of a webcam? For that, we have Bodyfuck.

If you do create a language of your own, tweet it, add it to the esolangs wiki, send it to *esoteric.codes*. Esolangs are better when they are shared.

—Daniel Temkin

Daniel is an esolanger, artist, and the writer of *esoteric.codes*, a blog about esolangs and self-expression in the text of code. Winner of the *ArtsWriters.org* grant from Creative Capital and the Warhol Foundation, *esoteric.codes* has been exhibited at ZKM and written in residence at the New Museum's NEW INC incubator.

ACKNOWLEDGMENTS

Piglet noticed that even though he had a Very Small Heart,
it could hold a rather large amount of Gratitude.
–A. A. Milne

I want to thank all the good folks at No Starch Press for believing in the book and helping it to become a reality. Particular thanks goes to Alex Freed, whose gentle nudges and suggestions have made the book all the better; Daniel Temkin for the foreword; and my brother, Bob Kneusel, for taking the time to offer his clarifications of technical matters (in other words, pointing out my errors). If any errors remain, they are solely my fault for not listening to the sage advice of others.

INTRODUCTION

My first exposure to programming came in the summer of 1980. It involved an Apple II+ computer. As principal of the local high school, my father was able to bring it home for us to play with over the summer. It was the only personal computer in the school. I already knew about video games and had an Atari 2600 game console. But the idea of being able to make the machine do whatever I wanted it to was amazing and seductive.

The Apple II+ included a version of unstructured BASIC in ROM called Applesoft. As far as BASIC programming languages go, it was somewhat limited. However, it opened a new world to me, and I ran with it, writing small program after small program as I explored what the Apple II+ was and could do. It could ask questions, interpret answers, calculate formulas, plot pictures, and make sounds. And all of that power was at the tips of my 14-year-old fingers.

Of course, I wanted one of these godlike machines for my own. My father, likely thinking it would put me off, told my younger brother, Bob, and me we could have one if we learned how to program it. Challenge accepted!

Months later, we did just that, and for Christmas in 1981, we got our own Apple II+. I still have it; it's sitting on a shelf some five feet from me as I type this. And it still works.

My brother and I both ended up in computer science. During high school, I taught myself BASIC, 6502 assembly, Pascal, and FORTRAN, all on the Apple II+. I fell in love with programming languages and became a programming language junkie. A high school friend showed me a cryptic and small but powerful language he had for his TRS-80 color computer. He said its name was "Forth." I kept that in the back of my mind for years until I encountered it again in the 1990s. Forth is one of the languages we'll explore in this book, and it was my go-to language for most of the 1990s, on a Macintosh no less. My other language at the time was Modula-2, a successor of Pascal.

Thousands of programming languages have been developed over the years. I suspect a thorough history of programming languages would occupy several volumes. However, the purpose of this book is not history. The purpose of this book is:

- To give you a sense of where programming languages came from and provide some context for the languages we use today and the structures they contain.

- To explain some of the essential elements of programming languages, so you become familiar with terms like *Turing machine* and *Turing complete*.

- To expand your thinking about what a programming language can be and how it can express thought and process in creative and elegant ways. We'll do this by exploring various programming languages ranging from the unusual to the downright bizarre.

- *To have fun!* We'll create our own programming languages, and see how we can use them to implement some algorithms. We'll even put one on a small computer for standalone projects (the BBC micro:bit).

The "unusual to downright bizarre" programming languages have a name. They're called *esoteric languages* or *esolangs*. Playing with and developing esolangs is a hobby for many, and even a serious pursuit for some. Most esolangs are not intended for actual work (whatever that might be). However, some languages that might be considered on the fringe of the esolang world *are* used for serious work. For example, Forth has been used for spacecraft control on several NASA missions, and NASA developed a language called CLIPS for expert system development. I consider languages like Forth and CLIPS to be "atypical" programming languages, with everyday languages like Python, Java, and C/C++ being typical languages. Naturally, these labels are subjective and open to debate.

Who Is This Book For?

This book is for all fans of programming languages. It's for people enamored with the idea of encoding thought in a form usable by a machine.

I hope anyone who codes finds something of value in this book. My primary goal is to help you expand your conception of what it means to code, what programming actually is, and how coding might be expressed.

This book is truly for anyone who does more than use a computer. If you are a professional developer, you'll appreciate the freedom that comes from thinking about your craft in unusual ways. If you are a student, you'll hopefully see that programming can be more than what you may perceive it to be based on your introductory programming courses, as necessary as they are. If you're a hobbyist, you're likely already somewhat familiar with esolangs and are looking to feed your passion. Come on in, the water's fine.

What Can You Expect to Learn?

You can expect to learn about where the programming languages you use—perhaps daily—came from. You can expect to learn about alternate ways to think about programming and, by extension, see your everyday programming in a new light.

You can also expect to learn about the essential elements of a programming language, something about what makes a programming language complete (that is, capable of expressing any program), and something about how we can even know such a thing.

You can expect to learn a little about a lot of programming languages, with a focus on esolangs and other "atypical" languages. As I indicated above, I used Forth almost exclusively for a decade to write everything from web CGI frameworks to scientific analysis tools for functional brain imaging (see Figure 1). I (not so) secretly hope a bright mind out there can see how to merge the rule-based expert system power of CLIPS with the power of modern deep learning. I suspect there's a case to be made about why the two should work together.

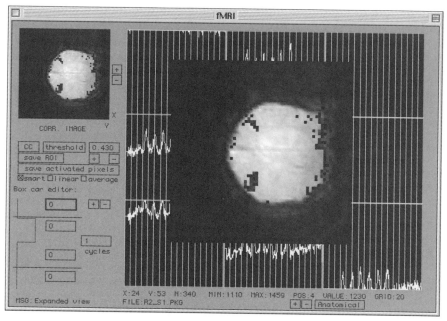

Figure 1: A functional brain imaging analysis program written in Forth (circa 1998)

It's my belief you'll learn that developing a programming language is fun, even if the language itself is not overly useful. The Filska and Firefly languages we'll create have different potential uses, but if nothing else, Filska can crunch numbers, and Firefly can make pretty pictures on a BBC micro:bit. The appendix demonstrates that even simple languages like Firefly can be useful for more "advanced" pursuits, like genetic programming.

I also expect you'll take what we do here and expand on it yourself. For example, the micro:bit has two pushbuttons. Why not enhance Firefly to use them? Or make additions to the ABC implementation beyond what we'll add in the book, as it's so simplistic that it's begging for additions. If you do, please share your results to *rkneuselbooks@gmail.com*.

What I Expect You to Know Already

I expect you are already familiar with programming at some level. We'll use Python to implement several esolangs, so it will help if you know something about Python. Beyond that, I don't have any expectation of prior knowledge. The most important thing you can bring to this book is curiosity.

It's said curiosity killed the cat, but you're not a cat. For us, curiosity is what made humans conquer fire, and develop stone tools, civilizations, art, music, mathematics, science, and ultimately, a car-sized robot wandering the surface of Mars—a robot we named "Curiosity."

If you're curious, if you wonder "why?", then you've got all the background you need to engage with the material in this book.

What This Book Is Not

Many books tell you what they are. Few tell you what they are not. I think this one should clarify itself, at least a little.

There are university courses and textbooks with titles like "Principles of Programming Languages" or just "Programming Languages." These courses and books are highly mathematical treatments of what programming languages are. They are fascinating, but very technical, and involve a lot of math and logic. I put them in the category of theoretical computer science. This book is not one of these texts. You won't find any deep mathematics here. The logic is implicit in the code, not formal. This book is about programming languages from a historical, practical, and, of paramount importance, fun perspective—with additional emphasis on the fun.

The end of the book points you toward more academic treatments of programming languages. Please do investigate. However, please don't put this book down believing you need to be a computer science graduate student to follow it. You don't. If you happen to be a computer science graduate student, please don't put the book down, either. I promise you'll have fun with it.

About This Book

The book reads well straight through. However, after Chapter 3, you can pretty much hop around as you wish. The first three chapters provide background and context. After that come three chapters on atypical programming languages (Forth, SNOBOL, and CLIPS) followed by five on esolangs (ABC, FRACTRAN, Piet, Brainfuck, and Befunge).

In the two chapters after those, we define, implement, and experiment with our first homegrown esolang, Filska. The two chapters after that do the same for Firefly. Lastly, the book ends by pointing you to more—there's always more to know.

The appendix explores genetic programming with Firefly. Genetic programming evolves programs instead of writing them by hand. The simplicity of Firefly makes it well-suited to such experiments—take a look and see.

Operating Environment

We assume Linux as our operating system. Specifically, we assume an Ubuntu distribution, at least version 20.04. None of the languages we'll explore require much in the way of external libraries, so it's highly likely future versions of Ubuntu will work without much effort.

We won't give explicit instructions here, but many macOS users will be able to install the languages as well. Windows users might need to work in a Unix-like environment like Cygwin, and will have to expend more effort to find some of the language tarballs and work through the installation process. Other options are using the Windows Subsystem for Linux or simply running Ubuntu in a virtual machine, both of which are easier than using Cygwin.

We need a C compiler to build some of the languages. Ubuntu usually comes with the gcc compiler suite for C and C++. You can test it with

```
$ gcc --version
gcc (Ubuntu 9.3.0-17ubuntu1~20.04) 9.3.0
Copyright (C) 2019 Free Software Foundation, Inc.
This is free software; see the source for copying conditions.  There is NO
warranty; not even for MERCHANTABILITY or FITNESS FOR A PARTICULAR PURPOSE.
```

Almost any version of gcc will work.

If gcc is not installed, and you get an error from the command above, the simplest way to install it is

```
$ sudo apt update
$ sudo apt install build-essential
```

Once you've done this, repeat the command above to verify that gcc is now present.

We'll also implement some of the languages ourselves using Python 3. The exact version of Python 3 is not critical. Ubuntu 20.04 comes with version 3.8.5,

```
$ python3 --version
Python 3.8.5
```

so version 3.8.5 or later will suffice.

Now, in the immortal words of Ms. Frizzle, "Take chances, make mistakes, and get messy!" Ready? Let's go.

PART I

ON PROGRAMMING LANGUAGES

1

A CHERRY-PICKED REVIEW OF PROGRAMMING LANGUAGES

This book's primary goal is to explore new ways to think about coding. Doing so will help you become a better coder, regardless of what language you are using. To that end, it makes sense to review existing programming languages, especially the languages that first introduced a particular coding paradigm or strongly influenced later languages.

The languages discussed in this chapter are not esolangs. Instead, they are serious approaches to the process of coding, meaning the process of translating thought into something a computer can use to solve a problem. Some of these languages are still in use. Others flowered briefly and then died. Still others evolved into something new. All of these languages have things to teach us, in addition to being fun to learn about and work with.

We'll begin the chapter with a bit of programming language paleontology. Following that, we'll consider the first programming languages. Even if you are still relatively new to coding, you already have a conception of what coding is and how to do it. That wasn't always the case—the very idea of coding had to come from somewhere. It's worth our time to take a look.

The remainder of the chapter is a series of vignettes, in roughly chronological order, that introduce us to a collection of programming languages we should keep in the back of our minds as we move through the book. We'll spend the next few chapters exploring select languages in still more detail before diving into esolangs proper.

There are thousands of programming languages (see *http://www.info .univ-angers.fr/~gh/hilapr/langlist/langlist.htm*), so why this particular set? I selected languages that were important to the development of future languages and, as such, often represent a new conception of programming, or languages that were novel in some way that will help us when we get to esolangs.

All of the languages presented in this chapter were invented before the year 2000. Of course, that's not to say programming language development stopped with Y2K. There are a plethora of new languages: Rust, Scala, Julia, Go, Kotlin, and Swift are all examples of languages developed after 2000. There will be no end to developing new programming languages. However, the current trend in language design leans toward multi-paradigm languages that take the best of what came before and mix it in some way with the hope of creating synergy. In other words, something greater than the sum of its parts. This trend validates our review of older languages with novel ideas as that is precisely what new languages are doing.

Let's begin.

Programming Language Paleontology

Paleontology, literally the study of ancient being, is concerned with the history of life on Earth as well as the equally important diversity of life, that is, the number and kind of species. An important event studied by paleontologists is the *Cambrian explosion*, which was the sudden appearance of a huge assortment of animals in the fossil record.

The best-known fossil site related to the Cambrian explosion, from a time just after it, is the Burgess Shale of western Canada. The Burgess Shale is a priceless fossil site, half a billion years old, where the soft body parts of a myriad of animals, most unlike any living today, are preserved.

Burgess Shale fauna, entirely marine, has familiar representatives, like trilobites, which are favorites of fossil collectors. But the real stars of the Burgess Shale are weird animals like *anomalocaris*, a large predator so unusual that its various body parts were originally classified as separate animals, or the five-eyed Opabinia, with its single, trunk-like arm and claw. Then there is Hallucigenia, a spiny, worm-like creature initially described upside down as if it were walking the sea floor on its spines.

Later life, which for us means more mainstream life, is definitely more familiar, if less diverse. Fish dominated the later Paleozoic seas and eventually wandered out of the water onto land to become the first tetrapods, a body plan that land-dwelling vertebrates from crocodiles to pterosaurs, dinosaurs, elephants, and humans have maintained virtually unchanged ever since.

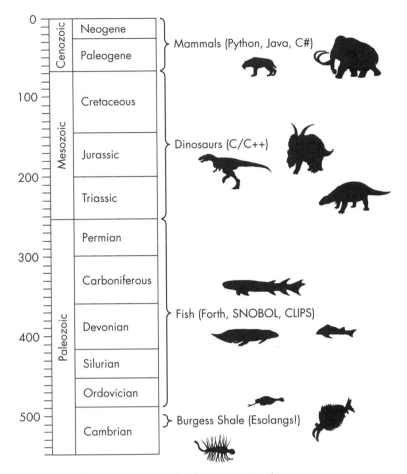

Figure 1-1: A geologic time scale of programming languages

Figure 1-1 shows a time scale of geologic history with programming languages marked at various places.

The silhouettes in Figure 1-1 indicate the type of life dominant at the time. What is important for us is not so much the time scale, but the diversity of life. Modern life, signified by the mammals during the Cenozoic era, such as Smilodon, the famed sabre-toothed cat, and the mighty mammoth, are related to newer languages like Python, Java, and C#. These languages are familiar and not at all surprising to us.

For the Mesozoic we have dinosaurs, including Alectrosaurus, a hunter who terrorized the late Cretaceous. Also present are a living tank, Edmontonia, and Achelousaurus, the prehistoric equivalent of a buffalo, but with fearsome horns. Although different in some ways, and perhaps a bit old, dinosaurs are familiar, so I've placed C and C++ in their company. Lest you think I'm slighting C and C++, do remember that the dinosaurs ruled the land for more than 100 million years and continue to rule the air even now, for birds are dinosaurs.

The later Paleozoic era, the Age of Fishes, seems a good place for unusual, but still not entirely alien, programming languages like Forth, SNOBOL, and CLIPS, all three of which we'll explore in this book. The fish silhouettes from the time are Eusthenopteron, the lobe-finned Sarcopterygii, and the jawless and armored Ostracoderm.

The Burgess Shale, the time of Anomalocaris, Opabinia, and Hallucigenia, is also marked. The diversity and unusual body plans of the Burgess Shale seem a perfect analogy for esolangs—experimental, perhaps evolutionary dead ends, but important all the same because they pushed the boundaries of what could be, before natural selection's heavy hand decided who continued and who didn't.

To me, esolangs are like the weirdly wonderful animals of the Burgess Shale. Like those animals, esolangs are experiments, forays into what could be, existing and thriving even if not destined to endure. The animals of the Burgess Shale made paleontologists rethink and reevaluate how they approached ancient life. Similarly, esolangs, if we let them, make us rethink and reevaluate how we approach programming.

Esolangs are weird, often very strange and alien, but that's the point. Like the beautifully bizarre animals of the Burgess Shale, esolangs explore niches in novel, unusual ways that might not be practical, but are definitely interesting and, most of all, fun.

There you have it: geology and computer science living together, sans mass hysteria. Hopefully, Figure 1-1 provides some food for thought, or at least an alternative viewpoint. We'll refer to Figure 1-1 from time to time throughout the book, but for now, let's move on and explore the first programming languages.

The First Programming Languages

What was the first programming language? That's a difficult question to answer without defining *programming language*. We'll define what we mean by a programming language in Chapter 2. For now, we'll use an intuitive definition: a programming language is a means by which an algorithm can be encoded to control a machine, specifically a computer.

Programming Before Computers

The idea of a programmable machine predates the idea of a programmable computer. The *Jacquard loom*, a loom that used punch cards for control, was introduced in 1804. The pattern of dots on the card controlled the movement of threads in the loom to specify the pattern woven. There is a language there, something that can be varied to produce a different output. Change the pattern of holes on the card and a new pattern emerges from the machine. The rolls for a player piano work in much the same way.

In fact, the first "modern" computer design, Charles Babbage's *Analytical Engine*, was influenced by the Jacquard loom. Although the Analytical Engine was never built, the engine had all the key components found in a modern computer and was programmable using punch cards. In 1843, while translating a set of lecture notes on the Analytical Engine from French to English, Ada Lovelace, Babbage's long-time friend and daughter of the famous poet Lord Byron, wrote about the capabilities and potential uses of the Analytical Engine. She envisioned using the Analytical Engine for computation, but went further, imagining that the engine could be used for composing music and would release scientists from tedious computation, thereby freeing them for more advanced thinking. Ada was correct on both counts.

The translation, and more importantly, Ada's insightful and brilliant notes, are in "Sketch of the Analytical Engine" in volume III of *Taylor's Scientific Memoirs* (1843, pp. 666–731). An online search will quickly locate a PDF version. I highly recommend reading through Ada's notes, at least Note A. However, Ada's Note G is most important to us. There, she applied an algorithm to the engine to compute Bernoulli numbers to demonstrate how the engine would compute the result. Bernoulli numbers are used in different areas of mathematics, but how they are used is unimportant to us. What matters is that Ada took an algorithm and structured it for the Analytical Engine—that is, she wrote a program for a general-purpose computer. It then seems fair to claim that Ada wrote the world's first computer program in 1843. The programming language she used was the *diagram of development* notation she introduced in Note D.

Figure 1-2 presents Ada's program. It details the sequence of steps, the variables involved, and how they change during the computation. Various people have translated her program into modern programming languages. Of particular interest is that she seems to have made an error, the world's first computer bug.

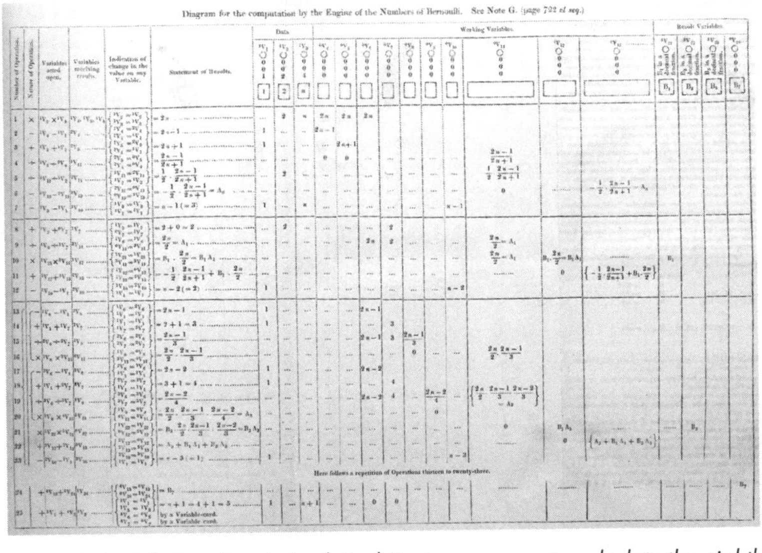

Figure 1-2: Ada Lovelace's Analytical Engine program to calculate the eighth Bernoulli number (1843)

Step 4 of Figure 1-2 calculates v5 / v4; however, the correct calculation is v4 / v5. With that modification, translations into modern languages produce the correct result: −1/30. Translations into C and Python are available on the internet. To learn more about Ada's life, I recommend *Ada's Algorithm*, by James Essinger (Melville House, 2015). She was ahead of her time, even though her own life was so short.

The First Modern Programming Languages

The first programming language in the modern sense was *Plankalkül*, developed by Konrad Zuse around 1943, 100 years after Ada's first program. Plankalkül is German for "plan calculus" or "plan calculation." Zuse used Plankalkül as a high-level programming language, though it was not implemented for any of his "Z" series computers. The language supported structured programming with for and while loops, floating-point arithmetic, arrays, and other features found in modern programming languages. Interestingly, the syntax of Plankalkül is 2D, with symbols written above other symbols. Zuse's word for a program was "rechenplan," which means "arithmetic" or "computation" plan. A good summary of Plankalkül can be found in "The Plankalkül of Konrad Zuse: A Forerunner of Today's Programming Languages," by Bauer and Wössner, Communications of the ACM 15, no. 7 (1972).

Lovelace and Zuse, respectively, deserve credit for the first program and the first programming language. But neither program nor language worked on actual, physical computers. The first programming language for a working computer is likely up for much debate. Early computers like ENIAC were programmed by rewiring. The Manchester Baby, circa 1948, was the first stored-program computer, so in that sense, it had a programming language—the instructions stored in its memory. We call the low-level instructions understood by a processor *machine language* or *machine code*. Machine code is a programming language, as are the assemblers that generate the machine code from *assembly language*.

Machine code and assembly aside, the first programming language used on an actual computer is probably *Short Code*, developed by John Mauchly in 1949 and implemented by William Schmitt for the UNIVAC I in 1950. Short Code supported arithmetic, including branching and a set of library functions like square root and absolute value. Expressions were transliterated from algebra to code and then manually packed into six 2-byte groups to fit the 12-byte words of the UNIVAC. Short Code was interpreted and parsed the meaning of an instruction from a tokenized representation of the program. In other words, Short Code worked much like the BASIC that interpreters built into early home computers of the 1980s. Running on a computer from the 1950s, interpreted Short Code must have been exceedingly slow to execute.

The first proper compiler, at least as credited by Knuth and Pardo in "The Early Development of Programming Languages" in *A History of Computing in the Twentieth Century* (Academic Press, 1980) is *AUTOCODE* by Alick E. Glennie at the University of Manchester, circa 1950–52. Unlike

Short Code, AUTOCODE was compiled, meaning it was translated into equivalent machine code instructions. Visually, AUTOCODE looks a bit like machine code with text thrown in here and there.

While AUTOCODE and its successors were under development in the UK, in the US, Grace Hopper, Margaret H. Harper, and Richard K. Ridgeway were working on their compilers for the UNIVAC: A-0 to A-2. In 1954, John Backus defined "The IBM Mathematical FORmula TRANslating system, FORTRAN," and by 1957, the first *FORTRAN* compiler was released.

The development of FORTRAN was a watershed moment. Programming language design kicked into high gear in the late 1950s. Most notable of the languages defined in the later 1950s, besides FORTRAN, is John McCarthy's *Lisp* in 1958. It is truly impressive that both FORTRAN and Lisp are still in widespread use today. High-performance computing (HPC) makes frequent use of FORTRAN. Later in the book, we'll use a version of Lisp to implement a *FRACTRAN* interpreter. We'll focus on FRACTRAN, perhaps the most unusual of esolangs, in Chapter 8.

The last pre-1960 programming language of note is *COBOL*. It was designed by a committee in 1959, with the first version appearing a year later. Rightly or wrongly, COBOL is still in use today. Unlike FORTRAN, a language for research scientists, and Lisp, a language for computer scientists, COBOL was a language intended for business use. COBOL programs are highly structured, rigid, and verbose. For example, consider this snippet from the COBOL 60 report defining the language:

```
IF X EQUALS Y THEN MOVE A TO B;
OTHERWISE IF C EQUALS D THEN MOVE A TO D AND
IF Y EQUALS Z THEN ADD B TO C
```

The early years of programming language development resulted in the basic form and concept of a general-purpose programming language. The three critical languages to come out of this era are FORTRAN, Lisp, and COBOL. All three are still in use.

FORTRAN was a natural choice for what is still a primary use of computers: number crunching. COBOL is an early example recognizing that commercial use of computers was something apart from their scientific use. Lisp was far in advance of its time, but slow, resource-limited computers made it difficult for Lisp to live up to its potential.

Let's now examine 10 different programming languages. These languages represent major transitions in the evolution of programming languages because of what they introduced or how they grew in popularity or opened the arcane art of coding to a larger population.

ALGOL

The first language we'll consider, *ALGOL*, gave rise to entire generations of programming languages and still influences programming languages today. ALGOL, like COBOL, was designed by committee.

ALGOL is a compiled, structured, imperative programming language, meaning it looks familiar to modern programmers. Subsequent programming languages inspired by ALGOL include Simula, PL/I, and Pascal, all mentioned later. ALGOL captured the essentials of what *imperative programming* is: a structured way to give step-by-step instructions to the computer.

Listing 1-1 is a simple program to compare two integers.

```
#  Ask for two ints and report their relationship #
( print("enter an integer: ");
  INT a = read int;
  print("now enter another integer: ");
  INT b = read int;
  IF (a > b) THEN
    print((a, " is greater than ", b, new line))
  ELSE
    IF (b > a) THEN
      print((b, " is greater than ", a, new line))
    ELSE
      print((a, " is equal to ", b, new line))
    FI
  FI )
```

Listing 1-1: Comparing numbers in ALGOL 68

Even without knowing the language, the form should be familiar to you if you know any modern structured programming language. Notice that the program begins with (and ends with) instead of BEGIN and END. The latter works as well and is what users of Pascal or Modula-2 expect to see, but ALGOL's free-form approach allows parentheses to denote code blocks.

If you're interested in trying ALGOL, you should look to Marcel van der Veer's "Algol 68 Genie" implementation (see *https://jmvdveer.home.xs4all.nl/en.algol-68-genie.html*), which runs on Linux and Windows. You'll find extensive documentation on his site, all you need to learn the language. The Ubuntu package is algol68g. Listing 1-1 is in *bigger.a68*. To run it, enter

```
> a68g bigger.a68
```

Figure 1-3 shows ALGOL's descendants.

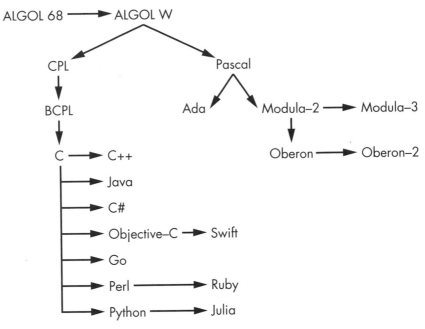

Figure 1-3: The ALGOL family tree

Naturally, programming languages can have multiple influences, but this tree seems quite reasonable.

APL

In 1962, Kenneth E. Iverson published *A Programming Language*, detailing a new programming language designed with arrays in mind that, in a show of boundless creativity, came to be called *APL*. One of the defining characteristics of APL is its nonstandard character set. That fact sometimes turns off would-be learners. For us, Iverson's use of alternative characters is an excellent reason to include APL in our list of programming languages. However, the real reason to include APL is that it was the first *array-processing language*. Array-processing is a paradigm we'll encounter in a later chapter, but, in a nutshell, it involves wholesale operations on arrays in a compact way. For a modern comparison, consider Matlab or Python with NumPy.

APL sessions are typically interactive. Listing 1-2 shows GNU APL in action. The user's input is indented and the system's responses are not.

```
      x ← ι10
      10 × x
10 20 30 40 50 60 70 80 90 100
      y ← 4 4 ρ 16 ? 100
      y
97  5 92 67
49 74 63 29
23 85 56 33
78 77 98 81
```

Listing 1-2: APL in action

The first line of Listing 1-2 assigns (←) whatever $ι100$ returns to the variable, x. APL's many operators each have two modes. If used in a unary fashion (that is, on a single operand), then the use is *monadic*. If used in a binary fashion (on two operands), then the use is *dyadic*. In this case, the monadic use of $ι$ returns the vector 1 2 3 4 5 6 7 8 9 10, which is exactly how it would be entered manually. Thus, the first line is equivalent to x = np.arange(1,11) in Python using NumPy. The second line in Listing 1-2 multiplies each element of x by 10.

The dyadic form of $ι$ searches for its second argument in the first. For example, consider the following APL code:

```
      x ← 10?10
      x
7 9 4 2 10 5 6 3 8 1
      xι10
5
```

Here we use the dyadic form of ? to set x to a 10-element vector of random integers from 1 to 10, without repeats. Next, the dyadic form of $ι$ searches x for the number 10 and returns its index, 5. APL indexes from 1, not 0. If the dyadic form of ? returns vectors of random integers between 1 and some upper limit, what might the monadic form of ? do? If you guessed return a random integer, you are correct: $?n$ returns a random integer in $[1, n]$.

The second assignment in Figure 1-2 sets y to a 4×4 matrix of random integers in $[1, 100]$. We use ? to ask for 16 numbers, and then use $ρ$ (rho) to reshape the 16-element vector into a 4×4 matrix before assigning it to y. To index a vector or array, use ⌷ (vertical rectangle) as in 3 ⌷ x to access the third element of vector x or 2 3 ⌷ y to access y_{23} of matrix y.

One quirk of APL is that expressions are evaluated from right to left, with no operator precedence rules. As a consequence, parentheses must be used to enforce desired behavior. For example, according to APL, the first of the two expressions below is completely correct.

```
      3 × 6 + 2
24
      (3 × 6) + 2
20
```

Virtually every other programming language will tell you that both expressions equal 20 because multiplication is performed before addition. However, APL parses the first expression as "add 2 and 6 to get 8, then multiply by 3 to get 24."

APL is compact and powerful but also cryptic, and thus comes with a high learning curve. This, to say nothing of the early difficulties in using its alternative character set, has limited its use. Perhaps because of these difficulties, Iverson and Roger Hui developed *J*, an ASCII version of APL in the early 1990s (*https://www.jsoftware.com/*). J retains the power of APL and expands on its capabilities to be more useful on modern computer systems. However, like APL, J has a high learning curve, creating the potential for high reward in learning a new way to think about what it means to code.

BASIC

Almost everyone who used a microcomputer in the 1980s is at least somewhat familiar with *BASIC*. The "Beginner's All-purpose Symbolic Instruction Code" was developed at Dartmouth College in 1964 by John G. Kemeny and Thomas E. Kurtz. BASIC was originally an unstructured programming language, meaning it used gotos to control program flow, and was intended for students and non-professionals. In the late 1970s, when the microcomputer revolution took off, most computers included BASIC, usually in ROM. The first programming language many current software engineers learned was unstructured BASIC on a personal computer from the 1980s. As a result, BASIC's impact on software development is significant and continues to this day.

BASIC was interpreted and often stored in memory as tokens, much like Short Code, described above. BASIC lives on as *Visual Basic*, which uses structured programming and is fully object-oriented. Visual Basic is still one of the most widely used programming languages.

Listing 1-3 shows a simple BASIC program for the Apple II to simulate coin flips.

```
10   HOME
100  REM COIN FLIPPER
110  PRINT : INPUT "HOW MANY FLIPS:";N
120  IF N < 1 THEN  END
130  K = 0:T = 0:H = 0: PRINT
140  C = . INT (2 *  RND (1))
150  IF C = 0 THEN  PRINT "T";:T = T + 1
160  IF C = 1 THEN  PRINT "H";:H = H + 1
```

```
170 K = K + 1
180  IF K < N THEN  GOTO 140
190  PRINT : PRINT
200  PRINT H;" HEADS AND ";T;" TAILS"
210  PRINT "DO YOU WANT TO TRY AGAIN?": INPUT A$
220  IF A$ = "Y" THEN  GOTO 10
230  HOME : END
```

Listing 1-3: An Applesoft BASIC program to simulate coin flips

BASIC used line numbers, required for every line, to provide targets for GOTO statements. Different dialects of BASIC provided various commands, but all had GOTO and many had ON-GOTO to provide a simple computed goto construct. BASIC also supported subroutines via GOSUB, though most did not support recursion. Although perhaps scoffed at by many more serious programmers back in the 1960s and onward, the fact that BASIC continues today validates its utility.

PL/I

PL/I (Programming Language 1) was developed by IBM in the mid-1960s as a general-purpose programming language for all uses, scientific to business. As such, it competed directly with FORTRAN and COBOL. IBM has maintained PL/I and it's currently available for IBM mainframe computers. The language itself is structured and imperative, and borrowed concepts from ALGOL, FORTRAN, and COBOL, as one might expect from a jack-of-all-trades language of the time. PL/I was in steady use from the late 1970s through the mid-1990s and represents one of the first languages intended to meet all programming needs.

Even though PL/I survives on IBM mainframes, its use elsewhere is negligible. New development in PL/I is likely equally insignificant. As an example of the language, Listing 1-4 shows a simple loop that outputs "Hello, world!" repeatedly.

```
hello:proc options(main);
  declare i fixed binary;
  do i = 1 to 10;
    put skip list("Hello, world!");
  end;
end hello;
```

Listing 1-4: A PL/I greeting

This example is quite readable, even now, though wordy, requiring four words to declare a simple integer variable. The influence of FORTRAN and ALGOL is evident via FORTRAN's DO loop and ALGOL's END.

Logo

In 1967, Wally Feurzeig, Seymour Papert, and Cynthia Solomon gifted generations of students with *Logo*, a "simplified" version of Lisp intended to teach programming concepts. Logo, which means "word" or "thought" in Greek, is intended to foster thinking about programming, especially thinking about how the Logo turtle will behave given the commands the students enter.

Figure 1-4 shows a simple Logo session. The user enters commands at the bottom of the screen, and the triangular "turtle" responds.

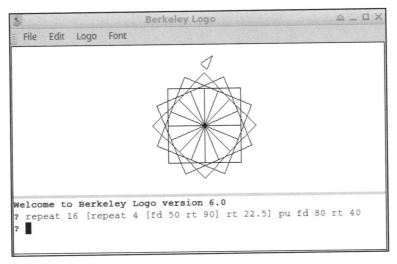

Figure 1-4: Drawing with the Logo turtle

Most commands are easy to understand, even if you've never seen Logo before. The commands in Figure 1-4 are, with comments

```
repeat 16 [          ; repeat commands in [ ] 16 times
    repeat 4 [       ; repeat commands in [ ] 4 times
        fd 50        ; turtle forward 50 pixels
        rt 90        ; turtle turn right 90 degrees
    ]
    rt 22.5          ; turn right 22.5 degrees
]
pu                   ; pen up
fd 80                ; forward 80 pixels
rt 40                ; right turn 40 degrees
```

The inner repeat command draws a square with the turtle ending where it began. The 22.5 degree right turn tilts the turtle to draw another square. Since 16 × 22.5 = 360, 16 repetitions completes the pattern. The final instructions move the turtle off the pattern. Note that this particular Logo example is for Berkeley Logo. The exact form of the commands might be slightly different for another implementation. Logo is still used to teach programming concepts to children; see "Turtle Academy" (*https://turtleacademy .com/*). As Logo represents one of the first attempts to develop a programming language designed for teaching children, it deserves a place in our pantheon of languages.

Simula

The first object-oriented language was *Simula*, developed by Kristen Nygaard and Ole-Johan Dahl. As the name suggests, Simula was first used for discrete-time simulations and evolved into a general-purpose language by 1967 (Simula 67). Simula brought the world classes, objects, and inheritance. The description that follows is specific to Simula 67. I tested the examples with the GNU cim compiler (*https://www.gnu.org/software/cim/*), which is a bit tricky to build (at least version 5.1 is, which is the latest version available as of this writing). The cim compiler translates Simula to C before calling the standard gcc compiler to build the final executable.

The "Hello, world!" program in Simula isn't particularly impressive.

```
comment Hello world;
begin
    OutText("Hello, world!");
    OutImage;
    OutText("How are you today?");
end
```

It's immediately clear that OutText prints something, and it's reasonable to guess that OutImage acts like a newline, which it does. Structurally, Simula is part of the ALGOL family, with blocks denoted by Begin and End and semicolons to separate statements. Simula isn't case sensitive, so Begin and BEGIN are equivalent. Comments begin with comment or an exclamation point and end with a semicolon, like other statements. If you're familiar with Modula-2 or Pascal, then Simula syntax should look familiar.

Simula is a structured language, like ALGOL, so both for and while control structures are present. Simula's for is more flexible than in most other languages. For example, for iterates over a list of values, some of which may specify ranges. Consider the program

```
begin
    integer r;
    for r:= 1,1, 3 step 3 until 18, -12 do
    begin
        OutInt(r,5);      OutText(" ");
        OutInt(r*r,5);    OutText(" ");
        OutInt(r*r*r,5); Outimage;
    end
end
```

which outputs a table of squares and cubes:

```
   1     1     1
   1     1     1
   3     9    27
   6    36   216
   9    81   729
  12   144  1728
  15   225  3375
  18   324  5832
 -12   144 -1728
```

Here, r is 1 for the first two iterations of the loop, then runs from 3 through 18 by threes, and ends with −12.

However, if this were all Simula offered, it wouldn't be worth discussing. Simula's true gift to the world is object-oriented programming (Listing 1-5), for which both Nygaard and Dahl received the Turing Award in 2001.

```
begin
  class Person;
  begin
    text first, last;
    integer age;
    procedure Print;
    begin
      OutText(first); OutText(" ");
      OutText(last); OutText(", age");
      OutInt(age,3); Outimage;
    end;
  end;

  Person class Pal;
  begin
    text nickname;
    procedure Print;
    begin
      OutText(nickname);
      OutText(" is ");
      This Pal Qua Person.Print;
    end;
  end;

  ref(Person) Fred, Barney;
  ref(Pal) Wilma, Betty;

  Fred :- new Person;
  Barney :- new Person;
  Wilma :- new Pal;
```

```
Betty :- new Pal;

Fred.first :- "Fred";              Barney.first :- "Barney";
Fred.last :- "Flintstone";         Barney.last :- "Rubble";
Fred.age := 37;                    Barney.age := 34;

Wilma.first :- "Wilhelmina";       Betty.first :- "Elizabeth";
Wilma.last :- "Flintstone";        Betty.last :- "Rubble";
Wilma.age := 35;                   Betty.age := 31;
Wilma.nickname :- "Wilma";         Betty.nickname :- "Betty";

Fred.Print;
Wilma.Print;
Barney.Print;
Betty.Print;
end
```

Listing 1-5: Using classes in Simula 67

Listing 1-5 shows us how to define and use classes. We define two classes, Person and Pal, a subclass of Person. Person uses the familiar class keyword and then defines first and last names as type text, a string object, along with age, an integer. Person defines one method, Print, to print the person's full name and age.

Pal is a subclass of Person. It adds nickname and overrides Print to output the nickname before throwing in the strange line

```
This Pal Qua Person.Print;
```

which is a way to call the Print method of the superclass, Person. The phrase This Pal is a reference to the object itself. It returns a reference to the current object much like this in C++. The phrase Qua Person.Print interprets the reference returned by This Pal as a Person object so the proper Print method is called. ("Qua" is derived from Latin and means "in the capacity of" or "as.")

To use instances of these classes, we must create reference variables and then use new to assign the references to the actual instances. The :- operator assigns objects created on the heap to references. The := operator assigns values to variables. Simula includes automatic garbage collection, so there is no need to delete objects when no longer needed.

To populate the objects, we use both :- and :=. Strings are objects, so :- assigns them to the text objects, whereas := is used to assign age as it is an integer. First we populate the two instances of the parent class, Fred and Barney, with names and ages. Then we populate the two Pal subclass instances, Wilma and Betty, in much the same way, this time including nicknames.

The goal of all of Listing 1-5 is to call the Print methods of the now populated objects, which produces

```
Fred Flintstone, age 37
Wilma is Wilhelmina Flintstone, age 35
Barney Rubble, age 34
Betty is Elizabeth Rubble, age 31
```

Notice that the proper Print method is called on each object to produce the desired output string.

Simula was well ahead of its time. Object-oriented programming took well over a decade after Simula 67 to catch on and, arguably, 20 years to become widely employed in the commercial software world. Simula's strong association with simulation hurt the adoption of the language. As we've seen here, Simula is much more than a simulation language and even now fits into what we expect an object-oriented language to be.

Pascal

Niklaus Wirth released Pascal in 1970. It is a direct descendant of ALGOL and was widely used into the 1980s, primarily to teach structured programming concepts. After unstructured BASIC, many software engineers learned Pascal as their first "serious" programming language. Early versions of the Macintosh operating system were written, at least partially, in Pascal. UCSD Pascal, followed by commercial products like Turbo Pascal, brought the language to microcomputers. As with BASIC above, Pascal has strongly influenced a generation of developers, to say nothing of programming language development as a whole, so it deserves a place in the pantheon as well.

Look again at Figure 1-3. There are two main branches of the ALGOL family of languages, one based on C and the other on Pascal. The Pascal branch leads to Modula-2, which overcame Pascal's shortcomings but was never particularly popular, at least in North America. Ada was created by the US Department of Defense (DoD) as a standard for all development in the 1980s (Ada is named after Ada Lovelace). The DoD required the use of Ada for projects from 1991 to 1997. At present, Pascal has fallen into obscurity, and Modula-2 and its descendants, along with Ada, are even less popular. However, Pascal lives on as Delphi/Object Pascal. As a straightforward, structured programming language without object-oriented abilities, there was little reason to select Pascal after the rise of C and C++.

Listing 1-6 gives us a feel for the language.

```
program nonsquares;

var
    n : integer;

begin
    for n := 1 to 120 do begin
```

```
    write(n + trunc(0.5 + sqrt(n)):4);
    if (n mod 10) = 0 then writeln;
  end;
  writeln
end.
```

Listing 1-6: Generating the sequence of nonsquare integers

Pascal looks quite similar to ALGOL and Simula. This particular program produces a table of 120 numbers.

```
  2   3   5   6   7   8  10  11  12  13
 14  15  17  18  19  20  21  22  23  24
 26  27  28  29  30  31  32  33  34  35
 37  38  39  40  41  42  43  44  45  46
 47  48  50  51  52  53  54  55  56  57
 58  59  60  61  62  63  65  66  67  68
 69  70  71  72  73  74  75  76  77  78
 79  80  82  83  84  85  86  87  88  89
 90  91  92  93  94  95  96  97  98  99
101 102 103 104 105 106 107 108 109 110
111 112 113 114 115 116 117 118 119 120
122 123 124 125 126 127 128 129 130 131
```

Look carefully at the table; do you see what isn't there? The table contains every integer less than 132 *except* for all the perfect squares: 4, 9, 16, 25, 36, 49, 64, 81, 100, and 121. The program implements the sequence

$$n + \lfloor 0.5 + \sqrt{n} \rfloor, \quad n = 1, 2, 3, \ldots$$

which has the remarkable property of bypassing all perfect squares, as n is incremented from one.

Pascal programs begin with program followed by a variable declaration section beginning with var. Here we define one integer variable, n. The body of the program is between begin at the beginning and end. at the end. Note that the period is required for the final end. Blocks of code are also enclosed within begin and end.

The body of this program is a single for loop running from 1 to 120. The body of the loop is a write statement, which does not move to the next line when done. The number output is the equation above for the current value of n. The argument :4 tells Pascal to right-justify the output in four spaces. The code also tells the program to move to the next line if n is a multiple of 10.

Pascal was intended for teaching and wasn't suitable for system-level programming without nonstandard extensions. Wirth enhanced Pascal to make Modula-2, which was suitable for system-level programming. However, Modula-2 never reached its full potential in the commercial world. Regardless, Wirth's Pascal, and subsequent languages, rightfully earned him the Turing Award in 1984.

Prolog

Most programming languages are imperative. That is, programs are a recipe, a series of "do this" followed by "now do that." However, in *Prolog*, things are different. Prolog is a *declarative language*. Relationships are encoded as rules, and it's up to the Prolog engine to figure out how to accomplish the goal of answering a user query. Prolog was created in 1972 by Alain Colmerauer and Robert Kowalski and is still in limited use today.

A Prolog program is a series of *facts*, *rules*, and *queries*. We'll learn what these are in a bit. Thinking in Prolog is quite different from thinking in most languages. Imperative languages are natural, and object-oriented languages build on that. Even APL makes sense once you understand the odd characters. But Prolog is an entirely different beast. We'll only scratch the surface of it here. Later in the book, we devote an entire chapter to CLIPS, which is somewhat like Prolog, so we'll struggle with this mode of thinking then.

This section presents two small Prolog examples. I used SWI-Prolog (*https://www.swi-prolog.org/*), which is most easily installed on Ubuntu by typing the following command:

```
> sudo apt-get install swi-prolog-nox
```

Please see the Prolog website for the macOS and Windows versions.

Modeling Family Relationships

The canonical Prolog example involves family relationships. Our example is in *family.pl*, with the most important parts shown in Listing 1-7.

```
male(uranus).
male(cronus).
male(zeus).
--snip--
female(gaia).
female(rhea).
female(hera).
--snip--
parent(uranus, cronus).
parent(gaia, cronus).
parent(cronus, zeus).
--snip--
married(zeus, hera).
married(hephaestus, aphrodite).

father(X,Y) :- parent(X,Y), male(X).
mother(X,Y) :- parent(X,Y), female(X).
child(X,Y) :- parent(Y,X).
sibling(X,Y) :- parent(P,X), parent(P,Y), dif(X,Y).
brother(X,Y) :- sibling(X,Y), male(X).
sister(X,Y) :- sibling(X,Y), female(X).
```

```prolog
grandparent(X,Y) :- parent(X,A), parent(A,Y).
grandfather(X,Y) :- grandparent(X,Y), male(X).
grandmother(X,Y) :- grandparent(X,Y), female(X).
greatgrandparent(X,Y) :- parent(X,A), parent(A,B), parent(B,Y).
greatgrandfather(X,Y) :- greatgrandparent(X,Y), male(X).
greatgrandmother(X,Y) :- greatgrandparent(X,Y), female(X).
cousin(X,Y) :- sibling(A,B), parent(A,X), parent(B,Y), dif(X,Y).
aunt(X,Y) :- sister(X,A), parent(A,Y).
uncle(X,Y) :- brother(X,A), parent(A,Y).
wife(X,Y) :- female(X), (married(X,Y); married(Y,X)).
husband(X,Y) :- male(X), (married(X,Y); married(Y,X)).
paramour(X,Y) :- child(A,X), child(A,Y), \+ married(X,Y), dif(X,Y).
```

Listing 1-7: Family relationships in Prolog

Let's walk through the code in Listing 1-7 before exploring what Prolog can do with it. The first portion of the code builds a knowledge base, which is a listing of facts. The code presents facts about the relationships between the classic Greek gods. For example, according to mythology, the parents of Cronus are Gaia and Uranus, so the knowledge base uses the lines `parent(uranus, cronus).` and `parent(gaia, cronus).` to state this.

Note that Prolog doesn't have a `parent` function' thus, the statements are facts relating two *atoms*. Atoms are generic names, a collection of characters treated as a symbol and acting as a single unit. There is a relationship called `parent` and `gaia` and `cronus` share it. We read the fact as "Gaia is the parent of Cronus." Similarly, the knowledge base also labels the sex of the gods. Read `female(hera).` as "Hera is female." Notice that facts, and later rules and queries, end with a period. The knowledge base identifies the sex, parents, and whether or not two gods were considered married. Again, these are the facts that Prolog will work with. To do anything interesting, we need some rules to go with the facts. That's the second part of Listing 1-7.

Using family relationships helps because we are all so familiar with them. For example, we define a rule to decide if X is the father of Y, where atoms beginning with a capital letter are logical variables. Prolog will try to satisfy rules by locating values for these variables. The rule defines the relationship as "If *X* is the parent of *Y* and *X* is male, then *X* is the father of *Y*."

The left-hand side of `father(X,Y)` is true *if* the right-hand side is true. The right-hand side is true *if* `parent(X,Y)` is true *and* (comma) `male(X)` is true. Prolog uses a comma for "and" and a semicolon for "or." With just this bit of knowledge, we can read the rest of the rules. A mother is a parent and female. Someone, X, is the child of Y if Y is the parent of X.

The rule for `sibling` says two people are siblings if they share a parent. That much makes sense. The last part of the rule is `dif(X,Y)`. It adds "and *X* and *Y* are not the same" to the rule. This is there because we don't normally think of ourselves as our own siblings.

The rule for `wife` uses parentheses and a semicolon for "or." X is a wife if she is female and married to Y. Prolog doesn't intuitively know that the rule `married(X,Y)` implies `married(Y,X)`, so either case is checked.

The final rule is `paramour`, because, after all, we're talking about ancient Greek gods. Here, X is a paramour of Y if A is a child of both X and Y, X and Y are not married (\+ is like "not"), and X and Y are different. Read through the rules in Listing 1-7 until you feel comfortable with what they express.

Prolog programs are not loaded, but are rather *consulted*. The line

```
> swipl family.pl
```

consults *family.pl*, after which Prolog presents its prompt and waits patiently for user input. Let's ask Prolog some questions about the gods and see if it can answer them based on the facts and rules we fed it (see Listing 1-8).

```
?- married(zeus,hera).
true.
?- wife(X,zeus).
X = hera ;
false.
?- mother(hera,W).
W = ares ;
W = hephaestus ;
W = eris.
?- mother(X,hera).
X = rhea.
?- mother(X,zeus).
X = rhea.
?- father(zeus,W).
W = ares ;
W = hephaestus ;
W = eris ;
W = athena ;
W = hermes ;
W = apollo ;
W = artemis ;
W = dionysus.
```

Listing 1-8: Exploring family relationships

Listing 1-8 shows a Prolog session where *family.pl* has been consulted. User input is in bold with Prolog's replies following. First, we ask Prolog if Zeus and Hera are married. Prolog replies `true`, as this is simply a fact in its knowledge base.

Next, we ask Prolog to find an X such that X is the wife of Zeus. Notice that the rule is defined such that X is the wife of Y so the query is `wife(X,zeus)` and not `wife(zeus,X)` which would be asking the question "who is Zeus the wife of?" Prolog finds one match, one binding for X that makes the query true: Hera. The user then enters the bold semicolon. After Prolog finds a solution, if it can't decide that there are no other solutions to the query on its own, it pauses and waits for the user to enter a semicolon to tell Prolog to search for more solutions. The final `false` is Prolog telling the user that no more solutions were found.

Then we ask Prolog, "Hera is the mother of who?" and we're correctly told Ares, Hephaestus, and Eris. Next we ask, "Who is the mother of Hera?" and, again correctly, Prolog answers Rhea. The following query tells us that Rhea is also Zeus's mother. The ancient gods certainly had complex family relationships.

We next ask Prolog to identify the children of Zeus. Specifically, we ask, "Zeus is the father of who?" and are correctly told he is the father of eight other gods, much to the annoyance of Hera.

A few more examples will drive home how Prolog works. Listing 1-9 shows Prolog's response to the query "Who are Zeus's paramours?"

```
?- paramour(zeus,W).
W = metis ;
W = maia ;
W = leto ;
W = leto ;
W = semele.
?- grandmother(X,apollo).
X = rhea ;
false.
?- greatgrandfather(X,artemis).
X = uranus ;
false.
```

Listing 1-9: More family relationships

Notice that Leto is listed twice. The rule for paramour is

```
paramour(X,Y) :- child(A,X), child(A,Y), \+ married(X,Y), dif(X,Y).
```

meaning that X and Y are paramours if they are not married and have a child together. In mythology, Zeus and Leto have twins, Apollo and Artemis. Therefore, Prolog finds that Leto and Zeus are paramours in two different ways, once for Apollo and again for Artemis. There are ways to capture responses and return only unique solutions, but using them here would only cloud the example. The final two queries in Listing 1-9 illustrate that Prolog can resolve queries involving grandparents and great-grandparents.

Implementing the Fibonacci Sequence

Our last Prolog example shows how it works with numeric data and its support for recursion. Specifically, we'll implement the Fibonacci sequence,

```
1 1 2 3 5 8 13 21 34 55 ...
```

which is expressible recursively by saying that the next number is the sum of the previous two:

$$F_n = F_{n-1} + F_{n-2}, \quad F_1 = 1, \quad F_2 = 1$$

We'll discuss the Fibonacci sequence in more detail in Chapter 13. It's an easy target for esolang examples. For now, we'll use a recursive Python implementation as a guide for a Prolog version. In Python, the equation above can be implemented as

```
def fib(n):
    if (n <= 2):
        return 1
    else:
        return fib(n-1) + fib(n-2)
```

The nth Fibonacci number is the sum of the previous two, or if n is less than or equal to two, just one. This function tells us that $F_{11} = 89$, which is correct. So how can we express the rule for the Fibonacci sequence in Prolog? To do so, we first need two facts that act as the base cases, $F_1 = 1$ and $F_2 = 1$. Then we need to express the recursive relationship. Listing 1-10 has what we need.

```
fib(1,1).
fib(2,1).

fib(N,F) :-
    N > 2,
    N1 is N-1,
    N2 is N-2,
    fib(N1,F1),
    fib(N2,F2),
    F is F1 + F2.
```

Listing 1-10: Recursive Fibonacci numbers

The two base cases are facts. The first Fibonacci number is 1, and the second is 1. When Prolog is eventually trying to satisfy fib(2,1), it will find the fact. The "return value" is the second number. The query to find the 11th Fibonacci number is fib(11,F). or "What F value makes fib(11,F) true?" That's the 11th Fibonacci number.

The general rule is fib(N,F). The body is the conjunction (that is, clauses linked by "and") of several things. First, is it true that N > 2? Next come two "assignments," which are true when N1 is $n - 1$ and N2 is $n - 2$. So far, the statements make sense and are elements of the Python definition.

The next two lines, fib(N1,F1) and fib(N2,F2), are strange at first. These are the recursive calls, as it were. The first seeks to find F_{n-1} by finding an F1 such that fib(N1,F1) is true. Likewise, the second does the same for F_{n-2}. If these are found, then F1 and F2 have meaningful values, and the last line says that F, the actual number we've been looking for, is the sum of F1 and F2, which must be the previous two Fibonacci numbers.

The code for Listing 1-10 is in *fib.pl*. Let's start Prolog, consulting *fib.pl*, and ask it for the 11th Fibonacci number:

```
?- fib(11,F).
F = 89 .
```

We see that our example works, as it gives us the same answer as the Python version. Now, ask for fib(26,F) and see how long it takes Prolog to answer. On my machine, Python answers immediately with 121,393. Prolog also answers with 121,393 but takes 29 seconds to do so. The double recursive call makes this Fibonacci implementation inefficient. However, Prolog's exceedingly slow response validates a common criticism of the language: its performance. Moreover, the Unix utility, top, reported that during the search, Prolog used 0.5 percent of system memory, or about 42MB, which seems excessive for such a simple task.

Tracing lets us watch Prolog work through a query. For example, here's the output tracing the query fib(3,F).

```
?- trace.
true.
[trace]  ?- fib(3,F).
   Call: (8) fib(3, _4072) ? creep
   Call: (9) 3>2 ? creep
   Exit: (9) 3>2 ? creep
   Call: (9) _4296 is 3+ -1 ? creep
   Exit: (9) 2 is 3+ -1 ? creep
   Call: (9) _4302 is 3+ -2 ? creep
   Exit: (9) 1 is 3+ -2 ? creep
❶ Call: (9) fib(2, _4304) ? creep
   Exit: (9) fib(2, 1) ? creep
❷ Call: (9) fib(1, _4304) ? creep
   Exit: (9) fib(1, 1) ? creep
   Call: (9) _4072 is 1+1 ? creep
   Exit: (9) 2 is 1+1 ? creep
   Exit: (8) fib(3, 2) ? creep
F = 2 .
```

First, we activate trace and enter the query: fib(3,F). At each step, Prolog pauses, waiting for a command. Pressing ENTER moves to the next step and displays creep. Therefore, each line above represents entering or exiting a subgoal of the rule. Temporary variables have names like _4072.

The first line of the trace is the query with a temporary name for F. The 8 is similar to a call depth indicator, as it increases as the query is evaluated and decreases back to its initial value when the query is satisfied.

If you walk through the trace, you'll see that each step works to satisfy the particular subgoal, that is, a part of the right-hand side of the rule. The first pair, for example, indicates that 3 > 2 is true. The second pair says that $2 = 3 + (-1)$, which is also true. Interestingly, Prolog adds a −1 instead of subtracting 1.

The first recursive call ❶ is immediately satisfied because fib(2,1) is a known fact, one of the base cases of the recursion. The second recursive call ❷ is similarly satisfied because fib(1,1) is also a fact.

With the recursive calls satisfied, the final subgoal, F is F1 + F2, can be satisfied with F=2. Thus, the query, fib(3,2), is now satisfied and Prolog returns F = 2.

The trace for fib(3,F) produced 14 lines of output and the trace for fib(26,F), which took nearly 30 seconds to return, produced 1,456,706 lines, reaching a maximum depth 24 above the base depth.

We've been a bit unfair to Prolog. The double recursive Fibonacci algorithm is inefficient because it is not *tail recursive*. A tail-recursive call is one in which the last invocation is the recursive part. Tail-recursive functions can be implemented without storing the current call's stack frame. The recursion becomes essentially a jump to the beginning of the function without involving the call stack.

Listing 1-11 is a tail-recursive version of the Fibonacci program. You'll find it in the file *fib_tail.pl*.

```
fib(1,A,F,F).

fib(N,A,B,F) :-
    N > 0,
    N1 is N-1,
    B1 is A+B,
    fib(N1,B,B1,F).
```

Listing 1-11: Fibonacci numbers using tail recursion

This version of the code uses two additional variables as accumulators: the second and third arguments. The base case is any call matching fib(1,A,F,F), with F being the desired number, and A being any other value. Notice that the rule fib(N,A,B,F) has a recursive call as the final subgoal, unlike Listing 1-10, which has two recursive calls, neither of which is the final subgoal. Prolog can use tail recursion here because there is nothing in the body to come back to.

Run Listing 1-11 as fib(26,0,1,F) to find the 26th Fibonacci number. This time, Prolog will respond immediately with 121,383. Then try fib(266,0,1,F) to see that Prolog supports arbitrary precision integers. The trace command will show you how the accumulators are used to ultimately arrive at a call matching fib(1,A,F,F).

If our goal is to learn to think outside the box in terms of what it means to code, and it is, then Prolog promotes such thinking. Keep Prolog in the back of your mind. We'll see a similar approach later when we discuss CLIPS in Chapter 6.

Smalltalk

Smalltalk came to be in the early 1970s, a product of the Learning Research Group at Xerox PARC. It was designed by Alan Kay, Dan Ingalls, and Adele

Goldberg as a teaching language, much like Logo. Smalltalk is an object-oriented language. In fact, it is a *pure object-oriented language*, meaning that everything, even numbers, is an object. Pure object-oriented languages stand in contrast to impure languages like C++. In C++, *primitives*, such as integers, are not objects. Smalltalk objects communicate with each other by sending messages. If an object knows how to reply to a message, then that object is a valid receiver of the message.

Smalltalk classes support *duck typing* and may be extended at will. Duck typing allows any object that supports a particular method to be used where that method is expected. In other words, if it walks like a duck and quacks like a duck, it's a duck.

Even without knowing the syntax, we can understand that MyClass in the following example defines a method, A, to square its argument.

```
Object subclass: MyClass [
    A: n [ ^n*n ]
]
```

At any later time, even if objects of MyClass already exist, a new method to calculate cubes may be added.

```
MyClass extend [
    B: n [ ^n*n*n ]
]
```

The MyClass class, including any existing objects, now knows how to use the method B.

Many Smalltalk systems include an extensive graphical interface. This includes Smalltalk-80, the version we'll explore here. Modern Smalltalk systems, like Squeak (*https://squeak.org/*) or Pharo (*https://pharo.org/*), follow this tradition. If Smalltalk piques your curiosity, do take a look at one or both of these systems. However, the essence of the Smalltalk language is our focus, not its graphics abilities. Therefore, we'll work with GNU Smalltalk, which is graphics-free.

If you want to follow along yourself, install GNU Smalltalk by typing

```
> sudo apt-get install gnu-smalltalk
```

On macOS, you can install Smalltalk by typing

```
$ brew install gnu-smalltalk
```

For Windows users, I recommend a Linux virtual machine, Windows Subsystem for Linux, or, barring that, Cygwin.

Smalltalk supports integers, floating-point numbers, strings, and fractions (rationals). Smalltalk has 1D arrays, dictionaries, and many other container objects.

Our goal in this vignette is to learn what makes Smalltalk unique and a good addition to our collection of novel programming languages. First comes a brief discussion of what Smalltalk brings to the table. Then we'll work through a complete Smalltalk program to understand, at least super-ficially, how classes are defined and subclassed. Specifically, we simulate a race between four different animals, each its own Smalltalk class: bird, wolf, frog, and snail.

Basic Smalltalk Features

GNU Smalltalk is intended for scripting, just like Python or Perl. For example, this code shows our first example:

```
#!/usr/bin/gst
"Smalltalk 'Hello, world!' example"

'' displayNl.
'Hello, world!' displayNl.
'' displayNl.
```

The first line is not standard Smalltalk. It's the comment line used by Unix systems to make a script executable by pointing to its interpreter. Double quotes surround comments in Smalltalk, while single quotes surround strings.

The general syntax for calling a method on an object is *<object>* *<method>* or *<object>* *<method>*: *<argument>*. Everything's an object, including strings (even empty ones). Each line in the example above defines a string and then calls the displayNl method to print it. Notice the period at the end of each line. Smalltalk uses periods as statement separators. On a Unix-like system, chmod a+x hello.st makes *hello.st* executable. The GNU Smalltalk interpreter itself is gst:

```
gst
GNU Smalltalk ready

st> 2 + 3 * 6
30
st> 2 + (3 * 6)
20
```

You can exit the interpreter with CTRL-D.

The expressions above should give you pause. Smalltalk evaluates from left to right without respect to operator precedence. Therefore, the first expression is interpreted as 2+3*6 = 5*6 = 30. Recall that APL is similar but evaluates from right to left. In Smalltalk, use parentheses on expressions to enforce the desired evaluation ordering.

Smalltalk syntax is simple but leads to verbose statements. To define and make basic use of an array, use

```
st> x := Array new: 5
(nil nil nil nil nil )
st> x at: 1 put: 3
3
```

```
st> x at: 3 put: 'plugh'
'plugh'
st> x
(3 nil 'plugh' nil nil )
```

Smalltalk uses := for assignment, so the first line declares x to be an array of five elements. Smalltalk variables default to `nil`. The second line is x[0]=3 in most other languages. The method name is at and it accepts one argument, the index, and a keyword argument, `put`. Smalltalk arrays hold any object, as the remaining lines above demonstrate. Smalltalk indexes arrays from one.

It's possible Smalltalk would win first prize for the longest method name in a standard library. Consider the following, which counts how many times a substring appears in another string:

```
st> s := 'Nobody expects the Spanish inquisition!'
st> s countSubCollectionOccurrencesOf: 'i'
5
```

Graphical Smalltalk systems have a transcript window where messages are displayed. GNU Smalltalk uses this for normal output:

```
st> Transcript show: 'howdy'; cr; show: 'partner'; cr
howdy
partner
```

This little example illustrates several Smalltalk features. First, `Transcript` is the name of a class, so we're using class-level methods, not instance methods. Second, Smalltalk uses a semicolon to call methods using the most recent class or object, which in this case is `Transcript`.

Blocks

An important concept in Smalltalk is the *block*, which is code between square brackets. Blocks are similar to unnamed functions, as they can be assigned to variables and later executed. They also form the body of Smalltalk's control structures, which are nothing more than method calls on objects, like everything else in Smalltalk. Consider the following example.

```
st> b := [ 'I am a block. I am an island.' displayNl ]
a BlockClosure
st> b value
I am a block.  I am an island.
'I am a block.  I am an island.'
```

We define b to be a block. The block contains one statement to print a string. To execute the block, we call `value`, which prints the string. The second string in quotes is the value of the block, the last statement in it, which is the string here. In a running program, the second string would not be shown.

Blocks accept arguments and support local variables.

```
st> x := 'number 9'
'number 9'
st> b := [ :i | |y| y:=i. x:=y. z:=y ]
a BlockClosure
st> b value: 42
42
st> x. z. y
42
42
nil
```

It's important to understand this example. First, we have x, defined out-side of a block and set to a string. Next, we define block b. It accepts an ar-gument, i (the colon is necessary), and defines a local variable, y. Local variables are listed between vertical bars (pipes). The body of the block sets y to the argument, i, then uses y to assign to x and z.

The block is executed with 42 as the argument. Then we look at the value of x, z, and y. What happened? The block updated x, which already existed outside of the block. It also defined z *outside* the block. We didn't declare z to be local to the block, so it was defined globally. We did declare y to be local to the block, so it has no value outside of the block, hence nil. The moral of the story is: if you want what happens in the block to stay in the block, only use local variables. As an exercise, try this example in Python, defining a function called b(i) in place of the block. Variables defined in the function do not alter variables defined globally unless you use global explicitly. Smalltalk blocks allow unintended consequences, so care is necessary.

Control Structures

Smalltalk has the expected control structures, but their syntax is unusual because they are really methods. Let's look quickly at conditional statements, while loops, and iterated loops. We can't cover all combinations, especially with iteration, but you'll get the gist of what's going on.

Examine this short program:

```
v := stdin nextLine asInteger.

(v < 0) ifTrue: [
    a := -1
] ifFalse: [
    (v > 0) ifTrue: [
        a := 1
    ] ifFalse: [
        a := 0
    ]
].
```

It asks the user for an integer by reading the next line from standard input and interpreting the resulting string as an integer before assigning it to v.

Next, the code checks to see if v is less than 0, 0, or greater than 0 and sets the value of a accordingly.

The code above looks like an if-then-else construct, and it acts like one, but it isn't one. It's normal Smalltalk *<object> <method>*: *<argument>* syntax. The ifTrue method is applied to the Boolean returned by (v < 0). If the Boolean is true, execute the block that sets a to −1. Similarly, ifFalse fires if the Boolean value is not true. Nesting within the block is perfectly fine, so the first ifFalse block has its own pair of ifTrue and ifFalse method calls.

In Smalltalk, while loops act similarly. Consider

```
i:=1.
[i < 10] whileTrue: [ i displayNl. i := i + 1 ]
```

where, unlike ifTrue, whileTrue is applied to a block, [i < 10]. As expected, this code snippet displays the numbers 1 through 9. The same output is generated by

```
i:=1.
[i >= 10] whileFalse: [ i displayNl. i := i + 1 ]
```

which loops for as long as the code block returns false. Note that while loops are applied to a block, so the block need not be just a simple Boolean expression, but need only return a Boolean value. The following is a perfectly valid loop

```
i:=1.
[x:=i*i. i < 10] whileTrue: [ i displayNl. i := i + 1 ]
```

with the side effect of defining x and setting it to 100.

A basic for loop in Smalltalk is

```
1 to: 10 do: [ :i | i displayNl ]
```

As with if and while, the loop isn't a construct; it's a message to sends to the integer object, 1. The first part creates an Interval object, which is the entity that understands the do message. For example, the following code produces the same output as the previous.

```
j := 1 to: 10.
j do: [ :i | i displayNl ]
```

Notice that the argument to do is a block, with i being the argument that becomes the loop control variable. Therefore, we can do something like the following if we wish:

```
j := 1 to: 10.
b := [ :i | i displayNl ].
j do: b.
```

The first line defines j as an Interval object, the second defines b as a block (really a BlockClosure object), and the third uses do to apply the block to the interval.

We've hit the essentials of Smalltalk, though honestly we've barely put our little toe in the water. Smalltalk has a simple syntax and an extensive class library that we've ignored. However, we must press on. Smalltalk is all about objects and classes. Let's see how by going to the races.

Going to the Races

We'll create a small class hierarchy and use it to race four animals against each other. Our plan is this:

1. Define a base class, Animal, that responds to messages common to all the animals.

2. Define four subclasses: Bird, Wolf, Frog, and Snail. The subclasses respond to messages based on how the animals move: fly, run, hop, and crawl, respectively. The class ignores messages that it doesn't understand.

3. Create an instance of each animal and send randomly selected messages to them.

4. Display the distance each animal has moved and declare a winner.

The complete source code is in *race.st*. We'll present it in pieces as we walk through it. Please read through the full source code file first before proceeding. If you do, the discussion will be easier to follow. Recall that the first line of the file is not standard Smalltalk; it's Unix-speak to run the file as a script. The -g option disables the occasional garbage collection message.

We begin with the base class, Animal:

```
Object subclass: Animal [
    | increment distance letter |
    init: inc letter: l [
        letter := l.
        increment := inc.
        distance := 0
    ]
    getDistance [ ^distance ]
    print [
        (distance-1) timesRepeat: [ '-' display ].
        letter displayNl
    ]
]
```

All Smalltalk classes are subclasses of something. The top of the object hierarchy is the class Object, so Animal subclasses from it. There are three member variables: increment, distance, and letter. There are three methods: init, getDistance, and print.

The init method accepts inc as an argument along with letter, a keyword argument. In Smalltalk, instances of a class are usually created with new and initialized later; however, this process is flexible. We'll call init to set up our class instances. In this case, initialization sets the distance traveled to zero, the letter associated with the animal when printing, and how far the animal moves each time it does move.

The next method is getDistance. It returns the current value of distance. Smalltalk does not have a return statement; rather, it precedes the value to return with a carat (^).

The final method, print, displays the animal's distance traveled as a sequence of dashes ending with the animal's letter. It uses timesRepeat, a message sent to an integer to repeat a code block a set number of times.

Animal defines the base class. The specific animal classes come next:

```
Animal subclass: Bird [
    init [ super init: 6 letter: 'B' ]
    fly [ distance := distance + increment ]
    doesNotUnderstand: msg [ ]
]
Animal subclass: Wolf [
    init [ super init: 5 letter: 'W' ]
    run [ distance := distance + increment ]
    doesNotUnderstand: msg [ ]
]
Animal subclass: Frog [
    init [ super init: 4 letter: 'F' ]
    hop [ distance := distance + increment ]
    doesNotUnderstand: msg [ ]
]
Animal subclass: Snail [
    init [ super init: 3 letter: 'S' ]
    crawl [ distance := distance + increment ]
    doesNotUnderstand: msg [ ]
]
```

Each class defines init, which calls init of the superclass, Animal, passing in the increment and letter associated with the animal. For Bird, the increment is 6 and the letter is 'B'.

Each subclass defines a method based on how the animal moves. For Bird, it's fly. The move method adds the increment to the distance. The last method in each subclass is doesNotUnderstand. This method is called by Smalltalk when an object receives a message it has no method for. For example, if we pass the fly method to a Wolf object, doesNotUnderstand is be called. We want to ignore unknown messages, so the body of the method is empty.

The classes are defined, but no instances have been created. Let's create an instance of each and store the objects in an array.

```
animals := Array new: 4.
animals at: 1 put: (Bird new).
animals at: 2 put: (Wolf new).
animals at: 3 put: (Frog new).
animals at: 4 put: (Snail new).
1 to: 4 do: [ :i | (animals at: i) init ].
```

Each element of the array animals is set to the object returned by calling new. Doing this creates the objects, but they are not yet initialized. The final line loops over the array, calling each object's init method.

The animals are ready, so let's run the race.

```
moves := #('fly' 'run' 'hop' 'crawl').
50 timesRepeat: [
    m := moves at: ((1 to: 4) atRandom).
    1 to: 4 do: [ :i | (animals at: i) perform: m asSymbol ].
].
```

There are four movement methods: fly, run, hop, and crawl. We want to select one of them at random and send it to each animal. If the animal knows how to respond to the message, it does; otherwise, it quietly ignores it.

First, moves is set to an array of the method names. This syntax is a shortcut for the at:put: syntax used above. The timesRepeat loop sets the number of moves that will happen. The interval, (1 to: 4), is sent atRandom to return a random integer in $[1, 4]$. This is the index in moves to set m to a randomly selected method string. The do loop sends the message in m to each animal by first converting the string to a symbol representing the method before passing it to the object itself via perform. Because each animal only responds to one of the move messages, only one animal will move during each pass through the timesRepeat loop.

The race is now over. To see how the animals did, we use the code below to call the print method of each animal:

```
Transcript cr; show: 'Race results:'; cr; cr
1 to: 4 do: [ :i | (animals at: i) print ].
'' displayNl.
```

To declare a winner, we need to find which of the four moved the farthest. For that, we'll use a Dictionary,

```
dist := Dictionary new.
1 to: 4 do: [ :i |
    animal := animals at: i.
    dist at: animal put: animal getDistance
].
```

where the keys are the object instances and the values are the distance each animal moved. To declare a winner we find the maximum distance.

```
d := (animals at: 1) getDistance.
winner := (animals at: 1) class displayString.
dist associationsDo: [ :pair |
    ((pair value) > d) ifTrue: [
        d := pair value.
        winner := (pair key) class displayString.
    ]
].
Transcript show: 'The winner is '; show: winner; cr; cr.
```

To loop over a dictionary, use `associationsDo`, which passes a key-value pair to the body of the loop. The `value` of the pair is the distance that animal traveled and the key is a reference to the object. The phrase `class displayString` converts the name of the object class to a string for display.

The output of *race.st* looks like this:

```
Race results:


-----------------------------------------------------------B
------------------------------------------------------------W
---------------------------------------------------------F
--------------------------S


The winner is Wolf
```

The bird will win most often as it flies the farthest each time it moves. The wolf wins next most often and the snail least often. The file *run.py* runs 10,000 races tracking how often each animal wins. For example, one run produced

```
Bird wins  0.6373
Wolf wins  0.2802
Frog wins  0.0760
Snail wins 0.0065
```

The bird won nearly 64 percent of the races, followed by the wolf, who won 28 percent. The poor snail only won about one race in two hundred.

Standard ML

Our final language is *Standard ML* (SML), an early functional language based on ML. *Functional languages* use composition of functions—that is, functions applied to the output of other functions—to implement algorithms. We'll get to what makes SML a functional language in a later chapter when discussing programming language paradigms.

The version of SML we'll work with, SML-NJ (NJ stands for "New Jersey") largely conforms to the language standard promulgated in 1997 (*https://sml family.github.io/sml97-defn.pdf*).

To follow along, install SML on Ubuntu using the command

```
> sudo apt-get install smlnj
```

Versions for macOS and Windows are available at *http://www.smlnj.org/dist/working/110.99/index.html*.

Run **sml** to start the interpreter. As with Smalltalk, use CTRL-D to exit.

```
Standard ML of New Jersey v110.79 [built: Tue Aug  8 23:21:20 2017]
-
```

Ensure that the version number is at least that shown here. The interpreter is waiting for us to type something; try "scary movie";. The interpreter responds with

```
val it = "scary movie" : string
```

This tells us that "scary movie" is of type string. Moreover, the interpreter has defined the variable it and assigned the string to it. SML statements end with a semicolon and SML is a typed language; however, one of its strengths is that it infers types in most cases.

One characteristic of functional languages like SML is *referential transparency*, meaning that a function returns the same value for the same input regardless of the state of the system as a whole. For example, consider the following Python session:

```
>>> x = 359
>>> def f(y):
...     return x+y
>>> f(2)
361
>>> x = 42
>>> f(2)
44
```

The value returned by f(y) depends on the current value of the variable x. Now consider the equivalent in SML.

```
- val x = 359;
val x = 359 : int
- fun f(y) = x+y;
val f = fn : int -> int
- f(2);
val it = 361 : int
- val x = 42;
val x = 42 : int
- f(2);
val it = 361 : int
```

In this case, the function uses the value of x as it was when the function was defined. Changing x later does not affect the function value. SML is referentially transparent, but Python is not. SML functions are defined with fun, followed by the function name and argument list in parentheses. At least they can be defined that way. We'll encounter other ways below.

SML supports the common primitive data types: integers, reals, and strings. It also supports lists and tuples, along with more advanced user-defined data structures resembling classes. Every member of an SML list must be of the same data type. Tuples may mix data types; however, SML functions consider tuples to be a compound type rather than a collection of the same type.

SML is perhaps the only language that requires you to write threatening code.

```
- val x = true;
- val y = false;
- x orelse y;
val it = true : bool
- x andalso y;
val it = false : bool
```

SML uses orelse where most other languages use or. So to check if one or the other conditional expression is true, you use orelse. Similarly, andalso replaces and.

SML supports *unnamed functions*, or *lambda functions* as they are sometimes called. For example, the following code defines an unnamed function to add 1 to its argument and then immediately applies it to the number 11.

```
- (fn x => x+1) 11;
val it = 12 : int
```

SML treats functions as *first-class objects*. This means they can be assigned to variables and returned from functions. One use of this ability is to return a partially evaluated function in which some of the arguments are bound but others are not. This is known as *currying*, after Haskell Curry, an American mathematician who worked in logic. The Haskell programming language is named after him.

Before we see currying in action, consider the following two function definitions:

```
- fun add(x,y) = x+y;
val add = fn : int * int -> int
- add(11,22);
val it = 33 : int
- fun add x y = x+y;
val add = fn : int -> int -> int
- add 11 22;
val it = 33 : int
```

We define add twice with the second definition replacing the first. Both definitions take two arguments and add them together, so add(11,22) produces the same output as add 11 22. Look carefully at what SML returned after each function definition.

The first definition produced

```
fn : int * int -> int
```

which means that add is a function that accepts two integers and returns an integer. The second definition produced

```
fn : int -> int -> int
```

meaning that add is now a function that accepts an integer and produces *a function* that accepts an integer and returns an integer. Defined in this form, add enables currying. Consider:

```
- fun add x y = x+y;
val add = fn : int -> int -> int
- (add 11) 22;
val it = 33 : int
- val add11 = add 11;
val add11 = fn : int -> int
- add11(22);
val it = 33 : int
- add11;
val it = fn : int -> int
```

We define add as above and apply it to 11 to return a function that we then apply to 22 to get 33.

Currying allows us to fix the first argument, the x, and bind the returned function, now expecting only the y, to a variable. The new function, add11, accepts an integer argument and returns that argument plus 11. Lastly, we see that add11 is indeed a function mapping an integer to an integer.

SML functions can use patterns, much like Prolog. For example, consider these definitions:

```
fun hello () = print "Hello, world!\n";

fun greetA(n) =
    if (n = 1) then hello()
    else (hello(); greetA(n-1));

fun greetB 1 = hello()
  | greetB n = (hello(); greetB(n-1));
```

This example is in the file *hello.sml*. You can load it with **sml hello.sml** or by entering **use "hello.sml";** if you're already in the interpreter. Either way, you'll see SML's output as to the functions and their types.

```
[opening hello.sml]
val hello = fn : unit -> unit
val greetA = fn : int -> unit
val greetB = fn : int -> unit
```

The first function, hello, accepts no arguments and returns nothing. In SML, nothing is represented by unit. The hello function is used solely for its side effect of printing "Hello, world!" Therefore, hello accepts unit and returns unit. Both greetA and greetB accept an integer and return nothing, hence unit.

Look at the definition of greetA. It uses a recursive call to greetA to print "Hello, world!" repeatedly. If the argument is 1, call hello and return. Otherwise, call hello then call greetA again after subtracting 1 from the argument.

Now look at greetB.

```
fun greetB 1 = hello()
  | greetB n = (hello(); greetB(n-1));
```

This function uses a pattern. The first pattern is greetB 1, meaning that if the argument is one, the pattern matches, so call hello. The pipe (|) marks the beginning of the next pattern. This pattern is checked if the previous pattern fails to match. Here, the pattern is any n that isn't 1. In that case, call hello and then call greetB again with n-1. This second pattern will repeatedly match until the first pattern matches. The first pattern returns nothing, so the return value of all recursive calls is nothing. This is why SML tells us that greetB maps an integer to unit. As an exercise, try implementing the recursive factorial function using a pattern.

The final piece of Standard ML we'll consider is *higher-order functions*. Higher-order functions are functions that accept functions as arguments. The most common higher-order function is map, which applies a function to every element of a list. Consider these examples:

```
- fun add x y = x+y;
val add = fn : int -> int -> int
- val add3 = add 3;
val add3 = fn : int -> int
- map add3 [0,1,2,3,4];
val it = [3,4,5,6,7] : int list
- map (fn x => "a " ^ x) ["boat", "car", "truck"];
val it = ["a boat","a car","a truck"] : string list
```

The first two definitions use currying to define add3, a function that adds 3 to its argument. The next line uses map to apply add3 to each element of the list [0,1,2,3,4], producing [3,4,5,6,7]. The final example applies an unnamed function to prefix a list of strings using ^, which concatenates two strings.

The function map is straightforward to understand. Let's now look at two more higher-order functions supplied by SML. They go by the names foldl and foldr. Review the following and try to work out what they do.

```
- val f = (fn (x,y) => y^x);
val f = fn : string * string -> string
- foldr f "a " ["boat", "car", "truck"];
val it = "a truckcarboat" : string
- foldl f "a " ["boat", "car", "truck"];
val it = "a boatcartruck" : string
```

The first line shows yet another way to define a function by assigning an unnamed function to a variable. The function f accepts two arguments and returns the first prepended by the second. Note the flip between x and y.

The next line calls foldr with f and two arguments: the string "a " and a list of strings. The result is a string. The following statement uses foldl in place of foldr. It also produces a string, but the order of the strings in the list is reversed from the foldr example. Do you see the pattern?

The foldl function traverses the list from left to right, so the foldl call is equivalent to

```
f("truck", f("car", f("boat", "a ")));
```

whereas foldr traverses from right to left

```
f("boat", f("car", f("truck", "a ")));
```

The fold higher-order functions are useful numerically as well.

```
- foldl op+ 0 [11,33,22,44];
val it = 110 : int
- foldl op* 1 [5,4,3,2,1];
val it = 120 : int
```

The notation op+ refers to the binary addition operator, so the first line sums a list of integers. Likewise, op* is multiplication, meaning the second line calculates the product of a list of integers.

There is much more to Standard ML, including an extensive library of data types. However, we've reviewed enough to get a feel for the language.

Summary

In this chapter, we compared programming languages to paleontology, a metaphor we'll return to throughout the book. Then, we briefly explored 10 programming languages to understand how they approach the idea of coding. The selected languages either introduced fundamental concepts or programming paradigms, like object-oriented programming, or were novel simply because they were first. In some cases, the language was foundational to a collection of future languages, like ALGOL. Reviewing what was and is helps us see where we might go and puts us in a frame of mind conducive to what esolangs have to offer.

The vignettes in this chapter are superficial, but necessarily so. Let's step back a bit now and consider what it means to be a programming language, to grasp at their essence.

2

THE ESSENTIALS OF
PROGRAMMING LANGUAGES

Attempting to compress the essentials of programming languages into a single chapter is an impossible task, but I'll do my best to convey what is essential about programming languages as background for the rest of the book. In reality though, this chapter should be either a book or a semester-long undergraduate course.

The vignettes of Chapter 1 were meant to give you an introduction to a few programming language concepts, but they left some big questions unanswered. For example, what exactly *is* a programming language? How are programming languages structured and implemented? What are programming paradigms? And so on. Potential questions abound. In this chapter, I'll provide sufficient answers to these questions, and others, to give us what we need to work through the languages we'll encounter and implement later in the book.

We'll begin this chapter with a working definition of *programming language*. Then we'll cover syntax and semantics—how to speak in a programming language and what the speech means. After that, we'll briefly review the ways programming languages are implemented, or made real. We'll implement several esolangs in this book, so basic knowledge in this area will be useful.

We'll then explore data types and data structures, what sort of data the language works with, and how it organizes that data. We'll also explore variables and *scope*, which is the part of the language telling us what information can be seen and in what context.

All programming languages implement some form of *flow control*, that is, some way to do more than execute instruction after instruction in a linear fashion. We'll explore that before ending the chapter with a discussion of *programming language paradigms*, or the different ways programming languages approach coding. We encountered several different programming paradigms in Chapter 1. Here, we'll put names to the paradigms and discuss their characteristics. The paradigm, or paradigms, a language supports directly influence how we think in that language.

Defining Programming Language

A book about programming languages should include a definition of its subject. Therefore, let's be explicit about what we mean when we write the words *programming language*.

> A programming language is a vehicle that expresses thought and actualizes it as an algorithm to control a computer. A programming language consists of two things: *a set of instructions* and *rules for organizing those instructions*.

All of the languages in Chapter 1 meet our definition. Clearly, Short Code and everything created after it does: there are instructions and rules for organizing those instructions. Zuse's Plankalkül and even Ada's "diagram of development" meet this definition. Ada's diagram encodes an algorithm in a manner useful for the Analytical Engine. Some might quibble that the Analytical Engine would not have been able to use the diagram directly, but a modern computer can't use C, ALGOL, or Prolog source code directly, either. A programming language is abstract; it needs an interface between itself and the machine it seeks to control.

Syntax and Semantics

Syntax refers to how language elements can be combined to form valid statements in the grammar of a language. This is true for both human languages and programming languages. Most programming languages intended for real-world use have a formal grammar, that is, a specification of what is and isn't allowed as a statement in the language. These grammars guide the development of interpreters and compilers for the language.

The word *semantics* refers to the meaning of a syntactically correct statement. Syntax is concrete; a statement either is or isn't valid for the language. Semantics, on the other hand, is harder to pin down; it depends on what the programmer (speaker) intends, which may differ from the effective meaning.

In a human language context, this is a misunderstanding; in a programming language context, this is often a bug.

To help understand the difference between syntax and semantics, let's consider a while statement in Pascal:

```
while <boolean-expression> do <statements>
```

This is an expression of the while statement's syntax. Pascal's formal grammar must define <boolean-expression> and <statements>. A <boolean-expression> is an expression that returns a value that is true or false and <statements> is a single statement or a sequence of statements with begin and end around them (a block statement).

Therefore, syntactically, this is a correct Pascal statement:

```
while i < 10 do i := i - 1;
```

However, semantically, this statement is unlikely to be correct. Its meaning is likely not what the programmer intended. If i is greater than or equal to 10, the while loop never executes because the condition is false. If i is less than 10, the while loop does execute, but would never end because i is less than 10 and is only getting smaller. In practice, the while loop will eventually end when i wraps around from the largest negative to the largest positive supported by the integer data type. In Pascal, the largest negative integer is −32,768 and the largest positive is 32,767. In Pascal, an integer is signed and 16 bits wide. This statement is, at best, a highly inefficient way to do i := 32767, and is likely not at all what the programmer intended.

Remember: syntax refers to grammatically correct statements and semantics refers to the meaning of a statement.

Implementing Programming Languages

Konrad Zuse's Plankalkül was a programming language, but he didn't implement it. Zuse expressed thought through it, but he couldn't actualize the thought encoded because there was no interface, that is, no implementation of the language for a physical machine. Programming languages can exist without a computer to run them, but to control a machine, there must be an implementation. In this section, we'll discuss the ways programming languages are implemented.

There are two main methods for implementing a programming language. An *interpreter* takes the program text, breaks it up into pieces called statements—that is, sets of instructions with meaning—and performs the actions implied by the instructions. On the other hand, a *compiler* takes the program text, breaks it up into pieces with meaning, and translates those pieces into another language, often the computer's machine language.

The output of a compiler is a set of machine instructions that the computer can execute directly. Compilers are programs that translate one programming language into another. Interpreters are programs that implement the meaning of the instructions implied by the program text.

Interpreters are like work crews. They get the work order and make it happen. Compilers are like translators. They map meaning from one programming language to another. Interpreters run programs; compilers produce programs to run later.

There is a clear conceptual break between what an interpreter does and what a compiler does. Unfortunately, in practice, this line isn't as distinct as we might hope. For example, many new languages are both interpreted and compiled at the same time. This includes Python and Java, among others. There is a good reason for this: namely, portability between different hardware platforms. Languages that do this make use of *bytecode compilers*, which are compilers that translate from the high-level source language (like Python) to a low-level target language that can be interpreted very quickly. The compiler portion does the hard work of extracting the meaning of the program text while the interpreter concentrates on performance. The net result is a language implementation that is portable—just rewrite the interpreter part for a new target machine—and much faster than an old-style interpreter that mindlessly re-derived the meaning of the code, over and over, as it was executed.

Tokens, Lexers, and Parsers

Neither interpreters nor compilers work with source code text as typed. The text is first processed by a *lexer* to split the text into *tokens*, which are strings representing the elements of the programming language. The lexer often attaches extra information to the tokens, such as whether the token is a number or a keyword of the language.

The output of the lexer is usually passed to a *parser*, which groups the tokens into meaningful language statements, often in the form of a tree. The interpreter or compiler then uses that tree to evaluate the statement (interpreter) or transform the statement into the target language (compiler).

For example, consider this Pascal statement:

```
y := m * x + b;
```

The lexer splits the statement into tokens and then adds the associated information.

Token	Associated information
y	Variable, type real
:=	Assignment
m	Variable, type real
*	Multiplication
x	Variable, type real
+	Addition
b	Variable, type real
;	End of statement

The parser uses this to construct an *abstract syntax tree* (see Figure 2-1).

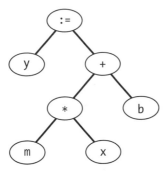

Figure 2-1: An abstract syntax
tree for y := m*x + b

The tree is a representation of the statement in a form the interpreter or compiler can process. An interpreter would evaluate the right side of the tree using the current value of the variables m, x, and b to assign a new value to the variable y. A compiler would use the tree to generate a series of assembly language or machine code instructions that, when executed, implement the assignment.

Lexers and parsers for real programming languages can be quite complex. Most people use parser generators like flex/bison or ANTLR to automatically generate code from the language specifications. Fortunately for us, the esolangs we'll explore are often so simple that lexing is removing whitespace and comments and parsing is examining the next character in the string output by the lexer. For example, this is precisely how the ABC language of Chapter 7 is processed by its interpreter.

Interpreters

Interpreters are usually easier to write than compilers. Computer scientists spent decades learning how to write optimizing compilers that produce highly efficient and fast code. The downside of an interpreter is that it's often slow compared to the machine code generated by a compiler. All of the esolangs we'll work with in this book are interpreted, though compilers do exist for some of them (for example Brainfuck; see *https://github.com/Wilfred/bfc/*).

Later in the book, we'll write interpreters in Python for simple esolangs like ABC, FRACTRAN, Filska, and Firefly. By design, their syntax is simple enough that complex lexing and parsing are not necessary.

A complete example of an interpreter, with a specified language grammar and a complete lexer and parser, is beyond what we can present here. However, I do recommend attempting to do that yourself at some point. If you do, think clearly and be prepared for some level of frustration before you succeed. For now, let's look at what an old BASIC interpreter does to parse a simple program.

The Apple II computer came with BASIC in ROM. BASIC was both the command line and the programming language of the machine. Users entered a line of the program, which BASIC immediately parsed and stored in memory. Programs were stored in memory as a linked list, which is why every line needed a line number. It was so BASIC knew where to insert the line in the list.

Consider this simple program entered line by line at the prompt (]):

```
] 10 FOR X = 1 TO 10
] 20 PRINT X, X*X
] 30 NEXT X
```

If this program is RUN, it produces a table of squares.

```
]RUN
1      1
2      4
3      9
4      16
5      25
6      36
7      49
8      64
9      81
10     100
```

The tokenized representation of this program occupies 30 bytes of the Apple II's memory (Listing 2-1).

```
0801: link: 080D
      0A 00 -- line number 10, uint16, lo/hi
      81 token "FOR"
      58 ASCII character, "X"
      D0 token "="
      31 ASCII character, "1"
      C1 token "TO"
      31 30 ASCII characters, "10"
      00 end of line
080D: link: 0818
      14 00 -- line number 20, uint16, lo/hi
      BA token "PRINT"
      58 ASCII character, "X"
      2C ASCII character, ","
      58 ASCII character, "X"
      CA token "*"
      58 ASCII character, "X"
      00 end of line
0818: link: 081F
      1E 00 -- line number 30, uint16, lo/hi
```

```
      82 token "NEXT"
      58 ASCII character, "X"
      00 end of line
081F: 00 00 -- end of program
```

Listing 2-1: A tokenized Applesoft BASIC program

The program begins at memory location 0x0801, with the link to the next line beginning at 0x080D. The line number is stored as a 16-bit unsigned integer, with the low-order byte first: `0A 00` = 0 × 256 + 10 = 10. The parsed line of code comes next, where known BASIC commands like `FOR` have been replaced by a single-byte token (0x81). Interestingly, the numbers, like 1 and 10 for the `FOR` loop limits, are not stored as numbers but rather as ASCII characters. The `PRINT` statement is also stored as ASCII characters, including the name of the variable, `X`.

BASIC must do a significant amount of work to interpret a line, and do so repeatedly in this case because a loop is involved. Because of this, BASIC was notoriously slow. However, to be fair, the Apple II's BASIC interpreter was written in assembly language for a simple 8-bit microprocessor to run on a machine with as little as 16KB of RAM. We'll use Python to implement our languages, so our task will be significantly easier and proportionately less impressive.

Compilers

One of the best books about compilers is the classic "Dragon Book" by Aho, Lam, Sethi, and Ullman: *Compilers: Principles, Techniques, and Tools*, 2nd edition (Addison Wesley, 2006). It's called the Dragon Book because of the cover illustration. If you are at all curious about compiler design, I recommend this book.

Section 1.2 of the Dragon Book enumerates the phases of a compiler:

1. Lexical analyzer
2. Syntax analyzer
3. Semantic analyzer
4. Intermediate code generator
5. Code optimizer
6. Code generator

Interpreters perform at least phases 1 through 3, and possibly some form of phase 4, and then execute the program. Compilers perform all or most of the phases to produce machine code output.

Let's look at the code produced by a simple compiler called `pico`. It compiles a simple stack-based language to assembly code for Microchip 10F2xx series microcontrollers. The 10F2xx series are perhaps the cheapest microcontrollers on the market. As of this writing, a single 10F200 can be yours for a mere 0.66 USD.

The compiler is in the file *pic0.py*, and implements phases 1 through 5 above. Phase 6, final code generation, uses the gpasm assembler (see *https://gputils.sourceforge.io/*).

The file *timer.pic0* (Listing 2-2) contains a PIC0 program to toggle an LED attached to the microcontroller.

```
p10f200
IntRC_OSC
WDT_OFF
CP_OFF
MCLRE_OFF

equ[ count 0x12 ]

[ main
  asm{ movwf OSCCAL }        ;  store oscillator calibration value
  OSCCAL/0                    ;  disable INTOSC/4 on GPIO.2
  0 GPIO!                     ;  clear GPIO
  0b00001000 R0->W tris       ;  set GPIO directions

  ;  Clear TMR0 and reset prescaler
  0 TMR0!  clrwdt 0b11000111 R0->W option

  ;  Loop forever
  {
    ;  Wait for the timer to overflow 100 times
    100 count! {
        TMR0@ 0if
          count--  count@ ?0break
        then
    }

    ;  Toggle LED
    if(GPIO^2) GPIO/2 else GPIO^2 then
  }
]
```

Listing 2-2: A PIC0 program to toggle an LED

The compiler takes this file as input producing *timer.asm* as output (Listing 2-3). For the final compilation phase, gpasm takes *timer.asm* as input to produce several output files: *timer.cod*, *timer.lst*, and *timer.hex*.

```
    processor   10F200
    include     <P10F200.inc>
    __CONFIG    _IntRC_OSC & _WDT_OFF & _CP_OFF & _MCLRE_OFF

GP0     equ     d'0'
GP1     equ     d'1'
```

```
GP2     equ     d'2'
GP3     equ     d'3'
R0      equ     d'16'
R1      equ     d'17'
count   equ     d'18'

main
        movwf   OSCCAL
        bcf     OSCCAL,0
        movlw   d'0'
        movwf   GPIO
        movlw   d'8'
        movwf   R0
        movf    R0,w
        tris    GPIO
        movlw   d'0'
        movwf   TMR0
        clrwdt
        movlw   d'199'
        movwf   R0
        movf    R0,w
        option
A_0000
        movlw   d'100'
        movwf   d'18'
A_0002
        movf    TMR0,w
        movwf   R0
        movf    R0,f
        btfss   STATUS,Z
        goto    A_0004
        decf    d'18',f
        movf    d'18',w
        movwf   R0
        movf    R0,f
        btfss   STATUS,Z
        goto    A_0006
        goto    A_0003
A_0006
A_0004
        goto    A_0002
A_0003
        btfss   GPIO,2
        goto    A_0007
        bcf     GPIO,2
        goto    A_0008
```

```
A_0007
    bsf      GPIO,2
A_0008
    goto     A_0000
A_0001
    sleep
    END
```

Listing 2-3: PIC0 compiler output

The file *timer.hex* contains code actually loaded onto the microcontroller.

```
:020000040000FA
:1000000025000504000C2600080C30001002060034
:10001000000C21000400C70C300010020200640C28
:100020003200010230003002430710D0AF2001202C2
:100030003000300243071D0A1E0A110A4607220A31
:0A0040004604230A46050F0A0300D8
:021FFE00EB0FE7
:00000001FF
```

Listing 2-2 may seem somewhat cryptic, but it's likely more readable than Listing 2-3 even though both programs achieve the same goal. To learn more about PIC0, see *PIC0_Manual.pdf* in the same directory as *timer.pic0*.

Bytecode Compilers

Modern interpreters blur the line between interpreter and compiler by compiling the high-level language to a low-level language that can be interpreted quickly. In essence, these languages produce code for a machine that doesn't exist: a machine simulated via an interpreter. To muddy the waters still further, some bytecode compilers perform *just-in-time compilation* (JIT) to produce actual machine code instead of interpreting the bytecode itself. Do we still call those languages interpreted?

Bytecode compilers are not new, though they may not have been called that at first. For example, the UCSD Pascal system used in the late 1970s produced *p-code*, a bytecode that was then interpreted by programs written for a specific system. This made the output portable as only the interpreter needed to be rewritten for a new system. The Pascal system, including the compiler, was written in Pascal and already compiled to p-code.

As mentioned above, Python is also bytecode compiled. Python supplies a module, dis, showing us the bytecode for any function. For example, this function generates factorials recursively:

```
def fact(n):
    if n == 0:
        return 1
    else:
        return n * fact(n-1)
```

To see the bytecode Python actually runs, we can add

```
import dis; dis.dis(fact)
```

This produces

```
2           0 LOAD_FAST            0 (n)
            2 LOAD_CONST           1 (0)
            4 COMPARE_OP           2 (==)
            6 POP_JUMP_IF_FALSE   12

3           8 LOAD_CONST           2 (1)
           10 RETURN_VALUE

5    >>    12 LOAD_FAST            0 (n)
           14 LOAD_GLOBAL          0 (fact)
           16 LOAD_FAST            0 (n)
           18 LOAD_CONST           2 (1)
           20 BINARY_SUBTRACT
           22 CALL_FUNCTION        1
           24 BINARY_MULTIPLY
           26 RETURN_VALUE
           28 LOAD_CONST           0 (None)
           30 RETURN_VALUE
```

Again, even without studying the meaning of each part of the disassembly, we can follow the flow of the function by examining the tokens on the far right and the names of the instructions in the middle. For example, POP_JUMP_IF_FALSE must examine the result of applying ==, and if not true, jumps to 12, which clearly implements the else portion of the function.

Notice the final two lines of the disassembly? They return None, which is the default value Python returns from a function. To us, it is obvious that the function never ends by exiting the if, as both branches use return, but the Python compiler must not detect this, so it adds code to handle leaving the function without executing return.

Programming languages, both compiled and interpreted, must operate on data. Let's now explore how languages manipulate and store data.

Data Types

The phrase *data type* refers to the organization of data in a programming language. Is the data element a number? A character? A structure made up of other data pooled together? How data is processed and stored depends on the data type.

Programming languages fall into different categories based on how they deal with data types. A language may be strongly typed or weakly typed. Similarly, a language might be statically typed or dynamically typed.

In a *strongly typed language*, the type of a variable will not, at a minimum, be automatically changed behind the scenes for a particular use of the variable. Python is a strongly typed language, as is Java. For example, in Python, adding an integer and string will result in a runtime error, even if the string is actually a number. You can see this by running `1 + '2'`, which should generate a `TypeError`.

A *weakly typed language* will change data types implicitly in different situations. In Chapter 5, we'll explore SNOBOL. In SNOBOL, for some string operations, a numeric value is implicitly converted into a string. Similarly, a string that represents a number will be implicitly converted into a number if the expression expects a number. In SNOBOL, the expression `1 + '2'` isn't an error. It correctly evaluates to 3 by quietly converting `'2'` into a number behind the scenes. Therefore, SNOBOL is a weakly typed language.

A *dynamically typed language* does not require the programmer to declare the type of data a variable holds before using it. Python is a dynamically typed language. If the variable contains a number, it can be assigned a string at any time, for example. Therefore, Python is both strongly and dynamically typed. Smalltalk variables are not given a type before use, so Smalltalk is also a dynamically typed language.

A *statically typed language* forces the programmer to declare what kind of data a variable will hold. C, C++, Java, Pascal, ALGOL, and FORTRAN are all statically typed languages. FORTRAN still supports implicit variable typing, which superficially looks like dynamic typing, but it isn't. Unless otherwise instructed via `implicit none`, FORTRAN automatically treats variables beginning with the letters I through N as integers and all other variables as reals (floating-point). The type is still specified indirectly. Therefore, FORTRAN is statically typed as well.

As with many things in programming languages, absolute statements are fraught with peril. Nonetheless, for pedagogical purposes only, let's categorize languages by whether they are dynamic or static and strongly or weakly typed. The result is Table 2-1.

Table 2-1: Languages by Strong/Weak and Dynamic/Static Typing

	Dynamic	Static
Weak	JavaScript, Perl, SNOBOL	C, C++, Pascal
Strong	Python, Ruby, Smalltalk, APL	Scala, Java, Ada, ALGOL, FORTRAN, COBOL, Simula

Some languages don't have a place in Table 2-1. For example, in Chapter 4 we'll explore Forth, which is a stack-based language.

Forth has no concept of data type beyond the number of bits used by the values on its stack; however, some Forth systems have a separate floating-point data stack. The stack value might be a number, or it might be the address of a structure, which in Forth is only an agreed upon partitioning of some amount of memory. Forth is an *untyped* language and enforces nothing related to types.

Data types and their study are an important part of theoretical computer science. Please see the reference material at the back of the book for information on where you can go to dive as deeply into the world of data types as you wish. Here, we'll only concern ourselves with primitive data types and *records*, which are user-defined collections of other data types.

Primitive Data Types

Primitive data types are the atoms of a programming language. They are what you expect languages to work with: numbers, both integers and floating-point values, along with characters (C) and strings (Python). C doesn't have strings as a primitive data type. Instead, it uses arrays of characters to represent strings. In Python, strings are primitive, along with Booleans (True or False). Additionally, Python supports complex numbers, which are usually represented internally as pairs of floating-point values, one for the real part and another for the imaginary part. Some languages, like Scheme, support fractions as a primitive data type. We'll use this to good effect in Chapter 8 when we implement FRACTRAN in Scheme.

Computers use multiple methods for representing numbers in memory. Depending on the language, a programmer might need to know explicit details of how a number is stored. This is often true for C when used in an embedded setting, such as on a microcontroller or single-board computer. In Listing 2-1, we saw how the Apple II stored the 16-bit integer used to represent the line number with its lowest-order byte first followed by the higher-order byte.

NOTE *Storing integers with the lowest-order byte first is known as little-endian. As you might guess, the reverse is known as big-endian (or sometimes network order). For a detailed presentation of how computers store and operate on numbers, please see my book* Numbers and Computers *(Springer, 2017). To understand the origin of "little-endian" and "big-endian," read* Gulliver's Travels *by Jonathan Swift.*

Records

If you use a programming language for any length of time, you'll eventually want to group different data types into a meaningful unit. A *record*, also known as a *structure*, is just that. Languages supporting records include the ALGOL family, both the Pascal and C branches (Figure 1-3), along with many others, like SML. Exactly how a language supports this concept varies, and in some cases, the words *record* and *structure* are not synonymous. This is the case with C#, where a record is immutable but a structure is not. Let's look at how Pascal and C implement records.

Pascal Records

A program to store information on people for later reference would benefit from a record grouping a person's name, birthday, address, and phone number into a single unit. We might then define an array of these records to hold the same set of information for many different people. In Pascal, such declarations might look like this:

```pascal
type
    PhoneNumberType = record
        area, exchange, number : Integer;
    end;

    BirthdayType = record
        month, day, year : Integer;
    end;

    PersonType = record
        first, last : string;
        address : string;
        phone : PhoneNumberType;
        bday : BirthdayType;
    end;
```

The type `PersonType` combines several strings along with instances of `PhoneNumberType` and `BirthdayType`. A variable of type `PersonType` is a single variable with multiple fields.

```pascal
var  person : PersonType;
```

Fields are accessed by name using dot notation.

```pascal
person.first := 'Melvin';
person.bday.year := 1953;
```

The nested `BirthdayType` is referenced first by accessing `bday`, and then by field of `bday`.

A simple example using `PersonType` is in the file *lbb.pas*. To compile it, use the Free Pascal compiler (*https://www.freepascal.org/*), which is easy to install on Ubuntu.

```
> sudo apt-get install fp-compiler-3.0.4
```

See the website for macOS and Windows versions. Once installed, compile *lbb.pas* with `fpc lbb.pas`. The program generates a random database of 100 different people. We'll skip listing *lbb.pas* to save space, but do read through the file to understand what is going on.

C Structures

C structures are similar to Pascal records. The person structures look like:

```c
typedef char string[32];

typedef struct {
    int area, exchange, number;
```

```
} phone_number_t;

typedef struct {
    int month, day, year;
} birthday_t;

typedef struct {
    string first, last;
    string address;
    phone_number_t phone;
    birthday_t bday;
} person_t;
```

As C has no primitive string type, we first define one using a fixed array of 32 characters called string. The declarations use typedef to create a named type for each structure (struct). The names follow the C convention of using underscores and _t at the end to denote a type.

Some languages allow a structure to use the same region of memory to represent multiple fields with different types. I suspect the original motivation for this was to save memory for cases where fields were mutually exclusive. A C union works this way. For example, the following code defines a union where the same memory location is sometimes interpreted as a 32-bit float or a 32-bit unsigned integer.

```
typedef union {
    float f;
    unsigned int d;
} fp_t;
```

Which interpretation is used depends on which field is accessed, f or d. The code below declares a variable fp to be of type fp_t, and then assigns the floating-point field the value of π before referencing the same memory as an unsigned 32-bit integer.

```
fp_t fp;
fp.f = 3.14159265;
printf("%0.8f in hex is %08d\n", fp.f, fp.d);
```

Data Structures

A *data structure* is a way to organize data in memory. A record is a data structure, but the term is usually used to describe more complex ways of managing data. Data structures are necessary but somewhat masked by modern programming languages, as their intrinsic data structures, like Python's lists and dictionaries, are so powerful that more elaborate data structures are not necessary as often as they used to be. Still, for C and C++ programmers, understanding data structures is critical. Data structures are a book in their own right, like many topics in this chapter. Sadly, we must give data structures short shrift by providing only quick summaries.

Arrays

At its simplest, an *array* is nothing more than a block of contiguous memory partitioned into chunks of equal size. An array of 100 32-bit integers occupies a block of $100 \times 4 = 400$ bytes because each integer is 4 bytes long. For example, in C, int A[100] declares A to be such an array. The C sizeof operator reports that A uses 400 bytes of memory, as expected.

The variable A refers to the first 4-byte block of memory allocated for the array. As C knows the size of each element of the array, finding the address of any index of the array is as simple as multiplying the index by four and adding that number to the base address of the array. This is why many programming languages index arrays from 0. That way the offset to the first array element is 0 bytes from the base address.

Multidimensional arrays are still stored as a single block of memory. For example, Pascal defines a 2D array like this:

```
var A : array[0..7, 0..7] of integer;
```

The array A is an 8×8 array, or matrix, of integers (think of a chessboard). In memory, it's still a contiguous block of memory, this time using $8 \times 8 \times 2 = 128$ bytes. To index the array, we use two indices, A[i,j], and calculate the address of the desired element as 8 * i + j added to the base memory address. The eight is the number of elements in one row of the array, that is, the number of columns. Indexing basic arrays, even multidimensional arrays, is trivial and fast as long as the array is stored as a contiguous block of memory.

Linked Lists

Linked lists are the next simplest data structure. They are a collection of nodes, usually allocated on the heap, holding the data of interest along with a pointer to the following link in the chain. A *doubly linked* list also keeps a pointer to the previous node.

Inserting and removing elements of a linked list is easy once the proper node has been located. Locating a node in the first place is relatively slow by comparison because, in the simplest version of a linked list, the list must be traversed node by node from the beginning to find the target. Because of their conceptual simplicity, linked lists are a favorite homework assignment for introductory programming courses.

It might be tempting to wonder if Python lists are sophisticated instances of a linked list. However, this is not the case. Python lists are dynamic arrays of pointers to the objects they contain. Python lists can deliver good performance when indexing by cleverly managing how the arrays grow when new elements are added. They use the simple equations above to locate elements, bypassing the slow, node-by-node traversal of a linked list. That said, dynamic arrays of object pointers are still too slow for many scientific applications, which was the motivation behind powerful array-processing libraries for Python, like NumPy.

Trees

Trees are elaborate hierarchical data structures, usually built dynamically in heap memory. There are many different kinds of trees, and they offer excellent performance in terms of inserting or removing information and locating information quickly. We saw an example of a tree earlier in the chapter in Figure 2-1, where the parser for a programming language builds trees representing the structure of program statements.

Recursive algorithms exist for quickly traversing trees. Trees are ubiquitous in computer science, but again, they are now less often used in day-to-day scenarios because modern languages support robust data structures implicitly or via libraries. Thus, programmers are freed from implementing their own trees except in the most demanding of cases.

Hash Tables

In a *hash table*, a *hash*, the output of a *hash function*, is used to map a block of data to a single value. The idea behind a hash function is to map the data to a unique value, an integer in a specified range. For example, under the hood, Python dictionaries are hash tables. The key is given to the hash function to calculate a unique integer representing the key. Then, the table is indexed by the hash value to return the data associated with the key.

If two different keys generate the same hash value, a *collision* has occurred. There are different options for handling collisions. Python dictionaries randomly probe the table to locate an open position for the key in case of a collision. A good hash function, plus a thorough knowledge of the probabilities behind hash collisions for a specified table size, lets Python manage hashes efficiently to minimize collisions while not wasting memory.

Of course, there are many more types of data structures. The references at the end of the book will point you toward resources where you can explore data structures in more depth. For now, let's learn about how programming languages decide which variable to access when referenced in a program.

Variables and Scope

Variables exist in some context, in a relationship to other variables and regions of the code. The region of code where a variable is visible is known as the variable's *scope*. Programming languages fall into two main camps when it comes to scope: lexical scoping and dynamic scoping. The majority of programming languages use lexical scoping. A smaller subset uses dynamic scoping, and a few, like Perl, use both. Each language has its own, sometimes rather complex, scoping rules. In this section, we'll restrict ourselves to the difference between lexical and dynamic scoping and leave the minutiae of a particular language's scoping rules out of the discussion.

Lexical Scope

In *lexical scoping* (also called *static scoping*), a variable reference is tied back to a declaration or assignment based on the structure of the program when the program was written, that is, the structure seen by a compiler. In this case, the relationships between variable references and which variable is used are static and fixed by the source code's structure.

For lexical scoping, the variable corresponding to a reference follows a simple resolution algorithm: local block or function, next outer block or function, next outer, and so forth to the global level. Python is statically scoped. Consider the following example.

```
def a():
    def b():
        def c():
            def d():
                x = 20
❶                print('d() says', x)
❷            print('c() says', x)
                d()
❸        print('b() says', x)
            c()
        x = 15
        print('a() says', x)
        b()

x = 10
print('main says', x)
a()
```

The output of this program is

```
main says 10
a() says 15
b() says 15
c() says 15
d() says 20
```

Python allows nested function declarations, so the function a contains b, which contains c, which in turn contains d. The outermost level, global scope, defines x=10, as the first print informs us. We then call a, which sets x=15 locally, as a's print tells us. Then we call b, which does not define x locally. Therefore, to understand the reference to x ❸, Python must search for x in an enclosing scope. Python finds x in a, so b uses a's value, 15. When c is called by b, c must search for an x as well ❷. Python doesn't find x in b, so it searches the next higher enclosing scope, that of a, where it does find x=15. Lastly, c calls d which defines x=20 locally, as d reports ❶.

Lexical scoping makes sense without excessive tracing of the program to understand which value is used for which reference. That's why most languages, especially newer or more widely used commercial languages, use it.

Dynamic Scope

Dynamic scoping uses the current state of the program to decide which value goes with which reference. This means it isn't always easy to see which value of a variable will be used by a function, as it depends on the context in which the function is used.

Let's do a little experiment. We'll write what is, more or less, the same program in four different languages: lexically scoped Python and C, dynamically scoped SNOBOL, and Perl, which, as we'll see, is both lexically and dynamically scoped. We'll then see if we can explain the output in each case. The presentation below lists the source code on the left and the program's output on the right.

Python

We know that Python is lexically scoped, as we demonstrated it above. Therefore, let's use Python as our base case, the one that shouldn't surprise us in any way.

Code	Output

``python
x = 10
def f():
    return x
def g():
    x = 20
    return f()
print(g())
``
	10

The code first defines x globally, then f, which does nothing more than return x. Next, the code defines the function g, which defines x=20 locally, within the scope of g, and then returns whatever f returns. The main part of the code prints whatever g returns.

Look at the definition of g. There is a local x defined before the call to f. So why wasn't the output 20? After all, that's what x is set to immediately before the call to f. The output isn't 20 because when f is defined (compiled), x exists globally as 10. Therefore, that's the value used for f, regardless of any local x defined by g.

Review this example, if necessary, to make sure you follow it. When you are ready, read on.

C

C, like Python, is also lexically scoped. Therefore, this example should be much like the example above. Let's take a look.

Code	Output
``c	`h() = 10`
int x = 10;	`g() = 20`
int f() { return x; }	
int g() {	
x = 20;	
return f();	
}	
int h() {	
int x = 15;	
return f();	
}	
void main() {	
printf("h() = %d\n", h());	
printf("g() = %d\n", g());	
}	

For this example, begin at the bottom, with the function main. In C, main must exist and is the entry point for all programs. The function main prints two values: whatever h returns followed by whatever g returns.

The function h defines a local x=15 and then calls f to return whatever f returns. The function f can only see the global x=10, so that's what it returns. The first output line makes sense.

What about the output of g? Does that make sense? The function g is much like h, but the assignment to x=20 doesn't have an int type in front of it. When compiling this function, C realizes there is no locally defined x in g, so it goes up one level in scope to find x (in this case at global scope) and updates that x. So g has a side effect: it alters the value of x globally. This is why f now returns 20 instead of 10.

SNOBOL

SNOBOL, the subject of Chapter 5, is a text-processing language from the 1970s. SNOBOL is dynamically scoped. Its syntax is strange, which is fitting for such a quirky language. For now, we need know only a few things about SNOBOL:

- Functions are declared with define and return whatever value is assigned to their name.

- Variables are declared as local to a function by adding them after the name and arguments in the define statement.

- Printing in SNOBOL is assigning to output.

The code we'll consider is

Code	Output
| ```
    x = 10
    define('f()')      :(ef)
f   f = x              :(return)
ef
    define('g()x')     :(eg)
g   x = 20
    g = f()            :(return)
eg
    output = 'global x = ' f()
    output = 'local  x = ' g()
    output = 'global x = ' x
end
``` | ```
global x = 10
local  x = 20
global x = 10
``` |

This program defines two functions: f and g. The first returns whatever x is, and the second, which defines x as local to g, returns f's return value. The main program begins with x = 10.

The first line of the output is much like we saw earlier: x is global and f returns its value. The second line isn't what we saw earlier. Instead of f using the value of x that existed when f was defined, it uses the value of x set by g, even though g's x is local to g. The function f uses the context in which it is called, at runtime, to locate the value corresponding to x. This is dynamic scoping.

The final line is there to show that x has not been updated by g, so this isn't the situation we encountered with C where, in that case, g did update the global value of x.

Perl

Our final scoping example uses Perl. Perl is known for flexibility, so Perl supports both static and dynamic scoping, whichever suits the programmer's fancy. Let's see how.

Code	Output
| ```
$x = 10;
sub f { return $x; }
sub g {
    local $x = 20;
    return f()
}
sub h {
    my $x = 15;
    return f()
}
print g()."\n";
print h()."\n";
``` | ```
20
10
``` |

The form of this program is familiar. We see f, g, and h, just like the C example above. The program prints the output of g followed by h's output. The only difference between g and h, besides the value assigned to x, is that g uses local and h uses my.

Both local and my define a variable local to a function. The difference lies in which type of scoping is applied to the variable. When my is used, scoping is static, so h returns what f sees via static scoping, namely, x=10. However, for g, Perl has been told, via local, to use dynamic scoping with x, so the call to f from g uses g's context to figure out which x to use, that is, the x local to g, thereby returning x=20. The lesson is clear: read Perl source code carefully.

Variable scoping is intimately linked with program flow. Investigating how programming languages implement and manipulate program flow is next on our list.

Controlling Program Flow

All programming languages implement some form of *flow control*, which is some means for modifying the sequence of instructions executed in response to different conditions. The discussion in this section focuses on *control structures* commonly encountered in programming languages. We'll divide languages into two main groups: unstructured and structured. Let's learn something about the characteristics of each.

Unstructured Languages

Unstructured languages use goto, in some form, as the only way to modify program flow. Along with goto, these languages have some mechanism for testing different conditions. The combination of goto and conditional testing is sufficient to implement any algorithm, but that doesn't mean doing so will be clear or easy to debug or verify.

Old-style BASIC, like the example in Listing 1-3, is unstructured. There are if statements and a goto statement (of potentially different kinds). Likewise, assembly language is unstructured. Review Listing 2-3, which includes instructions to test different conditions (btfss) and gotos.

SNOBOL is also unstructured. Every line in SNOBOL either succeeds or fails, and a label can be given to instruct SNOBOL where to go in either case. SNOBOL does not have a structured if statement, but instead has predicates that either succeed or fail, allowing a goto to handle either case.

Most of the esolangs we'll explore in later chapters are unstructured languages. Most use simple tests and branching or goto, like machine code. Some, like the Firefly language we'll develop in Chapter 15, or Chapter 8's FRACTRAN, lack any form of goto beyond restarting the program from the beginning.

Structured Languages

Edsger Dijkstra's famous 1968 letter "Go To Statement Considered Harmful" sounded the alarm on how goto as a flow control option is generally a bad idea. In the decades since, unstructured languages have faded and have largely been replaced by languages that implement *structured programming*, meaning languages that use the now-familiar control structures and eschew goto and the like.

Selection

Selection refers to using the result of a Boolean expression, or the equivalent, to alter program flow. The most common selection structure is the if-then-else construct. For example, in Pascal, and most modern languages, the syntax is virtually the same.

```
if <condition> then <statements1> [else <statements2>]
```

Here, `<condition>` returns a Boolean value. If `<condition>` is true, `<statements1>` are executed; otherwise, `<statements2>`, if present, are executed. Variations on if statements exist, like elif in Python to combine a nested if:

```
if x < 2:                      if x < 2:
    print("less")                  print("less")
else:                =>        elif x < 12:
    if x < 12:                     print("more")
        print("more")
```

Many languages support case or switch statements. Pascal uses case and C uses switch. For example, in C, a switch statement to check on the value of an integer, x, might look like this:

```
switch (x) {
    case 1:
        printf("one\n");
        break;
    case 3:  case 5:  case 7:
        printf("prime\n");
        break;
    case 2:  case 4:  case 6:
    case 8:  case 0:
        printf("even\n");
        break;
    default: break;
};
```

The break is necessary, as execution falls through to the next case if not present. The same construct in Pascal might look like the following:

```
case x of
  1 : writeln('one');
  3,5,7 : writeln('prime');
  2,4,6,8,0 : writeln('even');
end;
```

Scheme uses a cond statement in much the same way.

```
(cond
  ((= x 1) (display "one"))
  ((member x '(3 5 7)) (display "prime"))
  ((member x '(2 4 6 8 0)) (display "even")))
```

Here, each sublist of cond is (<condition> <statements>) and the statements are executed if the condition is true. The cond statement tests each condition in order until one of them is true.

Repetition

By *repetition*, I mean any form of looping structure. Specifically, we'll discuss four kinds of loops: top-tested, bottom-tested, counted, and infinite. We'll use Modula-2 for Listing 2-4, as it supports all four kinds. Modula-2 is a successor of Pascal.

```
MODULE loops;

FROM StrIO IMPORT WriteString, WriteLn;
FROM NumberIO IMPORT WriteCard;

VAR
❶ i : CARDINAL;

BEGIN
  WriteString("Top tested:");  WriteLn;
  WriteString("  index:");
❷ i := 0;
  WHILE (i < 6) DO
    WriteCard(i,3);
    i := i + 1;
  END;
  WriteLn;

  WriteString("Bottom tested:");  WriteLn;
  WriteString("  index:");
❸ i := 0;
  REPEAT
    WriteCard(i,3);
```

```
      i := i + 1;
    UNTIL i = 6;
    WriteLn;

    WriteString("Loop:");  WriteLn;
    WriteString(" index:");
❹ i := 0;
    LOOP
      WriteCard(i,3);
      i := i + 1;
      IF i = 6 THEN
        EXIT;
      END;
    END;
    WriteLn;

    WriteString("Counted:");  WriteLn;
    WriteString(" index:");
❺ FOR i := 0 TO 5 DO
      WriteCard(i,3);
    END;
    WriteLn;
END loops.
```

Listing 2-4: Loops in Modula-2

Listing 2-4 presents all four kinds of structured programming loops. The preamble loads required functions from the standard library. A single variable, i, is all we need ❶. Modula-2 distinguishes between integers and cardinals, which are positive integers.

The first loop is a *top-tested* WHILE loop ❷. The loop executes while the condition is true. Because the test on the condition is at the top of the loop, there is the possibility that the loop will never execute.

The second loop ❸ is a *bottom-tested* loop. The test on whether to continue the loop happens after the body of the loop; therefore, this loop executes the body at least once, regardless of i's initial value. Modula-2 uses UNTIL for the bottom test, meaning the loop body repeats until the condition is true. Some languages, like C, use a while for the bottom test, so the loop executes while the condition is true.

Modula-2 is one of the few high-level languages with an explicit *infinite* loop structure ❹. A LOOP executes the body forever, or until EXIT is executed. A while loop that is always true has the same effect.

The last example is a FOR loop ❺. Modula-2's FOR is virtually identical to that of many other languages. The loop index has an initial value and continues incrementing until it reaches its ending value. There are many variants of this kind of loop, called the *counted loop*. In this category, I'm including loops like Python's for that iterate over any object supporting iteration.

Program flow is influenced by the way the programming language is structured and its approach to coding. Let's conclude the chapter with a review of important coding paradigms used by programming languages.

Programming Paradigms

A *programming paradigm* is the way a language approaches the act of coding. The most important paradigms are imperative, object-oriented, and declarative, to which we'll add my personal favorite, array processing. Let's discuss the high-level characteristics of a few paradigms and give some examples of languages supporting each paradigm. Many practical languages support more than one paradigm.

Imperative

Imperative programming languages instruct the computer step by step. Almost all languages, especially those you'll encounter as a professional developer, use this paradigm, or at least support it somewhat. And that makes sense: this is the most natural way to think about coding. To achieve a goal, certain things must happen in a specific order. That's imperative programming: the programmer issues commands to the computer via the programming language.

Think of a popular programming language. It's almost undoubtedly imperative: Java, Python, C/C++, C#, JavaScript, and so on. All of the languages we encountered in Chapter 1, except for Prolog and SML, are imperative languages.

Imperative languages are often further subdivided into structured and unstructured. A structured imperative language uses structured programming, which we just discussed in the previous section. Therefore, Pascal, C, Modula-2, and so on, are all structured imperative programming languages. An unstructured imperative language does not use structured programming. This includes assembly, but also higher-level languages like SNOBOL.

All the esolangs we'll encounter and develop are imperative languages. It's the most obvious way to do things.

Object-Oriented

Object-oriented languages employ encapsulation, polymorphism, and inheritance. In a sense, object-oriented languages are imperative languages plus a higher level of organization. The leap from imperative programming to object-oriented is relatively straightforward.

Encapsulation means that objects are both data and methods—they have their own data, separate from other objects, and their own methods for operating on that data. This hides information from outside of the object. This separation between objects adds security and reliability to programs. It is less likely that changes in one part of the program will adversely and subtly affect another part of the program in an object-oriented language.

Polymorphism is perhaps best understood by example. Imagine a class called Shape that has a method called draw. Now imagine subclasses of Shape, such as Rectangle, Square, and Circle. Each of these subclasses supplies a draw method appropriate for its particular shape. This creates an object hierarchy (see Figure 2-2).

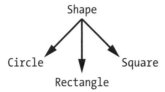

Figure 2-2: Hierarchy of objects in an object-oriented language

In this diagram, Rectangle, Square, and Circle are all children (subclasses) of Shape. If we now make a function accepting a Shape argument, and call the draw method of that Shape, we can pass any subclass of Shape to the function and the proper draw method will be called. This is polymorphism.

FUNCTION OVERLOADING

Polymorphism also happens during *function overloading*, a situation where multiple functions using the same name are defined, but each accepts a different type of argument. For example, consider this C++ code:

```
#include <iostream>
using namespace std;

double CtoF(int C) {
    return (9*C)/5 + 32;
}
double CtoF(double C) {
    return (9.0/5.0)*C + 32.0;
}

int main() {
    cout << CtoF(37) << endl;
    cout << CtoF(37.0) << endl;
}
```

The function CtoF is defined twice. The first definition accepts an integer and returns a double. The second definition accepts a double (64-bit float) and returns a double. The main function then calls CtoF, first with an integer argument, and then again with a floating-point argument. The C++ compiler uses the argument type to match which function is called.

(continued)

The program outputs

```
98
98.6
```

The first line is from the integer version of CtoF and the second is from the double version. Note that in C++, if the only CtoF available to the compiler is the double version, both calls will return 98.6, as the compiler is smart enough to know it can automatically change the integer to a double to make the call succeed. This is not the case in general and is an example of weak typing in C++. Function overloading is an example of *compile-time polymorphism* because the compiler selects which function is evaluated while building the output executable.

The final hallmark of an object-oriented language is *inheritance*. This means a class can inherit, or acquire, the methods of another class. We saw this above with Shape and Circle, which is a subclass of Shape. The class Circle will inherit any methods Shape shares, gaining that functionality for free. We also saw inheritance at work in the Simula example of Chapter 1, where the class Pal inherited the member variables of its parent class, Person.

Declarative

Declarative programming, in which the programmer states *what* instead of explicitly *how*, comes in several flavors. We already explored one flavor in Chapter 1—logic programming—when we discussed Prolog. In Prolog, the goal is presented as what needs to happen without explicit step-by-step instructions as to how to make it happen.

Functional programming languages, like SML, also from Chapter 1, fall under the declarative category as well. SML is a good example of how difficult it can be to assign a language to just one paradigm. Functional languages use functions and recursion to express the what of a program rather than imperative control structures like while loops. However, SML supports while loops, a concession to imperative programming. Other languages that are often called "functional" include Lisp and Scheme, and, sometimes, even Python. However, it seems better to say Python includes functional programming elements but isn't a functional language.

Hallmarks of functional programming include treating functions as *first-class objects*, meaning they can be assigned to variables, and *higher-order functions*, functions that accept functions as arguments or return functions. Let's review two examples with Python.

In Chapter 1, we saw an example of currying in SML. Now, let's see how currying works in Python.

```python
def factory(x):
    def mult(y):
        return x*y
```

```
❶ return mult

❷ mult2 = factory(2)
  mult11 = factory(11)

  print(mult2(4))
  print(mult11(3))
```

First, we define a function called factory, which takes an argument and returns a function. Look carefully at factory. The function, mult, is defined within factory and accepts one argument, y. However, the body of mult returns x*y, with x being the argument to factory. The value of x used by mult is the value of x passed to factory when factory is called.

Now look at the return value of factory ❶: it is the function, mult. Moreover, it is mult in the environment of factory, which means mult is using the value for x passed to factory. Now we see why I chose the name: factory is a generator of functions where one argument, x, is fixed. Returning a nested function creates a *closure*, a function with a specific environment bound to it—namely, the value of x.

The variable mult2 is assigned whatever factory(2) returns ❷. However, factory(2) returns a function, mult, with x=2. The variable mult2 holds a function that multiplies its argument by 2. Likewise, mult11 holds a function multiplying its argument by 11. Therefore, the code prints 8 and 33 as output.

Our second functional example involves decorators, Python syntactic sugar for a higher-order function that wraps another function.

```
❶ def mydecorator(f):
      def decorate(*args, **kwargs):
          return "Per your request, the result is " + str(f(*args,**kwargs))
      return decorate

❷ @mydecorator
  def afunc(x):
      return x**2 + 3*x + 4

❸ def bfunc(x):
      return x**2 + 3*x + 4

  dfunc = mydecorator(bfunc)
```

This example defines four functions: mydecorator, afunc, bfunc, and dfunc. The first function ❶ accepts a function, f, and returns a new function, decorate, that wraps the result of f. Much like how the factory example above created a closure binding the value of x, decorate binds f to the function passed to mydecorator. Using *args and **kwargs is Python-speak for an arbitrary collection of positional and keyword arguments. Therefore, mydecorator is a higher-order function because it accepts a function as an argument and returns a function (a closure).

The definition of afunc ❷ is preceded by @mydecorator. This is the syntactic sugar part, a readable way to use mydecorator with afunc. To show this is so, ❸ defines bfunc identical to afunc and then assigns the output of mydecorator (bfunc) to dfunc.

Now, consider how afunc and dfunc work, assuming the code to be in the file *decorator.py*.

```
>>> from decorator import *
>>> print(afunc(23.4))
Per your request, the result is 621.76
>>> print(dfunc(23.4))
Per your request, the result is 621.76
```

Both calls return the expected value wrapped by the string 'Per your request...', demonstrating that the decorator @ syntax is, in reality, a function application. Decorators enable adding new functionality to a function without altering the original function or altering source code that uses the function. Any code depending on afunc would still work as expected, assuming the decorator did something more valuable than intercepting the return value and printing.

Many modern languages have adopted elements of functional programming. Pure functional languages—those that are only function calls without side effects like updating variable values directly—have yet to make much of a dent outside of academic circles. Computer scientists like pure functional languages because they are friendly to proving a program to be correct. In contrast, software engineers like some aspects of functional languages but still need the ability to easily and more directly implement in code thinking that conforms to how we operate—executing an algorithm, step by step, to reach a desired outcome.

Array Processing

Scientific programming makes frequent use of numerical data, which is often most easily organized as some form of array, be it a vector, matrix, or higher-order tensor. For example, image processing and deep learning with convolutional neural networks use 2D, 3D, and even 4D data.

Given this, it would make sense for programming languages to process entire arrays en masse without explicit loops. Such languages are known as *array-processing* languages. In Chapter 1, we briefly explored the first one, APL. Since APL, many array-processing languages have been developed.

Suppose I'm a deep learning researcher with a dataset of images I need to work with. If the images are each 512 rows by 512 columns, I can store the images in an array. If the image is grayscale, meaning each pixel is represented by a single integer, often in the byte range of $[0, 255]$, then I can use a 2D array. If I have a stack of images, all the same size, I can store them one on top of the other in a 3D array. If the images are color, I need an extra dimension for the channels, implying a 4D array.

A common operation with deep neural networks is scaling the input so it lies in the range [0, 1]. If I have 100 images, each 512 rows by 512 columns, I can store the stack in an array that is 100 by 512 by 512. In that case, the scaling operation in a language like Pascal becomes

```
var
  A : array[0..99,0..511,0..511] of real;
  i,j,k : integer;
begin
  (* Load the array with the images *)

  for i:= 0 to 99 do
    for j:= 0 to 511 do
      for k:= 0 to 511 do
        A[i,j,k] := A[i,j,k] / 255.0;
```

In order to access every element of the array, we need a triple loop over the indices of the array. It would be nice to write A := A / 255.0; and have the language just "know" that A is an array and automatically apply the scaling operation to every element of it. This is precisely what an array-processing language provides.

Most deep learning researchers use Python with the NumPy library. NumPy adds high-speed array processing to Python. Native array-processing languages are in widespread use as well. For example, IDL and Matlab, or their respective open source counterparts, GDL and Octave, were built from the ground up for array processing.

Let's use GDL to see array processing in action. On Ubuntu, install GDL with the following command:

```
> sudo apt-get install gnudatalanguage
```

If using macOS or Windows, see the Github page for installation instructions at *https://github.com/gnudatalanguage/gdl/*.

Listing 2-5 contains GDL code to manipulate a small collection of public domain test images.

```
❶ pro display, a, b, f
    compile_opt idl2, logical_predicate
    tvscl, a, 0
    tvscl, b, 1
    write_png, 'images/'+f, tvrd()
  end

  pro arraydemo
    compile_opt idl2, logical_predicate
    window, 0, xs=1024, ys=512

❷   i0 = read_png('images/barbara.png')
    i1 = read_png('images/boat.png')
```

```
    i2 = read_png('images/cameraman.png')
    i3 = read_png('images/zelda.png')

❸ display, i2, 255-i2, 'cinvert.png'

❹ m03 = bytscl(1.0*i0 + i3)
    m12 = bytscl(1.0*i1 + 2*i2)
    write_png, 'images/bzelda.png', m03
    write_png, 'images/cboat.png', m12

❺ t = i3/255.0
    m = t^3 - t
    display, i3, m, 'zelda_ghost.png'

❻ k = [[0,1,0],[-1,0,1],[0,-1,0]]
❼ im = convol(i1, k)
    display, i1, im, 'boat_edges.png'
    k = [[0,-1,0],[-1,5,-1],[0,-1,0]]
    im = convol(i0, k)
    display, i0, im, 'barbara_sharp.png'
❽ k = 5*(randomu(seed,3,3)-0.5)
    im = convol(1.0*i2, k)
    display, i2, im, 'camera_random.png'
    print, k
end
```

Listing 2-5: Image processing in GDL

The code above is in *arraydemo.pro*. To run it, enter

```
> gdl -quiet
GDL> arraydemo
```

The -quiet command line argument suppresses GDL's startup message. Use CTRL-D to exit GDL.

Listing 2-5 shows two procedures, display and arraydemo. The procedure display ❶ uses GDL commands to show two images, a and b, side by side before writing them to disk as one image. The tvscl command displays an image with scaling to [0, 255]. The tvrd function returns the image in the current window.

All the action is in arraydemo. First, we read the test images into 512×512 pixel arrays ❷. We then take the cameraman image and invert it by subtracting it from 255, the largest value in a byte image ❸. The expression 255-i2 returns a new 512×512 array in which each element is the difference between 255 and the corresponding element of i2. The entire image has been processed with no explicit loops.

Next, we alpha-blend the test images ❹. Alpha-blending is a technique that merges two images into one, like the image on the right in Figure 2-3.

Figure 2-3: The test images (left) and a sample alpha-blend (right)

The variable m03 holds the merged *barbara.png* and *zelda.png* images. Note that GDL respects data types, so we first multiply one of the images by the floating-point value 1.0 to convert the entire expression to floating-point, thereby avoiding the overflow that would happen if we left everything in the byte range. The bytscl function maps its input to $[0, 255]$ to make the result fit as a grayscale image.

The next bit of code merges the cameraman and boat images. Unlike the previous blend, the images are given unequal weighting, making the cameraman image twice as intense as the boat image. Do review the output images created by arraydemo to see the full effect.

For ❺, we apply a mathematical expression to the *zelda.png* image. The image is first scaled to $[0, 1]$, and then each output pixel is assigned via $m_{ij} \leftarrow t_{ij}^3 - t_{ij}$ for all array elements ($i, j = 0, 1, \ldots, 511$). The indices are not needed because GDL knows to apply the same operation to every array element. In a non-array processing language, the expression would be a double loop over i and j.

A standard image processing technique involves convolving a kernel over an image. Convolution means sliding a smaller array (the kernel) over the larger array (the image), where for each position of the kernel, the output value is the sum of the product of the kernel with the currently overlapped image region for all elements in the kernel. Convolution produces an output image showing how the image responds to the kernel. In ❻, we apply three kernels. The first detects edges, the second sharpens the image, and the last is randomly generated, so each run of *arraydemo.pro* produces a different output. The actual convolution uses GDL's convol library routine. The random kernel comes from randomu, which returns a random array in $[0, 1]$.

Array processing is a powerful paradigm, especially for scientific applications. Without array processing, writing code, especially research code not meant for long-term use, would be exceedingly tedious and error prone.

Summary

In this whirlwind chapter, we presented cherry-picked essentials related to programming languages meant as background for the remainder of the book. We discussed syntax and semantics and how programming languages are implemented, both interpreters and compilers. We then explored data types, including primitive types and records/structures, after which we followed a summary of more complex data structures like lists, trees, and hash tables. Next, we covered variable scope and learned the difference between lexical and dynamic scope. We then reviewed control structures, which are ways of controlling and modifying program flow. The chapter then reviewed several important programming paradigms, including imperative, object-oriented, declarative, and array processing.

Next, let's move on and explore a bit of computer science theory related to what "computability" means.

3

TURING MACHINES AND TURING COMPLETENESS

Spend enough time around programming languages, and two phrases inevitably appear: "Turing machine" and "Turing completeness." In this chapter, we'll explain what these phrases mean and why they are important. Specifically, we'll introduce the halting problem and discuss Alan Turing's fantastic solution to it. That will set the stage for discussing Turing machines and Turing completeness. We'll end by simulating a Turing machine in Python.

The topics of this chapter fall under the heading "theoretical computer science," which is a branch of mathematics, not software engineering. As we'll see below, theoretical computer science predates the availability of physical computers.

The Halting Problem

Early 20th-century mathematicians had a problem. They were several decades into a serious effort to put all of mathematics on a logical foundation. As part of this program, in 1928, David Hilbert and Wilhelm Ackermann issued their "Entscheidungsproblem" (German for "decision problem"). When given a statement in some formal system, the problem asked for an algorithm that would infallibly return "yes" or "no" as to the validity of that statement. In other words, the problem asked for an algorithm that would say whether the statement can be proven from the axioms of the system, which are those statements accepted as true without proof. It's important to note that Hilbert and Ackermann's challenge was for a universal algorithm, that is, one that will always give the correct answer for all applications.

In 1936, a young Alan Turing, not quite 24 years old, published what became the foundational paper of theoretical computer science: "On Computable Numbers, with an Application to the Entscheidungsproblem." In this paper, Turing demonstrated that there is no general solution to the Entscheidungsproblem. That is, there is no algorithm that can always correctly decide on the validity of a statement.

To do this, Turing addressed a specific problem: the *halting problem*. There are different ways to describe the halting problem, but we'll use this definition:

> Find a program, *P*, that when given as input the source code of another program, *T*, and an input for that program, *I*, will always output "yes" if *T* will eventually stop for input *I*, or "no" if *T* will run forever for input *I*.

This is a halting problem. We want to know if a program will eventually stop, or run forever for a given input. The program in question is *T* and the input is *I*. The program that decides, that outputs "yes" or "no," is *P*. The definition above uses the word *program* for *P*, with the implicit understanding that algorithms can be encoded in programs. After all, that is what programming is all about: encoding algorithms (thought) in a form that can instruct a machine. We'll come back to this equivalence between algorithm and program below.

Turing's paper, which is quite readable and easily found online with a search for the title above, showed that there is no *P*. It doesn't exist. As the halting problem is a decision problem, Turing thereby established that the Entscheidungsproblem has no solution either.

At virtually the same time as Turing, indeed, slightly before, Alonzo Church arrived at the same conclusion using a formal system known as λ-calculus (lambda calculus). If you read Turing's 1936 paper, the introduction concludes with a reference to Church's "recent paper" using λ-calculus to show what Turing was about to demonstrate. In the end, Turing became Church's student at Princeton, completing his PhD there in 1938.

Turing's proof that there is no solution for the halting problem required several iterations. The version in his 1936 paper is somewhat buggy. The essence of the proof is by contradiction.

Assume we have a program, *P*, a program that accepts another program, *T*, and an input for it, *I*. *P* tells us whether *T* will halt on *I*. The output of *P*, as we stated above, is "yes" or "no."

Now, we make a slight change to *P* so it accepts a single input and uses that input as both *T* and *I*. Additionally, when *P* is about to return "yes" to indicate that *T* does halt on input *I*, we add an infinite loop before the return. If we call this slightly edited program *Q*, what happens when we use *Q* as the argument to itself?

There are two cases. Suppose *Q* does halt with *Q* as input. If so, *P* would return "yes." However, we added an infinite loop before the return, so *Q* doesn't halt. Now suppose that *Q* doesn't halt with *Q* as input. In that case, *P* returns "no" to indicate that *Q* with *Q* as input doesn't halt. However, by issuing "no," *Q* does, in fact, halt. We're left with a contradiction: *Q* given *Q* as input halts if and only if *Q* given *Q* as input does not halt. This is an impossibility, and as *Q* is really *P* with a tiny addition to the case where the argument does halt, it means that *P* cannot exist either. Thus, the halting problem has no solution.

Turing's proof that the halting problem has no solution is foundational, but what concerns us more, practically, is what he introduced along the way. He introduced, in 1936, before any physical computer existed, a *model of computation*. That is, a straightforward machine that captures the essence of what we mean by the word *algorithm*—in other words, a Turing machine. Let's take a look.

Turing Machines

A *Turing machine* is a simple computer consisting of an infinite tape partitioned into squares and a read/write head that moves along the tape. A table of states, sometimes called the *instruction table*, specifies the operation of the machine. Each step involves searching the instruction table for a match between the current state and the symbol presently on the tape beneath the head. For each match, the table specifies an action, a direction to move, and a new state. There are three allowed actions: print a symbol on the tape, erase the symbol already on the tape, or do nothing. The direction is either move left, move right, or don't move. The machine is initialized by loading a tape, which may be blank or already marked, and positioning the head over the starting position, usually the beginning of the tape. Figure 3-1 presents an abstract representation of a Turing machine.

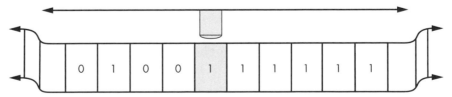

Figure 3-1: A conceptual Turing machine

To run the machine, we follow these steps:

1. Search the table for a match between the current state and the symbol beneath the tape head.

2. Perform the action given for that combination: do nothing, print a symbol, or erase a symbol.

3. Move the tape head to the left or right one square if specified in the table.

4. Set the current state to the new state read from the table and repeat from Step 1.

As simple as this machine is, it can implement any algorithm; but no one said anything about efficiency or ease of implementation. The *Church–Turing thesis* goes even further and states that the very definition of algorithm is that which can be implemented by a Turing machine. That is, a problem can be solved by an algorithm if (and only if) it can be solved by a Turing machine. Note that this statement is a *thesis* and not a *theorem*. A thesis is something believed, with good reason, to be true, but a theorem is something that has been proven to be true.

Section 3 of Turing's paper lists example machines. His first example is a machine that fills the tape with the pattern "0 1 0 1 0 . . ." The machine prints a 0, moves to the right twice to leave a blank space, prints a 1, and then moves to the right twice, repeating forever.

The tape is initially empty, meaning there is no input to this machine. The head starts at the first square and the initial state is 0. To make a move, we need the instruction table that tells us what the next step is. The instructions for this machine are in Table 3-1.

Table 3-1: Turing's First Example

State	Symbol	Print	Move	New state
0	*blank*	0	R	1
1	*blank*	*blank*	R	2
2	*blank*	1	R	3
3	*blank*	*blank*	R	0

The machine starts in state 0 with a blank tape. Searching the table for this configuration produces a match with "0 *blank*." For this case, the table says to print a 0, move to the right, and set the machine to state 1.

The next step searches for state 1 and whatever is under the tape head, which is a blank. There is a match for this configuration. The match says to print a blank, move to the right, and set the machine to state 2. State 2 matches, prints a 1, moves to the right, and moves to state 3. Lastly, state 3 matches, prints a blank, moves to the right, and goes back to state 0. At this point, the process repeats forever as there is no halt state. We'll explore other Turing machine examples below.

It isn't immediately obvious or, for that matter, obvious in any sense of the word, that a Turing machine embodies the concept of an algorithm. In fact, Turing himself believed that the Church–Turing thesis was not amenable to mathematical proof. In its favor, beyond multiple approaches leading to the same situation, is the fact that decades of attempts to disprove the thesis have been unsuccessful.

In his 1936 paper, Turing makes several arguments to help convince the reader that a Turing machine can implement any algorithm. My favorite is his comparison between a human computer (someone who performs calculations and the original meaning of the word *computer*) and a Turing machine. Turing describes a situation where a human computer is working on a problem in a manner similar to the configuration of a Turing machine and using a tape to hold results. He then describes a situation where the computer interrupts the work in progress:

> It is always possible for the computer to break off from his work, to go away and forget all about it, and later to come back and go on with it. If he does this, he must leave a note of instructions (written in some standard form) explaining how the work is to be continued. This note is the counterpart of the "state of mind." We will suppose that the computer works in such a desultory manner that he never does more than one step at a sitting. The note of instructions must enable him to carry out one step and write the next note. Thus the state of progress of the computation at any stage is completely determined by the note of instructions and the symbols on the tape.

Here, Turing is appealing to our intuition. If a human can implement any algorithm with pen and paper, and a human is capable of following the process a Turing machine follows, then we should expect a Turing machine to be able to implement any algorithm as well.

Universal Turing Machine

If a Turing machine is capable of implementing any algorithm, then a Turing machine should be able to implement another Turing machine. In other words, it should be possible to construct a *universal Turing machine (UTM)* that accepts another Turing machine and tape as input and executes it. Turing introduces this idea in Sections 5 through 7 of his paper.

A Turing machine includes an instruction table and an input tape, which may be blank. A UTM accepts two things: a Turing machine, meaning the instruction table, and an input tape. The input Turing machine must be encoded in some way and Turing developed such an encoding in Section 5 of his paper.

A Turing machine described by an instruction table like Table 3-1 can be mapped to what Turing called the *standard description (S.D.)*. The sequence of instructions are written one after the other using letters with a semicolon between them.

For example, the instructions of Table 3-1 are 5-tuples that Turing writes in *standard form* as $q_i S_j S_k R q_m$;, where q_i is the current state, S_j is a symbol under the read head, S_k is a symbol to print, R means move right (there's also L for left or N for stay put), and q_m is the new state. The semicolon ends the instruction.

To find the S.D. of an instruction, q_i is written as D followed by i As. Similarly, the S_j symbol is written as D followed by j Cs. The movement letter is written as itself: R, L, or N. Thus, the first instruction of Table 3-1 is

0   blank   0   R   1

which Turing would write as $q_1 S_0 S_1 R q_2$;, as he numbers states from one and uses a set of allowed symbols, S = {blank, 0, 1}. Here, S_0 is a blank, S_1 is zero, and S_2 is one. The S.D. of this instruction is therefore *DADDCRDAA*;, and the entire S.D. of the machine specified by Table 3-1 is

DADDCRDAA;DAADDRDAAA;DAAADDCCRDAAAA;DAAAADDRDA;

After calculating the S.D. of a machine, Turing goes further to generate what he calls a *description number (D.N.)*, which is a single integer that fully specifies the Turing machine. To calculate the D.N., begin with the S.D. and replace each possible letter in the S.D. with an integer.

$$A \to 1, \; C \to 2, \; D \to 3, \; L \to 4, \; R \to 5, \; N \to 6, \; ; \to 7$$

For example, the S.D. above becomes

31332531173113353111731113322531111731111335317

The D.N. mapping means that every computable sequence, that is, anything computable by a Turing machine, has at least one D.N., and each D.N. specifies only one computable sequence. The net result is that the number of Turing machines is enumerable. Turing is writing about computable numbers, which are real numbers that can be computed by an algorithm, but by showing that the number of Turing machines is enumerable (could be counted), he shows that there are infinitely many real numbers that are not computable, that is, numbers for which no algorithm exists. Here he's building on Georg Cantor's famous proof that the real numbers are not countable. For a summary of Cantor's proof, see *https://mathworld.wolfram .com/CantorDiagonalMethod.html*.

In Section 8 of his paper, Turing uses the fact that the number of Turing machines is countable to contemplate a machine for checking description numbers, a machine that knows whether or not the Turing machine associated with the description number will halt or not for all possible inputs. Through an attempt to apply a mathematical process used by Cantor, Turing arrives at a contradiction, proving that no such machine exists. This is his proof that the halting problem is undecidable—that there exists no algorithm that will tell you if program *P* halts on input *I* for all possible inputs.

To recap, a UTM is a Turing machine that accepts encoded Turing machines and input tapes as its input. The UTM then runs the supplied Turing machine on the provided tape to produce the output of the Turing machine. Thus, a UTM is a program that runs other programs. Does this sound familiar? The UTM is a general-purpose computing machine—a computer—and it can run programs given as inputs. The UTM is a stored-program computer, that is, a computer that puts programs and data in the same memory (its input) and executes the program. This is what every modern computer does: specifically, every *von Neumann architecture* computer. For those familiar with computers—presumably everyone reading this book—this is a no-brainer idea; that's just what computers do. However, the idea wasn't a no-brainer in 1936. It was foundational and groundbreaking.

Turing machines are not the only possible models of computation. Others, like *finite-state machines* and *Minsky register machines*, do exist. At best, these other models are equivalent to Turing machines (Minsky machines) or demonstrably less powerful (finite-state machines). Comparing models of computation is part of *automata theory*. The significant result for us is that Turing machines are the top of the heap, and there are no models of computation that can perform actions beyond what a Turing machine can implement. This most likely includes quantum computers. We'll encounter a Minsky register machine in Chapter 8 when we discuss FRACTRAN.

Turing machines are the best known model of computation, and perhaps the best model possible if the Church–Turing thesis is correct. Let's see how equivalence to a Turing machine is helpful for our exploration of esolangs.

Turing Completeness

A Turing machine can implement any algorithm. If a programming language can do the same, the language is called *Turing complete*. Specifically,

> A *Turing complete* system can simulate all Turing machines, that is, can simulate a universal Turing machine.

If a programming language is Turing complete, it can, in theory, implement anything a Turing machine can, and therefore any algorithm at all. As you might expect, widely used programming languages are Turing complete. In the next section, we'll implement a Turing machine simulator in Python, which demonstrates that Python is Turing complete.

Imperative programming languages need only two things to be Turing complete:

1. Some form of looping based on a conditional, like a `while` loop or a combination of `if` and `goto`.
2. The ability to manipulate an arbitrarily large amount of memory.

The second requirement is, of course, not met for any real-world programming language *as implemented*, but it is easily met when the language is *specified*. For example, there is nothing in Python's specification that says "a list may contain at most one million items." In the language itself, there is no limit on how many items a list may contain, even if an implementation must, to be realized in the physical world, have such a limit.

Why should we care about Turing completeness? Turing completeness is particularly interesting when dealing with esolangs. Esolangs are all about pushing boundaries and thinking in novel ways. Therefore, it makes sense to ask whether an esolang is Turing complete. If it is, then a design goal might well have been achieved: the language is, in theory, capable of implementing any algorithm, regardless of how difficult it might be to do so in practice. Not every language we'll explore in this book is Turing complete; however, not being Turing complete does not mean useless. By itself, HTML is not Turing complete; yet, HTML is, as the basis for web pages, extremely useful.

It is also possible to demonstrate Turing completeness by providing a translator between the language in question and another language known to be Turing complete. This is often used to illustrate Turing completeness for different esolangs. For example, the Nopfunge esolang (*https://esolangs .org/wiki/Nopfunge*), which is based on the Befunge esolang we'll explore in Chapter 11, shows Turing completeness by translating a Minsky machine into Nopfunge. Minsky machines are known to be Turing complete. Therefore, if Nopfunge can implement a Minsky machine, then Nopfunge can implement any Turing machine.

The requirements for Turing completeness are so minimal that many systems not originally intended to be Turing complete have been shown to be so. For example, each of the following is Turing complete:

- The mov instruction for the x86 architecture (see *https://github.com/ xoreaxeaxeax/movfuscator/* for a C compiler that generates only mov instructions)
- Minecraft
- *Magic: The Gathering* card game
- The Dwarf Fortress video game (see *https://youtu.be/j2cMHwo3nAU/* for a video showing Space Invaders running in Dwarf Fortress)
- PowerPoint (see *http://www.andrew.cmu.edu/user/twildenh/PowerPoint TM/Paper.pdf*)
- The vim text editor (see *https://github.com/ealter/vim_turing_machine/*)

This list is by no means exhaustive.

Let's put theory into practice and implement a basic Turing machine simulator in Python.

Let's Build a Turing Machine

Perhaps the best way to understand how a Turing machine works is to implement one. In a way, Turing machines are the first esolangs. They are capable of everything, but are impractical for serious use. Turing machines are rather general, as they work with an arbitrary set of symbols, but we'll restrict ourselves to a machine using only 0 and 1 as symbols, along with blank for an empty space. Likewise, we'll represent the instruction table as shown in Table 3-1, where each row of the table is a 5-tuple describing the state and tape condition followed by the action, move, and new state. For example, we'll express Table 3-1 in Python with Listing 3-1.

```
((0,' ','0','R',1),
 (1,' ',' ','R',2),
 (2,' ','1','R',3),
 (3,' ',' ','R',0))
```

Listing 3-1: Turing's first example in Python

The rows of Table 3-1 match the rows of Listing 3-1. The first entry in the table describes state 0 and a blank. The action is to print a 0, move right, transfer to state 1, and then repeat. For our machines, all actions are to print something, and all movements are to the right or left; there is no standing still. All possible combinations of state and the current symbol, the first two elements of every instruction, should be present in the table; otherwise, the program is incomplete because there are state and symbol combinations with no defined actions.

Let's take our Turing machine for a spin and then dive into the code.

The Simulator

The code for our Turing machine simulator is in *turing.py*. It begins with a small catalog of example programs in PROGS along with a brief description in NAMES.

Running *turing.py* without arguments gives us

```
> python3 turing.py
turing <prog> [<M> | <list>] [-t]

  <prog> - program # [0,4]
  <M>    - blank tape of size M
  <list> - initial tape (list: 0,1,2=blank)
  <-t>   - trace, if present

programs:
    0: Turing's first example
    1: change 0's to 1's
    2: unary increment: 111 -> 1111
    3: binary increment
    4: unary subtraction: 11111 111 -> 5 - 3
```

The output tells us to select an example program from the list below and then specify the size of the blank tape, or manually enter an initial tape configuration as input. The optional final argument, -t, enables tracing, allowing us to step through the program to see the effect of each instruction.

Let's run Turing's first example (Program 0).

```
> python3 turing.py 0 20
Program complete: (state=0, tc=20)
```

```
[0 1 0 1 0 1 0 1 0 1 ]
```

Program:
```
    0, ' ' ==> '0', 'R',  1
    1, ' ' ==> ' ', 'R',  2
    2, ' ' ==> '1', 'R',  3
    3, ' ' ==> ' ', 'R',  0
```

We told the simulator to use a blank tape with 20 spaces. As conceived, Turing machines never run out of tape. The output shows the pattern of 0s and 1s as expected. We're also told that the machine stopped in state 0 and that the tape counter (tc) was at position 20. In other words, we ran out of tape, so the simulation stopped. The selected program's instruction table is printed below the output showing the state and symbol matched followed by the print action, movement, and new state.

In *turing.py*, the main function parses the command line arguments to select the program run along with the size of the blank tape or the initial tape configuration entered by the user. We'll see how to enter a tape below. The machine itself is contained in the class TuringMachine.

Listing 3-2 shows the TuringMachine class with the Result method omitted to save space.

```
class TuringMachine:
    def Step(self):
        found = False
❶      for p in self.prog:
            if (p[0] == self.c) and (self.tape[self.tc] == p[1]):
                found = True
                break
        if (not found):
            raise ValueError("No match found for current state:
                (%d,'%s')" % (self.c,self.tape[self.tc]))
❷      w,m,c = p[2:]
        if (w != ''):
            self.tape[self.tc] = w
        if (m == 'R'):
            self.tc += 1
        elif (m == 'L'):
            self.tc -= 1
        self.c = c

❸   def Done(self):
        if (self.c == -1) or (self.tc < 0) or (self.tc == self.M):
            return True  # end state or fell off the tape
        return False
```

```
❹ def Run(self):
       while (not self.Done()):
           if (self.trace):
               s = "".join(self.tape)
               t = " "*self.tc + "^"
               print("%s, (state=%d, tc=%d)" % (s,self.c,self.tc))
               print("%s" % t)
               _ = input("?")
               if (_.lower() == "q"):
                   quit()
           self.Step()

   def Result(self):
       --snip--

❺ def __init__(self, prog, tape=None, M=100, trace=False):
       if (tape is None):
           self.tape = [' ']*M
           self.M = M
       else:
           tape.append(' ')  # extra blank added
           self.tape = tape
           self.M = len(tape)

       self.c = 0          # start in state 0
       self.tc = 0         # start at position 0
       self.prog = prog    # state table, i.e. the program
       self.trace = trace  # trace or not
```

Listing 3-2: The TuringMachine class

The constructor ❺ accepts the program (prog) and the initial tape (tape), if any, or the size of the blank tape. If a tape is supplied, we add an extra blank as several example programs expect an ending blank. The constructor sets up the default state (c) and tape counter position (tc) and then saves the program.

The Run method is short and sweet as most of it implements tracing ❹. Running a program is performing step after step until done. Done returns True if we fall off the tape or hit negative state, which we'll interpret as a halt instruction ❸. All the action takes place in Step.

Step first locates the instruction table entry corresponding to the current state and the symbol under the tape head ❶. Once found, we then extract the action, movement, and next state ❷. We then update the current tape position with the action. After that, we increment or decrement the tape counter based on the move character (R or L). Lastly, we update the state to complete the instruction step.

There are additional comments in *turing.py* explaining the code in more detail. Please review them. The catalog of examples is in PROGS. To add more examples, place them there and add a description in NAMES. Note that our machine follows Turing's original paper, meaning we move the tape head along the tape. If you examine other Turing machine simulators, and there are many far more sophisticated than ours, be aware that many move the *tape* instead. Therefore, if you want to transfer a program for such an implementation to *turing.py*, you must change all R characters to L and vice versa.

The Examples

We described Turing's Program 0 above. Now let's walk through the other examples using a sufficient level of detail to understand the process encoded in the instruction table.

Program 1: Change 0s to 1s

This example is straightforward. The instructions convert all 0s to 1s and the program stops when a blank or one is encountered.

```
((0,'0','1','R', 0),
 (0,'1','1','R',-1),
 (0,' ',' ','L',-1)),
```

There is only one state, state 0, with a rule for all allowed symbols: 0, 1, and blank. To be specific, the first row of the table says, "if in state 0 and the symbol under the tape head is a 0, print a 1, move to the right, and remain in state 0." This instruction will continue for as long as the symbol under the tape head is 0. It replaces the 0 with a 1 and moves to the next symbol again and again.

The remaining two instructions capture what to do if the symbol under the tape head is a one or a blank. In both cases, the matched symbol is printed again to leave that square unchanged. The critical point is that the next state is -1. Our machine stops if the state is negative, so -1 means "halt."

Combined, these states move to the right along the tape, changing every 0 into a 1 until the program reads a 1 or a blank. Let's see if our interpretation is correct by running the program with different input tapes. Initial tape configurations are passed on the command line as Python lists using 0 and 1, with 2 representing a blank. For example:

```
> python3 turing.py 1 [0,0,0,0,0]

Program complete: (state=-1, tc=4)

[11111 ]

> python3 turing.py 1 [0,0,0,0,0,1,1]
```

```
Program complete: (state=-1, tc=6)

[1111111 ]

> python3 turing.py 1 [0,0,0,0,0,2,1]

Program complete: (state=-1, tc=4)

[11111 1 ]
```

In each case above, the output matches what we expect from the program. All consecutive 0s are now 1s and blanks, and 1s are unchanged.

Program 2: Unary Increment

Binary numbers use two digits: 0 and 1. Unary numbers are tallies, that is, repeated instances of 1.

1	1
2	11
3	111
4	1111
5	11111

Program 2 increments the unary number already on the tape:

```
((0,'1','1','R', 0),
 (0,'0','1','L',-1),
 (0,' ','1','L',-1)),
```

This program is quite similar to the program to map 0s to 1s. The first instruction marches along the tape, keeping every 1 a 1 and moving right until it finds a 0 or blank. The program turns the first 0 or blank into a 1 and then halts.

Let's run this program with tracing to see how it moves. Press ENTER at each prompt to continue.

```
> python3 turing.py 2 [1,1,1] -t

111 , (state=0, tc=0)
^
?
111 , (state=0, tc=1)
 ^
?
111 , (state=0, tc=2)
  ^
?
111 , (state=0, tc=3)
   ^
```

```
?
Program complete: (state=-1, tc=2)

[1111]
```

Tracing shows the current tape, three 1s, and a blank added at the end as well as the current state and tape counter. The following line prints a carat under the current tape position. Pressing ENTER three times moves along the 1 to the blank. Pressing ENTER one more time fills that blank with a 1, after which the program halts. The initial input was 3 (111), and the output tape is now 4 (1111).

Program 3: Binary Increment

Binary numbers use 0 and 1 as digits. The addition rules for binary are simple and can be expressed as

$$0 + 0 = 0$$
$$0 + 1 = 1$$
$$1 + 0 = 1$$
$$1 + 1 = 10 \text{ (carry)}$$

Note that the sum of 1 and 1 produces a carry. Program 3 implements a Turing machine that adds one to the binary number on the input tape. Its instruction table is

```
((0,' ',' ','L', 1),
 (0,'0','0','R', 0),
 (0,'1','1','R', 0),
 (1,' ','1','R', 2),
 (1,'0','1','L', 2),
 (1,'1','0','L', 1),
 (2,' ',' ','L',-1),
 (2,'0','0','R', 2),
 (2,'1','1','R', 2)),
```

Program 3 uses three states. It isn't readily evident from looking at the instruction table alone what the states are doing. So let's run an example with tracing to see the instructions in action. We'll add one to $1011_2 = 11_{10}$. The command line is

```
> python3 turing.py 3 [1,0,1,1] -t
```

Table 3-2 contains the trace, step by step. The program generates $1100_2 = 12_{10}$, as expected.

Table 3-2: Tracing Binary
Increment for 1011

1011 , (state=0, tc=0)	
^	
1011 , (state=0, tc=1)	
^	
1011 , (state=0, tc=2)	
^	
1011 , (state=0, tc=3)	
^	
1011 , (state=0, tc=4)	
^	
1011 , (state=1, tc=3)	
^	
1010 , (state=1, tc=2)	
^	
1000 , (state=1, tc=1)	
^	
1100 , (state=2, tc=0)	
^	
1100 , (state=2, tc=1)	
^	
1100 , (state=2, tc=2)	
^	
1100 , (state=2, tc=3)	
^	
1100 , (state=2, tc=4)	
^	

The first five steps of Table 3-2 move along the input, looking for a blank marking the end of the binary number. state 0 is sufficient for this part. When the program finds the blank in this state, it decrements the tape counter to look at the rightmost digit of the binary number, after which state 1 becomes active.

With state 1 active, if the symbol under the tape head is a 0, it is replaced by a 1, the tape head moves to the left, and state 2 becomes active. This is equivalent to adding 1. If the symbol under the tape head is a 1, the program replaces it with 0 as 1+1 = 0 with a carry of 1. The machine then remains in state 1 after moving left. The carry is implied by state 1 and the fact that the state moves left, replacing 1s with 0s. The 0 and 1 instructions of state 1 together process the number right to left and handle the carry by remaining in state 1 until a 0 is found. Adding 1 to 0 does not produce a carry, so the machine would move to state 2 and the increment would be complete.

State 2 moves the tape head back right along the number until a terminating blank is found, at which point the state becomes −1 and the machine halts. The action of state 2 is only to position the tape head. If we're not interested in positioning the head at the end of the number, we could transition to −1 from state 1 as soon as a 0 is updated to a 1. Try this example with different inputs until you are comfortable with how it works.

Program 4: Unary Subtraction

Adding 1 to a unary number was quite simple. This next example implements unary subtraction with the larger number first, followed by a blank, and then the smaller number. For example, an input of [11111 111] returns [11   ], which is 5 − 3 = 2, using blanks to overwrite any extra digits.

Let's run this example with tracing. We won't list the many steps required, but I suspect that you will see for yourself what the instructions are doing. It's quite clever. Run the example with the following command:

```
> python3 turing.py 4 [1,1,1,1,1,2,1,1,1] -t
```

State 0 finds the blank between the first and second number and then transitions to state 1. State 1 finds the blank after the second number and transitions to state 2. State 2 moves left over the smaller number, changing the first 1 found into a 0 and then moving to state 3. State 3 finds the blank between the two numbers and moves to state 7. State 7 makes the first 1 of the larger number a 0 and moves back to state 0. This state 0, 1, 2, 3, 7 cycle repeats until state 2 no longer finds a 1 in the smaller number.

At this point, all the 1s of the smaller number are 0s, as are the same number of rightmost 1s of the larger number. In essence, the subtraction is complete. The remainder of the program changes 0s to blanks, so the only symbols on the tape when the program ends are the remaining 1s of the larger unary number. States 4, 5, and 6 accomplish this and then transition from state 6 to −1 when there are no more 0s.

Try Your Hand

Running *turing.py* without command line arguments shows five example programs. There is actually a sixth, Program 5, but it was intentionally left out of the list as an exercise. Program 5 calculates the two's complement of the binary number on the input tape. Computers store negative integers in two's complement format so hardware only needs to implement addition. Subtraction of two integers is addition using two's complement form.

Finding the two's complement of a binary number is easy: change all 0 bits to 1s and all the 1s to 0s, and then add 1 to that result. For example:

$$01011011 \rightarrow 10100100 + 1 \rightarrow 10100101$$

The challenge of this section is to create the instruction table for a Turing machine that converts its input to two's complement format. We have a Turing machine that adds 1 to a binary number. We also have a Turing machine that converts 0s to 1s. The required machine will flip 0s and 1s before adding 1. Try writing the two's complement instruction table yourself. When ready, take a look at the last entry in PROGS and compare it with your table. You can run Program 5 easily enough.

```
> python3 turing.py 5 [0,1,0,1,1,0,1,1]

Program complete: (state=-1, tc=7)

[10100101 ]
```

The output is what we found for the example above.

Summary

This chapter explored Turing machines and the idea of Turing completeness. We began with the halting problem and then moved on to Turing
machines, the mechanism Turing used in his famous 1936 paper where
he demonstrated that the halting problem was undecidable. We then explored the idea of a UTM, which led directly to the concept of a stored-
program computer.

Next, we discussed the concept of Turing completeness, something we'll
refer to throughout the book as we explore esolangs. The idea that many
systems are accidentally Turing complete is simple enough. Lastly, we implemented a Turing machine simulator in Python and worked through several
example programs.

This chapter concludes Part I of the book. We move on now to consider what I'm calling "atypical programming languages," by which I mean
languages meant for serious use but that are sufficiently different from the
pack in their approach to warrant a detailed examination as a precursor to
the esolangs that follow. We will begin with Forth, a stack-based language.

PART II

ATYPICAL PROGRAMMING LANGUAGES

4

FORTH

Forth is the quintessential minimalist programming language. Parsing Forth is nothing more than extracting tokens separated by whitespace. There is no interpretation of formulas and everything is a discrete word operating on the stack. Programs are a collection of functions, called *words*, that are compiled, function by function, to an ever expanding memory space known as the *dictionary*. Words are executed when encountered, or compiled to the dictionary when defined. This is in contrast to languages like Python, C++, or Java, which require sophisticated parsers and compilers and a rigid structure, and are well-abstracted from the hardware of the computer.

In this chapter, we'll install Forth, discuss the origins and philosophy behind the language, and then dive into the language itself. We'll include some examples along the way and end with a discussion.

Installation

Installing Forth is particularly easy.

```
> sudo apt-get install gforth
```

Forth runs interactively. To see if our installation is working, we can type

```
> gforth
Gforth 0.7.3, Copyright (C) 1995-2008 Free Software Foundation, Inc.
Gforth comes with ABSOLUTELY NO WARRANTY; for details type `license'
Type `bye' to exit
```

Forth is quietly waiting for us to type something. Forth interprets tokens separated by one or more spaces. If the token is a known word, that is, a defined function, it is executed. If the token is a number, then it's pushed on the stack. Input lines are executed when you press ENTER. Try the following command:

```
cr 1 2 + 3 * .
9  ok
```

This will tell Forth to move to the next line (cr), push 1 on the stack followed by 2, and then add (+) the 1 and the 2, leaving 3 on the stack. Next, we push another 3 on the stack and multiply them (*). Lastly, the period (.) prints the top stack value, which is now 9. Forth signals it's ready for more commands with the ok prompt. To exit, enter **bye**.

Forth uses *postfix notation*, meaning the operator comes after the operands. To get 1 + 2, we entered 1 2 +. Postfix notation was developed by Jan Łukasiewicz in 1924 and, because of his nationality, is often known as *reverse Polish notation* or *RPN*. Some early desk calculators also used postfix notation. The nice thing about postfix is that it never requires parentheses.

Origins and Philosophy

Forth was created by Charles "Chuck" Moore and evolved through the 1960s, coming of age in the early 1970s. As an interactive system in an age of punch cards, Forth was ahead of the curve. One of its primary uses early on was telescope control. Over time, Forth found its niche in small systems, though full-blown, object-oriented Forths appeared for personal computers.

Forth, originally spelled FORTH, was meant as a fourth-generation programming language, but the assembler only allowed five-character names. So instead of "FOURTH," it was "FORTH," and later "Forth." The term *fourth generation* dates to when programming languages were grouped by the vague concept of a generation. The first generation was machine code and the second was assembly. Languages like C were the third generation. And that's where the term *generation* started to falter—most languages were third generation.

Freedom to the programmer sums up Forth's philosophy. The extreme openness of the language includes extending the compiler itself, which is functionality seldom seen in other languages. We'll see how to do this later in the chapter.

Forth conceives of programs as documents written in a custom language using words (functions) compiled into a dictionary. The dictionary stores all the words needed to implement the program, along with all necessary data. Each new word or block of data is added to the end of the dictionary.

Historically, the Forth community frowned upon code reuse. Building a library for later use was deemed a recipe for disaster. The modern approach of pulling pieces from many different libraries of pre-built code, like the standard modules of Python or the standard template library of C++, was alien to Forth and considered distasteful. A "good" Forth programmer developed the appropriate set of words to implement the specified task: no more and no less. If done well, the code itself reads much like a document. Good Forth is self documenting.

I ran across an email signature many moons ago, source long lost, that read: "C makes you think it is the best programming language in the world. Forth makes you think you are the best programmer in the world." This captures the philosophy of Forth quite nicely. Instead of only using what the language designers gave, the Forth programmer manipulates the raw material of Forth, turning it into the ideal language for the task at hand.

The Language

Forth is, in essence, a system and not simply a compiler or interpreter. Early Forths *were* the operating system. They accessed disks in 1024-byte blocks—there was no filesystem—and they compiled code from those blocks. There is a top-level *REPL* (read, evaluate, print, loop) that, by convention, uses ok as the prompt. Forth programs are a sequence of tokens separated by whitespace. In most Forths, any combination of characters, excluding space, tab, and newline, is a valid token.

Tokens are evaluated as encountered. If the token is found in the dictionary, it is executed. If the token is not in the dictionary, Forth tries to interpret it as a number. If Forth fails at this, Forth throws an error message and returns to the ok prompt.

Executing a word when encountered makes sense. But what does Forth do with numbers? Forth pushes them on the *stack*. All operations use the stack, either pulling arguments from or pushing results onto the stack. Tokens interpreted as numbers are pushed onto the stack. Words often pull values from the stack, operate on them, and push new values onto the stack.

The stack is central to Forth and several of the esolangs we'll encounter later in the book, so let's spend a bit of time understanding what a stack is and how to work with one.

Understanding the Stack

Stacks are basic computer science data structures, often referred to as *last in, first out*, or *LIFO*, data structures. They are the opposite of a queue, which is a *first in, first out*, or *FIFO*, data structure. I think of the stack of trays at a buffet. When trays are put on the stack, the first tray is set down, then the second, then the third, and so on. When someone takes a tray, they don't take the first tray; they take the last one put on the stack. In contrast, the first thing out of the queue is the first thing put into it, not the last.

Most programming languages use stacks. An example is the return stack for function calls. Forth uses a stack for data and, as we'll see below, a separate one for returning from function calls. It's the data stack that Forth programmers use most frequently, though they can temporarily use the return stack with care.

Figure 4-1 illustrates the operation of the stack.

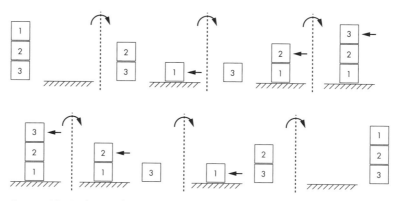

Figure 4-1: Pushing values on the Forth stack (top), and popping values off (bottom)

Let's walk through Figure 4-1, beginning with the top row going from left to right. We have three values—1, 2, and 3—and an empty stack. Next, we *push* 1 on the stack. The top item on the stack is marked with an arrow. Then we push 2 on the stack, which is now on top of 1 and is thus the new top stack item. Lastly, we push 3 on the stack, making it the top stack item.

To remove items from the stack, we *pop* them. This is shown in the bottom row of Figure 4-1. Again, moving from left to right, we pop the stack to get 3. Notice that 3 was the *last* item pushed onto the stack, so it is the first item popped off of the stack. We then pop the stack again to get 2, and pop one last time to get 1, leaving the stack empty. Attempting to pop an empty stack is a common Forth error. You'll make it yourself, eventually.

Using the Stack

Manipulating the stack is perhaps the most frustrating part of Forth. However, Forth comes with many intrinsic words to help you control the stack. Let's introduce some of them and see how they work. We'll start with a simple example.

```
> gforth
1 2 3  ok
```

```
. 3  ok
. . 2 1  ok
bye
```

First, we push 1, then 2, then 3 on the stack. To pop the stack and print the popped value, use a period (.). Doing so gives us 3, the last item pushed on the stack. Popping and printing the stack two more times gives us 2 and then 1, leaving the stack empty. To exit Forth, enter **bye**. Forth is case insensitive, so BYE works just as well.

Table 4-1 introduces several words and an essential Forth convention.

Table 4-1: Stack Manipulation Words

Word	Effect	Description
dup	(a -- a a)	Duplicate the top stack item
drop	(a b -- a)	Drop the top of stack item
swap	(a b -- b a)	Swap the top two stack items
2dup	(a b -- a b a b)	Duplicate the top two stack items
2drop	(a b c -- a)	Drop the top two stack items
over	(a b -- a b a)	Copy the next to top of stack item
rot	(a b c -- b c a)	Rotate the top three stack items
nip	(a b c -- a c)	Drop the next to top of stack item
.s	(--)	Print the stack without altering it

The words are somewhat descriptive, and Forth is case insensitive, but the Effect column is important. The Effect column contains *stack-effect comments*, which we'll describe below. Forth comments begin with a left parenthesis, (, and end with a right parenthesis,). Note that a space after the (is required. Forth ignores anything after (until the first). Comments may not be nested. Many Forth systems, including ours, use \ as a comment running to the end of the line, like // in C++.

The comment itself illustrates how the word affects the stack. On the left is the stack as the word expects it with the top stack item on the right, next to the dashes. On the right of the dashes is the stack as the word leaves it, again with the top stack item on the right. There are conventions for the characters used, though they are more like guidelines than actual rules.

For example, dup duplicates the top stack item, so a becomes a a. If the word does not affect the stack, the empty (--) comment is used. By convention, every word definition has a stack-effect comment after its name, much like the convention of adding a documentation string after the definition of a function in Python.

Table 4-1 includes the word .s to print the contents of the stack without changing it. As you work with Forth, especially when getting a feel for the stack words, you'll use .s often. It's a good idea to use it to check that your words are not leaving extra junk on the stack.

Let's explore the stack some more.

```
1 2 3 .s <3> 1 2 3  ok
dup .s <4> 1 2 3 3  ok
2drop .s <2> 1 2  ok
3 nip .s <2> 1 3  ok
swap .s <2> 3 1  ok
2drop .s <0>  ok
```

The example above ends by calling 2drop to remove the remaining two stack items, which is why .s shows no items on the stack (<0>). Work with the stack until you feel comfortable with the stack manipulation words.

All Forth systems support integer arithmetic using the expected operators: addition (+), subtraction (-), multiplication (*), division (/), and modulo (mod). Many Forth systems, including gforth, work with floating-point numbers as well.

As practice, you might try implementing the following expressions using the standard arithmetic words:

$$(1200 \times 3) \div 4 \qquad (\text{ans} : 900)$$
$$8 \times (127 - 9) \div 11 \qquad (\text{ans} : 85)$$
$$8 \times (127 - 9) \bmod 11 \qquad (\text{ans} : 9)$$
$$((33 - 45) \div (7 + 9)) \times 3 \qquad (\text{ans} : -3)$$

You'll need to convert the expressions into postfix, meaning instead of $a + b$ you'll write $a\ b\ +$, and so on. Leave subexpression values on the stack and combine them with operations later: $(a + b) \times (c + d)$ becomes $a\ b\ +\ c\ d\ +\ \times$.

To use floating-point with gforth, you must do two things. First, enter floating-point constants using scientific notation. So to push 3.1415 on the floating-point stack, separate from the data stack, which is integer only, use 3.1415e0. For example, to calculate $1/1{,}121$ using first integer then floating-point math, enter the following:

```
1 1121 / . 0  ok
1e0 1121e0 f/ f. 0.000892060660124888  ok
```

For simplicity, we'll stick with integer operations for the remainder of this chapter.

FORTHS NOT FORTH

You've likely noticed by now that I've referred several times to "Forths" instead of just "Forth." There is a reason for that. The "freedom to the programmer" philosophy extends to Forth itself. Excluding the minor differences between versions, there is only one Python. Similarly, C++ is C++ and Java is Java. In contrast, there are, or were, legions of Forths. Most are now forgotten or virtually unusable because the computers they were written for are long gone. For

---

Now let's learn how to define our own Forth words.

Words and Loops

"Hello, world!" in Forth is

```
: hi ( -- ) ." Hello, world!" cr ;
```

Here, we've defined our own word to print `Hello, world!`. Word definitions begin with a colon (:), followed by the name of the word, which in this case is `hi`. Next comes the stack-effect comment, which isn't required, but strongly encouraged.

The word `hi` consumes nothing from the stack and leaves nothing on the stack, so the comment is empty: (--). The next token is ." which begins compiling a string to print. Don't forget the space after ."; it's required. The string ends with a double quote ("), followed by `cr` to move to the next line. The definition ends with a semicolon (;). We just defined our first word. To use it, enter `hi` at the `ok` prompt. Not too exciting, but it's a start.

What if we are feeling particularly happy today and want to greet the world repeatedly? That's easy to do as well. We just need a word that knows how to say `hi` many times:

```
: hello ( -- ) 10 0 do  hi  loop ;
```

The new word, `hello`, uses a do loop. This is Forth's version of a for loop, and may only be used within a word definition.

The general form of a do loop is

```
<end> <start> do <body> loop
```

Here, the ending and starting values are on the stack, with the ending value first, then the starting value, followed by the word `do`, the body of the loop, and the word `loop` to end the loop. Why so convoluted? It has to do with how Forth works. Comments about Forth being the exposed core of a compiler aren't all that far from the truth. The words `do` and `loop` are not keywords, but rather words that execute immediately when encountered by Forth. Their action sets up the code to make the loop. All of Forth's flow control words operate this way. The core Forth compiling words are no different from those a programmer might create, which is why the Forth compiler can be extended on the fly if desired.

Some Forth systems, especially those implemented in C, define most of Forth in Forth using a small core set of words to build the rest of the system. For example, lbForth (*https://gist.github.com/lbruder/10007431/*) is one such C-based Forth in the public domain. Here's how it defines do and loop in terms of other Forth words.

```
: do here @ ' swap , ' >r , ' >r , ; immediate
: loop ' r> , ' r> , ' swap , ' 1+ , ' 2dup , ' = , ' 0branch , here @ - , ' 2drop , ; immediate
```

Many of the words in these definitions will not make sense right now, but they will over time if you continue to work with Forth. The immediate tag after ; marks the word to make sure it is executed when encountered, even when defining another word. Also, the single quote (') takes the next token, looks up its execution address in the dictionary, and places that address on the stack. The comma (,) adds the top-of-stack number to the end of the dictionary, which in this case is the address of the word before it. The word here places the address of the end of the dictionary on the stack. Thus, do's net effect is to put the current end of the dictionary address on the stack and then compile references to order and store the loop limits that are already on the stack on the return stack. That's swap >r >r. I mentioned above that the return stack, which holds the address of where to go after the current word ends, is available to programmers if they are careful and remove anything they place on it.

Notice how loop pulls the limits from the return stack with r> and orders them, after which it increments the lower limit and compares it with the upper limit. If the limits are not equal, a branch back to the initial starting address placed on the stack by do happens courtesy of 0branch. The number of bytes to branch backward is calculated with here @ -.

A firm understanding of how these words operate isn't required. I've only highlighted them so we notice how even the compiler itself is Forth. The openness that allows flow control words like do and loop to be implemented in Forth is available to all Forth programmers. I know of no other programming language that is so open in this way.

The loop of hello above ran 10 times even though the limits were 0 and 10. This is because the upper limit is not included, making the do loop act like a C for loop:

```
for(int i=0; i < 10; i++)
    printf("Hello, world!\n");
```

The C code above used i as the loop counter. In Forth, the word i supplies the loop counter. Consider the following:

```
: counter ( -- ) 10 0 do i . loop ; ok
counter 0 1 2 3 4 5 6 7 8 9 ok
```

In this example, note that do uses i to access the current value of the loop counter.

There are times when incrementing by one isn't sufficient. Forth uses +loop in those cases, with the increment on the stack. The following example counts by threes.

```
: counter2 ( -- )  20 0 do i . 3 +loop ;   ok
counter2 0 3 6 9 12 15 18  ok
```

It is also possible to use the index as the increment.

```
: counter3 ( -- )  100 1 do i dup . +loop ;   ok
counter3 1 2 4 8 16 32 64  ok
```

Nested do loops are allowed. Use i to access the counter of the inner-most loop and j to access the counter of the next outer loop.

```
: nested0 ( -- ) 3 0 do 3 0 do j . i . space loop loop ;   ok
nested0 0 0  0 1  0 2  1 0  1 1  1 2  2 0  2 1  2 2   ok
```

In this example, i refers to the counter of the inner loop and j the outer. The word space prints a blank, as you likely surmised from the output. Note that we're writing the double loop in one line for simplicity. Forth is quite happy if you split up the code in a way that is easier to read.

```
: nested0 ( -- )
  3 0 do
    3 0 do
      j . i . space
    loop
  loop ;
```

Let's experiment a bit more with i and j. Consider the following:

```
: nested1 ( -- ) 5 1 do i 0 do j . loop loop ;   ok
nested1 1 2 2 3 3 3 4 4 4 4  ok
: nested2 ( -- ) 5 1 do i 0 do i . loop loop ;   ok
nested2 0 0 1 0 1 2 0 1 2 3  ok
```

Look at the definition of nested1. There are two do loops here. The first loop goes from 1 up to, but not including, 5. The inner loop runs from 0 up to, but not including, the current value of i. The output reflects the counter of the outer loop and runs the inner loop that many times: first once, then twice, then three times, and so on, each time printing the value of the outer loop because of j.

Now, look at nested2. In this case, the inner loop references i, which is the counter of the inner loop. Therefore, the first pass of the outer loop sets i to 1, causing the inner loop to iterate one time from 0. This explains the first 0. On the next pass, i is 2 in the outer loop, thereby causing the inner loop to run twice. The inner loop then references i as well; however, this time, the second i refers to the *inner* loop counter, which is why the output, on separate lines, is

```
0
0 1
0 1 2
0 1 2 3
```

What if you have three or more nested loops? How do you get the outermost counter? There is no Forth word for that, so you'd need to stash the counter with i before starting the next two nested loops and access it that way. You can either leave it on the stack, push it to the return stack, or dump it to a variable and reference it when needed.

What Is Truth?

Forth is unusual, so it should come as no surprise that Forth's definition of truth is unusual as well. In most languages, if there is no explicit Boolean data type, like False and True in Python, 0 is false and 1 (or not 0) is true. In Forth, false is 0, but true is −1. Forth also supports the usual comparison operators such as < and >.

```
1 2 < . -1  ok
-123 321 < . -1  ok
45 3 > . -1  ok
3 45 > . 0  ok
```

The above tells us that 1 < 2, −123 < 321, and 45 > 3 but not 3 > 45.

To test for equal and not equal, use = and <>.

```
1 2 = . 0  ok
1 2 <> . -1  ok
```

Forth works with both signed and unsigned integers, but the comparison operators above work only with signed integers. However, Forth also supports unsigned versions, indicated with a letter u before the operator.

```
1 2 u< . -1  ok
-123 321 u< . 0  ok
```

The first result makes sense, but the second might not; however, it is correct. The unsigned comparison looks only at the bit pattern representing −123. In two's complement format, assuming 16-bit integers even though our Forth system uses 64-bit integers, the bit pattern for −123 is 1111111110000101 whereas the bit pattern for 321 is 0000000101000001. This means that −123 is greater than 321 when using an unsigned comparison.

Forth wouldn't be of much use without some form of conditional expression. Thankfully, it supports if, else, and then. The general format for a conditional expression is

```
<condition> if <true_instructions> then
<condition> if <true_instructions> else <false_instructions> then
```

Here, *<condition>* is a condition flag on the stack, with 0 indicating false and −1 indicating true. If true, the words in *<true_instructions>* are executed. If there is an else and the condition is false, the words in *<false_instructions>* are executed.

For example, Goldilocks might want to know something about the state of the bowl of porridge she's just stumbled upon based on its temperature. In Python, she might write the following:

```python
def porridge(n):
    print("The porridge is ", end="")
    if (n < 90):
        print("too cold")
    elif (n > 100):
        print("too hot")
    else:
        print("just right")
```

In Forth, she might write what's shown in Listing 4-1.

```forth
: porridge ( n -- )
  ." The porridge is "
  dup  90 < if  drop ." too cold"  else
       100 < if  ." just right"     else
                 ." too hot"
  then then cr ;
```

Listing 4-1: Too cold, too hot, or just right

She'd then test her Forth code like so:

```
80 porridge The porridge is too cold
 ok
99 porridge The porridge is just right
 ok
111 porridge The porridge is too hot
```

Let's walk through the example in Listing 4-1. The word porridge expects a number on the stack, which in this case is the porridge's temperature in degrees Fahrenheit. With the temperature still on the stack, porridge prints the first part of the output sentence. Note that there is no cr, so by default, the output does not move to the next line.

Next comes the set of nested if statements. Let's start with the first one.

```forth
dup  90 < if  drop ." too cold"     else
```

The word dup duplicates the temperature. This is necessary, as < will consume it along with 90 to test $n < 90$. The result, either 0 or −1, is then pushed onto the stack. The value is consumed in this test, so if the first if fails, the nested second if will need a copy of *n* for its test.

At this point, the stack contains *n* and the output of <. Next, if consumes the 0 or −1. If −1, porridge prints the rest of the sentence: too cold. What's the drop doing there? Because *n* was duplicated to preserve it in case the first if failed, it's still on the stack. Therefore, it must be dropped before porridge exits.

The second if is like the first; it checks to see if *n* is less than 100. If so, the porridge is just right; otherwise, it's too hot. Note that there is no dup before the second if as *n* is not needed after the comparison, so it's consumed by <.

The way Listing 4-1 is written follows classic Forth convention. As mentioned, early Forths accessed disks in 1024-byte blocks, so writing compact code was essential. The Forth editor split the 1024 bytes of a block, a *screen*, into 16 lines of 64 characters each.

Modern Forth is more flexible. The following code works just as well as Listing 4-1.

```
: porridge (n -- )
  ." The porridge is "
  dup 90 < if
    drop ." too cold"
  else
    100 < if
      ." just right"
    else
      ." too hot"
    then
  then cr ;
```

Some Forth systems, including gforth, support a case selection structure that mirrors switch in C. For example, in a menu-driven program, the proper action to take depends on which option the user selects—a natural place to use case.

```
: menu ( n -- )
  case
    0 of ." option 0" endof
    1 of ." option 1" endof
    2 of ." option 2" endof
    ." bad option"
  endcase ;
0 menu option 0 ok
1 menu option 1 ok
2 menu option 2 ok
5 menu bad option ok
```

Notice that case expects the option to be on the stack when the word is executed. Forth then searches through the cases looking for a match.

If a match is found, Forth executes the case's body, which consists of the words between of and endof. If no case matches, Forth can use a default case ("bad option").

Other Control Structures

Forth's remaining control structures include a top-tested loop, a bottom-tested loop, and an infinite loop.

```
begin <condition> while <body> repeat
begin <body> <condition> until
begin <body> again
```

The first two are similar to while and do-while in C, but the last one is a bit curious. It's an infinite loop, which is easily written in other languages by making the while condition always true. However, when considering Forth implemented in Forth, it's easy to see why begin-again might exist:

```
: begin here @ ; immediate
: again ' branch , here @ - , ; immediate
```

Both begin and again are immediate words, that is, those that execute even when defining a word; begin places the current end-of-dictionary value on the stack, and again branches backward from the end of the dictionary to the location that begin initially placed on the stack. The branch is backward because again happens after the body of the loop, so here will report a higher address than the address placed on the stack by begin. I won't show it here, but with a little imagination, one can guess how while, repeat, and until might be implemented as Forth words.

A simple example of begin-again is

```
: infinity ( -- ) 0 begin  dup . cr 1+  again ;
```

The word infinity places 0 on the stack, duplicates it so it can be printed, and then increments it and starts repeating until you press CTRL-C or the power goes out.

Of more immediate utility are the top- and bottom-tested loops. A top-tested loop, the while loop, tests its condition before executing the body of the loop. Therefore, the body of the loop might never execute if the condition fails initially. For a bottom-tested loop, the body executes at least once to get to until. Let's see while in action.

One way to estimate the square root of a number using integer operations is to start at 0, square 0, and ask if that result is equal to or greater than the number. If it isn't, move on to try 1, then 2, 3, 4, and so on. Eventually, we'll get to the point where the number squared is equal to or greater than the given number. Listing 4-2 implements this inefficient algorithm with while.

```
: dsqr ( n -- )  0 begin  2dup dup * > while 1+ repeat nip ;
```

Listing 4-2: A brute-force square root word

We'll call the word dsqr for "dumb square root" because it implements the simplest algorithm possible. The word pushes an initial 0, which is the counter, and then starts the loop with begin. Note that the number we want the square root of, *n*, is already on the stack.

There are two pieces to the while loop: the condition and the body. Here the condition is 2dup dup * >. We have the given number and 0 on the stack for 2dup to duplicate. Next, dup duplicates the counter so it can be multiplied by itself to square it. This sets up >, which leaves a 0 or −1 on the stack. Remember, because of 2dup, the given number and counter are still on the stack.

Next, while uses the condition's state to decide whether or not to execute the body of the loop, 1+, which increments the counter still on the top of the stack. The repeat word does nothing as far as the loop is concerned, but again, we've seen enough of the internals of Forth to know that repeat is calculating how far back in the dictionary to branch to start again at begin. The word completes once the square root is found by removing the given number, the second-to-top stack item (nip).

As dumb as it is, dsqr works and is exact for perfect squares (but not for other numbers). Later, we'll implement a different integer square root algorithm, one that is surely less computationally demanding (we think).

In Forth, begin-until loops always execute the body of the loop at least once. For example, here's a word that plays a little guessing game.

```
: guess ( -- ) 0 begin 1+ key 15 and 7 = until . ." guesses" ;
```

Execute guess and press keys on the keyboard. The game ends when the lowest four bits of the ASCII character code for the key are 7. The counter is initially 0 and placed on the stack before begin. It is immediately incremented (1+) as there will always be at least one guess. Next, a keystroke is read and placed on the stack with key. The lowest four bits of the key's character code are kept by anding with 15 (0xF = 1111 in binary). That's 15 and. If the result is 7, = leaves −1 on the stack for until. If the result isn't 7, until branches back to begin.

Earlier, I said that begin-until is similar to do-while in C; however, there is an important difference. Consider the C equivalent of guess:

```
int main(int argc, char *argv[]) {
    int count = 0;

    do {
        count++;
    } while ((key() & 0xF) != 7);

    printf("\n%d guesses\n", count);
    return 0;
}
```

This program uses do-while, but the condition on the while part is written so it is *true* if the low-order nibble (that is, the lowest four bits) of the key entered is not 7. The Forth loop condition is *false* until the condition is met. In C, the logic is reversed: the do-while loop continues while the condition is true and the begin-until loop continues while the condition is false. Note that key() is not a standard C library function; it's just a stand-in for a function that waits for a keystroke and returns the ASCII key code without requiring a newline.

This example introduced key to wait for a character from the keyboard. We'll examine other Forth input and output functions later in the chapter. For now, let's get a handle on how Forth works with memory.

How Forth Uses Memory

Forth relies heavily on its stack, but that's not the only means it has to work with data. Forth supports constants and variables natively, and can allocate space on the dictionary for any use. Let's see how.

Variables and Constants

To define constants and variables, use code like what's shown in Listing 4-3.

```
variable f
variable c
32 constant b
: c2f c @ 9 * 5 / b + f ! ;   ok
: f2c f @ b - 5 * 9 / c ! ;   ok
212 f !   f2c   c @ . 100  ok
22 c !   c2f   f @ . 71  ok
32 f !   f2c   c @ . 0  ok
```

Listing 4-3: Variables and constants in Forth

The first two lines define variables f and c. The next line defines a constant, b, which is set to the top stack value, in this case 32.

Two short definitions come next. The first converts Celsius to Fahrenheit, $F = (9/5)C + 32$, and the second does the opposite, $C = (5/9)(F - 32)$. Both definitions use the variables f and c instead of the stack—a very *un*-Forth-like thing to do. As an exercise, rewrite c2f and f2c to use the stack.

The word definitions in Listing 4-3 have strange @ and ! characters in them. When a Forth variable is referenced, the value of the variable is *not* placed on the stack; only the address of the variable goes on the stack. To get at the value, the address must be dereferenced, just like in C, where a pointer must be dereferenced to get at the thing it points to. Therefore, the expression c @ first places the address of c on the stack, then executes @, which is the word that takes an address and returns the 64-bit integer at that address. Equivalent C code for c @ is *&c, assuming that c is declared to be an int. First, use & to get the address of c, then use * to return the contents of c.

Look again at the definition of c2f in Listing 4-3. The definition ends with f !. As you've likely already guessed, ! stores values at the address on the top of the stack, in this case the Fahrenheit temperature. The stack effect for ! is (n a --) to store value *n* at address *a*.

There is an elegance to how Forth handles variables, as other data areas also leave their address on the stack. However, all the @ and ! characters flying around quickly become distracting. For example, to increment a variable x by 1, use x @ 1+ x !, which isn't particularly easy to read. Note that 1+ is not a typo. Incrementing the top stack item is common enough that Forth implements a special word for it that executes faster than 1+ will. In truth, though, I'm being a bit unfair here. Forth does have the word +!, which adds a value to a variable. So x @ 1+ x ! might be written as 1 x +!, which is slightly more readable.

Forth supplies, at a minimum, two other words for memory access: c@ and c!. Here the c refers to "character," meaning old 8-bit ASCII. These words access *bytes*, not 64-bit integers. Consider this code:

```
variable x   ok
hex 1122334455667788 x !   ok
x @ . 1122334455667788   ok
x c@ . 88   ok
x 1+ c@ . 77   ok
x 2 + c@ . 66   ok
x 3 + c@ . 55   ok
x 4 + c@ . 44   ok
x 5 + c@ . 33   ok
x 6 + c@ . 22   ok
x 7 + c@ . 11   ok
```

First, we define x as a variable. Then, we assign a value to x by introducing a new word, hex, to place Forth in hexadecimal mode. All numbers will be interpreted as base-16 until decimal is executed to restore base-10. So the second and third lines when written in C become

```
long long x = 0x1122334455667788;
printf("%llx", x);
```

What of all the lines with c@ in them? As x pushes the *address* of x on the stack, using c@ returns the first *byte* at that address. Because Intel machines are little-endian, the first byte at the address of x is the lowest-order byte, 0x88 (to use C notation). Adding 1 to the address of x before accessing it moves to the next byte in memory to return 0x77, and so on for all eight bytes of x.

This freedom makes it easy to modify memory in interesting ways. For example, the following code defines x as before, but then uses c! to modify the low-order byte of x, changing it from 88 to ee:

```
variable x hex   ok
1122334455667788 x !   ok
x @ . 1122334455667788   ok
ee x c!   ok
x @ . 11223344556677EE   ok
```

Constants are just that: constants. Once fixed, they cannot be changed. Forth enforces this rule as well. However, consider these words:

```
1 constant 2   ok
4 constant 1   ok
1 1 + . 8   ok
2 2 * . 1   ok
```

Not every Forth system will allow this, but gforth does. What on Earth is happening? Recall what Forth does when it encounters a token on input. If it finds the token in the dictionary, it executes it; otherwise, it interprets it as a number and pushes it on the stack. The first two lines above define constants, 2 and 1. In this case, the constants' names really are "2" and "1" as characters. The value of the constant "2" is 1, and the value of the constant "1" is 4.

So the next time "2" is encountered, Forth first searches the dictionary, finds a constant with that name, and dutifully executes it to place a 1 on the stack. The same is true for "1" to place a 4 on the stack. Therefore, while confusing, Forth is perfectly correct to present output that seems to us to say 1 + 1 = 8 and 2 × 2 = 1.

There is a historical reason for allowing such shenanigans. Let's face it: old computers were slow. Programmers were always on the lookout for tricks to speed things up. When dealing with a new token, Forth scans the dictionary from beginning to end, so many Forth programs started with strange definitions like 0 CONSTANT 0 because it was faster to look up zero as a word than scan the entire dictionary and then interpret the token as a number.

Allocating Memory

We'll introduce several new words in this section. There will be a table at the end that contains all of them.

Forth puts all new data at the end of the dictionary. This includes word definitions, variables, and constants. To allocate arbitrary amounts of dictionary space, say for a buffer or a sequence of data structures of some kind, Forth provides several useful words: create, does>, allot, cells, a comma (,), and c,. Let's see how they work.

The word create defines a word that does nothing more than place its address on the stack. For memory allocation, create is often followed by allot, like so:

```
create buf 1000 allot   ok
```

The word buf is created, and immediately following it, 1,000 bytes of dictionary space are allocated. Effectively, this means there is a 1,000-byte buffer at the end of the dictionary, and the first byte of the buffer is the address that buf leaves on the stack when executed. This alone is already useful, as shown next.

```
1 buf c!  ok
2 buf 1+ c!  ok
3 buf 2 + c!  ok
buf c@ . 1  ok
buf 1+ c@ . 2  ok
buf 2 + c@ . 3  ok
```

The first three lines store byte values 1, 2, and 3 in the first three bytes of the 1,000-byte buffer pointed to by buf. We're using buf as an array of bytes. Continuing with the example above, try the following:

```
123456789 buf 3 + !  ok
buf 1+ c@ . 2  ok
buf 3 + @ . 123456789  ok
```

The first line stores a 64-bit value beginning at byte 4 of buf. The next line shows that the second byte of buf is still 2, as we set it above, and the third line that there is still a 64-bit value beginning at byte 4 of the buffer.

Although it's definitely possible to work with a block of memory byte by byte, it's tedious and error prone. Listing 4-4 shows how create works with allot and does> to create a word that defines 1D arrays:

```
: bArray ( n -- )  create allot does> + ;  ok
100 bArray x  ok
123 0 x c!  ok
124 1 x c!  ok
125 2 x c!  ok
1 x c@ . 124  ok
0 x c@ . 123  ok
2 x c@ . 125  ok
```

Listing 4-4: Defining a byte array

The first line defines bArray, which expects a number on the stack, which is the number of bytes to allot. First, create makes the new word and leaves the stack untouched. Next, allot reserves *n* bytes of dictionary space. So far, this makes sense; we saw this above. However, things get interesting when does> is executed.

The word bArray has two parts. The first part uses create and allot to reserve dictionary space for the byte array. This happens when bArray is executed. However, the does> portion is *not* executed just yet. The word does> details what happens when a word defined by bArray is itself executed. Additionally, when the word is executed, it pushes its address on the stack, after which does> the rest of the definition. Let's walk through it.

The second line, 100 bArray x, creates a byte array word, x. The create and allot words have executed to create x and reserve 100 bytes of dictionary space. When x itself is executed, its address is pushed on the stack, and the remainder of the definition of bArray, the part after does>, is also executed.

For bArray, there is a plus (+) after does>. The address of the word, x, is on the top of the stack, so the + adds the address to the value just below it on the stack (n a -- a+n), with *a* representing the address and *n* the value below, that is, an offset. Adding an offset to a base address is precisely how almost all programming languages index into arrays stored in contiguous memory. So if we supply an index before x, after x is executed, the stack contains the address of an element in the byte array assigned to x. Now the c! and c@ lines in Listing 4-4 make sense: 125 2 x c! is equivalent to x[2] = 125 in other languages. Likewise, 2 x c@ . is print(x[2]), if using Python. The combination of create and does> has allowed us to create words that implement byte arrays. Excellent. But what if we want not an array of bytes, but an array of integers? The word array does what we want:

```
: array ( n -- )  create cells allot does> swap cells + ;   ok
100 array y  ok
111111 66 y !  ok
222222 67 y !  ok
333333 68 y !  ok
66 y @ . 111111  ok
68 y @ . 333333  ok
67 y @ . 222222  ok
```

The only difference between bArray and array is the appearance of cells. In Forth, the basic unit of memory is a *cell*. For gforth, a cell is 64 bits or 8 bytes. If we want an array to store 100 values, we should allocate 800 bytes. Likewise, to index the array, we need addresses that are not just the base plus the index, but the base plus the index times the size of a cell. The word cells expects a number on the stack and returns the number of bytes in that many cells: 100 cells . returns 800.

So adding cells after create simply calculates the number of bytes allot should reserve at the end of the dictionary. When we index, the part after does>, we first convert the index from cells to bytes and add the result to the base address. That's what swap cells + accomplishes. After these changes, array works just like bArray, but one should use ! and @ to set and get values from the array.

Sometimes, allocating the array isn't all that we want. We also want to initialize it at the same time. The Forth way to do this uses a comma (,) or c,. These words compile the top stack item into the dictionary, either as a 64-bit integer or a byte. For example,

```
create ABCDEF 65 c, 66 c, 67 c, 68 c, 69 c, 70 c,
```

creates ABCDEF and allocates six values, the ASCII values for ABCDEF. The same is true if using the comma, but instead of bytes, it allocates cells (64-bit integers). These words are useful for setting up tables of constants or even arrays of words.

```
: one ." one" ;  ok
: two ." two" ;  ok
```

```
: three ." three" ;   ok
create tbl ' one , ' two , ' three ,   ok
tbl 2 cells + @ execute three ok
tbl 1 cells + @ execute two ok
tbl @ execute one ok
```

This example introduces two new words: single quote (') and execute. The first takes the execution address of the next token, a word, and places it on the stack. The next word, execute, runs the word whose execution address is on the stack. So tbl is an array of three "function pointers" as it were, to use C terminology. Once the proper offset to tbl is known, and the execution address is on the stack courtesy of @, execute calls the word.

Table 4-2 summarizes the words we introduced in this section.

Table 4-2: Forth Words for Manipulating Memory

Word	Effect	Description
@	(a -- n)	Get the 64-bit integer at address *a*
!	(n a --)	Store a 64-bit integer in address *a*
,	(n --)	Compile an integer into the dictionary
c@	(a -- b)	Get the byte at address *a*
c!	(b a --)	Store a byte in address *a*
c,	(b --)	Compile a byte to the dictionary
create	(--)	Create a new word
does>	(-- a)	Define the word's behavior
allot	(b --)	Allocate dictionary space (bytes)
cells	(n -- b)	Convert cells to bytes

Let's set memory aside for now and investigate Forth's input and output mechanisms.

Input and Output

A programming language without input or output is essentially useless. Forth, of course, has words for basic input and output, to say nothing of low-level I/O via serial and other mechanisms. We saw key in the begin-until example above. Modern Forth, like gforth, also has file access words as part of its interface to the operating system. We'll ignore those here to save space. Additionally, we already mentioned classic Forth's block-level disk access. Surprisingly, gforth emulates this, if desired, using a disk file as a representation of the disk itself. Therefore, if you care to explore it, gforth will let you relive the classic Forth experience.

We already know ., which prints the top stack item as a signed integer. To print the top stack value as an unsigned integer, use u.:

```
hex -aa dup . cr u. cr decimal -AA
FFFFFFFFFFFFFF56
```

This example works in hexadecimal to make it easier to understand what is happening. We push -0xAA on the stack, duplicate it, and print it twice, once with . as a signed integer and again with u. as an unsigned integer.

As expected, . produces -AA. However, u. produces FFFFFFFFFFFFFF56, a large, positive number, which is the value found by interpreting the signed 64-bit binary value as a positive number.

Forth grew up in an age of terminals and teletypes. Therefore, it supports many words that are variations of . and u., including words for highly structured formatting. One useful variation is u.r. It prints right-justified unsigned numbers (n d --), with n the number and d the width of the field. For example:

```
create x 10 , 100 , 1000 , 10000 , 100000 ,   ok
: aligned cr 5 0 do  i cells x + @  6 u.r cr  loop ;   ok
aligned
    10
   100
  1000
 10000
100000
```

First, we create a small array, x, with five numbers. Next, we define aligned to iterate through the array using u.r to display each number.

The word key reads a key from the user and pushes its character code on the stack. The analogous output word is emit, which takes the character code on the stack and displays it.

```
: alpha 26 0 do  [char] A i + emit loop cr ;   ok
alpha ABCDEFGHIJKLMNOPQRSTUVWXYZ
```

The word alpha displays the alphabet using emit to output the characters. We've also introduced [char], which is used during compilation to take the next character token, which here is A, and push its code on the stack. We could just as easily have used 65 instead of [char] A, as that is the ASCII code for "A."

To get a string of input from the user, use accept, which expects two values on the stack: the address of where the string should go and the maximum number of characters to input.

```
create str 80 allot   ok
str 80 accept (press enter here) How now brown cow?   ok
. 18   ok
```

accept returns the number of characters actually entered. The buffer, str, now holds the text. To see it, use type.

```
str 18 type How now brown cow? ok
```

This also expects the address and count on the stack.

Creating a special buffer for input is a bit tedious, so Forth provides pad, a pre-allocated buffer of at least 84 characters (for gforth). Let's use pad to learn how to input numbers instead of strings.

```
pad 80 accept (press enter here) -2211333  ok
pad swap evaluate . -2211333  ok
```

The first line reads a character string of up to 80 characters and puts it in pad. Recall that accept returns the actual number of characters read, which is used in the next line.

The second line puts the address of pad on the stack, swaps to make the number of characters entered the top stack item, and calls evaluate to interpret the string as a number.

We could spend many more pages describing all the various, sometimes quirky, input and output options Forth provides, but the examples discussed so far are a good start.

Square Root Redux

In this section, we'll make good on a promise made earlier in the chapter. While discussing dsqr above, we said we'd develop a better method for finding integer square roots. To see that we can, let's do it now.

dsqr found the square root of an integer by testing all options to see which one was the square root. Although this approach works, it's at first blush quite computationally inefficient. Instead, let's try an implementation based on Equation 4.1:

$$\sum_{i=0}^{n-1} 2i + 1 = n^2 \tag{4.1}$$

This equation says that the sum of the first n odd numbers is n^2. Therefore, if we count the number of times an increasing odd number can be subtracted from another number, we'll have an estimate of the square root of that number.

Listing 4-5 implements the algorithm implied by Equation 4.1.

```
: sqrt ( n -- sqrt[n] )
  0 >r 1 swap begin
    dup 0 >
  while
    over - swap 1+ 1+ swap r> 1+ >r
  repeat 2drop r> ;
```

Listing 4-5: Integer square root in Forth

The stack contains n, the number whose square root is sought, and x, an ever-increasing odd number, first 1, then 3, 5, 7, and so on. Each iteration sets $n \leftarrow n - x$ and $x \leftarrow x + 2$. When n is less than or equal to 0, the loop ends. To get the square root, we count the number of passes through the loop and use the return stack to hold the counter, initializing it with 0 >r and incrementing it with r> 1+ >r. When the loop ends, *n* and *x* are dropped, and the count is returned.

A few examples demonstrate that sqrt works as advertised (with 7 as the estimated square root of 42).

```
25 sqrt . 5  ok
36 sqrt . 6  ok
42 sqrt . 7  ok
144 sqrt . 12  ok
152399025 sqrt . 12345  ok
```

Surely, sqrt is a better option than dsqr from Listing 4-2. Let's set up a test and see. The code we want is in the *examples* directory in the file *sqrt.4th*.

```
( Park and Miller PRNG )
variable seed  8675309 seed ! ( default seed )
: rand ( -- n ) 48271 seed @ * 2147483647 mod  dup seed ! ;
: random ( m -- n ) rand swap mod ;

( Time to find the square root by method )
variable x
utime drop dup seed ! x ! ( keep seed )

: run0 ( -- ) 100000 0 do  1000 random 1+ dup * sqrt drop  loop ;
: run1 ( -- ) 100000 0 do  1000 random 1+ dup * dsqr drop  loop ;

: main ( -- )
  utime  run0  utime 2swap d- d. cr
  x @ seed !  ( use the same sequence )
  utime  run1  utime 2swap d- d. cr ;

main  bye
```

Listing 4-6: Testing sqrt and dsqr

Listing 4-6 presents the relevant portion of *sqrt.4th*. The file first defines sqrt and dsqr (not shown) before defining a simple 32-bit linear congruential pseudorandom number generator. The word random takes an upper limit, which is never returned, and replies with a random integer in the range $[0, n)$.

Gforth uses utime to return a double-precision (128-bit) time value, the lower 64 bits of which become the seed for the random number generator. A copy of the seed is kept in x as well so we can repeat the sequence later.

Two short words come next: run0 and run1. Both calculate the square root of 100,000 random values in $[1, 10^6]$, each of which is a perfect square. We don't actually want the answers; we're only interested in how long the calculation takes, so each square root is immediately discarded (drop). Next, run0 uses sqrt and run1 uses dsqr.

The `main` word grabs the start time, leaving it on the stack, calls `run0`, and prints the time it takes to run in microseconds (`2swap d- d.`). It then resets the pseudorandom seed and repeats the calculation using `run1`.

Executing *sqrt.4th* 10 times (`gforth sqrt.4th`) gives us the following mean runtimes for the two square root methods.

```
SQRT: 0.7457714
DSQR: 0.4978122
```

Time is now in seconds. Clearly, our intuition was incorrect. The more elegant algorithm takes about 1.5 times longer to execute, on average, than the brute-force method. This reminds me of physicist Ludwig Boltzmann's famous quote: "If you are out to describe the truth, leave elegance to the tailor." In this case, elegance loses out to raw computing power. It is simply faster to check all possibilities compared to the number of calculations and stack manipulations necessary to implement the subtraction method.

Is this the final word, though? There is one more algorithm we can try: Newton's method. Newton's method finds the roots of equations, the values of x that make the equation zero. If the equation is $x^2 - n$, then it's clear this equation is zero when $x = \sqrt{n}$.

Newton's method is iterative based on an initial guess. It is powerful and converges quickly. Equation 4.2 shows us how to iterate with

$$x_{i+1} \leftarrow x_i + \frac{1}{2}\left(x_i + \frac{n}{x_i}\right) \tag{4.2}$$

for some initial guess, $x_0 = n/2$.

The code we need, also in *sqrt.4th*, is

```
: step ( n xi -- n xi x_{i+1} )
  2dup dup rot swap dup 0= if 2drop else / + then 2/ ;
: newton ( n -- sqr[n] )
  dup 2/ step begin 2dup swap < while nip step repeat drop nip ;
```

The word `step` performs one update step (Equation 4.2) with n and x_i on the stack as input and n, x_i, x_{i+1} as output. The `if` handles things if x_i is 0.

`newton` performs the iterations for as long as $x_{i+1} < x_i$. The first `dup 2/` sets the initial guess, x_0. The body of the loop keeps x_{i+1} as the new x_i and then takes another step. After the loop, the last x_{i+1} is dropped, along with n, leaving only x_i as the answer.

Running `newton` 10 times lets us complete our list of average runtimes.

```
SQRT:   0.7457714
DSQR:   0.4978122
NEWTON: 0.0493205
```

We have a clear winner. Newton's method is, on average, an order of magnitude faster than the brute force method. Boltzmann is wrong in this case; elegance and truth do go together.

Discussion

What should we make of Forth? It's definitely a curious language, but with its own charm. However, it seems best suited to a computing environment that is largely bygone. Figuring out how to manipulate the stack to accomplish what can be done in a simple statement or two in other languages is both frustrating and rewarding, but not particularly practical for day-to-day use. Forth's learning curve is rather high, though experts can do amazing things with it.

Because the code can be difficult to read, Forth is often characterized as a "write-only" programming language. Expert practitioners will disagree, and strict adherence to Forth style guidelines might mitigate some of the effects, but the charge is not without merit.

Back in the Introduction, you can see Figure 1, which shows a functional brain imaging system I wrote in Forth for the Macintosh nearly 25 years ago. It worked well, and I used it often. Now, some 25 years later, thanks to the power of open source emulators like BasiliskII, I was able to run the code and pull out the source. Here's the code for accessing a single pixel of what amounts to a 3D block of data, a time series of magnetic resonance images.

```
: }Pixel ( x y z -- n )
  ( Return value of x,y pixel in image z of current slice )
  rot matsize @ m* zTmp 2! swap s>d zTmp 2@ d+ 2dup d+ zTmp 2!
  s>d d>f imgsz 2@ d>f f* f>d  ( z*image_size )
  zTmp 2@ d+  ( offset into slice )
  slcoff 2@ d+  ( slice offset )
  mem 2@ dl@ d+ l@ ;  ( fetch pixel value )
```

I agree that this probably deserves the label of write-only code. The comments explain what is happening, but I doubt anyone would say it's easy to read. For comparison purposes, here's how to do the same thing in Python with NumPy: n = images[z,x,y].

Lest readers think me unfair in my criticism, I still use Forth for different projects, usually to simulate the small microcontrollers that a larger system communicates with via RS-232 serial. Forth works well in this case, even on old Apple II computers.

The Forth words of this chapter took time and some effort with pen and paper to work out. However, that adds to the charm of achieving success with the language, even as it subtracts from the practical utility.

Forth's popularity has definitely waned in recent years. However, the embedded development world still holds a place for Forth. There are small, single-board computers that run Forth as well as C, but they are few and far between. Increasingly, the embedded world is moving to tiny computers supporting more modern languages. Later in this book, for example, we'll use the BBC micro:bit, which uses Python as its primary language, though hobbyists have developed a version of Forth that runs on the micro:bit. Full-blown Linux environments for small boards, like the Raspberry Pi Zero and BeagleBoard, are common. The world that motivated the development of Forth has changed.

So why consider Forth?

Because Forth is a perfect exemplar for what this book intends to present to you: an opportunity to look at programming in a new light.

To succeed with Forth, you must think not only at the higher level of algorithm, though that is still necessary, but also at the lower level of *how* each algorithm step can be implemented, in minute detail.

Forth is close to what the computer is doing and not abstracted away from it like Python or Java. Bytes, addresses, order of operations on a stack, and how much limited dictionary memory is available all require a different kind of thinking, a more parsimonious approach to programming.

Those bitten by the Forth bug seldom recover. I recall many times reading posts on the old comp.lang.forth newsgroup (remember those?) that were almost spiritual in their expression of the joy one might feel when working with Forth. A tad excessive, perhaps, but there is definitely a joy to using Forth. Please do continue to play with the language.

Summary

This chapter introduced Forth, a unique language with a long history. We explored the language, how it works, its programming model, and its philosophy. We looked at some examples and saw that Forth is often implemented in Forth, building itself by pulling itself up by its bootstraps.

Thinking in Forth takes time and effort. Indeed, *Thinking FORTH* is the name of a classic Forth text by Leo Brodie (*http://thinking-forth.sourceforge.net/*). Take a look. If you want, you might also take a gander at Brodie's *Starting FORTH* (*http://www.exemark.com/FORTH/StartingFORTHfromForthWebsitev9 _2013_12_24.pdf*). Between these two books, you'll get a thorough understanding of what it means to work with Forth.

Now, it's time for something completely different. We leave the low-level world of Forth behind and move into the oddly wonderful world of text processing with SNOBOL.

5

SNOBOL

SNOBOL is a text pattern matching language developed in the 1960s. Modern programmers might find its syntax quaint, and maybe even a tad frustrating, but I suspect the power of the language will shine through in the end as we explore its features, some of which are still with us in modern languages like Python.

SNOBOL, like Forth, is a denizen of the later Paleozoic. SNOBOL and Forth are of similar vintage, but they are extremely different. Forth is minimal and low level. SNOBOL is abstract and surprisingly powerful, though quirky.

In this chapter, we'll explore SNOBOL, specifically SNOBOL4, the latest dialect of the language. SNOBOL is known for its pattern matching and string processing abilities, but it is a general-purpose language. As we'll see, SNOBOL's data handling facilities are surprisingly sophisticated and include an atypical level of flexibility. As Michael Shafto put it in 1982, "SNOBOL4 is the Alice's Restaurant of programming languages: you can get anything you want" (see "Artificial Intelligence Programming in SNOBOL4," available on this book's GitHub site).

Let's explore SNOBOL by reviewing the structure of the language and the interesting abilities it provides. We'll walk through its features, look at examples, and finish by building a simple machine learning classifier to link our explorations with the hopes of at least some computer scientists from the 1980s. As before, we'll end with some closing thoughts.

Installation

To install SNOBOL, download it from *http://ftp.ultimate.com/snobol4/* by grabbing *snobol4-2.3.1.tar.gz*, or any later version you see on that site. Save the file in a subdirectory called *SNOBOL*. Once you have the file, expand it and build the SNOBOL executable as follows:

```
$ tar xzf snobol4-2.3.1.tar.gz
$ cd snobol4-2.3.1/
$ ./configure
$ make
```

The commands above generate a lot of output. Some are from the C compiler, including a few warnings we can safely ignore. The rest are from SNOBOL test scripts. When all is said and done, if you see a message about sending timing info to `timing@snobol4.org`, you'll know that SNOBOL was successfully built and is running correctly.

Origins and Philosophy

SNOBOL ("StriNg Oriented and symBOlic Language") was developed during the 1960s at AT&T Bell Laboratories by David Farber, Ralph Griswold, and Ivan Polonsky. The name *SNOBOL* is a backronym, meaning the developers began with the acronym they wanted and worked backward to ensure they got it.

According to Farber, the original name for the language was "Symbolic EXpression Interpreter," or SEXI. In the 1960s, running a computer program meant walking to the machine room with a stack of punch cards. Typically, the program name and username were marked on the deck. So Farber handed the young woman running the programs a stack labeled "SEXI Farber." She read the name and laughingly said, "That's what you think." Clearly, a new name was needed. After much frustration, someone complained that they didn't have a snowball's chance in hell of coming up with a name; thus "SNOBOL" was born. The spelling pays homage to other similarly named languages of the time like COBOL and ALGOL. (Farber posted this story to his Interesting-People mailing list in December 2008.)

SNOBOL's claim to fame is its powerful pattern-matching abilities. Current programming languages often rely on regular expressions, which have a separate history from SNOBOL, but SNOBOL's matching skills were perfectly suited to the sort of highly structured data processing that was the focus of most computer mainframe use at the time. We'll explore pattern matching throughout the chapter.

SNOBOL's philosophy might best be summed up as "all the world's a string." Strings are almost everything in SNOBOL. Data in the 1960s was typically textual, like records with fixed sizes and fields. SNOBOL's pattern matching made processing such data (relatively) straightforward.

Even though SNOBOL manipulated structured text data, it did not itself make use of structured programming. Thus, there are no for or while loops in SNOBOL. For that matter, SNOBOL lacks even basic if-then constructs. The only way to control program flow is by using what amounts to a goto statement. However, in SNOBOL, gotos are rather flexible. One of SNOBOL's unique concepts is that every line of code either succeeds or fails and where the program goes next depends on that fact. We'll see this in action as we work through the examples. In SNOBOL, failure is definitely an option. In fact, it's a requirement.

SNOBOL is dynamically typed and able to create new variables and data structures on the fly. SNOBOL can even create new code on the fly, though we won't be so ambitious here. SNOBOL supports powerful arrays and tables, the latter of which are much like Python dictionaries. User-defined data structures are also available.

The best way to learn SNOBOL is to use SNOBOL. It really must be seen to be believed. So without further ado, let's take a walk in the snow.

The Language

We'll begin by learning how to get SNOBOL to do basic things like print "Hello, world!" Once we've figured that out, we'll move to variables and user-defined data types. Next come arrays and tables, SNOBOL's intrinsic data structures. Patterns follow, though some pattern use will already have snuck in. Patterns are the traditional reason for using SNOBOL, and are perhaps the one part of the language that best distinguishes it from most other languages.

SNOBOL allows user-defined functions. We'll see how to define them and learn why the process is, to be blunt, ugly. Then we'll close with disk files and command line arguments. We'll learn how to control a SNOBOL program's flow as we work through the examples, as that's the best way to learn it. All the files mentioned in the following sections are in the *examples* directory under *SNOBOL*.

Running SNOBOL

SNOBOL runs interactively if started without a filename. This mode is available for quick calculations and testing ideas, but SNOBOL was meant to run code from a file or, originally, a stack of punch cards.

Listing 5-1 gets us started with *hello.sno*.

```
*  hello.sno
   output = 'Hello, world!'
   output = 'Hello, '  "world!"
   output = 'Hello #' 9
   output =
```

```
        output = "Goodbye!"
end
```

Listing 5-1: A SNOBOL greeting

This short program already has much to say about SNOBOL. First, comment lines begin with an asterisk (*). However, unlike in other languages, the asterisk *must* be in column 1. Either the entire line is a comment, or none of it is.

To print something in SNOBOL, we assign it to the special variable output. SNOBOL is not case sensitive, so output and OUTPUT are treated the same. The thing assigned to output is a string or something SNOBOL will implicitly convert into a string, like a number.

Concatenation is such a common operation in SNOBOL that space is used as the operator. So the first output statement in Listing 5-1 assigns a string enclosed in single quotes while the second concatenates two strings together. Note the use of double quotes. Like Python, SNOBOL allows both kinds. As you can see from the next line, SNOBOL implicitly converts numbers, which may be integers or floating point, into strings. Lastly, to output a blank line, assign nothing. Assigning nothing is also the SNOBOL way of removing things from a string. We'll see that in action when using patterns.

All SNOBOL programs end with end. Note that end is in column 1 and all the output statements are indented. SNOBOL doesn't care how far statements are indented, only that they don't begin in column 1. The only things allowed in column 1 are * for comments, + for line continuation (which is seldom used now), and labels, including end.

You can run *hello.sno* like you'd run a Python script.

```
> snobol4 hello.sno
```

This should give you the following output:

```
Hello, world!
Hello, world!
Hello #9

Goodbye!
```

The output of Listing 5-1 implies that SNOBOL always prints the string assigned to output on a line. There is no easy way to output a partial line followed by more text before ending the line. SNOBOL is line oriented, both for output and input. Thus, it is up to the programmer to build the entire line first before assigning it to output.

Now run Listing 5-2, *hello2.sno*.

```
*  hello forever
loop  output = "You say goodbye and I say hello"   :(loop)
end
```

Listing 5-2: Hello, hello, hello

When you get bored, use CTRL-C to interrupt the program. This is our first SNOBOL loop. In SNOBOL, every line has the opportunity to execute a goto. The first part of the line, in column 1, is a label, loop. Labels are the targets SNOBOL uses when the goto portion of a line is executed. Labels, and other identifiers, must start with a letter. After that, letters, numbers, and underscores are allowed. Note that labels are global. That is, they must be unique across the entire program. Also, SNOBOL lines get rather lengthy and full of spaces, so we'll remove extra spaces present in the source code files to save space in the text.

The goto portion of a SNOBOL line comes at the end. The number of spaces before the goto can vary, but no code comes after the goto. The colon (:) begins the goto. Target labels are enclosed in parentheses. We'll encounter more sophisticated gotos as we proceed. Note that if there is no goto, control proceeds to the next line of code as in most programming languages.

One more item is worth noting here. The goto in Listing 5-2 always executes whether the line succeeds or fails. Granted, this line will never fail, but we'll see other lines that do and that indeed must fail. It's part of how the language works. Forgetting to distinguish between success and failure and using a goto that always executes can lead to strange behavior. Of course, the potential dangers of goto statements are well known—see Edsger Dijkstra's famous 1968 paper "Go To Statement Considered Harmful" (*https://homepages.cwi.nl/~storm/teaching/reader/Dijkstra68.pdf*). However, with SNOBOL, it's all we have to work with.

Listing 5-3 introduces a few new SNOBOL concepts.

```
*  A bit of interaction
again output = "Name?"
  name = input
  output = differ(name, null) "Greetings, " name  :f(again)
  output = "Shall we play a game?"
  output = "On second thought, nah"
end
```

Listing 5-3: A bit of interaction

The first new concept is showing how to get input from the keyboard by referencing input; it returns a string that is assigned to the variable name. Notice that the variable name was not declared. Like Python, SNOBOL is dynamically typed, meaning that variables are created on demand and can hold whatever data is assigned to them.

The next line needs parsing. It's an assignment to output, so it will ultimately print something on the screen. We see a constant string followed by name. There is space between them, so we expect the two to become a string using the name entered by the user. But what's this differ thing? And the goto section is new, too.

Let's start with the goto. It's :f(again). The colon begins the goto. The f stands for failure. If the line fails, goto again, the line that asks for the user's name. Okay, this seems reasonable; if the user's input isn't valid, ask again.

Now for the `differ` part: `differ` is a SNOBOL predicate. Like all predicates, its purpose is to determine whether something is true or false. However, unlike in any other programming language I've ever encountered, SNOBOL predicates don't return true or false. If the predicate is false, the function *fails*, and if any portion of a SNOBOL line fails, the entire line fails. If a line fails and there is a goto for a failure condition, that goto is then executed. So if `differ` fails, the line fails, and flow continues with the line labeled `again`.

Truth in SNOBOL is the null string. I'm sure there's a deep, philosophical implication to truth being null and empty, but we'll stick with computer programming and avoid the headache. SNOBOL predicates that are true return the null string. So `differ` takes two objects and asks if they are not the same. Here the objects are whatever was assigned to `name` and SNOBOL's constant for an empty string, `null`.

This line, then, is checking to see if the user pressed ENTER without typing anything. If so, `differ` fails and program flow returns to `again`. If the user enters some text, `differ` succeeds and returns the empty string, which, because it's separated from the string constant by a space, is concatenated with the string and the name. Concatenating a null string doesn't change anything. It's like adding zero. So the line succeeds and `output` is assigned. The trick of using a predicate that concatenates a null string to a line is a common one in SNOBOL. However, the predicate doesn't need to be used that way; it can be on a line by itself. For example, the following code works just as well:

```
differ(name, null)          :f(again)
output = "Greetings, " name
```

If the `differ` is false, it fails, and the loop happens. If `differ` is true, the null string has no effect and the `output` proceeds.

We have figured out how to print strings and get user input and store it in a variable. We were also introduced to the overall structure of a SNOBOL program and learned a bit about gotos. Let's continue our exploration by concentrating on variables and data types.

Variables and Data Types

As we've already seen, SNOBOL variables are created on demand and can hold any value. Strings, integers, and floats are SNOBOL's primitive data types. In this section, we'll work with these primitives and then go beyond them to create custom data types. This is the SNOBOL equivalent of structures in other languages like C.

Integers and Floats

Listing 5-4 presents *temperature.sno*, a simple menu-driven program to convert between Fahrenheit and Celsius temperatures.

```
menu   output =
       output = "(1) F to C or (2) C to F, 'q' to quit:"
       menu = input
       ident(menu,'2')                      :s(CtoF)
       ident(menu,'q')                      :s(end)

* F to C
       output = "Fahrenheit temperature?"
       F = input
       C = (5. / 9.) * (F - 32.0)
       output = F " F = " C " C"            :(menu)

* C to F
CtoF   output = "Celsius temperature?"
       C = input
       F = (9. / 5.) * C + 32.0
       output = C " C = " F " F"            :(menu)
end
```

Listing 5-4: Temperature conversion

The menu asks for the type of conversion or q to quit. The variable menu holds the user's selection. Next comes a new predicate, ident. As you likely surmised from the name, ident is the opposite of differ; it's true when the arguments are identical. Notice that menu is compared to the string constant '2' and not just 2. This is one place where SNOBOL's permissive automatic string conversion is not applied. The value returned by input is always a string, so we must use a string with ident. If we did use 2 and not '2', there would be no error, but the predicate would fail, and because there is no fail goto defined, SNOBOL would proceed to the next line instead.

The ident line shows us a new form of goto, :s(CtoF). The s means success, and tells SNOBOL where to go if the line does not fail. In this case, not failing means the user selected option two. Thus, the program jumps to the label CtoF to convert Celsius to Fahrenheit. Likewise, the following line jumps to the end if the user entered a q. If the user entered neither 2 nor q, execution falls through to the code marked F to C.

The conversions ask the user for a temperature, perform the proper conversion, report the result, and then jump back to menu. The conversions also do something subtle behind the scenes. The requested temperature is assigned to either F or C, which are then used in the conversion equation. In this case, SNOBOL does automatically convert the input to a number. Unless the user explicitly enters a decimal point or uses scientific notation, the resulting number is an integer; otherwise, it's a float. This means the programmer is responsible for ensuring that expressions perform the proper conversion as to type. To make the input an integer, multiply by 1. To make the input a float, multiply by 1.0 or use the convert function, which shows up later in this chapter.

There is more to notice in Listing 5-4. Look carefully at how we've written the conversion formulas. First, we use decimal points to force floating-point computation. Without them, the division operation would use integer math, though the expected promotion from integer to float happens if there is a float in the expression. However, be careful because each subexpression needs a float as well. In that case, (9 / 5) * 100.0 + 32.0 would be 132 rather than 212 because the fraction is pure integer math returning 1 instead of 1.8.

Notice that there are spaces around each of the operators in the conversions. These are not just for readability; SNOBOL requires them. Forgetting a space before or after an operator is an error, as SNOBOL will happily point out to you. Lastly, SNOBOL lacks the format specifiers found in languages like C and Python. SNOBOL expects the programmer to convert the number to a string with appropriate spacing and justification to format output. You're on your own when formatting output in SNOBOL.

Listing 5-4 implemented a simple menu by checking the user's input with ident. SNOBOL also allows *computed gotos*. A computed goto uses an expression to determine the target label. Listing 5-5 shows *menu.sno*, which implements a simple menu with a computed goto.

```
loop    output = "Select your entree:"
        output = "  0) Green eggs and ham"
        output = "  1) Purple pizza"
        output = "  2) Plaid tacos"
        output = "  3) Blue snocone"
        output = "  4) Quit"
        menu = input
        order = "You ordered "        :($('menu' menu))

menu0   order = order "green eggs and ham"   :(print)
menu1   order = order "a purple pizza"       :(print)
menu2   order = order "plaid tacos"          :(print)
menu3   order = order "a blue snocone"       :(print)
print   output =
        output = order
        output =                             :(loop)
menu4
end
```

Listing 5-5: Using a computed goto

The menu loop asks the user to select an entrée, then outputs the name of the selected entrée. Not a particularly useful program, but it does have one interesting feature: ($('menu' menu)).

The label matching the string formed by the expression inside $(...) is the goto's target. The $(...) syntax is a form of indirection that tells SNOBOL to build the target label on the fly using the expression inside the parentheses. The expression is 'menu' menu, which concatenates the word *menu* with the user's number. Naturally, an actual application would validate the user's input first.

Jumping to the proper label updates order and the desired entrée is displayed before jumping back to loop. If the user selects option four, the program jumps to label menu4, which falls through to end to exit the program.

Indirection

Consider the following sequence of SNOBOL instructions from an interactive session.

```
snobol4>  a = 123
snobol4>  b = .a
snobol4>  c = 'a'
snobol4>  output = a
snobol4>  output = b
snobol4>  output = c
snobol4>  output = $b
snobol4>  output = $c
snobol4>  output = $.a
snobol4> end

123
A
a
123
123
123
```

The first line assigns 123 to a. The second uses the *name operator* (.) to assign the name of a to b. In SNOBOL, the name of a variable is similar to the address of a variable in languages like C. The third line sets c to the string 'a'. Then come a series of output statements.

The first displays a returning 123, as expected. The second outputs b, which returns the name of a, A. SNOBOL is case insensitive, so the name of a variable is shown in all caps. The third output prints the string 'a', again, as expected.

The last three output statements are more interesting. They all use indirect references ($) to output not the value of the variable, but the value of the variable whose name is in the first variable. The variable b was assigned to the name of a, meaning it is the string 'A'. So the indirect reference looks to b to get the string 'A' and then looks for a variable called A, finds it, and returns *its* value. So the output of $b is 123, the value of a. Using a string with the variable name works as well, which is why the output of $c is also the value of a. Lastly, the name operator and indirect reference are inverses of each other, so $.a means "name of a indirectly referenced back to a," resulting in the value of a.

Listing 5-6 shows another indirection example, that of the file *indirect.sno*.

```
cosa1 = 'thing1'
cosa2 = 'thing2'
```

```
$cosa1 = 'mea1'
$cosa2 = 'mea2'
$thing1 = 'kitu1'
$thing2 = 'kitu2'
output = cosa1 ' ' cosa2
output = thing1 ' ' thing2
output = $thing1 ' ' $thing2
output = mea1 ' ' mea2
output = $$cosa1 ' ' $$cosa2
end
```

Listing 5-6: Another indirection example

Take a look at the listing before reading further to see if you can guess what the output will be. Notice that the output statements use string concatenation to output two variables on one line with a single space between them. Read on when ready to see what SNOBOL says the output should be.

SNOBOL reports the following as the output of Listing 5-6:

```
thing1 thing2
mea1 mea2
kitu1 kitu2
kitu1 kitu2
kitu1 kitu2
```

The first line of Listing 5-6 shouldn't be mysterious. It's normal variable output; cosa1 and cosa2 are the literal strings 'thing1' and 'thing2'.

At first glance, the second output line is a bit of a surprise. The code assigns variables thing1 and thing2 to output, but those variables are not explicitly defined in the code. The lines that create them are

```
$cosa1 = 'mea1'
$cosa2 = 'mea2'
```

where the indirect reference is used to assign not to cosa1 and cosa2, but to the variables created by the current value of cosa1 and cosa2, which are 'thing1' and 'thing2'. Therefore, thing1 equals 'mea1' and thing2 equals 'mea2'.

The next pair of lines in Listing 5-6 are similar.

```
$thing1 = 'kitu1'
$thing2 = 'kitu2'
```

To create two new variables, mea1 and mea2 assigned 'kitu1' and 'kitu2', respectively. This explains why the third line of output is kitu1 kitu2. The indirect reference on thing1, containing 'mea1', returns the value of mea1, which is 'kitu1', and likewise for thing2. Because they were created by assigning to $thing1 and $thing2, the next output line makes sense, too.

The final assignment uses indirection twice on cosa1. The first indirection, that is, the rightmost $, returns thing1. The second indirection on thing1 returns mea1's value, which is 'kitu1'. The same is true for $$cosa2.

SNOBOL's indirection and dynamic creation of variables during runtime are quite powerful and equally confusing if not used carefully. For the curious, *cosa* means "thing" in Spanish. Likewise, *mea* is Hawaiian for "thing" and *kitu* is Swahili for, you guessed it, "thing."

User-Defined Data Types

User-defined data types are created with the function data, which accepts a *string* as its argument. The string defines the name of the new type and the names of the elements of the type. SNOBOL creates a function to generate new instances of the type and functions with the names of the type elements. The latter functions are used to access elements of the type when it is used.

For example, consider the following instructions:

```
snobol4>  data('complex(real,imag)')
snobol4>  a = complex(1.5, 3.3)
snobol4>  b = complex(2.3,-0.4)
snobol4>  output = a
snobol4>  output = b
snobol4>  output = real(a) ' ' real(b)
snobol4>  output = imag(a) ' ' imag(b)
snobol4>  end

COMPLEX
COMPLEX
1.5 2.3
3.3 -0.4
```

The first line defines a new data type, complex, which has two elements real and imag. We can use this data type to hold a complex number. A complex number has two parts: a real part and an imaginary part. The real part is a floating-point number corresponding to a number on the number line. The imaginary part is also a floating-point number which is multiplied, conceptually, by the square root of −1. The square root of −1 doesn't exist. No number multiplied by itself is negative, so it's "imaginary." Even though complex numbers don't correspond to anything in the physical world, their properties are such that they make certain calculations vastly simpler. For our purposes, all we care about is that this new complex data type has two elements. Notice that the definition of complex is given as a string. Because of this, SNOBOL can create new data types on the fly at runtime, perhaps in response to user input or data read from a file. Also, and this is important, the data type string *must not* contain spaces. Thus, 'complex(real,imag)' works, but 'complex(real, imag)' generates an error.

After defining complex, we immediately create two instances of it, a and b. To create an instance, use the name of the data type and supply a value for all the elements. Next are four output statements, the first two of which use a and b. In this case, SNOBOL prints the name of the data type, COMPLEX.

The final two `output` statements use the `real` and `imag` functions SNOBOL created for us when `complex` was defined. We'll learn how to create user-defined functions below. Here, SNOBOL does us a favor by making functions automatically. The functions return the respective elements of the `complex` variables passed to them. We'll revisit the `complex` data type when we explore user-defined functions below.

Arrays and Tables

SNOBOL supports multidimensional arrays with flexible indexing. Array elements are not typed and any data can be stored in an array element, including another array. This means SNOBOL supports nested arrays—arrays within arrays. Few languages have such flexibility with arrays.

SNOBOL also supports associative arrays—or, to use modern terminology, dictionaries—though in SNOBOL they are called *tables*, a collection of key-value pairs. Like arrays, tables are not restricted in terms of the data they contain. However, unlike arrays, tables are not fixed in size and may grow as needed to accommodate more entries.

Arrays

SNOBOL arrays are created with the `array` function. The function's argument determines the number of dimensions, the range of the indices for each dimension, and a default value for each element. Let's examine different arrays to understand how they are defined and accessed. There are many small examples, so each will be presented as a code snippet and the resulting value of the element accessed. Most of the examples are in *array.sno*.

The following declarations create different versions of the array A:

```
A = array(10)
A = array('0:9')
A = array('0:7,20,-1:1')
A = array('128,128',0)
```

The first is a 1D array with 10 elements indexed from $[1, 10]$. Like FORTRAN, SNOBOL indexes arrays from 1 unless told otherwise. The second is also a 10-element vector with indices in $[0, 9]$. Notice that the array specification is a string. This is required to specify nonstandard index ranges. The third line defines a 3D array. The indices of the first dimension are in $[0, 7]$. The second dimension uses the defaults, $[1, 20]$. Lastly, the third dimension uses -1, 0, and 1 as indices. The final line defines a 2D array with indices in $[1, 128]$, specified as a string, with each element initialized to 0.

SNOBOL manages memory independently, meaning that this sequence of array declarations is allowed as a sequence of SNOBOL statements. Each new array declaration destroys the previous, automatically freeing its memory. If you try allocating a large array and get the `Insufficient storage to continue` error, the `-d` command line option tells SNOBOL to reserve more memory.

```
> snobol4 -d 10m big.sno
```

Here, the argument 10m allocates 10MB worth of *descriptors*, each of which uses 16 bytes. On my system, -d 300m took about 15 seconds to initiate an interactive session and used about 4.8GB of system memory. The price paid for SNOBOL's array flexibility is speed and memory use compared to standard fixed-data type arrays.

Let's see a SNOBOL array in action (Listing 5-7).

```
A = array('0:9')
A[0] = 'one'
A[1] = 3.141592
A[2] = 123456
A[3] = array(6)
A[3][1] = 'nested'
output = 'A[2]    = ' A[2]
output = 'A[1]    = ' A[1]
output = 'A[0]    = ' A[0]
output = 'A[3]    = ' convert(A[3],'string')
output = 'A[3][1] = ' A[3][1]
```

Listing 5-7: A 1D array

Listing 5-7 defines a 1D array of 10 elements with indices in [0, 9]. The next three lines assign the array's elements, first to a string, then a float, and lastly, an integer. The next line assigns A[3] to an array of six elements with indices in [1, 6]. This is a nested array because it is part of the larger 10-element array, A. To assign elements of the nested array requires first selecting the nested array with A[3] and then selecting the desired element of the nested array, here the first: A[3][1] = 'nested'.

The five output statements display the assigned values. There is something new here, the convert function, which changes a variable's type. The output statement is concatenating a string with the value of the array element. However, A[3] is not something automatically converted into a string. Therefore, convert is used to represent it as a string. The first argument to convert is the object to be converted and the second argument is a string naming the target type, in this case a string. We'll use convert again later to change between arrays and tables.

Now consider Listing 5-8.

```
B = array('128,128',0)
B[11,22] = 5555
B[12,45] = array('11,11')
B[12,45]<5,6> = 'how are you?'

data('complex(real,imag)')
B[12,45][1,2] = complex(3,0.141592)
output = real(B[12,45][1,2]) '+' imag(B[12,45][1,2]) 'i'
```

Listing 5-8: A 2D array

The array B is 2D with both indices in [1, 128] and all elements are initialized to 0. Assignments follow using both indices. Note that SNOBOL has no limit on the number of dimensions an array may use. Element B[12,45] has been assigned a nested 11×11 array. The assignment to B[12,45]<5,6> seems unusual, but it isn't. SNOBOL allows < and > in place of square brackets for indexing arrays. Consider them a relic of the 1960s.

The following two lines define the complex data type we saw above and then use it to store a complex number in B[12,45][1,2]. The output statement displays the complex number using the real and imag functions to extract the real and imaginary parts before piecing them together as 3+0.141592i, which is the usual way imaginary numbers are displayed.

NOTE   *Some languages, like Python, use j in place of i to indicate a complex number. Engineers do this because i usually refers to electric current in their world. Mathematicians prefer i because electric current doesn't exist in their world.*

Now consider Listing 5-9 with two blocks of code.

```
A = array('0:5')
A[0] = 'xyzzy'
D = A
D[0] = 12345
output = 'A[0] is now ' A[0]

A[0] = 'xyzzy'
E = copy(A)
E[0] = 'plugh'
output = 'E[0] is ' E[0]
output = 'A[0] is still ' A[0]
```

Listing 5-9: Array references and copying

The first block defines A and sets A[0] to the string 'xyzzy'. Next, it creates D by assigning A, after which it immediately sets D[0] to 12345. The question is: what does the following output statement display? The answer is:

```
A[0] is now 12345
```

This is because simple assignment of an array does not copy it; it only makes D refer to the same object as A. This behavior is typical of most programming languages. As arrays might occupy a significant portion of memory, it is best to copy them only when essential.

Now consider the second code block of Listing 5-9. It restores the original value of A[0] and creates E using the copy function before assigning E[0] the string 'plugh'. Then come two output statements. We might guess the output at this point.

```
E[0] is plugh
A[0] is still xyzzy
```

The copy function duplicated A, so updating E[0] did not alter the original array. However, be aware that copy makes only *shallow* copies. In a shallow copy, nested arrays are not copied, only referenced.

Tables

SNOBOL tables are like Python dictionaries. They associate a key with a value, which can also be any type of data. A few examples should suffice to illustrate their use (see Listing 5-10).

```
data('complex(real,imag)')
t = table()
t[1] = 'one'
t[2.0] = 'two'
t[complex(2,3)] = 'three'
c = complex(2,3)
t[c] = 'four'
output = t[1]
output = t[2.0]
output = t[complex(2,3)]
output = t[c]
```

Listing 5-10: Using a table

Listing 5-10 shows almost all that is needed to understand a table. It first defines the now familiar complex data type, followed by a table, t. Four assignments to t follow, each with a different data type as the key. The four output statements produce

```
one
two

four
```

This might not match your expectations, as there is no three in the output. To recover the value for a key, the key used must match exactly. The key for three was complex(2,3). That's a perfectly valid key, but passing another instance of complex(2,3) will not find its value because the two do not evaluate to the same object in memory. Using c as a key does allow four to be recovered because c references the same data structure in memory. The last lesson from Listing 5-10 is that referencing a key that doesn't exist returns null but is not an error. To check whether a key is in the table, use the ne predicate to check the value returned against null.

The table declaration accepts up to two arguments. The first is the table's initial size, the number of entries for which memory has already been allocated. Tables are dynamic, meaning they grow as needed. The second argument is the number of entries to grow by whenever the table must grow. If no arguments are given, table() is equivalent to table(10,10). If you know the table will be large but mostly fixed when established, use a large first argument and a smaller second argument. Conversely, if you don't know how large the table will be but expect that many entries will be added, use a small initial size and a larger second argument.

Listing 5-11 defines a table with initial room for 100 entries, z.

```
    z = table(100,25)
    z['one'] = 1
    z['two'] = 2
    z['three'] = 3
    z[3.14159265] = 'pi'
❶   a = array(10)
❷   a[7] = z
❸   z[a] = a
    output = z['two']
    output = z[a]
    output = z[3.14159265]
❹   output = z[a][7][a][7][a][7][3.14159265]
```

Listing 5-11: Another table example

The first four assignments to z are straightforward, though recalling the value of π to eight decimals so it can be used as a key to remember the string 'pi' is admittedly rather silly. The example gets worse. We define an array, a ❶, and assign the table, z, to its seventh element ❷. Then, in the next line, we put a in the table ❸. We've have an odd situation: the table we just placed a into is referenced by a itself.

The output statements generate

```
2
ARRAY('10')
pi
pi
```

We get the integer 2, the array a, the name pi from its floating-point value to eight decimals, and then the final output, also pi. The final output was generated by ❹. Because a is in z, and z is in a, we can use an arbitrary number of pairs of references, first [a] to return the array followed by [7] to get z from the array, to finally arrive again at z and recover pi. Of course, this is a ludicrous thing to do, but SNOBOL doesn't judge.

How can we know what keys a SNOBOL table has? In Python, we can use the keys method. In SNOBOL, we convert the table to an array to get at the keys. Likewise, we can convert a properly structured array into a table. Listing 5-12 illustrates an example of each.

```
❶   t = table()
    t['one'] = 1; t['two'] = 2; t['three'] = 3.3
❷   x = convert(t, 'array')
❸   i = 1
loop output = 'key: ' x[i,1] ', value: ' x[i,2]   :f(cont)
    i = i + 1      :(loop)
```

```
❹ cont a = array('3,2')
      a[1,1] = 'one'; a[1,2] = 1
      a[2,1] = 'two'; a[2,2] = 2
      a[3,1] = 'three'; a[3,2] = 3
❺ y = convert(a, 'table')
   output = y['one']
   output = y['two']
   output = y['three']
```

Listing 5-12: Converting tables to arrays and arrays to tables

We first create a table ❶ and add three entries. Next, we call convert to change the table into an array, x. The array has $n \times 2$ dimensions if there are n entries in the table. The first column is the key and the second column is the value. The keys and values are printed using a simple loop ❸. Notice that the loop ends when accessing the array fails because the index, i, is too large. In SNOBOL, you code for failure.

To go the other way and convert an array into a table, consider ❹. A 2D array is created with the first column as the key and the second column as the value. Another call to convert makes the properly structured array a table ❺.

SNOBOL arrays and tables are flexible and more advanced than many other languages of the time.

And now for something completely different.

A Blizzard of Patterns

In this section, we'll introduce patterns, though a thorough understanding of patterns is beyond what we can hope to cover in a single chapter. There are two types of pattern statements in SNOBOL. The first applies a pattern to a string. The second applies a pattern to a string and updates the portion of the string that matched the pattern. We'll learn about patterns in B. F. Skinner fashion, a little bit at a time, with examples.

A First Example

Consider Listing 5-13, which presents a simple program accepting lines of text from the user until the string 'hello' appears in one of the lines.

```
loop  input 'hello'         :f(loop)
      output = "Greetings!"
end
```

Listing 5-13: A simple pattern example

The first line of the program calls input to return a string. The second string, which at first might appear to be concatenated because of the space, is a pattern, with the pattern matching a constant string. If the text returned by input has 'hello' anywhere within it, the pattern match succeeds. If not, it fails, and the goto for failure asks the user for another string.

Listing 5-13 is an example of the first type of pattern matching statement: a *text pattern*. In a pattern, success or failure of the match decides what happens next; however, as we'll see, a pattern can generate new variables that hold pieces of the matched pattern. This means that many pattern matching statements are assigning data even if they don't have explicit gotos.

The pattern matches only an explicit string of characters. If we want to check for other options, we use alternation, | (with spaces!). Therefore, to accept either 'hello' or 'aloha', use 'hello' | 'aloha' as the pattern.

As you might expect, SNOBOL has many bits and pieces for matching various patterns. The ones we'll examine are len, span, pos, any, and break.

Matching and Updating Strings

The second pattern statement matches a pattern and updates the text matched with new text. See Listing 5-14.

```
color = 'brown'
animal = 'cow'
text = 'how now brown cow?'
text color = 'blue'
text animal = 'giraffe'
output = text
end
```

Listing 5-14: Matching and updating a string

The output of this program is how now blue giraffe?, where color matched to change brown to blue, and animal matched to change cow to giraffe. If the match fails, the string is not updated. Note that a match succeeds when the first success happens. Therefore,

```
text = 'The brown bear approached the brown car'
text 'brown' = 'black'
output = text
```

produces The black bear approached the brown car. To update all matches, use a loop.

```
     text = 'The brown bear approached the brown car'
loop text 'brown' = 'black'              :s(loop)
     output = text
```

This example loops for as long as the pattern 'brown' is found, replacing it with 'black' each time. The output is now The black bear approached the black car.

Extracting Information from a String

What if we want to extract the matched text? When used in a pattern, the name operator (.) extracts the matched text to a variable. See Listing 5-15.

❶ dpat = span(',: ')
❷ lpat = (break(',:') . last) dpat

```
❸ fpat = (break(',:') . first) dpat
❹ apat = (rem . address)
❺ text = 'Caesar,   Julius:  1313 Mockingbird Ln   '
❻ text lpat fpat apat
❼ output = first ' ' last ', address: ' trim(address)
   end
```

Listing 5-15: Capturing the matched text

Several new things are happening in Listing 5-15, so let's go through it carefully. Structurally, the program consists of four pattern definitions, which are the variables ending in pat. This is followed by a piece of example text with a first name, last name, and address. Our goal is to break this text apart into its individual fields. The pattern matching line comes next, followed by an output statement to print the data in a new format.

Let's explain what's happening, line by line. First, we define dpat ❶. This is a pattern to match one or more instances of a comma, colon, or space. That's what span does; it matches the longest possible sequence consisting of nothing but the characters in its argument.

Next comes lpat ❷. This pattern matches characters up to, but not including, the first occurrence of a comma or colon. That's what break does. If the string is abcde:f, then break(',:') matches the string abcde, but not the colon.

The break is next to the name operator, followed by last, with the entire expression surrounded by parentheses. The expression matches characters up to, but not including, the first comma or colon, and stores them in the variable last. Looking at line ❺ makes it clear that lpat matches the last name.

However, ❷ has a dpat hanging at the end. It's there to match the comma or colon that ended the break. As SNOBOL attempts to match a pattern, internally, it's moving a *cursor* over the string, character by character, forward and sometimes backward to try other options. When the break of lpat matches, the cursor is looking at the comma or colon that ended the break. So we use dpat to skip it.

The definition of fpat ❸ is nearly identical to ❷; however, the matched text is stored in first. That is, fpat matches the first name. As before, a dpat at the end of the pattern consumes the comma or colon that ended the break.

The internal cursor has now matched the last name and first name. The remaining pattern, apat, uses the special pattern, rem, to match the remainder of the line and assign it to address ❹.

To test the patterns, we define text to be a string with a last name, first name, and address using a comma and a colon as delimiters along with some extra spaces ❺.

Lastly, we apply the patterns to text ❻. Notice that, at first glance, ❻ is just a sequence of four variables in a row. However, SNOBOL knows to parse this as a string followed by a pattern. The string is text; therefore, the remaining variables form the pattern. The overall pattern is built by concatenating lpat, fpat, and apat. We might, for clarity, put parentheses around the three pattern variables. If we wanted to concatenate two or more text strings and then apply a pattern, the parentheses would be placed around those variables.

When ❻ executes, the last name, first name, and address are extracted. To prove this, ❼ dumps the same information rearranged to be first name, then last name, followed by the address. Notice that address is passed to trim, the SNOBOL function to remove trailing spaces from a string. The output of Listing 5-15 is 'Julius Caesar, address: 1313 Mockingbird Ln'.

More Elaborate Pattern Matching

Let's look at three more quick pattern matching examples. The first two manipulate a file of dates. The last one updates Lewis Carroll's *Alice's Adventures in Wonderland* to give "Bob" a chance to put himself in the story.

Listing 5-16 maps numeric dates in North American format (month, day, year) to European-style dates (day, month, year).

```
*   Map North American dates to European dates
    ❶ pat = len(2) . month ('/' | '-') len(2) . day ('/' | '-') len(4) . year
loop  text = input                    :f(end)
    ❷ text pat = day '/' month '/' year  :f(bad)
      output = text                   :(loop)
bad   output = "unknown format"       :(loop)
end
```

Listing 5-16: Manipulating dates with patterns, take one

The pattern, pat, uses len to match the specified number of characters, regardless of what they are. The first two characters are assigned to month, followed by a slash or dash; then the next two characters are put in day, followed by another slash or dash and a four-character year.

Listing 5-15 is in the file *dates.sno*. There is another file in the same directory called *dates.txt* that contains a set of numeric dates. For example, the first few lines of the file are

```
10-14-1066
10/12/1492
04/15/1912
07-24-1969
04/04/1968
11-23-1963
```

with some dates using slashes and some using dashes. A few even use a mix. Listing 5-15 uses a loop to read the file, line by line. Each line is read with input using command line redirection and placed into text. If there is nothing left to read, the input command fails and SNOBOL jumps to the end.

If the read succeeds, the pattern is applied to text, but this time in the form string pattern = update, where the text matched by pattern is replaced by the text in update. Here, the replacement text is constructed from the day, month, and year matched by pat, using slashes between elements ❷.

Notice that ❷ has a goto for failure. If the pattern doesn't match, the input string is not a valid date format, so the program jumps to bad to output unknown format before jumping back to the loop to process the next input. If the pattern match doesn't fail, text has been updated so it's output before jumping to loop to read the next date.

Run *dates.sno* with

```
> snobol4 dates.sno <dates.txt
```

to produce

```
14/10/1066
12/10/1492
15/04/1912
24/07/1969
04/04/1968
23/11/1963
...
11/04/2020
03/01/1892
13/12/1989
09/04/1865
16/11/1093
unknown format
```

The final unknown format line corresponds to an input of AVCDe-224*, which is clearly not a valid date.

The next example uses dates.txt, but produces full dates instead of numeric dates. See Listing 5-17.

```
*   Map numeric dates to full dates
        pat = len(2) . month ('/' | '-') len(2) . day ('/' | '-') len(4) . year
        m = array(12)
        m<1> = "January";  m<2> = "February";  m<3> = "March";
        m<4> = "April";    m<5> = "May";       m<6> = "June";
        m<7> = "July";     m<8> = "August";    m<9> = "September";
        m<10> = "October"; m<11> = "November"; m<12> = "December"

loop    text = input                                :f(end)
        text pat                                    :f(bad)
        output = m<month> ' ' (1 * day) ', ' (1 * year)   :(loop)
bad     output = "unknown format"                   :(loop)
end
```

Listing 5-17: Manipulating dates with patterns, take two

The pattern, pat, is the same as in Listing 5-16. Additionally, we define m, an array holding the names of the months.

The code runs in the same way as Listing 5-16 but outputs a full date using the number of the month as the index into the array of names. Also, notice that both day and year are multiplied by 1. The text matched is a string. To output the day and year without leading 0s, as there are a few three-digit years in dates.txt, we convert the strings to integers. Listing 5-17 is in the file *dates2.sno*. Run it to produce this output:

```
October 14, 1066
October 12, 1492
April 15, 1912
July 24, 1969
April 4, 1968
November 23, 1963
...
April 11, 2020
January 3, 1892
December 13, 1989
April 9, 1865
November 16, 1093
unknown format
```

For our final pattern example, with apologies to Lewis Carroll, we'll update the first part of *Alice's Adventures in Wonderland* to be *Bob's Adventures in Wonderland*. The text we'll work with is in the file *alice.txt*, and consists of the beginning part of Chapter 1.

The code we need is in *alice.sno* and Listing 5-18.

```
*     Convert from Alice to Bob
         p = null | any(' .,?!)')
         s = pos(0) | ' ' | '('
loop     text = input                              :f(end)
s0       text s . a 'Alice' p . c    = a 'Bob' c    :s(s0)
s1       text s . a 'her' p . c      = a 'his' c    :s(s1)
s2       text s . a 'Her' p . c      = a 'His' c    :s(s2)
s3       text s . a 'herself' p . c  = a 'himself' c  :s(s3)
s4       text s . a 'Herself' p . c  = a 'Himself' c  :s(s4)
s5       text s . a 'she' p . c      = a 'he' c     :s(s5)
s6       text s . a 'She' p . c      = a 'He' c     :s(s6)
         output = text                             :(loop)
end
```

Listing 5-18: Making Bob's Adventures in Wonderland

Listing 5-18 begins by defining two patterns, p and s. The first uses alternation to match nothing (null) or any single character that is a space, period, comma, question mark, exclamation point, or right parenthesis. The second pattern uses pos to match cursor position zero, that is, the beginning of a line, a space, or a left parenthesis.

The remainder of the program is a loop from input to output via loop. Between the input and the output there are seven lines, s0 through s6. Each of these lines is a loop (notice the success gotos) and has a similar format.

```
text s . a 'string1' p . c = a 'string2' c
```

The first part is the text read from the input file, text. The rest of the line up to the equals sign is a pattern. The pattern looks for a match to a word, such as the name 'Alice', storing the character before the word in a and the character after in c.

The matched text, if any, is replaced by the same leading and trailing character with the matched word updated. Thus, "Alice" is replaced with "Bob," "her" is replaced with "his," and so on. Recall that a match is successful after the first one is found, so if there are multiple occurrences of "Alice" in the line, only the first will be replaced with "Bob." So we must loop until the match fails to replace all occurrences.

After all seven patterns are tested and matched as much as possible, the updated text is output and the loop begins again until there is no input left.

The first paragraph of *alice.txt* is

```
Alice was beginning to get very tired of sitting by her sister on the
bank, and of having nothing to do: once or twice she had peeped into
the book her sister was reading, but it had no pictures or
conversations in it, "and what is the use of a book," thought Alice
"without pictures or conversations?"
```

The same paragraph after the "Bob" conversion is

```
Bob was beginning to get very tired of sitting by his sister on the
bank, and of having nothing to do: once or twice he had peeped into
the book his sister was reading, but it had no pictures or
conversations in it, "and what is the use of a book," thought Bob
"without pictures or conversations?"
```

The conversion isn't foolproof, but that isn't SNOBOL's fault. There are cases in English where the word "her" should be changed to "his" and cases where it should become "him." The code of Listing 5-18 knows nothing of the context, so it always uses "his."

There is much more to discover concerning SNOBOL patterns. An excellent place to learn more is Chapter 2 of Griswold, Poage, and Polonsky's *The SNOBOL4 Programming Language* (Prentice Hall, 1971). Versions of the second edition are floating around the internet if you care to take a look.

Let's move on to SNOBOL's user-defined functions, perhaps the least elegant part of the language (aside from relying solely on goto for flow control).

Functions

SNOBOL would be a weak language indeed if it had no facility for users to define functions. Thankfully, it does, though the syntax is a bit strange. In this section, we'll learn how to define and use functions.

We'll jump right in with Listing 5-19. This program, in the file *poly.sno*, defines a function to implement arbitrary polynomials of the form

$$y = ax^2 + bx + c$$

which we use to output (x, y) pairs for plotting the function.

```
* Define a function
      ❶ define('poly(a,b,c,x)')                :(epoly)
poly      poly = a * x ** 2 + b * x + c      :(return)
epoly

* Main body of the code
          x = -10
loop      output = x ' ' poly(1,2,2,x)
          x = x + 1
          ge(x,8)                              :f(loop)
end
```

Listing 5-19: A user-defined function

SNOBOL functions begin with a define statement ❶. There are a couple of important things to notice about ❶. First, the function declaration is a string. It begins with the name of the function (poly), followed by an opening parenthesis, the list of arguments, and a closing parenthesis. If the function uses local variables, they are listed next, separated by commas, as part of the string. Note that the string portion of the define statement *must not* include spaces. No spaces between the arguments, no spaces in the list of local variables, no spaces anywhere.

The next thing to notice is that the define statement ends with a goto (epoly). This label must jump to just beyond the end of the function's body, that is, it must not include any code that is part of the function. The function's body is the code between the define statement and the ending label, which here is epoly.

The function body begins with a label matching the function's name, which is poly in this case. The body of the function is free to use the arguments, any local variables, and any global variables. The value returned by the function is assigned to a variable of the same name, as is sometimes done in other programming languages. In Listing 5-19, the variable poly is assigned the value of the quadratic.

To exit the function, SNOBOL defines two special goto labels: return and freturn. Use the former if the function was successful and the latter if not. The function poly always succeeds, so we use return to exit.

SNOBOL allows recursion, as shown in Listing 5-20, which implements the factorial function. The factorial of an integer, n, is $n! = n(n-1)(n-2)\ldots 1$. For example, $5! = 5 \times 4 \times 3 \times 2 \times 1 = 120$.

Another way to think about the factorial of n is that it's n times the factorial of $n-1$, which is itself $n-1$ times the factorial of $n-2$, and so on down to 1. That's the recursive version. In Python, we might write this process as

```python
def fact(n):
    if (n < 1):
        return 0
    else:
        return n * fact(n-1)
```

where fact calls itself to solve the simpler problem. All recursive functions need a base case, something that stops the recursion. In this case, it's checking if n is less than 1. This catches the edge case of $0! = 1$.

Translating the recursive formula into SNOBOL leads to Listing 5-20.

```
* Recursive factorial function
        define('fact(n)')        :(efact)
fact    fact = eq(n,0) 1         :s(return)
        fact = n * fact(n - 1)   :(return)
efact

        output = "Enter a number:"
        n = input
        output = convert(n,'integer') "! = " fact(n)
end
```

Listing 5-20: A recursive factorial function

The definition accepts n. The first line of the body implements the base case. If $n > 0$, then eq(n,0) fails, so fact is not assigned and the next line is executed. If $n = 0$, eq(n,0) succeeds, so we return from the function via s(return).

The second line of fact implements the recursion. It assigns fact to n times whatever fact(n - 1) returns and then it returns via (return).

The main code asks the user for a number and returns the factorial. Run it and enter integers in $[0, 20]$. Beyond 20, integers overflow; however, if you enter a floating-point number, you can estimate larger factorials. Also, notice the use of convert to force n to be an integer for display purposes.

Let's write a function to swap the value of two variables. This should be easy. Our first attempt is

```
        define('swap(x,y)t')     :(eswap)
swap    t = x
        x = y
        y = t                    :(return)
```

```
eswap
        a = 3
        b = 5

        output = "a = " a ", b = " b
        swap(a,b)
        output = "a = " a ", b = " b
end
```

which defines swap. The value of x is kept in t, then y is assigned to x and t is assigned to y, followed by a return. The main body of the program sets $a = 3$ and $b = 5$, outputs their values, calls swap, and then outputs them again. Running the code produces

```
a = 3, b = 5
a = 3, b = 5
```

This is clearly incorrect. The values haven't changed. Why? The algorithm in swap is correct, so why didn't the values change?

SNOBOL passes simple variables by *value*, meaning the value of a is assigned to x. So when x is updated in the body of swap, a is not affected. To update the variables, we need to pass the data by *reference* so x is really a synonym for a. After that, updates to x will affect a. Note that SNOBOL passes arrays and tables by reference.

The code above is wrong. I don't want you to use it. However, the code in Listing 5-21 does work correctly.

```
* Function to swap two variables
        define('swap(x,y)t')          :(eswap)
swap    t = $x
        $x = $y
        $y = t                        :(return)
eswap

        a = 3
        b = 5
        output = "a = " a ", b = " b
  ❶ swap(a,b)
        output = "a = " a ", b = " b
  ❷ swap(.a,.b)
        output = "a = " a ", b = " b
  ❸ swap('a','b')
        output = "a = " a ", b = " b
end
```

Listing 5-21: Passing variables by reference

Let's focus on swap. It looks much like the wrong version, but it uses the indirection operator ($) before each argument, $x. Recall that indirection means "not this variable, but the variable named by this variable." Think of indirection as dereferencing a pointer in other languages. The swap function is now working directly with names passed to it rather than copies of the variables.

The main body of Listing 5-21 will clarify. The first call to swap passes a and b ❶. The second call uses the name operator to pass the names of a and b ❷. The last call passes the literal strings 'a' and 'b'.

Running Listing 5-21 produces

```
a = 3, b = 5
a = 3, b = 5
a = 5, b = 3
a = 3, b = 5
```

The first output line shows us the original values of a and b. The second output line shows the effect of ❶ in Listing 5-21. There is no effect. The variables are unchanged because we passed their values rather than their names, so the indirection operator failed.

The third output line shows the effect of ❷. Now swap is working. The name operator passed the strings 'a' and 'b', which the indirection operator can interpret to mean that a and b are swapped.

The final output line shows the effect of ❸. Here we pass the literal strings naming a and b. This is really what the name operator is doing, so swap works and swaps a and b again to restore them to their original values.

To sum up, SNOBOL passes simple variables by value, requiring the use of indirection to update them. However, arrays and tables are always passed by reference.

We know how to set up SNOBOL programs and how to create custom functions and data types. Now, let's take a quick look at disk files.

Input and Output

We've seen input and output many times already. In this section, we'll see how they work with disk files.

Listing 5-22 presents code to make an uppercase copy of a text file.

```
* Uppercase a file
        input('read', 10, 132, host(2,2))
        output('write', 11, 'W', host(2,3))
❶ loop   text = read                          :f(close)
        text = replace(text, &lcase, &ucase)
      ❷ write = text                          :(loop)
close   endfile(10)
        endfile(11)
end
```

Listing 5-22: Uppercasing a disk file

There's a lot here, so let's walk through the code line by line. First, open the source text file by supplying arguments to input. The first argument is not the name of the file. Instead, it's the name of a variable SNOBOL associates with the file. It's what we use to read data from the file, so let's call it read. The next argument is a unit number. This is a throwback to old-style programming where unit numbers were associated with operating system devices. The unit number needs to be unique for each open file. Use numbers of at least 10 or higher. Think of the unit number as a file reference.

After the unit number comes the maximum line length. Input lines longer than this are truncated. Remember, this is a text file, and SNOBOL works with lines of text. The final argument is the name of the disk file. We're using host(2,2), which is specific to our version of SNOBOL. This is a link to the actual operating system. The first argument, 2, refers to command line arguments. The second number refers to items on the command line. The second item is the first argument after the script name. Therefore, host(2,2) gives us the name of the first file.

To open the output file, we use output. As with input, the first argument is the name of a variable to which we will assign the output. We use unit 11 for output. The third argument is 'W' to write a text file. Use 'A' to append a file. The last argument is the name of the output file, here host(2,3), which uses the second argument passed to the SNOBOL program.

The files are now open, so let's read lines from the input, uppercase them, and write them to the output. At ❶ we use read, tied to the input file, to get a line in text. If the read fails, the input file is exhausted, so we jump to close. Otherwise, proceed to apply the intrinsic replace to the text to uppercase the line; replace updates all occurrences of characters in the second argument by the corresponding character in the third argument. To save typing, we use the predefined strings of lowercase and uppercase letters. SNOBOL variables beginning with & are system-supplied variables. The output of this line uppercases text.

To dump the text to the output file, assign it to write, which is the variable associated with the output file ❷. After dumping the newly uppercased text, we jump back to loop to continue.

Lastly, we need to close the input and output files before using endfile to exit.

Listing 5-22 is in the file *uppercase.sno*. Let's run it on the *Alice's Adventures in Wonderland* text to uppercase it.

```
> snobol4 uppercase.sno alice.txt uppercase.txt
```

The file *uppercase.txt* now contains ALICE in all caps.

The example above worked with a text file. SNOBOL can also work with binary data. Let's write a simple file copy program to read and write binary data. Listing 5-23 shows *copy.sno*.

```
*    Copy a file using the command line
        src = host(2,2)
        dst = host(2,3)
        input('read', 10, 'B,4096', src)
        output('write', 11, 'B', dst)
```

```
❶ loop    write = read         :f(close)s(loop)
  close    endfile(10)
           endfile(11)

end
```

Listing 5-23: Copying a file

Listing 5-23 is quite similar to Listing 5-22, but the input and output files are opened in binary mode. For `input`, where before we supplied the maximum line length, we now have `'B,4096'`. This specifies binary mode, meaning no line endings are interpreted, and a buffer of 4096 bytes. This means the source file will be read in 4096-byte chunks, or fewer if there aren't at least 4096 bytes left to read. For output, use `'B'` to indicate binary mode.

The loop, in this case, is a one-liner ❶. Read a 4096-byte chunk of the input and immediately assign it to `write` to write it to the output file. When `read` fails, jump to close the files. Otherwise, jump back to this same line of code to continue the loop.

To test *copy.sno*, try the following:

```
> snobol4 copy.sno src.png dst.png
```

This should copy the given *src.png* image to *dst.png*. The image is of a young raccoon and is taken from the open source SciPy toolkit.

Machine Learning with SNOBOL

Let's work through a little SNOBOL project to implement a simple machine learning classifier. Modern artificial intelligence is far removed from what computer scientists had in mind back when SNOBOL was new. Machine learning existed then, but the term "artificial intelligence" was not used to describe it for the most part.

Artificial intelligence now most often refers to that part of machine learning known as deep learning, that is, advanced neural networks, often with millions to billions of connections between the nodes (neurons). SNOBOL is not a good choice for such models. However, classical machine learning includes basic algorithms that are sometimes quite straightforward to implement and that sometimes perform quite well despite their simplicity.

Therefore, the goal of this section is to build a complete SNOBOL application to classify datasets using a simple machine learning technique—a *nearest neighbor* classifier.

Machine Learning 101

Machine learning maps feature vectors to class labels. A *feature vector* is a collection of numeric values called *features*; that's our input. We take this input and try to assign it a *class label*, that is, a category or class. For example, one of the datasets we'll work with relates to iris flowers. This dataset is perhaps the oldest in machine learning and one of the easiest to work with. It consists of 150 measurements of three different species of iris flowers.

There are four measurements per flower: two measuring the petal length and width and two measuring the sepal length in width. These four measurements are the features and the three different species are the classes.

Machine learning models must be trained so they can place an unknown sample into the correct class. *Training* involves learning the parameters of the model using a training set, a collection of feature vectors (x) and corresponding class labels (y). This is what the iris dataset gives us. The training set has 50 examples of each class, that is, each species of flower. We'll use 100 of these 150 examples to train the classifier and the remaining 50 to test the model to see how well it learned to distinguish between iris species.

We hope that when given a set of features for a new flower the trained model will be able to place the new flower into the correct class (in other words, correctly identify the species). The nearest neighbor classifier treats the feature vector as a point in a multidimensional space, in this case a 4D space for the iris dataset, as there are four features per sample. The idea is to find the training set sample whose feature vector is the closest to the feature vector of the unknown input and then assign the unknown input to the training sample class. In this case, closest means the training sample with the smallest *distance* to the unknown input.

There are many concept words in the paragraphs above, so let's make sure we know what they mean. Once we do, the operation of the classifier will become apparent or even obvious. Table 5-1 presents a brief machine learning glossary.

Table 5-1: A Brief Machine Learning Glossary

Term	Meaning
Feature	A measurement or characteristic of the data
Feature vector	A collection of features describing an instance
Class	The label, or group, the instance belongs to
Model	A means for mapping feature vectors to class labels
Training	Using known feature vectors to teach the model
Distance	The straight-line distance between two points

All machine learning models implement two phases: training and inference. During training, the training set, that is, the collection of feature vectors and their known class labels, is used to adjust the model's parameters to the task at hand. Once trained, the model can be used for inference to assign class labels to new, unknown feature vectors. For the nearest neighbor classifier, training is so trivial as to be nonexistent: we use the training set as it is, as there are no parameters to learn.

To classify feature vectors, we scan through the training set to calculate the distance between the unknown feature vector and each of the training samples to find the closest training sample. We use that training sample's class label as the class label for the unknown feature vector.

For example, if we have a new set of measurements for an iris flower but don't know its species, the nearest neighbor classifier searches the list of training set feature vectors for the sample closest to the unknown feature vector. It then declares the unknown input to be of the same class.

The word *distance* has been mentioned a few times now. Let's put a formula to the word, so we have a way to measure the distance between two feature vectors.

There are different types of distances, but the one we'll use here is the *Euclidean distance*, which is a generalization of the Pythagorean theorem. For example, in 4D, the distance between two points, (x_0, y_0, a_0, b_0) and (x_1, y_1, a_1, b_1), is

$$d = \sqrt{(x_0 - x_1)^2 + (y_0 - y_1)^2 + (a_0 - a_1)^2 + (b_0 - b_1)^2}$$

If we have 3D feature vectors, the distance between two points, (x_0, y_0, z_0) and (x_1, y_1, z_1), is

$$d = \sqrt{(x_0 - x_1)^2 + (y_0 - y_1)^2 + (z_0 - z_1)^2}$$

For *n*-dimensional feature vectors, the distance is

$$d = \sqrt{\sum_{i=0}^{n}(x_i - y_i)^2}$$

for two feature vectors, x and y. In the equation above, i is an index into the components of the vector. When we implement the Euclidean distance in code, i will be an index into an array.

The training set and the Euclidean distance are all we need to implement the nearest neighbor classifier, but how will we know if it's working? For that, we need test data. This is another dataset like the training set, but one that wasn't used to train the model.

We know the feature vectors and the correct class label for the test set. We'll run each test set feature vector through the model, comparing the classifier's predicted label with the correct class label. There are many ways to characterize the performance of a machine learning model, but in this case, all we need to measure is the model's accuracy.

$$\text{accuracy} = \frac{\text{number correctly assigned}}{\text{number of test samples}}$$

A classifier that randomly guesses class labels will only be correct, on average, one time in c, where c is the number of classes in the dataset. There are three classes for the iris flowers, so we'd expect, if guessing, to be correct one time out of three, or about 33 percent of the time, meaning the accuracy is 0.3333. A perfect classifier makes no mistakes and has an accuracy of 1.0 or 100 percent.

We now have enough background to get started. We have a model and we know how to train it and test it. Let's write some code.

Implementing the Classifier

Let's implement the classifier. Here's our plan of attack:

1. Load the training and test datasets into SNOBOL arrays.
2. For each test sample, assign the class label of the closest training set sample.
3. Compare the assigned labels to the known test labels.
4. Report the classifier's accuracy.

The code that follows is in the file *classify.sno*.

Loading the Data

This book's GitHub site contains several datasets. Let's walk through an example using the iris dataset. We'll classify the others later.

The iris dataset is in four text files in the *datasets* directory:

```
iris_train_data.txt
iris_train_labels.txt
iris_test_data.txt
iris_test_labels.txt
```

The first two contain training data and the associated class labels. The second two hold test data.

For example, the training datafile begins with

```
6.70000 3.00000 5.00000 1.70000
5.10000 3.50000 1.40000 0.30000
4.80000 3.40000 1.60000 0.20000
6.10000 2.80000 4.70000 1.20000
6.00000 3.40000 4.50000 1.60000
```

with the associated class labels

```
1
0
0
1
1
```

meaning the first feature vector is a class 1 instance, whereas the second feature vector is an instance of class 0, and so on. The test dataset files are structured similarly.

We need SNOBOL code to load these text files. We'll develop generic code, a SNOBOL function to load any datafile arranged such that each row represents a sample and each column represents a feature. Most machine learning datasets are structured this way.

The iris training data results in a 2D array with 100 rows and four columns because there are four features per sample and 100 samples in the training set. The training labels will become a 2D array as well, with 100 rows and one column. This simplifies the implementation.

Listing 5-24 shows a function to load datafiles. It's the most complex piece of code we need to develop, so it's best to start with the worst, knowing that things will get easier later.

```
        ❶ define('loadfile(name)pat,r,text,c,v')    :(eloadfile)
loadfile  input('reader', 10, , name)
        ❷ pat = break(' ') . v span(' ')
          r = 0
load_102  text = reader ' '                          :f(load_100)
          c = 0
load_103  text pat =                                 :f(load_101)
          c = c + 1                                  :(load_103)
load_101  r = r + 1                                  :(load_102)
load_100  endfile(10)
        ❸ loadfile = array(r ',' c)
          input('reader', 10, , name)
          r = 1
load_107  text = reader ' '                          :f(load_104)
          c = 1
load_106  text pat =                                 :f(load_105)
        ❹ loadfile[r,c] = 1.0 * v
          c = c + 1                                  :(load_106)
load_105  r = r + 1                                  :(load_107)
load_104  endfile(10)                                :(return)
eloadfile
```

Listing 5-24: Loading a datafile

The function accepts the name of the text file to load ❶. Notice the list of local variables. This prevents hard-to-detect errors whereby the function might alter a global variable. The function itself consists of two loops. The first loop, from label loadfile through label load_100, reads a line of text from the input file and parses it to count the number of features per sample. When the program reaches label load_100, the number of rows in the file is in r and the number of columns is in c.

To extract a number from the current line, we do two things. First, we add a blank space to the input line (see label load_102). Next, we perform a pattern match and update (see label load_103). The pattern ❷ uses break to match all text up to the first blank, storing it in v, and then matches any number of blanks with span. The net effect of pat is to grab the text representing a feature value and end with the cursor at the beginning of the next feature. Label load_103 assigns nothing to the matched text, thereby removing it from text. This process repeats, with c incremented until the line is empty and the match fails to cause a jump to label load_101 to increment r and advance to the next line of the input file. When the input file is exhausted, control moves to label load_100 to close the file.

The purpose of the first loop is to learn the file's dimensionality; it's in r and c. The return value of the function is defined as an array of the appropriate size ❸.

The input file is opened a second time, and the same read process happens again. This time, each matched feature value in v is placed into the array as a floating-point number ❹. When the input file is again empty, the function returns.

Calculating the Distance

Classifying an unknown sample requires computing the distance between pairs of feature vectors. The code to do this is in dist. See Listing 5-25.

```
          define('dist(x,y,i,j)sum,k')        :(edist)
dist      k = 1
dist_100  sum = sum + (x[i,k] - y[j,k]) ** 2  :f(dist_101)
          k = k + 1                           :(dist_100)
dist_101  dist = sqrt(sum)                    :(return)
edist
```

Listing 5-25: Calculating the Euclidean distance

The arguments to dist are the two datasets, x and y, which are 2D, and the rows to work with, i and j. The distance is the sum of the differences of each feature for the given rows. These are the columns of the arrays that we index with k.

The label dist_100 does all the work. It adds the square of the difference between the kth columns of x and y for the given rows to the existing sum. The loop fails when k exceeds the array's bounds. The return value is the square root of this sum (the label dist_101).

Some readers might be a bit confused by Listing 5-25, as sum is updated without being initialized. There is no error. SNOBOL treats undefined variables as null and adding a number to null returns the number, so there is no need to initialize sum explicitly.

Finding the Nearest Training Sample

We need to find the training sample that is closest to a given test sample. For that, we use the function nearest. See Listing 5-26.

```
          define('samples(a)pat')                   :(esamples)
samples   pat = break(',') . samples
          prototype(a) pat                          :(return)
esamples
```

```
          define('nearest(xtrn,ytrn,xtst,ytst,idx)s,i,mc,md,d')  :(enearest)
```

```
nearest    i = 1
           s = samples(xtrn)
           nearest = ytrn[i,1]
           md = dist(xtrn, xtst, i, idx)
near_l01   i = i + 1
           le(i,s)                                    :f(return)
           d = dist(xtrn, xtst, i, idx)
           lt(d,md)                                   :f(near_l01)
           nearest = ytrn[i,1]
           md = d                                     :(near_l01)
enearest
```

Listing 5-26: Finding the nearest training sample

Listing 5-26 actually defines two functions, nearest and samples (which is used by nearest). Let's start with samples. It returns the number of rows in a 2D array. Given how we organize the data, that's a sample, a feature vector.

The samples function defines a pattern (pat), matching text up to the first comma and storing it in the function name (samples). It then applies this pattern to whatever is returned by the SNOBOL prototype function. This function returns a string specifying the dimensionality of an array. Recall that arrays are declared using a string to specify the number and size of the dimensions. Our arrays are 2D, so prototype returns a string like '100,4'. The pattern extracts the first number. We won't use it, but *classify.sno* also defines features, which is a function to return the number of features, the second number returned by prototype. Do take a look.

The algorithm for nearest scans through the training data, calculating the distance between the current training sample and the specified test sample. If that distance is smaller than the smallest found so far, it keeps track of the distance and the training sample's class label. When the algorithm completes its pass through the training data, it returns the class label of the smallest distance; nearest classifies a given test set sample.

The long list of parameters to nearest passes the training set, both data (xtrn) and labels (ytrn), along with the test set data and labels, and idx, which is the current test set sample to classify.

The loop over the training set tracks md, which is the smallest distance found so far, storing the associated class label in nearest, the function value. The loop ends when le(i,s) fails where i is the row index and s is the number of samples in the training set. If lt(d,md) succeeds, the algorithm updates md and nearest.

The Main Code

The sections above describe the functions implementing each phase of the classification task. The main code, at the bottom of *classify.sno*, pulls these pieces together (see Listing 5-27).

```
*   Train and test datasets
            x_train = loadfile(host(2,2))
            y_train = loadfile(host(2,3))
            x_test = loadfile(host(2,4))
            y_test = loadfile(host(2,5))

*   Run the test data against the training to find the nearest neighbor
            i = 1; nc = 0; n = samples(x_test)
loop     le(i,n)                                                      :f(stats)
            c = nearest(x_train, y_train, x_test, y_test, i)
      ❶ nc = eq(c, y_test[i,1]) nc + 1
            star =
            star = ne(c, y_test[i,1]) ' **'
            output = "test " i ": assigned " c ", actual " y_test[i,1] star
            i = i + 1                                                :(loop)
stats    output =
            output = 'accuracy ' (nc / (1.0 * n)) ' (' nc ' out of ' n ' correct)'
            output =
end
```

Listing 5-27: Putting the classifier together

Listing 5-27 first loads the training and test data. The feature vectors are in x_train and x_test, respectively. The associated class labels are in y_train and y_test. The filenames are passed on the command line, after *classify.sno*, with the training data and labels first, followed by test data and labels.

The following code is a loop that runs through each test sample. The call to nearest returns the assigned class label for test sample i. If the classification is correct, it increments the number correct counter, nc ❶. Note that the SNOBOL construct of using the eq predicate in the same update statement. If the classification is wrong, eq fails, and the rest of the statement is skipped. There is no failure label, so execution continues with the next line. When all test samples have been classified, the overall accuracy is displayed before exiting.

The implementation is complete. Now the million-dollar question: does it work? Let's see.

Using the Classifier

Let's run *classify.sno* against the examples in the *datasets* directory. These datasets can be found on the UCI Machine Learning Repository website (*https://archive.ics.uci.edu/ml/index.php*). I downloaded the datasets and processed them to be in the form expected by *classify.sno*. The full dataset was randomly partitioned into training and test datasets using an 80/20 split. Feature vectors are in the "data" files, with the class labels, matching line for line, in the "labels" files.

The available datasets include those shown in Table 5-2.

Table 5-2: Available Datasets

Dataset	Features	Classes	Description
banknote	4	2	Real or counterfeit notes
cancer	10	2	Breast cancer histology slide features
ecoli	7	8	Characterizing *E. coli* bacteria
haberman	3	2	Five year breast cancer survival
iris	4	3	Types of irises
seeds	7	3	Types of seeds
wine	13	3	Wine origin

Let start with the irises. To run the classifier, use the following command line:

```
> snobol4 classify.sno iris_train_data.txt iris_train_labels.txt
         iris_test_data.txt iris_test_labels.txt
```

The output begins with

```
test 1: assigned 0., actual 0.
test 2: assigned 0., actual 0.
test 3: assigned 1., actual 1.
test 4: assigned 2., actual 2.
test 5: assigned 1., actual 1.
test 6: assigned 2., actual 2.
test 7: assigned 0., actual 0.
test 8: assigned 1., actual 1.
test 9: assigned 2., actual 2.
```

and ends with

```
test 45: assigned 1., actual 1.
test 46: assigned 1., actual 2. **
test 47: assigned 1., actual 1.
test 48: assigned 0., actual 0.
test 49: assigned 1., actual 1.
test 50: assigned 2., actual 2.
```

```
accuracy 0.96 (48 out of 50 correct)
```

There are 50 test samples and the assigned and actual class labels are displayed for each sample. If the classifier made a mistake, the output is followed by ** to mark it.

The overall accuracy was 96 percent, with only two mistakes. For such a simple classifier, this is not too shabby. Note that both errors were confusing between class 1 and class 2. For the iris dataset, class 0 is easily distinguished from the other two, but class 1 and class 2 are relatively similar, so they are more likely to be confused.

Run the other example datasets in the same way. Table 5-3 shows the statistics, including the accuracy, number correctly classified, number tested, and the size of the training set.

Table 5-3: Nearest Neighbor Classifier Accuracies by Dataset

Dataset	Accuracy (%)	Correct	Test	Train
banknote	100.0	275	275	1097
cancer	94.2	129	137	546
ecoli	86.8	59	68	268
haberman	67.2	41	61	245
iris	96.0	48	50	100
seeds	92.9	39	42	168
wine	83.3	30	36	142

The results range from perfection (banknotes) to a low of 67 percent (haberman). However, all things considered, this simple classifier performed quite well on these datasets.

There is another name for the nearest neighbor classifier: 1-nearest neighbor, where the *1* means only the nearest training sample is considered. This classifier can be generalized to consider the *k*-nearest neighbors where $k > 1$ and is odd. For a *k*-nearest neighbor classifier, the *k*-nearest neighbors are located. The assigned class is the result of voting among the *k*-nearest neighbors. In the event of a tie, select one of the neighbors at random. Although nearest neighbor classifiers are seldom used, *k*-nearest neighbor classifiers are still an active research area in machine learning. I leave it as an exercise for the reader to convert *classify.sno* into a *k*-nearest neighbor classifier.

NOTE *The world of machine learning offers much more than the tiny bit we've explored here. Witness the rapidly expanding world of deep learning, which has already greatly affected our daily lives and will continue to do so for years to come. If your interest has been piqued, please take a look at my deep learning books* Practical Deep Learning: A Python-Based Introduction *(2021) and* Math for Deep Learning: What You Need to Know to Understand Neural Networks *(2021). Both are available from No Starch Press.*

Discussion

What should we make of SNOBOL? I'll admit, I like the language. The flexibility of its arrays and the table data structure are surprisingly "modern." I also like its pattern-matching abilities, dynamic data typing, and automatic memory management.

But SNOBOL's complete lack of structured programming abilities hurts. The only way to directly control program flow is with a goto. There are no structured control statements like for or while.

Forth gets a bad rap for being a write-only programming language, but Forth uses structured programming, which is not even an option in SNOBOL. Using the success or failure of a statement as an essential element of program flow control is novel and intellectually engaging, but it ultimately makes working with the language difficult. However, I suspect much of that difficulty would fade with practice. The fact that SNOBOL labels are global is especially painful. Even some assemblers for old 8-bit microprocessors support local labels, something that would greatly benefit SNOBOL.

Historically, SNOBOL had a reputation for being slow. Thus, a simple timing test comparing SNOBOL and Python seems in order.

Listing 5-28 shows two equivalent programs to initialize a 1,000,000-element array/list 20 times, first in Python and then in SNOBOL.

```
Python:
        a = [0]*1000000
        for k in range(20):
            for i in range(1000000):
                a[i] = i


SNOBOL:
        a = array(1000000)
        k = 1
loop0   i = 1
loop1   a[i] = i                 :f(break1)
        i = i + 1                :(loop1)
break1  k = le(k,20) k + 1       :s(loop0)
end
```

Listing 5-28: Comparing SNOBOL and Python

The median runtime on my machine over 10 runs each is 2.363 seconds for Python and 3.548 seconds for SNOBOL. So yes, SNOBOL is slower, but not dramatically so. Note that to run the SNOBOL code, use **-d 1m** on the command line to reserve enough memory for the array.

In what ways does SNOBOL help us expand our conception of what it means to code? Several come to mind. SNOBOL uses global labels and is unstructured. This requires programmers to think clearly about the *entire* scope of the project, or at least to implement a disciplined approach to coding, one that is not enforced by the language itself as in other, newer programming languages. Without a global conception of the program, label confusion or spaghetti code is inevitable. Thus, clarity of thought is essential.

SNOBOL's robust pattern matching and string update abilities enable a novel approach to string manipulation. As a result, some of the burden incumbent on the programmer regarding string manipulation in languages like C++, Python, or Java is alleviated. This means thinking in terms of strings and their evolution becomes a new paradigm for implementing algorithms.

Lastly, SNOBOL requires thinking in terms of statement success *and* statement failure. Typically, coding is for success, as we don't want failures to happen. Error control in SNOBOL is fine grained, which is both helpful and perhaps a bit dangerous.

All in all, SNOBOL is a surprisingly "modern" programming language. In many ways, it was well ahead of its time. SNOBOL itself evolved into Icon, also by Griswold, which uses structured programming constructs. Icon never caught on, but readers who are so inclined can learn more at *https://www2.cs.arizona.edu/icon/*. Regardless, SNOBOL is worth a bit of continued effort on our part. Indeed, we'll see SNOBOL again in Chapter 10 when we use it to implement Brainfuck.

Summary

This chapter introduced us to SNOBOL, a quirky pattern matching programming language from the 1960s. We worked through the language from its overall structure to specifics of its key features, with numerous examples. We learned about its unique approach to flow control and saw a tiny portion of its powerful text pattern matching abilities.

We implemented a simple machine learning classifier in SNOBOL as an exercise and saw that it performed well against some small-scale machine learning datasets.

We ended the chapter by discussing the language, what we liked about it, and what we were less enthused about. Our ultimate conclusion was that SNOBOL well deserves of a place at our table as a novel language that can help us learn to think differently about coding.

Let's leave SNOBOL, with its successes and failures, and jump forward to the latter Mesozoic so we can experience the awe and mystery of CLIPS, a language designed for expert system development.

6

CLIPS

Back in the 1980s and 1990s, there was a hot new topic in artificial intelligence: *expert systems*, that is, programs that attempt to capture the knowledge of human experts in a particular domain in the form of rules, particularly if-then rules. In 1985, NASA developed CLIPS ("C Language Integrated Production System") to create expert systems. CLIPS has been developed and maintained since then, becoming public domain software in 1996.

In this chapter, we'll use CLIPS to get a feel for what an expert system is and how to create one, at least a primitive one. We'll introduce CLIPS, and with it, the concepts behind expert systems. Then we'll explore the language through a series of four examples: a calculator, a second look at the family relationships we explored with Prolog in Chapter 1, a simple factory simulation, and a complete expert system for the classification of iris flowers. We'll end the chapter with a brief discussion of CLIPS as an atypical programming language.

Installation

Installing CLIPS is similar to installing SNOBOL. First, we need the tarball, *clips_core_source_631.tar.gz*, which we download from *https://sourceforge.net/projects/clipsrules/files/CLIPS/6.31/*. Example files are in *examples_631.tar.gz*.

Expand the archive and build CLIPS.

```
> tar xzf clips_core_source_631.tar.gz
> cd clips_core_source_631/core/
> make
```

Next, run CLIPS to make sure it works.

```
> ./clips
        CLIPS (6.31 6/12/19)
CLIPS> (* (+ 1 2) 3)
9
CLIPS> (exit)
```

Note that the expression (1+2)*3 becomes (* (+ 1 2) 3). CLIPS, like Lisp, uses *S-expressions*, which are lists of items surrounded by parentheses. S-expressions are often nested, as in the example here, where the S-expression (+ 1 2) is nested inside the outer expression beginning with *.

The main CLIPS site is at *http://www.clipsrules.net/*. You can download the CLIPS 6.31 documentation from there, though we'll introduce the essential elements of the system as we use it. If you see a version later than 6.31, go ahead and use it. The probability of CLIPS changing to the point where our examples no longer work is extremely low.

Origins and Philosophy

To understand CLIPS, we must first better understand what an expert system is. Expert systems were popular in the 1980s, and it was hoped then that they would prove helpful as a more general approach to artificial intelligence. We'll discuss whether this hope was realized later in the chapter, but for now, note that the large-scale application of expert systems never happened.

An *expert system* is a computer program capable of inferring conclusions from a set of rules and facts. The rules are intended to capture the knowledge of a human expert in a specific domain, thereby allowing the software to perform similarly depending on the facts available. This is an abstract definition, and there is certainly room for other nuanced statements related to what an expert system is, but you'll appreciate what an expert system is as we explore CLIPS.

An expert system is a collection of facts, rules (a knowledge base), and an inference engine to use those facts and rules to reach conclusions. Expert systems use facts and rules to determine behavior. For example, an expert system monitoring a building might have a rule like the following:

```
if door-is-open and time-is-after-midnight then signal-the-police
```

Here, `door-is-open`, `time-is-after-midnight`, and `signal-the-police` are all facts. Note that the last fact is one that the rule puts into the knowledge base when the rule fires. In other words, the rule *asserts* the fact, which later might cause another rule to fire.

In CLIPS this might be written as

```
(defrule intruder
    ?x <- (door-is-open)
    ?y <- (after-midnight)
  =>
    (retract ?x ?y)
    (assert (signal-the-police)))
```

We'll get to the exact syntax of a CLIPS rule in a bit, but even now, we can start to see what is going on.

Put enough of these rules together and you have a system embodying a tiny knowledge domain. In other words, the system is an expert in that tiny domain. At least, that's the hope.

Viewed this way, an expert system might be thought of as a glorified set of `if-then` statements. And in a way, it is, but much can happen in the then part, thereby enabling the system to respond in a sophisticated manner, provided the developer captured the essential knowledge of the domain expert and properly arranged that knowledge in the form of rules firing in response to a particular set of facts.

Expert systems rely on forward chaining. This is in contrast to a language like Prolog, which uses backward chaining. *Forward chaining* systems process the data embodied in the facts they know to find valid conclusions. In contrast, *backward chaining* systems work from the goal to find true statements that support the goal.

A forward chaining system explores all known facts to select rules to evaluate, or *fire*. A system like CLIPS places rules to fire on an *agenda* and then uses *conflict resolution* to select which specific rule to fire. Firing a rule may update the set of known facts, causing other rules to fire, in which case, CLIPS continues to run until the agenda is empty or until it is explicitly told to stop.

Internally, CLIPS uses the *Rete algorithm* to perform inference, that is, to find conclusions by applying a set of rules to a collection of facts. Unlike the other programming languages we've explored (except Prolog), CLIPS incorporates advanced concepts in its inference engine that are worth digging into if you are curious; however, these concepts are well beyond what we intend to explore here. Our concern is the language and how to think in terms of it.

As you saw earlier, syntactically, CLIPS looks like Lisp, using S-expressions, or prefix notation, where $f(x, y)$ becomes $(f\ x\ y)$ so the function moves inside the parentheses.

CLIPS is a multiparadigm language: it is declarative at its base because of the inference engine and how code normally runs, but it is also procedural, with standard control structures, and object oriented, though we'll completely ignore that aspect of the language here. CLIPS runs from the command line with its REPL, which is how we'll use it; however, it's also possible to embed it in another application.

Let's see CLIPS in action and then walk through some examples to show us how to work with the system. Along the way, we'll introduce different aspects of the language.

The Language

Let's run one of the demos that comes with CLIPS. We won't look at the code—it's beyond what we want to consider—but it will show us how to work with the system and serves as a nice example of how an expert system works. The example is in *wine.clp*. The purpose of the expert system is to recommend a wine to go with a dinner we are preparing. The program will ask us questions and, based on our responses, generate a list of recommended wines with probabilities to select a good pairing.

Working with CLIPS

A typical session with *wine.clp* looks like this:

```
> clips
CLIPS> (load "wine.clp")
--snip--
CLIPS> (reset)
CLIPS> (run)
Do you generally prefer dry, medium, or sweet wines? dry
Do you generally prefer red or white wines? white
Do you generally prefer light, medium, or full bodied wines? light
Is the flavor of the meal delicate, average, or strong? average
Does the meal have a sauce on it? no
Is the main component of the meal meat, fish, or poultry? fish


        SELECTED WINES

    WINE                    CERTAINTY
    -----------------------------
    Chardonnay              58%
    Soave                   40%
    Sauvignon-Blanc         40%
    Chablis                 40%
    Geverztraminer          30%

CLIPS> (exit)
```

First, we load *wine.clp*. Not shown is CLIPS reporting the successful compilation of the various code components in the file. After loading, CLIPS must be reset before running. Resetting is necessary to configure CLIPS because it places a set of initial facts on the facts list. If the (reset) step is skipped, running *wine.clp* will display the SELECTED WINES banner and nothing more.

The wine demo asks the user a series of questions. Based on the user's response, the demo provides a list of selected wines with a probability of pairing with the indicated meal. Reset and run the demo a second time, enter the same responses, and the list should be the same. CLIPS is working through a set of rules and will arrive at the same conclusion each time the inputs match. There is nothing stochastic, no randomness, to what CLIPS is doing.

While the system is running, the set of facts may change and new inputs may be read. The agenda changes in response to rules that can fire. A reset configures CLIPS by defining the initial set of facts. For example:

```
> clips
CLIPS> (load "wine.clp")
--snip--
CLIPS> (run)

        SELECTED WINES

 WINE                    CERTAINTY
 -------------------------------

CLIPS> (facts)
f-0     (initial-fact)
For a total of 1 fact.
CLIPS> (agenda)
CLIPS> (reset)
CLIPS> (facts)
f-0     (initial-fact)
f-36    (attribute (name best-color) (value any) (certainty 100.0))
f-37    (attribute (name best-body) (value any) (certainty 100.0))
f-38    (attribute (name best-sweetness) (value any) (certainty 100.0))
For a total of 4 facts.
CLIPS> (agenda)
10000   start: *
For a total of 1 activation.
```

Here, we tell CLIPS to run the wine program without issuing a (reset) first. The header is shown, nothing more. Asking for the current set of facts returns only the default initial fact (f-0). Asking for the agenda returns nothing as the agenda is empty. When the agenda is empty, CLIPS stops. We then reset CLIPS and ask for the facts a second time. Now we see the initial set of facts defined by *wine.clp*. We don't need to understand the structure right now, only see that the list of facts has been configured. Asking for the agenda now shows one activation, start. An activated rule is one where the conditions have been met. The wine demo is now ready. When we call run, the start rule will become active.

Implementing Hello World

Let's implement our old friend, "Hello, world!" We'll write two versions. The first uses the inference engine by defining a rule that always fires. The second is purely procedural, proving that CLIPS does support imperative programming.

The file *hello0.clp* contains

```
(defrule hello
  => (printout t "Hello, world!" crlf))
```

We'll detail the syntax of defrule in the next section. For now, know that it defines a rule named hello. The portion of a rule after the arrow (=>) is the part that runs, which is the then portion. There is nothing to the left of the arrow because this rule always fires or fires if initial-fact, f-0 above, is defined, which it is by default.

To execute the rule we need only use (run) as there is nothing to configure regarding other facts and the agenda. Running the program looks like the following:

```
CLIPS> (load "hello0.clp")
CLIPS> (run)
Hello, world!
```

Excellent; our rule fired. However, you might have a question. If the rule hello is set to fire when initial-fact is present, which it always is, why doesn't CLIPS print "Hello, world!" forever? There is nothing removing the initial fact, so it's still present. Why doesn't the rule match again and again? This is because CLIPS fires a rule only once for each set of matching conditions. This is known as *refraction* (this term is borrowed from neuroscience, where it is related to the time delay after a neuron fires before it can fire again).

The file *hello0.clp* defined a rule and used CLIPS's inference engine to fire it. CLIPS allows imperative programming as well. The file *hello1.clp* contains the following:

```
(deffunction hello () (printout t "Hello, world!" crlf))
(hello)
(exit)
```

We can run this from the command line as follows:

```
> clips -f2 hello1.clp
Hello, world!
```

Use -f or -f2 to execute a program from the command line. The second option (-f2) disables load messages. Calling (exit) keeps the program from showing the CLIPS> prompt after running. The file *hello1.clp* uses deffunction to define a function named hello that is then called before exiting to print the message. The t after printout specifies the output file—in this case the terminal. CLIPS's support for imperative programming covers all the expected control structures like if-then and while. We won't discuss those elements here, but do consult the CLIPS documentation to learn about them. A good place for control structures is in the action part of a rule.

CLIPS manipulates facts with rules and input. The rules, when active, affect the agenda, and it is the agenda that drives a CLIPS program. Let's learn more about facts and rules.

Facts and Rules

You've already seen a bit about facts and rules, but to understand the examples that follow, we'll need a more thorough understanding. Let's dive in.

Facts

Facts are asserted (assert) and retracted (retract) as needed when rules fire. Simple facts are straightforward to add. For example:

```
CLIPS> (assert (emergency-brake-on))
<Fact-1>
CLIPS> (assert (roses-are red))
<Fact-2>
CLIPS> (assert (violets-are blue))
<Fact-3>
CLIPS> (facts)
f-0     (initial-fact)
f-1     (emergency-brake-on)
f-2     (roses-are red)
f-3     (violets-are blue)
For a total of 4 facts.
```

Three facts are asserted. The first might indicate to a running system managing a car that the emergency brake is on. The other two are the symbols roses-are and violets-are along with symbols for colors. Equivalent to an atom in Prolog, a *symbol* in CLIPS is a set of characters that represents itself, unlike a variable, which is a name given to a value. A symbol has no value. A set of facts may be defined at one time with deffacts. Facts defined this way are put on the facts list when (reset) is executed. Consider the following:

```
CLIPS> (facts)
f-0     (initial-fact)
For a total of 1 fact.
CLIPS> (deffacts arthropods (insects 6) (spiders 8) (trilobites 48))
CLIPS> (facts)
```

```
f-0      (initial-fact)
For a total of 1 fact.
CLIPS> (reset)
CLIPS> (facts)
f-0      (initial-fact)
f-1      (insects 6)
f-2      (spiders 8)
f-3      (trilobites 48)
For a total of 4 facts.
```

In this example, CLIPS has only the initial fact at first. Then, a deffacts statement named arthropods defines a set of facts. There are three facts defined, each a type of arthropod followed by the number of legs. (Of course, some arthropod enthusiasts may object that trilobites vary in the number of legs, but 48 isn't a bad guess.)

The next line uses (facts), but our newly declared facts are not present. When assert was used above, the facts appeared immediately. However, with deffacts, we must use (reset) first and then the facts appear. Any previously defined facts are lost as well.

Complex facts have many parts, some of which may be updated as CLIPS runs. CLIPS provides a mechanism for defining complex facts. For example, the file *coin.clp* defines a fact template for ancient Roman coins along with facts related to specific Roman coins:

```
(deftemplate roman-coin "Roman coin facts"
  (slot emperor)
  (slot denomination)
  (slot obverse)
  (slot reverse))

(deffacts coin-facts "ancient Roman coins"
  (ancient (emperor Otho)
           (denomination Denarius)
           (obverse "Emperor hd right")
           (reverse "Securitas std left"))
  (ancient (emperor Constantine)
           (denomination AE3)
           (obverse "IMP CONSTANTINVS MAX AVG")
           (reverse "VICTORIAE LAETAE PRINC PERP")) )
```

Here, deftemplate defines a fact template named roman-coin with an optional comment string. The fields of a fact are called *slots*. The template defines four fields: emperor, denomination, obverse, and reverse.

With roman-coin defined, we can then assert some facts about specific coins using deffacts. The first relates to a silver denarius of the first-century emperor Otho, one of the "Twelve Caesars" who ruled from January 15 to April 16 in the year 69. A denarius was the usual day's wage for a Roman soldier. The second coin is a small bronze coin, loose change of the time, minted by Constantine the Great around the year 325.

Let's inform CLIPS about these coins.

```
CLIPS> (load "coin.clp")
Defining deftemplate: coin
Defining deffacts: coin-facts
TRUE
CLIPS> (reset)
CLIPS> (facts)
f-0     (initial-fact)
f-1     (coin (emperor Otho)
               (denomination Denarius)
               (obverse "Emperor hd right")
               (reverse "Securitas std left"))
f-2     (coin (emperor Constantine)
               (denomination AE3)
               (obverse "IMP CONSTANTINVS MAX AVG")
               (reverse "VICTORIAE LAETAE PRINC PERP"))
For a total of 3 facts.
CLIPS> (retract 1)
CLIPS> (facts)
f-0     (initial-fact)
f-2     (coin (emperor Constantine)
               (denomination AE3)
               (obverse "IMP CONSTANTINVS MAX AVG")
               (reverse "VICTORIAE LAETAE PRINC PERP"))
For a total of 2 facts.
```

After loading *coin.clp*, we reset and look at the known facts. There are the new coins. During execution, CLIPS will often assert and retract facts. Here, we manually retract the first coin fact with retract, and after running (facts) again we see that it is no longer present. Notice that the fact numbers do not change after this. Fact f-2 is still fact f-2.

Rules

Rules are if-then constructs. The syntax for a rule is

```
(defrule <rule-name> "<optional-comment>"
  (<lefthand-side>) => (<righthand-side>))
```

The (<lefthand-side>), or LHS, is a set of zero or more conditions that attempt to match facts. The conditions are ANDed, which means that all must match for the rule to fire. When the rule does fire, everything on the (<righthand-side>), or RHS, is executed. These are the rule's *actions*. Typically, the actions alter the set of facts in some way to move the program forward. However, the actions may also have side effects, like printing information or requesting information from the user (this is where CLIPS's imperative coding abilities come into play). Rules with a matching LHS are placed on the agenda to execute their respective RHSs.

As rules match, they may also bind variables that are local to the rule. CLIPS variables follow the expected naming convention, but they must be referenced with a leading question mark. For example, ?x refers to the variable x. Binding on the LHS of a rule is useful as the bound variables may be used on the RHS. We'll see examples of this later in the chapter. To bind a variable directly, that is, to assign something to it, use the bind statement.

```
CLIPS> (bind ?x 1)
CLIPS> (bind ?y 1121)
CLIPS> (printout t (/ ?x ?y) crlf)
0.000892060660124889
```

Here's a hypothetical rule to react to a security breach.

```
(defrule react-security-breach "React to a security breach"
    ?r <- (security-breach ?typ)
  =>
    (retract ?r)
    (assert (log-security-breach ?typ))
    (printout t "!!! security alert !!!" crlf))
```

The rule name is react-security-breach. The LHS, the part before =>, is the condition that matches a fact of the form security-breach *<type>*, where the actual type is bound to ?typ. For example, (security-breach hacker) would match the rule and bind the symbol hacker to the variable ?typ.

The LHS has a funny bit of syntax: ?r <-. When the security-breach fact matches, it returns the fact number, which is bound to ?r. The RHS of the rule, the part after =>, uses ?r to retract the matched fact. As we are processing the security breach, we remove the trigger for this rule. Because of refraction, the rule will fire only once for the specific fact (security-breach hacker). Retracting the fact removes it, so when it is asserted again, the rule will fire once more.

The RHS of this rule asserts (log-security-breach ?typ) to add a new fact. Note the use of ?typ, which CLIPS extracted from the LHS of the rule. Asserting this fact acts as a trigger for another rule that will write some information to a logfile or perhaps send an alert email to the IT department. The final part of the rule prints the alert so we can see it.

If the rule is in *security.clp*, we load and run it as follows:

```
CLIPS> (load "security.clp")
CLIPS> (reset)
CLIPS> (assert (security-breach hacker))
<Fact-1>
CLIPS> (run)
```

```
!!! security alert !!!
CLIPS> (facts)
f-0      (initial-fact)
f-2      (log-security-breach hacker)
For a total of 2 facts.
```

To trigger the rule after reset, we must assert a security breach, which in this case is a hacker security breach. Running it shows us the security alert message indicating the rule fired. If we examine the known facts, we see a new one, f-2, which is the fact asserted by our rule.

CLIPS is large, powerful, and reasonably complex. Let's spend the remainder of the chapter exploring selected examples to illustrate how CLIPS works, at least at the level we'll use it.

CLIPS in Action

To build our intuition about CLIPS, in this section we'll walk through four examples. The first is an elementary calculator, just enough to get our feet wet. Next, we'll revisit the Greek god family tree from Chapter 1 to see CLIPS's take on it. Following that is a basic factory simulation, which illustrates how a CLIPS expert system might operate when monitoring something in the real world. Lastly, we'll build an expert system for iris flowers to compare a rule-based classifier with the SNOBOL nearest neighbor classifier of Chapter 5.

An Elementary Calculator

This example implements a calculator. For the calculator, we need four rules. The first rule handles the startup message and informs the user. The next rule handles binary operators like plus and multiply. Next, we need a rule for unary operations like sine and cosine. The final rule accepts input from the user and asserts the operation for the binary or unary rule to act upon. The source code is in *math.clp*.

Listing 6-1 contains the set of initial facts and the start rule.

```
(defrule start ""
  ?r <- (startup)
  =>
  (printout t "A simple calculator." crlf)
  (printout t crlf)
  (printout t "Enter <number> <op> <number> where" crlf)
  (printout t "<op> is +, -, *, /, ^, mod" crlf crlf)
  (printout t "Enter <function> <arg> where" crlf)
  (printout t "        <function> is: trig, log, exp, or sqrt" crlf crlf)
  (printout t "Type 'end' to exit and @ to use previous result." crlf)
```

```
  (retract ?r)
  (assert (get-next-operation)))

(deffacts initial-facts ""
  (@ 0)
  (startup))
```

Listing 6-1: Initializing the calculator

Here, there are two initial facts. The first is (startup), and the second is
@ 0. We'll use the @ fact to keep the result of the last operation.

The LHS of the start rule matches (startup), which is asserted when
CLIPS is reset because of deffacts. This rule does three things: first, it prints
a set of instructions for the user; second, it retracts (startup) so it is no longer
in the facts list; and third, it asserts (get-next-operation). We'll use this fact to
request input from the user.

Listing 6-2 shows the get-operation rule.

```
(defrule get-operation ""
  ?w <- (get-next-operation)
  =>
  (retract ?w)
  (printout t crlf "        ")
  (bind ?expr (readline))
  (if (eq ?expr "end") then (halt))
  (assert (operation (explode$ ?expr))) )
```

Listing 6-2: Processing user input

The get-operation rule fires only when (get-next-operation) is in the facts
list. As start places this fact on the list after it is done, the get-operation rule
will fire immediately after start ends. As CLIPS fires rules only once, when
matched, we retract (get-next-operation) so the rule will fire the next time it
is asserted.

The remainder of get-operation displays a prompt of spaces and then
binds ?expr to the string typed by the user. After a quick check to see if the
user entered end, the operation is asserted. The explode$ function takes a
string and splits it into a list, the elements of which become the fields of the
operation fact. CLIPS refers to lists as *multifields*.

The instructions tell the user to enter expressions carefully. A unary
expression is the function name followed by one or more spaces and an argument consisting of either a number or @ to use the previous result. A binary expression is the first operand, spaces, operation, spaces, and second
operand. When exploded, the operation fact will contain three fields if it's a
binary expression or two if it's a unary expression.

Now consider Listing 6-3, which processes unary expressions.

```
(defrule unary-math ""
  ?w <- (operation ?func ?x)
  ?at <- (@ ?last)
```

```
=>
(retract ?w)
(retract ?at)
(assert (get-next-operation))
(if (eq ?x @) then (bind ?x ?last))
(if (eq ?func cos) then (bind ?y (cos ?x)))
(if (eq ?func sin) then (bind ?y (sin ?x)))
(if (eq ?func tan) then (bind ?y (tan ?x)))
(if (eq ?func log) then (bind ?y (log ?x)))
(if (eq ?func exp) then (bind ?y (exp ?x)))
(if (eq ?func sqrt) then (bind ?y (sqrt ?x)))
(printout t ?y)
(assert (@ ?y)))
```

Listing 6-3: Processing a unary expression

The unary-math rule is triggered by an operation fact with two fields. The first is the function (?func) and the second is the argument to the function (?x). The last result is also part of the LHS, so we can pull it from the facts list. Both the operation and last result are retracted, meaning they will be asserted again later.

The rule asserts (get-next-operation) to fire get-operation again to acquire the next expression from the user. The remainder of the rule performs the requested operation. If ?x is @, ?x is updated to be the previous result (?last). The actual operation generates an output value, ?y, which is printed and asserted as the new previous result, which is the @ fact.

Binary expressions are processed by Listing 6-4.

```
(defrule binary-math ""
  ?w <- (operation ?a ?op ?b)
  ?at <- (@ ?last)
  =>
  (retract ?w)
  (retract ?at)
  (assert (get-next-operation))
  (if (eq ?a @) then (bind ?a ?last))
  (if (eq ?b @) then (bind ?b ?last))
  (if (eq ?op +) then (bind ?y (+ ?a ?b)))
  (if (eq ?op -) then (bind ?y (- ?a ?b)))
  (if (eq ?op *) then (bind ?y (* ?a ?b)))
  (if (eq ?op /) then (bind ?y (/ ?a ?b)))
  (if (eq ?op ^) then (bind ?y (** ?a ?b)))
  (if (eq ?op mod) then (bind ?y (mod ?a ?b)))
  (printout t ?y)
  (assert (@ ?y)))
```

Listing 6-4: Processing a binary expression

This rule is substantially the same as the unary expression case, but matches an operation with two arguments instead of one. CLIPS knows which rule to fire, unary-math or binary-math, because of the number of fields in the operation fact.

Let's see *math.clp* in action.

```
CLIPS> (load "math.clp")
CLIPS> (reset)
CLIPS> (run)
A simple calculator.

Enter <number> <op> <number> where
<op> is +, -, *, /, ^, mod

Enter <function> <arg> where
        <function> is: trig, log, exp, or sqrt

Type 'end' to exit and @ to use the previous result.

        111 * 123
13653
        @ + 5
13658
        @ / 23456
0.582281718963165
        cos @
0.835210036979047
        exp @
2.30529819530959
        @ ^ @
6.8579474467406
        end
```

User entries are in bold, demonstrating both binary and unary expressions, most of which use the previous result. Note that spaces are required between operands and operators.

This example exposes a general pattern: store information on the facts list and use assertions and retractions to arrange the flow of the program. The calculator begins with the startup message, which then asserts a fact to cause get-operation to fire, thereby acquiring and processing input from the user. In turn, that rule asserts the fact of the desired operation. The inference engine causes the proper binary or unary rule to fire to process the request. Those rules retract and reassert the last result, so the version in the fact list is always correct. They also reassert (get-next-operation) to acquire more input from the user. This keeps the program running until (halt) is executed.

Family Redux

In Chapter 1, we used Prolog to explore the sometimes unusual family relationships among the ancient Greek gods. Let's revisit that example now to understand what CLIPS might do with the same set of facts. This example is in *family.clp*. Let's walk through the code, then run it to see what manner of output we get.

Listing 6-5 is only partial. See *family.clp* for the complete set of facts.

```
(deffacts olympians
    (male uranus)
    (male cronus)
--snip--
    (female gaia)
    (female rhea)
--snip--
    (parent uranus cronus)
    (parent gaia cronus)
--snip--
    (married zeus hera)
    (married hephaestus aphrodite))
```

Listing 6-5: Some facts about the Olympians

As with Prolog, we declare some gods as male and other gods as female before listing parent-child relationships in the form (parent x y), which means X is a parent of Y. If gods were considered married, the facts list captures that as well.

Listing 6-6 gives us rules capturing basic family relationships.

```
(defrule father
    (parent ?x ?y)
    (male ?x)
  =>
    (printout t ?x " is father of " ?y crlf))

(defrule mother
    (parent ?x ?y)
    (female ?x)
  =>
    (printout t ?x " is mother of " ?y crlf))

(defrule wife
    (female ?x)
    (or (married ?x ?y) (married ?y ?x))
  =>
    (printout t ?x " is wife of " ?y crlf))
```

```
(defrule husband
   (male ?x)
   (or (married ?x ?y) (married ?y ?x))
  =>
   (printout t ?x " is husband of " ?y crlf))
```

Listing 6-6: Rules capturing basic relationships

As we can see in the first defrule in Listing 6-6, x is the father of y if x is a parent of y and x is male. The LHS of the rules captures the relationship from the facts binding variables. For example, the father rule binds both ?x and ?y, meaning it will fire if there is a set of (parent x y) and (male x) facts in the facts list where the same x is parent of y and also male. Therefore, for a rule's LHS, variables with the same name must be the same for every part of the condition to be true. When the rule fires, it simply outputs the now proven fact that x is the father of y. Notice that nothing is added to or removed from the facts list by these rules. These rules produce output only. Refraction will prevent the rule from firing more than once for the same set of facts.

The rule for mother is almost the same as father. The rules for wife and husband include a logical-OR because married might be specified as (married zeus hera) or (married hera zeus). Again, the rules make no change to the facts list.

Listing 6-7 shows us three more rules from *family.clp*.

```
(defrule sibling
   (parent ?p ?x)
   (parent ?p ?y)
   (test (neq ?x ?y))
  =>
   (assert (siblings ?x ?y)))

(defrule sister
   (siblings ?x ?y)
   (female ?x)
   (test (neq ?x ?y))
  =>
   (printout t ?x " is sister to " ?y crlf))

(defrule brother
   (siblings ?x ?y)
   (male ?x)
   (test (neq ?x ?y))
  =>
   (printout t ?x " is brother to " ?y crlf))
```

Listing 6-7: Rules capturing sibling relationships

The first rules capture the idea of siblings and the following two rules embody the ideas of sister and brother.

For x to be the brother of Y, x must be male and x and y must be siblings. To be siblings, x and y must have a parent in common. The rules of Listing 6-7 capture siblings and then assert that x and y are siblings. Once asserted, the brother and sister rules can fire because the new fact that x and y are siblings is now part of the fact list.

The LHS of the rules includes a test to make sure that x and y are not the same person, as we don't normally think of ourselves as our own siblings.

There is no startup rule in *family.clp* like we had for *math.clp*. Instead, the fact list is initialized by (reset), and (run) immediately begins using the fact list to satisfy the rules, place them on the agenda, and execute the RHS for all possible matches. Therefore, unlike Prolog, which gave us a result and waited patiently for us to request another or stop, CLIPS will run as long as it can match facts to rules and execute them.

If you load *family.clp* and execute (reset) and (run), you should see a flurry of output—119 lines' worth, to be exact. The output is all the possible relationships CLIPS was able to pull out of the initial set of facts. For example, the list begins with

```
hephaestus is husband of aphrodite
aphrodite is wife of hephaestus
zeus is husband of hera
hera is wife of zeus
uranus is father of aphrodite
aphrodite is sister to cronus
cronus is brother to aphrodite
semele is mother of dionysus
zeus is father of dionysus
dionysus is brother to artemis
--snip--
```

giving us a mix of husbands, wives, fathers, sisters, and so on. It would be nice to organize this list in some way, that is, to programmatically capture the relationships by type instead of dumping line after line. Fortunately, CLIPS is a full-service programming language. One way we can apply some order to the output is to capture instances of different types so we can report them at will.

```
(defglobal ?*brothers* = (create$))
(defglobal ?*sisters* = (create$))

(defrule sister
    (siblings ?x ?y)
    (female ?x)
    (test (neq ?x ?y))
  =>
    (bind ?msg (implode$ (create$ ?x is sister to ?y)))
    (bind ?*sisters* (create$ ?*sisters* ?msg)))
```

```
(defrule brother
    (siblings ?x ?y)
    (male ?x)
    (test (neq ?x ?y))
  =>
    (bind ?msg (implode$ (create$ ?x is brother to ?y)))
    (bind ?*brothers* (create$ ?*brothers* ?msg)))

(deffunction brothers ()
    (foreach ?bro ?*brothers*
        (printout t ?bro crlf)))

(deffunction sisters ()
    (foreach ?sis ?*sisters*
        (printout t ?sis crlf)))
```

Listing 6-8: Storing relationship output

The file *family2.clp* stores brothers and sisters in global lists. Only brothers and sisters are considered in this case, but it would be straightforward to include other family relationships. The essential pieces of *family2.clp* are in Listing 6-8. The initial set of facts has been excluded from the listing, as has the rule sibling, which is unchanged from the version in Listing 6-7.

Listing 6-8 begins with two new lines, instances of defglobal, which is CLIPS-speak for defining a global variable. CLIPS uses asterisks around the names of global variables, so we define two empty lists, the output of create$ with no arguments, to hold brothers and sisters: ?*brothers* and ?*sisters*.

To accumulate information about brothers and sisters, we modify the brother and sister rules. The LHS of each rule remains the same, but the RHS consists of two calls to bind. The first uses create$ to make a list of ?x, the symbols is, sister or brother, to, and ?y. This list is passed to implode$, which makes a string from a list. Therefore, the output of implode$ is a string, such as dionysus is brother to artemis, that we store in ?msg. The second bind again uses create$ to append the new string to the end of the existing list. In this way, every discovery of a brother or sister relationship is stored in the corresponding string.

If we load *family2.clp* and call (reset) followed by (run), we get no output. However, CLIPS did its job. To see this we need functions to print the lists. Enter the functions brothers and sisters. Neither function requires arguments and both use CLIPS's foreach loop to iterate over the lists to print one element per line.

Give *family2.clp* a try. First load, reset, and run as usual, and then list the sisters. For example:

```
CLIPS> (load "family2.clp")
CLIPS> (reset)
CLIPS> (run)
CLIPS> (sisters)
aphrodite is sister to cronus
```

```
eris is sister to dionysus
artemis is sister to dionysus
artemis is sister to apollo
artemis is sister to hermes
artemis is sister to athena
artemis is sister to eris
artemis is sister to hephaestus
artemis is sister to ares
--snip--
```

Calling (brothers) produces the other list. The *family2.clp* example shows how to combine procedural (imperative) programming with CLIPS's rules engine. Now, let's look at a factory simulation to see how rules can be ordered to fire in a specified sequence.

At the Factory

For this example, we'll simulate the monitoring of a factory. The factory has pumps that must be turned on and then turned off three seconds later. Additionally, from time to time, an emergency must be serviced before turning on the pumps. Our simulation's true purpose is to demonstrate *salience*, which determines the firing order for rules if multiple rules are on the agenda. Salience should be used with care, but it is sometimes necessary.

Listing 6-9 shows us a few necessary utility functions.

```
(defglobal ?*base* = (time))
(deffunction ftime ()
  (- (time) ?*base*))

(deffunction rand ()
  (/ (mod (random) 1000000) 1000000))

(deffunction pause (?delay)
  (bind ?start (time))
  (while (< (time) (+ ?start ?delay)) do))
```

Listing 6-9: Some utility functions

The first line defines a global variable, ?*base*, which holds the current epoch seconds value returned by (time). It's set when the program loads. We're using it with the ftime function to return the number of seconds since the program was loaded.

CLIPS has a function called (random) to return a random integer, which is really the return value of the C rand function. To get a floating-point value in [0, 1), we take the remainder of this integer when divided by 1,000,000 and divide that by 1,000,000. This approach is adequate for our purposes.

The system pauses before monitoring the state of the factory, hence defining (pause), which accepts the number of seconds and runs a while loop waiting for the time to elapse. This is very CPU intensive, but, again, it is acceptable for our purposes.

The rules responding to events in the factory are in Listing 6-10.

```
(defrule emergency "there is an emergency"
    (declare (salience 100))
    ?x <- (emergency-alert)
  =>
    (retract ?x)
    (printout t "  !!! emergency! !!!" crlf))

(defrule pumps-on "turn the pumps on"
    (declare (salience 5))
    ?x <- (pumps-on)
  =>
    (retract ?x)
    (printout t "  pumps on (" (ftime) ")" crlf)
    (assert (pumps-off-time (+ (ftime) 3))))

(defrule pumps-off "turn off the pumps"
    (declare (salience 5))
    ?x <- (pumps-off-time ?t)
  =>
    (if (>= (ftime) ?t) then
      (retract ?x)
      (printout t "  pumps off (" (ftime) ")" crlf)
    else
      (refresh pumps-off)))
```

Listing 6-10: The factory rules

There are three rules: emergency, pumps-on, and pumps-off. As before, the rules have a LHS and a RHS. There is also a new statement, declare, which sets the salience to an integer, which must be in the range [−10,000, 10,000]. Higher salience rules fire before lower salience rules when multiple rules are on the agenda. The default salience value is 0.

The first rule in Listing 6-10 uses a salience of 100. This is the emergency rule, and we want to ensure it fires immediately after being placed on the agenda; therefore, we give it a salience larger than any other rule. The pumps-on and pumps-off rules each have a salience of 5. Salience is for ordering execution on the agenda, and the numeric value has no other meaning. Therefore, the fact that emergency has a salience 20 times greater than that of the other rules doesn't mean anything other than that it fires first.

The emergency rule does nothing more than inform the user that an emergency condition exists, that is, the fact emergency-alert has been asserted. Notice that the fact has been retracted. If not, the rule would not fire again when a new emergency-alert is placed on the facts list.

The pumps-on rule displays the pump start time and then asserts pumps-off -time as three seconds beyond the current time. The assertion fires pumps-off.

This rule uses `if` to check whether the current time is beyond the desired stop time. If it is, the `pumps-off-time` fact is retracted and the off message displayed. If the full three seconds has not yet elapsed, `refresh` is used to cause `pumps-off` to fire again even though it already matched the `pumps-off-time` fact. Using `refresh` eliminates the need to retract the `pumps-off-time` fact only to assert it again.

The main factory monitor loop is the rule `monitor` (see Listing 6-11).

```
(defrule monitor "monitor the factory"
    (declare (salience 0))
    (monitor-loop)
  =>
    (if (< (rand) 0.2) then (assert (pumps-on)))
    (if (< (rand) 0.05) then (assert (emergency-alert)))
    (pause 0.2)
    (refresh monitor))

(deffacts initial
  (monitor-loop))
```

Listing 6-11: The `monitor` rule

The `monitor` rule uses a salience of 0, which is the default value. Doing this means the pump and emergency rules will always fire before this rule. The idea is to monitor the factory until something worthwhile happens and then react to the situation before returning to monitor the factory.

This is a simulation, so "monitor the factory" means use `(rand)` to assert events with random probabilities. For any execution of `monitor`, there's a 20 percent chance the pumps will be turned on. Likewise, there is a 5 percent chance an emergency alert will be issued. After a 0.2 second pause, the program refreshes the `monitor` rule to make it fire again. To prep the system, `deffacts` places `monitor-loop` on the facts list when `(reset)` is executed.

Now, let's run the simulation and see what it tells us.

```
CLIPS> (load "factory.clp")
CLIPS> (reset)
CLIPS> (run)
  pumps on (2.55227184295654)
  pumps off (5.55229592323303)
  pumps on (5.95234894752502)
  pumps off (8.95237803459167)
  !!! emergency! !!!
  pumps on (10.152487039566)
  pumps off (13.1525239944458)
  pumps on (14.5526268482208)
  pumps off (17.5526599884033)
^\Quit (core dumped)
```

This run activated the pumps and, as desired, turned them off after three seconds. There was one emergency alert. The factory simulation has no end condition, so use CTRL-\ to exit. This is the source of the Quit message in the listing above.

An Iris Expert System

In Chapter 5, we built a nearest neighbor classifier in SNOBOL. The nearest neighbor classifier is an example of machine learning, a statistical approach using training data to build a model that captures something essential about the data and allows for predictions when given new, unknown data.

An expert system attempts to encapsulate expert knowledge to capture enough about a particular domain to make informed decisions. This section uses "expert" knowledge of iris flowers to build a simple expert system. The result is a system that asks us questions about an unknown iris flower to decide what type of iris it is.

Unfortunately, I'm not an expert in iris flowers. But that isn't too much of a limitation in this case, as we can cheat a bit. We'll use machine learning to build a *decision tree* classifier for irises. A decision tree is a series of yes or no questions that ultimately lead from the tree's root to a leaf, which identifies the flower. Translating a decision tree into a simple expert system is straightforward, so we'll use the "expertise" captured by the decision tree to build the expert system. This isn't all that different from a human interviewing an iris expert to extract essential knowledge then encoded in a series of questions.

Therefore, our plan of attack is as follows:

1. Use the iris training data to build a decision tree classifier.
2. Use the associated test data to characterize the resulting tree's accuracy. Our expert system will use the same sequence of questions, so we'll get the same accuracy from CLIPS if we implement things correctly.
3. Translate the questions of the decision tree into a set of CLIPS rules.
4. Test the system with the iris test dataset.

First is the decision tree classifier. The code to train the classifier and output a tree representation is in the file *make_iris_tree.py*. You do not need to run it. The tree we'll work with is in *iris_tree.png*. If you want to generate a new tree, perhaps as an exercise in doing the translation to CLIPS yourself, you'll need to install scikit-learn (*https://scikit-learn.org/*) and Matplotlib (*https://matplotlib.org/*). scikit-learn uses some randomization when building the tree; therefore, each run of *make_iris_tree.py* results in a slightly different level of performance. The particular tree we're using here is 98 percent accurate on the iris test dataset (*iris_test_data.txt*).

Figure 6-1 shows us the decision tree classifier.

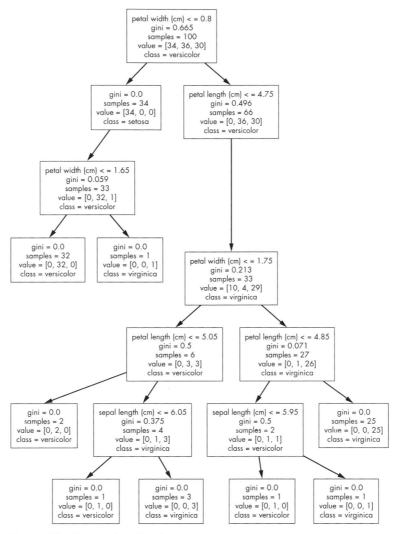

Figure 6-1: The iris classifier decision tree

The root of the tree is at the top, following normal computer science convention for representing a tree data structure. Each box is a node of the tree. If the box isn't a leaf, the first line of the box is a question asked of the user. If the answer to the question is "yes," move to the next lower box on the left. If the answer is "no," move to the lower box on the right. Answer enough questions and you'll eventually get to a leaf. The class label given there identifies the flower: *I. setosa, I. versicolor,* or *I. virginica.*

All boxes have additional lines of text. The *Gini score* is a measure used to generate the decision tree. Samples is a vector of three elements, one for each of the three iris flower types. It shows the split by type at that node when using the training data. The class label is the most correct label to give the flower if one stops at that node. For the leaves, the class label matches a value vector with only one class, meaning the decision tree was able to successfully partition the training data with 100 percent accuracy.

How do we use the decision tree? Let's walk through a test sample. The expert system will ask us about measurements made from an unknown iris flower. There are four measurements: sepal length, sepal width, petal length, and petal width, all in centimeters. See Figure 6-2 if you need a reminder of basic flower anatomy.

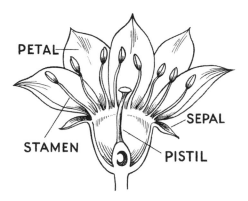

Figure 6-2: Basic flower anatomy

Our test case has the measurements

sepal length	6.8 cm
sepal width	2.8 cm
petal length	4.8 cm
petal width	1.4 cm

and is an instance of *I. versicolor* (class label 1). The path through the decision tree for this example is in Figure 6-3.

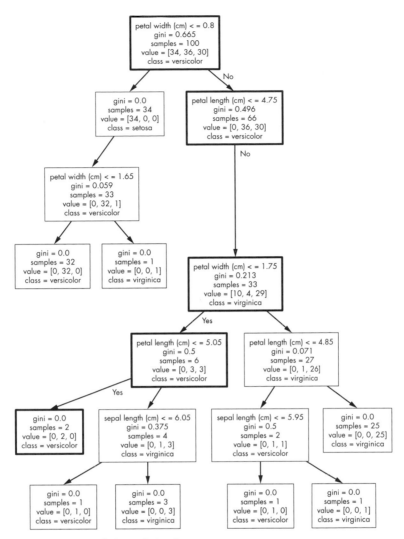

Figure 6-3: A path through the decision tree

We can place the questions asked at each node of the decision tree into Table 6-1.

Table 6-1: The Questions and Responses for the Iris Expert System

Question	Text	Yes	No
Q1	Is petal width ≤ 0.8?	setosa	Q2
Q2	Is petal length ≤ 4.75?	Q3	Q4
Q3	Is petal width ≤ 1.65?	versicolor	virginica
Q4	Is petal width ≤ 1.75?	Q5	Q6
Q5	Is petal length ≤ 5.05?	versicolor	Q7
Q6	Is petal length ≤ 4.85?	Q8	virginica
Q7	Is sepal length ≤ 6.05?	versicolor	virginica
Q8	Is sepal length ≤ 5.95?	versicolor	virginica

Each row of the table is a question. If the answer to a question is yes, we move to the indicated question or, if we now know the type, return the label. Notice that if the petal width is ≤ 0.8, the flower is an instance of *I. setosa* and there is no need to ask any further questions. This means of the three classes in the dataset, one is easily distinguished from the other two, but the remaining two need more work to tell apart. With the table, we now have what we need to implement the expert system. We begin with Q1, as that is the root of the tree, and move to other questions or endpoints based on the user's response to each question.

The full expert system is in *irises.clp*. We'll work through the code in sections beginning with the initial facts and helper rules (see Listing 6-12).

```
(deffacts initial-facts ""
  (question "Is petal width <= 0.80?")
  (state 1)
  (startup))

(defrule start "start the program"
  ?r <- (startup)
  =>
  (printout t crlf)
  (printout t "Iris classifier.  Please respond 'y' or 'n' to each question." crlf)
  (printout t crlf)
  (retract ?r))

(defrule ask-question "ask the user a question"
  ?p <- (question ?q)
  =>
  (retract ?p)
  (printout t ?q " ")
  (bind ?resp (readline))
  (assert (response ?resp)))
```

```
(defrule output-result "we have a label"
  (label ?label)
  =>
  (printout t crlf "The sample is an instance of ")
  (printout t ?label crlf crlf)
  (halt))
```

Listing 6-12: Facts and helper rules

The program begins with the start rule, which fires because initial-facts places it on the facts list when (reset) is run. It also defines a state fact, set to 1 for question Q1, and the text of the question itself. When startup fires, it prints instructions for the user and retracts itself. The presence of the question rule fires ask-question, which displays the question text and asserts the user's response: y or n. A full system would, naturally, validate the user's input. Rule output-result reports when we have a valid label and halts.

Asserting a response fact causes a question rule to fire. There are 16 of them, two each for Q1 through Q8 in Table 6-1, one each for a yes or no response. Let's look at the first pair of rules. You should review *irises.clp* yourself to see the entire program.

Listing 6-13 shows us the first two rules for Q1, that is, the first row of Table 6-1.

```
(defrule q1-yes ""
  ?q <- (state 1)
  ?r <- (response "y")
  =>
  (retract ?q ?r)
  (assert (label "setosa (0)")))

(defrule q1-no ""
  ?q <- (state 1)
  ?r <- (response "n")
  =>
  (retract ?q ?r)
  (assert (state 2))
  (assert (question "Is petal length <= 4.75?")))
```

Listing 6-13: Some iris rules

As you can see, if the user's response to Q1 is "yes," rule q1-yes fires. Table 6-1 says a "yes" response to Q1 means the sample is an instance of *I. setosa*. Therefore, rule q1-yes asserts label, causing output-result from Listing 6-12 to fire, tell us the iris type, and halt.

If the user's response to Q1 is "no," rule q1-no fires instead. Table 6-1 says to move to Q2 in this case, so the RHS of q1-no asserts state 2 and the proper question, which ask-question in Listing 6-12 dutifully asks.

As the user answers questions, CLIPS moves from state to state until it reaches a rule with a known label. For example, if we run *irises.clp* for the test sample above we get the output shown in Listing 6-14:

```
CLIPS> (load "irises.clp")
CLIPS> (reset)
CLIPS> (run)

Iris classifier.  Please respond 'y' or 'n' to each question.

Is petal width <= 0.80? n
Is petal length <= 4.75? n
Is petal width <= 1.75? y
Is petal length <= 5.05? y

The sample is an instance of versicolor (1)
```

Listing 6-14: Using the expert system

If you are patient enough, you can work through every example in the *iris_test_data.txt* file in the *SNOBOL/datasets* directory. Matching the reported labels against the known labels in *iris_test_labels.txt* will tell you that the iris expert system is 98 percent accurate, meaning it makes one mistake out of every 50 test samples. The SNOBOL nearest neighbor classifier is 96 percent accurate on the same test data using the same training data. Therefore, in this case, the expert system is quite good. Of course, our "expert knowledge" of iris flowers came from the training data in the first place, so we didn't implement a true expert system. We merely encapsulated knowledge synthesized from a statistical model. I'll have more to say about this in the discussion up next.

The examples in this section give us a good feel for CLIPS, but, as stated earlier, CLIPS is much more than we can explore here. For example, we ignored CLIPS's object-oriented abilities and the fact that CLIPS is designed to play nicely when integrated into other applications. A quick review of Google Scholar shows that academic papers referencing CLIPS are still being written, to say nothing of industrial uses for CLIPS that are likely never discussed in print.

Discussion

Expert systems are often considered "old-school" or even "failures," but that isn't fair. You won't hear the term *expert system* too much these days, but they are alive and well under the term *business rule management system.* For example, DROOLS (*https://www.drools.org/*) is an open source rules-based system in active development with a large user base and supporting documentation, including multiple books. As a general approach to artificial intelligence, expert systems are passé, replaced by the phenomenal success of deep learning and neural networks, which represent a connectionist view of cognition, not the computational view embodied by an expert system.

Expert systems are rigid. Once coded, they are not easily modified. Additionally, the rules often contain gaps, missing elements, or paths that are not specified. If a rule-based system claims to cover a topic, how would we know we've tested all the corner cases and all the possible sets of inputs? It becomes difficult, perhaps exponentially difficult, as the rules become more complex and intertwined.

The iris expert system shown earlier used "knowledge" extracted from a machine learning model. What if, instead, we needed to extract the rules from an expert gardener? The expert certainly knows how to identify iris flowers, but how do we get that knowledge out of the expert's head and into a set of rules for CLIPS? The process of mapping an expert's knowledge to rules is known as *knowledge extraction*, and it is an Achilles' heel of sorts for expert systems. The concept of an expert system is seductive, but the realization is difficult at best. To be sure, the iris expert won't know that a petal width less than 0.8 cm means the flower is almost certainly *I. setosa*, even if able to identify that species with almost perfect precision. How is that then captured and coded? Careful interviewing, which is highly time consuming, to say nothing of potentially irritating to the interviewee, might generate more general rules, but none would be as specific as those extracted by the decision tree. For example, one rule asks in a particular circumstance if the petal length is less than 4.75 cm, versus less than 4.85 cm in another. I doubt any expert would consider a millimeter difference in petal length of any importance.

CLIPS's use has faded as expert systems have fallen out of favor, but it is still maintained. There are likely many CLIPS-based expert systems out there, quietly running in the background and invisible to the general public.

Because of its multiparadigm nature, CLIPS is, of course, a Turing-complete language. Indeed, one could use CLIPS without any reference to the rules engine if desired. As a framework for an expert system, CLIPS has stood the test of time, so if you find yourself in a situation where an expert system seems appropriate, CLIPS is an option. For us, CLIPS is an atypical language, but one we should be familiar with and keep in our back pocket for those times when the appropriate situation arises. In terms of thinking about coding, CLIPS requires a different approach if we want to use the rules engine. That fact alone warrants including CLIPS in our explorations.

Summary

The CLIPS expert system was the focus of this chapter. We introduced the language and the concept of an expert system before exploring the basics: facts and rules. The bulk of the chapter saw us work through four examples illustrating the core of CLIPS. We learned how rules respond to facts by building an elementary calculator. We then re-explored family relationships to illustrate the difference between CLIPS and Prolog when generating inferences from collections of facts. The next example used a factory simulation to demonstrate arranging the firing sequence of rules by manipulating their salience. The final example was our most elaborate. We used a learned decision tree to implement a collection of rules, those that might have been created by an expert to let us categorize different types of iris flowers by answering a few yes or no questions.

CLIPS is our last atypical programming language. We move now to the first of our esolangs and into the realm of what I'm calling "eccentric programming languages." We'll begin with ABC, a tiny language that will serve us well to introduce the weirdly wonderful world of esolangs.

PART III

ESOTERIC PROGRAMMING LANGUAGES

7

THE ABCS OF ABCS

ABC (*https://esolangs.org/wiki/ABC*) was created by a programmer known as "Orange," an esolang fan with several entries in the esolangs wiki. Some are jokes, others more serious, and then there's ABC. I selected ABC because of its simplicity. Think of it as a starting point: something that is, but begs to be more. This chapter takes ABC from its unadorned description to a vanilla Python implementation, ultimately evolving it into something more via extensions to the language. This will be a warm-up for the esolangs that follow.

Specifically, we'll present and implement ABC as originally described. Then, we'll morph ABC into the cleverly named ABC2. We follow ABC2 and its implementation with some examples that help us think in this new language. As always, we'll end with a discussion of the languages.

ABC

Let's start slowly. In this section, we'll discuss what the ABC language entails, then we'll implement it in Python. It won't take much. After that, we'll test the implementation with some existing ABC examples.

The Language

The esolang wiki description of ABC is

```
a - Increment the accumulator
b - Decrement the accumulator
c - Output the accumulator

d - Invert accumulator
r - Set accumulator to a random number between 0 and
    accumulator
n - Set accumulator to 0

$ - Toggle ASCII output mode.  When on, the c
    instruction prints the accumulator as an ASCII
    character.
l - Loop back to the beginning of the program.
    Accumulator and ASCII mode does not reset.
; - Debug.  Prints out accumulator as a number and
    ASCII character.

Unknown instructions are treated as NOPs.
```

That's all there is; there isn't any more. However, that's all we need. The description tells us ABC uses an accumulator that can be incremented by one, decremented by one, or inverted (negated).

There isn't much here, but that's the charm of it—what can we do with something so simple?

An ABC Implementation

Implementing ABC shouldn't take too much effort on our part. The esolang wiki has an implementation in Java, but we'll use Python.

Listing 7-1 is the complete source code to our ABC implementation (see *ABC.py*).

```
import sys
import random
❶ t=open(sys.argv[1]).read()
tokens=["a","b","c","d","r","n","$","l",";"]
prog=""
```

```
    for c in t:
❷   if (c in tokens): prog+=c
    mode=False; A=0; k=0
❸ while (k<len(prog)):
      t=prog[k]
      if   (t=="a"): A+=1
      elif (t=="b"): A-=1
      elif (t=="c"):
        if (mode):   print("%s"%chr(A),end="")
        else:        print("%d"%A,end="")
      elif (t=="d"): A=-A
      elif (t=="r"): A=int(random.random()*A)
      elif (t=="n"): A=0
      elif (t=="$"): mode=not mode
      elif (t=="l"): k=-1
      elif (t==";"): print("{%d:(%d,%x,'%s')}"%(k,A,A,chr(A)),end="")
      else:          pass
      k+=1
    print()
```

Listing 7-1: A Python implementation of ABC

Python isn't normally written so compactly, but we're implementing a tiny language, so a tiny implementation seems appropriate. We'll admit one slight deviation from the language description. The r command should set the accumulator (A) to a random value in [0, A]. Instead, our implementation uses [0, A), which is closer to how pseudorandom generators are typically used—the upper limit is not usually included in the range. The effect on example code is minimal.

ABC reads a source code file from the command line ❶, keeping only characters representing ABC commands ❷. This means text that isn't a valid ABC command is fair game for comments. Channeling our inner COBOL, we adopt the convention of using uppercase letters with minimal punctuation for comments.

We store the program in the variable prog. Program state is set to the defaults of number output (mode==False), accumulator of zero (A=0), and program counter zero (k=0).

The main body of ABC now runs: a while loop with a nested if asking whether the current instruction (t) matches a command or not ❸. The program ends when all commands have been executed. By design, the l command causes an infinite loop, as there is no exit command.

Testing ABC

The esolang wiki page for ABC includes several example programs. Let's use them to test the implementation. The simplest one counts forever: acl.

With comments, it looks like this:

```
COUNT FOREVER
a   INCREMENT ACCUMULATOR
c   PRINT THE ACCUMULATOR AS A NUMBER
l   START AGAIN FROM THE BEGINNING
```

Other examples include *1337.abc*

```
acaaccaaaac
```

which prints 1337 (leetspeak). The program increments A to print 1, then two more times to print 3 twice, and finally four more times to print 7. Simple.

We also have *dice.abc*

```
aaaaaaarac
```

which rolls a standard die. The program increments until $A = 6$, then replaces it with a random integer in $[0, 6)$. A final increment sets $A \in [1, 7)$ before printing it. Note that *dice.abc* has an extra a before the r to accommodate our change in how r works.

The examples also include *hello.abc*

```
$aaaaaaaaaaaaaaaaaaaaaaaaaaaaaaaaaaaaaaaaa
aaaaaaaaaaaaaaaaaaaaaaaaaaaaaaaaacaaaaaa
aaaaaaaaaaaaaaaaaaaaacaaaaaaaccaaacnaa
aaaaaaaaaaaaaaaaaaaaaaaaaaaaaaaaaaaaaaaa
aacbbbbbbbbbbbbcaaaaaaaaaaaaaaaaaaaaaaaa
aaaaaaaaaaaaaaaaaaaaaaaaaaaaaacaaaaaaaa
aaaaaaaaaaaaaaaacaaacbbbbbbcbbbbbbbbcnaa
aaaaaaaaaaaaaaaaaaaaaaaaaaaaaaaac
```

which prints "Hello, world!" by setting ASCII output mode, then incrementing, decrementing, and starting from 0 to get the accumulator to hold the necessary ASCII codes for each letter. Note that the accumulator isn't reset for each character, but rather uses an offset from the last character's code. It's as easy as ABC.

The final example program, *phone.abc*, prints a randomly generated US-style telephone number:

```
ac                      COUNTRY CODE
naaaaaaaaaaradc         THREE DIGIT AREA CODE
naaaaaaaaaaarc
naaaaaaaaaaarc
naaaaaaaaaaaradc        THREE DIGIT EXCHANGE
naaaaaaaaaaarc
naaaaaaaaaaarc
naaaaaaaaaaaradc        FOUR DIGIT SUBSCRIBER
```

```
naaaaaaaaaaarc        NUMBER
naaaaaaaaaaarc
naaaaaaaaaaarc
```

The clever trick in this program is to add d to make the accumulator negative before printing it, thereby adding the dash between the parts of the number: 1-883-386-3219.

With that, ABC and its examples are finished. As mentioned, ABC begs to be more. Spend a lot of time with esolangs and you'll eventually get the itch to work on your own, and see how to take what exists and modify and enhance it. If you have that itch, scratch it; creativity is asking you to dance.

Let's have some fun rebuilding ABC. We'll maintain compatibility with what it is now, but we can add more.

ABC2

After much deliberation and several focus groups, the name we've selected for ABC's successor is ABC2. There is precedent: Modula became Modula-2 (and Modula-3), Oberon became Oberon-2, and so on. What should be done to ABC to make it ABC2? Existing ABC programs should run without modification, meaning that ABC2 is backward compatible. Of course, most anything could be done, but in the next section, we'll describe what we did and then follow with the updated Python implementation.

The Extensions

Extending ABC is fun. Here's what turned ABC into ABC2:

- An interactive mode if no program is supplied at the command line
- A second accumulator, B, and a command to toggle between A and B (^)
- A stack with arithmetic commands
- A command to exchange the top stack value and the active accumulator (x) as well as push (!) and pop (@) the stack
- A primitive conditional command (?) with <, >, and = commands
- A command to halt a program (q)
- A command to get a character from the user (k)
- A branch command (g)
- A command to toggle adding newline to output (e)

We'll discuss these changes and their effect on what ABC was and became in the final section of this chapter. For now, let's turn our attention to the implementation.

An ABC2 Implementation

ABC2 is in the file *ABC2.py*. It isn't as compact as *ABC.py*, but follows standard Python conventions. The structure of the interpreter remains the same: process each character in prog as a command until all have been processed. Some modification is necessary to allow a purely interactive mode. We'll present the code in pieces, starting with Listing 7-2, which shows the code to parse the command line:

```
if (len(sys.argv)==2):
    interactive = False
    t = open(sys.argv[1]).read()
    tokens = [
        "a","b","c","d","r","n","$","l",";",
        "e",">","<","g","+","-","*","/","x",
        "q","%","=","?","!","@","k","^",
    ]
    prog = ""
    for c in t:
        if (c in tokens):
            prog += c
else:
    interactive = True
```

Listing 7-2: Parsing program text in ABC2

The if loads and parses a program, keeping only actual command characters, or sets the interactive flag.

Next comes the default state and the modified main loop (Listing 7-3).

```
A = [0,0]
I = mode = cr = k = 0
stack = []
ops = ["+","-","*","/","%","<",">","="]
while (True):
    if (interactive):
        prog = input(": ")
        k = 0
    while (k < len(prog)):
        t = prog[k]
        # ... execute command in t ...
        k += 1
    if (not interactive):
        print()
        quit()
```

Listing 7-3: The ABC2 state and main loop

The single accumulator is now a pair of accumulators, both initially zero (A). The value of I toggles between them. Output defaults to numbers (mode=0) and no newline (cr=0). The stack is a standard Python list. We'll use the seldom seen pop method. All stack operations are in ops.

Next, two loops begin. The outer while loop runs forever. If interactive, prog is set to whatever sequence of commands the user enters. Note that the state is not reset, so whatever state is active when the entered commands are complete is still present for the next set. The second while loop is the same as in ABC proper: get the character of the command and evaluate it. When the program ends, if not in interactive mode, exit.

In the actual implementation, the second while loop contains a rather lengthy compound if statement to execute the command (Listing 7-4):

```
if (t == "a"):
    A[I] += 1
elif (t == "b"):
    A[I] -= 1
elif (t == "c"):
    if (mode):
        print("%s" % chr(A[I]), end="", flush=True)
    else:
        print("%d" % A[I], end="", flush=True)
    if (cr):
        print()
elif (t == "d"):
    A[I] = -A[I]
elif (t == "r"):
    A[I] = int(random.random()*A[I])
elif (t == "n"):
    A[I] = 0
--snip--
```

Listing 7-4: Executing ABC2 commands

A conceptually more elegant implementation would make ABC2 a class and use a dictionary of methods associated with each command in a small loop. Readers are invited to build such an implementation and share it. However, for pedagogical purposes, building on the existing ABC if statement approach seems easier to follow, even if it's less creative.

ABC2 is backward compatible with ABC, so we'll only describe the extensions. All previous commands operate as before, with A replaced by A[I] to use the active accumulator. Most of the extended commands require no more than one or two lines of code (see Table 7-1).

Table 7-1: Python Code for the Extended ABC2 Commands

Command	Implementation
^	`I ^= 1`
k	`A[I] = ord(getch())`
q	`quit()`
e	`cr ^= 1`
!	`stack.append(A[I])`
@	`A[I].stack.pop()`
g	`k = k + stack.pop() - 1`
?	`if (not stack.pop()):` `    k += 1`

x	`v = stack.pop()`
	`stack.append(A[I])`
	`A[I] = v`

stack ops	`if (t == "="):`
	`    t = "=="`
	`v=eval("%d %s %d" % (stack[-2],t,stack[-1]))`
	`if (type(v) is bool):`
	`    v = 1 if (v) else 0`
	`stack.pop(); stack.pop()`
	`stack.append(int(v))`

There is no need to walk through each of the little code snippets in Table 7-1, as most are self-explanatory. Note that sanity checks for things like popping the stack are not in Table 7-1; however, they are in *ABC2.py*, so please read through the full source code.

There is one piece of code in Table 7-1 we should discuss. The k command calls a function, getch, which returns a keypress without waiting for the user to press ENTER. This is not a standard Python function. The top portion of *ABC2.py* implements getch for Linux, macOS, and Windows.

Both the $ and ^ commands make use of an operator that might be unfamiliar to some: ^ (exclusive-OR or XOR). Exclusive-OR is a logical operation with the truth table

A	B	A^B
0	0	0
0	1	1
1	0	1
1	1	0

which states that the output of XOR is 1 when either of the inputs, but not both, is 1. This behavior makes toggling straightforward because `0^1 = 1` and `1^1 = 0`, meaning XORing a 0 or 1 with 1 results in 1 or 0, thereby flipping its state. As with other Python operators, `I ^= 1` is shorthand for `I = I^1`.

Our implementation is complete. Now, let's see what ABC2 can do.

ABC2 in Action

After surviving Forth, ABC2 will seem straightforward. Let's begin with the simplest of examples: adding two numbers. This is something ABC cannot do easily: you have to count up to the first value with as and then use more as to add a positive number before printing the result. ABC2 makes this a little easier. Consider *add.abc2*.

```
ADD TWO NUMBERS AND DISPLAY THE RESULT
e               NEWLINE MODE
aaaaaaaaaa!     10 TO STACK
bbb!            7 TO STACK
+@c             ADD STACK, PULL TO A AND PRINT
```

The comments clarify the actions, but the gist is to set newline mode to print one number per line of output, count up to 10, and push the accumulator on the stack. As the accumulator is already at 10, and pushing to the stack does not alter it, we count down to 7 and push that to the stack.

The last line calls + to put 10 + 7 = 17 on the stack before popping it off the stack to the accumulator to print with c. Note that only values in the accumulators, A and B, can be printed. There is no "print the top stack" item as in Forth. To run *add.abc2*, use

```
> python3 ABC2.py add.abc2
```

Well, that was easy enough. Let's try something similar using interactive mode. Launch ABC2 (**python3 ABC2.py**), but don't supply a filename. Then, enter the sequence of statements in Listing 7-5.

```
: aaaaa;
{5:0: (5,'')(0,'')} <0>:
: !;
{1:0: (5,'')(0,'')} <1>: 5
: !;*;
{1:0: (5,'')(0,'')} <2>: 5 5
{3:0: (5,'')(0,'')} <1>: 25
: @ec;
25
{3:0: (25,'')(0,'')} <0>:
: q
```

Listing 7-5: An interactive ABC2 session

Listing 7-5 might look like random noise at first, but there's a method to the madness. Let's walk through it. ABC2's interactive prompt is a colon (:). The first line shows five as followed by a semicolon (;). We know a; it adds 1 to the accumulator, so the accumulator now holds the number 5. The ; is the "debug" command from ABC. That's what produces the second line, {5:0: (5,'')(0,'')}.

There are four parts to the debug line. The first part shows the current program counter, which is the instruction number followed by a colon and a 0 or 1. In this case, the program counter is 5, as the ; is the sixth instruction entered (always count from 0). The next bit, 0:, tells us A is the current accumulator, A[0] in *ABC2.py*.

Next come two sets of parentheses. These are the current numeric value and value as a character for the two accumulators, A and B. In this case, A is 5, and B is its default of 0. Characters are shown if the accumulator is in [32, 127], which excludes 5 and 0, so no characters are shown.

After the closing brace comes the stack. The number of items on the stack comes first. In this case it's <0>, as the stack is empty. Any items on the stack follow.

The next set of commands entered, !;, store A on the stack and print the debug information again. This time we see <1>: 5 telling us that there is one item on the stack, a 5.

The following commands push A on the stack a second time, call debug, multiply the top two stack items, and call debug again, leaving 25 on the stack. Lastly, @ec; pops the stack, sets A to 25, moves to newline mode, and prints A. The q command exits ABC2. If you venture to try your hand at ABC2 code, and I strongly suggest you do, you'll find the interactive mode useful during program development.

Let's walk through three more ABC2 examples. Each example explores an additional capability of ABC2, culminating in a final program that serves as a tribute to an underappreciated early computing pioneer.

HELLO WORLD!

The Hello World Collection website lists versions of "Hello, world!" in more than 600 different programming languages (*http://helloworldcollection.de/*). It's become almost a moral obligation for every language capable of printing "Hello, world!" to do so at some point. Therefore, we'll be good citizens and do our duty.

The file *hello.abc2* contains the obligatory, and slightly grammatically incorrect, ABC2 version of "Hello, world!" Running *hello.abc2* produces

```
HELLO WORLD!
```

The ABC version incremented and decremented the accumulator to arrive at the necessary ASCII code for each character. ABC2 has a stack, which, as we learned in Chapter 4, is a LIFO data structure; the last thing in is the first thing out. Let's use the stack to store the characters we want to output, pushing them in reverse order so they print correctly when popped off the stack. Moreover, the stack supports arithmetic, so we don't need to count up to the values we want. We can take shortcuts to reach the necessary ASCII codes more quickly.

Listing 7-6 gives us the code.

```
HELLO WORLD
aaa!aaaaaaaa!*@!!!+@aa!
@!aaaaaaaa!@!aaaaaa!
@!bbb!@!aaaaaaaa!
naaaa!aaaa!*@!!!+
@aaaaaaaaaaaaaaa!
@!bbb!!bbbbbbb!aaa!
$@c@c@c@c@c@c@c@c@c@ce@c
```

Listing 7-6: "Hello, world!" in ABC2

The first line is, of course, the comment. Let's parse the first line after the comment aaa!aaaaaaaa!*@!!!+@aa!:

aaa!	3
aaaaaaaa!	3 11
*	33
@!!!	33 33 33
+	33 66
@aa!	33 68

Each line shows the ABC2 commands on the left and the state of the stack afterward. Look at the last line. The stack contains 33 and 68, the ASCII codes for ! and D, respectively, which are the final two characters to output. The program builds the output string on the stack in reverse order.

The remainder over HELLO WORLD! is similarly placed on the stack. When the second to last line of Listing 7-6 is complete, the stack contains

```
33 68 76 82 79 87 32 79 76 76 69 72
```

which the final line of Listing 7-6 outputs by enabling character mode ($) and repeatedly popping the stack and printing (@c). Before the final character is output, e turns on newline mode.

Now, let's do some math with ABC2.

A Slice of Pi

I'm writing this section on March 14th, which, using American-style dates, is 3/14—Pi Day. Therefore, in honor of everyone's favorite mathematical constant, our next example uses ABC2 to estimate the value of $\pi = 3.14159\ldots$ using nothing more than random integers.

The area of a circle is $A_{circle} = \pi r^2$, where r is the radius, the distance from the center to the edge. If we set $r = 1$, the area of the resulting circle is $A_{circle} = \pi(1)^2 = \pi$. A circle of radius 1 has a diameter of 2. If this circle is centered at the origin, the diameter goes from −1 to +1. Now imagine a square with a side length of 2 set over the circle. The square is *circumscribed* over the circle (see Figure 7-1).

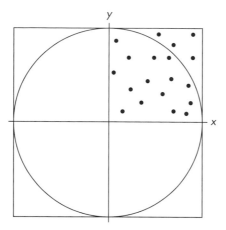

Figure 7-1: A square circumscribed over a circle of radius 1

We'll get to the dots in Figure 7-1 momentarily. For now, just consider the relationship between the square and the circle. If the square's side is 2, its area is $A_{\text{square}} = s^2 = (2)^2 = 4$.

The ratio between the areas of the circle and the square is $A_{\text{circle}}/A_{\text{square}} = \pi/4$. This ratio remains even if we only consider the first quadrant, that is, one quarter of the shapes (where the dots are in Figure 7-1). The area of the circle in quadrant one is one quarter of π, that is, $\pi/4$, and the area of the square in quadrant one is $4/4 = 1$, meaning the ratio between the two is $\pi/4/1 = \pi/4$.

Okay, so what? Well, if we had an estimate of the area of the circle and the square in quadrant one, we'd be able to divide the two and expect that it matches $\pi/4$. Here's where the dots in Figure 7-1 come into the picture. They represent random points in the range $[0, 1)$ in both x and y. What if we generate many of these random points? In a sense, the points will slowly fill in the area of both the circle and the square. If we count how many land within the circle and divide by those that land within the square, which is all of them because we are using $[0, 1)$, we'll have an estimate of the ratio between the circle and the square, which, as we just saw, is $\pi/4$. Therefore, if multiplied by 4, this ratio should give us an estimate of π, which is exactly what we want.

Great! Let's select random values in the range $[0, 1)$ and start counting how many land within the circle. How do we know if the point is within the circle? That's straightforward. It's really an application of the Pythagorean theorem: $c^2 = a^2 + b^2$, where a is x and b is y. The circle is centered at the origin and has a radius of 1. If $x^2 + y^2$—the distance from the origin to the randomly selected point—is less than the radius squared, then the point is within the circle. For the circle, $r^2 = 1$, so the point is within the circle if its distance from the origin is less than 1.

We need two counters. The first counts every randomly generated point because $[0, 1)$ covers the entire area of the square in quadrant one. This means that every point lands within the square so no test is needed. We'll call this counter S. The second counter is for all the points that land within the circle, (x, y), where $x^2 + y^2 < 1$. We'll call this counter C.

Here's the algorithm we want to code:

```
S = C = 0
Loop forever:
    x = [0,1)
    y = [0,1)
    S = S + 1
    if (x*x + y*y < 1):
        C = C + 1
    print 4*C/S
```

On every pass through the loop, the code selects a new (x, y) point, increments S, and if the point is within the circle, increments C. The ratio, then, will approach $\pi/4$, which when multiplied by 4 is an estimate for π.

Of course, you've likely already noticed the problem. ABC2 works with integers only. The algorithm expects floating-point numbers. Are we stymied? No, we're not. We want a ratio of two areas, one for the circle and one for the square. We aren't really restricted to the range $[0, 1]$. What if we use integers and select points in the range $[0, 1, 000, 000, 000)$? ABC2 has no difficulty working with integers in that range. If we scale the x and y by one billion, then the limit we check scales by the square of that. So instead of checking if $x^2 + y^2 < 1$, we check if $x^2 + y^2 < 10^{18}$, one billion squared. Again, ABC2, thanks to our Python implementation, has no difficulty with an integer like 10^{18}.

Therefore, our algorithm remains the same, and only the limits on the random numbers and the distance from the origin change. However, our output must change as well. We won't calculate 4*C/S, but instead display C/S *as a fraction*. That is, literally as C followed by a / and then S. At any point, we can take an output value, dump it in a calculator to get the actual floating-point ratio, and multiply by 4 to get the current estimate of π.

The code we need is in Listing 7-7 and *pi.abc2*.

!	PUT A ON STACK
naaaaaaaaaa!!*@!!*@!!*naaaaaaaaaa!*@	A IS 1 BILLION
r!!*	X SQUARED
naaaaaaaaaa!!*@!!*@!!*naaaaaaaaaa!*@	A IS 1 BILLION
r!!*	Y SQUARED
+	XX PLUS YY
naaaaaaaaaa!!*@!!*@!!*naaaaaaaaaa!*@!!*	10 TO THE 18TH
<+	INC C IF LESS THAN
^a^	INC S
@!c	PRINT C
naaaaaaaaaa!!+@!!+@aaaaaaa$c$	PRINT SLASH
^ece^	PRINT S
@l	LOOP

Listing 7-7: Estimating π with random numbers

We'll use accumulator B to hold S and the stack to hold C. When the program starts, accumulators A and B are both zero. So we push A on the stack to initialize the counter.

We'll use r to select a random integer in $[0, 10^9)$, so we need to make A one billion. That's what the second line of Listing 7-7 does. First A is 10, then after squaring by pushing it on the stack twice, A is 100. Then 100 × 100 = 10,000 and 10,000 × 10,000 = 100,000,000 on the stack. A final multiplication by 10 sets A to one billion. That was the painful part. Selecting a random value and squaring it is r!!* to select the value, push it on the stack twice, then multiply. The stack now contains (C x*x --). The next two lines of Listing 7-7 repeat the previous two to get y^2 on the stack so + can add them together.

The stack now contains C followed by the square of the distance of the random point, (x, y), from the origin. We must increment C if this distance is less than 10^{18}, so we use an approach similar to setting A to one billion to get 10^{18} on the stack. The stack is now (C x*x+y*y 10**18 --).

The less-than command, <, performs the comparison and leaves 0 or 1 on the stack. This is particularly convenient. If the comparison is false, that is, the distance isn't less than 10^{18}, we get 0; otherwise, we get 1, so the stack is (C 0|1 --). Either way, adding this result to C works. If the comparison is true, the 1 is on the stack, which increments C for us. Otherwise, there's no harm in adding 0 to C. Because of this happy arrangement, the only branching necessary is the loop at the end of the program to generate the next point.

We've incremented C, if necessary, but we still need to increment S. As it's in accumulator B, incrementing is particularly easy: switch to accumulator B, increment with a, and then switch back to accumulator A with ^a^.

We're ready to display our current estimate for $\pi/4$. First, we print C and return it to the stack so it isn't lost (@!c). Then, we set A to 47, the ASCII code for a slash, and display it with c. Lastly, we switch to accumulator B, toggle newline mode with e, and print S, remembering to turn off newline mode and toggle back to accumulator A.

The first instruction is ! to store A on the stack, meaning store C. Just before we loop, we pull C off the stack with @ and then loop with l.

The program runs forever, generating ever better estimates of $\pi/4$. Let's see how well it does. For one run of the program, the first few iterations output are

---

```
 1/1,    2/2,    3/3,    4/4,    5/5,
 5/6,    6/7,    7/8,    8/9,    9/10,
10/11,  11/12,  11/13,  12/14,  13/15,
14/16,  15/17,  16/18,  17/19,  18/20,
19/21
```

---

with the last iteration giving an estimate of $\pi \approx 4(19)/21 = 3.6190476$. Not too good, but the program's just started. The output a second or two later was $\pi \approx 4(992)/1280 = 3.1$, so it's heading in the right direction. After about 15 seconds, the estimate was $\pi \approx 4(44893)/57153 = 3.1419523$, which is definitely in the ballpark.

How quickly does the output approach π? If we capture the program's output and plot the estimate of π as a function of the iteration number, we arrive at Figure 7-2, which shows the convergence as iterations proceed. After some 100,000 iterations, the estimate was 3.1416803, which is accurate to nearly four decimals.

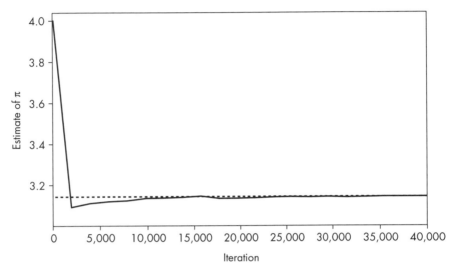

Figure 7-2: The estimate of π as a function of iteration number

Figure 7-2 shows that many iterations are necessary to get close to π—around 25,000 or so. This isn't too surprising, as we're trying to replace an actual area with a collection of random points. You might feel a little unsettled as a point has no area, so how can a collection of them have an area? I think of it this way: imagine that infinite space is actually discrete. In that sense, an area is a collection of (extremely) tiny cells (think pixels) where the random points fill in an ever-increasing set of cells. The difference here is that a cell *does* have an area, even if a tiny one, and all of the cells together tile the circle and square. From that point of view, we randomly fill cell after cell to arrive at a better and better estimate of the actual circle and square areas. We would expect over time to get a better and better estimate of $\pi/4$, and ultimately π.

I hope you enjoyed this little Pi Day example. It's nice that ABC2, for all its simplicity, can do something like this and that the logical operators for ABC2 happened to give exactly the right value in the right place (that is, on the stack above C) so no painful looping construct was necessary.

Now, let's develop our version of an early computing machine, and learn a bit about its remarkable, though largely unknown, inventor.

The Electromechanical Arithmometer

You've likely never heard of Leonardo Torres y Quevedo (sometimes written as Leonardo Torres Quevedo). Before I started writing my first book, I had never heard of him, either. If you have heard of him, fantastic.

Torres Quevedo was a Spanish inventor born in the mid-19th century. His many accomplishments include cable cars, dirigibles, an early form of remote control, a working chess-playing automaton, and, of most interest to us, the electromechanical arithmometer. An arithmometer is a 19th-century mechanical calculator. Torres Quevedo's version, presented in Paris in 1920 (see Figure 7-3), was electronic and mechanical.

Figure 7-3: The electromechanical arithmometer circa 1920. Image used with the kind permission of Francisco A. González Redondo, Universidad Complutense, Madrid.

On the right of Figure 7-3 is a typewriter. This was the keyboard used by the operator. The operator put paper in the typewriter and proceeded to type an expression such as 123 x 321 = to which the machine would respond by typing 39483 on the same line before advancing the paper to the next line. Recall that this was 1920, well before the first true electronic computers and before the pioneering work of Konrad Zuse. Torres Quevedo showed the electromechanical arithmometer and then put it aside. It was never marketed.

We'll get back to Figure 7-3 in a little bit, but, as this is a book on programming languages, it seems fitting to point out that not only did Torres Quevedo build such an impressive machine, he also, even earlier, worked through what it means to implement floating-point arithmetic in a machine-friendly way. In his 1914 work "Essays on Automatics," he writes that numbers should be stored as $n \times 10^m$, which is how we store floating-point numbers now: $n \times 2^m$. A problem with floating-point is that numbers in scientific notation are not unique: $3.1415 \times 10^0 = 0.31415 \times 10^1 = 31.415 \times 10^{-1}$. Torres Quevedo understood this, so he proposed the following rules to store numbers in a consistent way for a machine to process:

1. *n* will always be the same number of digits (six, for example).

2. The first digit of *n* will be in the order of tenths, the second in hundredths, and so on.

3. One will write each quantity in the form: *n;m*.

Modern computers store floating-point numbers with a fixed size *n*; for example, 52 bits for a C `double` (really 53 bits; a leading 1 is implied as the integer part of the significand, $1.b_{51}b_{50} \ldots b_0$). It's clear that Torres Quevedo was thinking in base-10, but the idea of fixing the significand size was key. Zuse, mentioned above, was likely the first to implement floating-point numbers in computers in base-2, much as we do now—see the IEEE 754 standard.

One last observation on Torres Quevedo's floating-point format before we get back to the electromechanical arithmometer. Notice that he suggests, again in 1914, that floating-point numbers be written as *n;m*. So using his rules, he would write π as 0.314159;1, meaning $0.314159 \times 10^1 = 3.14159$. This is very close to how floating-point numbers are entered today: 0.314159e1. The only difference is using a semicolon (;) for *e*.

Okay, this is all very interesting, but what does it have to do with ABC2? One feature of ABC2 we have yet to explore is the k command, the command that reads a character from the keyboard and places its character code in the current accumulator. Let's use this command to mimic Torres Quevedo's arithmometer. We'll restrict ourselves to multiplication only.

The code we'll work with is in *multiply.abc2*. This is the most complex ABC2 program we'll consider. Not only does it use k for input, it also uses ?, the only conditional command available in ABC2.

Let's begin with an outline of what we want to accomplish. Leonardo's arithmometer let the user type a number, an operation, and a second number. We're fixing the operation, multiplication, so what we need from the user are two numbers—specifically, two three-digit numbers—though the leading digits might be zero. The k instruction gets one character from the keyboard, so how will we turn characters into numbers?

The first thing to notice is that the ASCII code for zero is 48. The ASCII codes for the digits follow in order, meaning that 49 is one, 50 is two, and so on. Therefore, if the user presses 3, the accumulator will contain 51. Subtracting 48 from 51 leaves 3. To convert the ASCII code for a digit into the digit itself we would subtract 48. We now know how to get single digits. But what about a three-digit number?

We have a three-digit number, 451. In grade school, you likely learned how to write numbers in expanded form as

$$451 = 400 + 50 + 1$$

but there's another way to expand a number:

$$451 = (((4 \times 10) + 5) \times 10) + 1$$
$$= ((40 + 5) \times 10) + 1$$
$$= (45 \times 10) + 1$$
$$= 450 + 1$$
$$= 451$$

Expanding a number this way points us toward an algorithm for entering three digits and converting them to a three-digit number:

1. Get the first digit, multiply by 10, and store it on the stack.

2. Get the second digit and add it to the number on the stack.

3. Multiply the number on the stack by 10.

4. Get the third digit and add it to the number on the stack.

When these steps are complete, the stack contains the three-digit number the user entered character by character. Let's follow the steps and see if they work.

```
User enters 4,  stack: 4
Multiply by 10, stack: 40
User enters 5,  stack: 40 5
Add,            stack: 45
Multiply by 10, stack: 450
User enters 1,  stack: 450 1
Add,            stack: 451
```

The steps work. The user entered 4, 5, and 1, and the stack holds the number 451. When implemented in ABC2, there is one additional step: after the user enters the digit, we must subtract 48 to convert the character code to the digit value.

We know how to get a number from the user. To implement the "arithmometer," we must get two numbers from the user, each on the stack, and multiply.

Listing 7-8 shows all of *multiply.abc2*.

```
ENTER TWO THREE DIGIT NUMBERS AND MULTIPLY THEM
QUIT IF THE FIRST CHARACTER OF THE FIRST NUMBER IS ESC

^naaaaa!aaaaa!*@bb  B IS 48
^k!!                FIRST KEYPRESS
naaa!aaaaaa!*=?q    QUIT IF ESC PRESSED
@!$c$^!^-           FIRST DIGIT
naa!aaa!**          TIMES TEN
k$c$!^!^-+          SECOND DIGIT
naa!aaa!**          TIMES TEN
k$c$!^!^-+          THIRD DIGIT
```

```
naaaa!aaaa!*@$c          SPACE
aaaaaaaaaac              TIMES
bbbbbbbbbbc$             SPACE
k$c$!^!^-                FIRST DIGIT
naa!aaa!**               TIMES TEN
k$c$!^!^-+               SECOND DIGIT
naa!aaa!**               TIMES TEN
k$c$!^!^-+               THIRD DIGIT
naaaa!aaaa!*@$c          SPACE
!!+@bbbc                 EQUALS
naaaa!aaaa!*@c$          SPACE
*@ecel                   PRODUCT AND LOOP
```

Listing 7-8: Multiplying pairs of numbers

The first line has the comment B IS 48. This line switches to accumulator B (^) and makes sure it is 0, which is necessary because we loop. It then increments to 5, pushes it on the stack, and increments five more times to push 10 on the stack. Multiplying leaves 50 on the stack, which is popped off the stack to accumulator B (@) and finally decremented twice to leave B equal to 48. This is the constant we need to subtract from the digit ASCII codes the user will enter. For this program, we use B as a constant. When needed, we switch to accumulator B, push its value on the stack, and then immediately switch back to accumulator A.

The next line is FIRST KEYPRESS, ^k!!. The ^ statement toggles back to accumulator A. We read a character from the keyboard (k) and push it on the stack twice with !!. We push it twice because program will loop to ask the user for pairs of numbers repeatedly. For the first digit, if the user presses ESC (ASCII 27), we want to exit the program instead. We push the first digit twice, once to use in calculating the number as we did above, and a second time to compare the key to ESC.

The QUIT IF ESC PRESSED line checks if the top stack value is 27. First, we set A to 27 with naaa!aaaaaa!*. We increment A to 3 and push it onto the stack, and then increment six more times to 9 and push it onto the stack and multiply the two numbers to leave 27 on the stack with the ASCII code of the character the user entered immediately below it. Executing = checks if the top two stack items are equal. While ? pops the stack, if the top stack value is true (not 0), the program executes the command immediately after ?. Otherwise, it skips the next command and execution continues with the following command. In this case, the next command is q, quit, so if the key the user pressed was ESC, the = left true on the stack for ? to pick up and, because it's true, execute q to end the program.

We've checked whether the first key is ESC, but we have not yet displayed the key nor subtracted 48 to get its digit value. It's currently on the stack, so we load it back into accumulator A with @!: @ to pull it from the stack into accumulator A and ! to push it back to the stack because we need it there as well. Next, c prints the character by switching to character mode, printing with c, and switching back to number mode.

To subtract 48, we use ^!^-. This pattern repeats throughout the program every time we need to subtract 48. It switches to accumulator B, pushes B on the stack, switches back to accumulator A, and subtracts. The stack now contains the digit value, which must be multiplied by 10 via naa!aaa!**, which puts 2 and then 5 on the stack, multiplies them to get 10, and finally multiplies the digit value by 10. This pattern also repeats whenever a digit value must be multiplied by 10.

The first digit is a special case because we need to check for ESC. The remaining five digits are essentially the same: kc!^!^-+ to get the digit, display it, push it, push 48, subtract, and then add the digit value to the value already on the stack. If necessary, this pattern is followed by the multiply-by-10 pattern.

The other lines in Listing 7-8 handle necessary text output. The final line is *@ecel. The stack now contains the two numbers the user entered, so * multiplies them and @ pulls the result into accumulator A for display with ec, where e turns on newline mode. To go back and get another pair of numbers, we first turn off newline mode and then loop l.

The description above is necessarily dense. Do review the code to see what it does and try some of the patterns in interactive mode as well. Let's see what the output of *multiply.abc2* looks like; however, naturally, in print you won't see the flow.

```
123 * 321 = 39483
451 * 359 = 161909
999 * 999 = 998001
002 * 003 = 6
```

Although not as impressive as Torres Quevedo's electromechanical arithmometer, we might argue there's at least some utility to a little program like this. As an exercise, extend *multiply.abc2* to accept four-digit numbers. Note that there is no check to ensure that the key pressed is actually a valid digit. The program is happy with any keypress; however, the results will not be meaningful in that case.

Let's bid Torres Quevedo a fond farewell and conclude our ABC2 adventure with a short discussion.

Discussion

This chapter began with the esolang wiki description of ABC and our Python implementation. It is abundantly clear that as a programming language, ABC isn't even remotely Turing complete. Nor was it meant to be; it was just a cute idea for something capable of simple tasks. We then extended ABC to create ABC2. Is ABC2 Turing complete? No, it isn't. There are only two memory locations and a stack that cannot be accessed cell-by-cell like an array.

What might make ABC2 Turing complete? One might imagine ABC3, with the stack and, instead of two accumulators, an "infinite" set of accumulators accessible by index. In other words, an array. That scenario would use the stack much like the arithmetic logic unit of a CPU and the accumulators as memory. I suspect such a language might be Turing complete. I might make it as it wouldn't be difficult. Better still, you make it, and if you feel like sharing, send it to me and I'll put it on the book's GitHub site.

ABC2's stack is limited because there are no intrinsic commands to manipulate it like DUP, SWAP, ROT, and OVER in Forth. Or is that really the case?

ABC2 does not have stack manipulation commands, but we can create patterns that function like stack words, provided we don't need to preserve the contents of the accumulators.

For example, these ABC2 patterns act like the given Forth word:

@!!	DUP
@x!	SWAP
@	DROP
@^@x!^x!	ROT
^@^@!^!^!	OVER

Run ABC2 in interactive mode and give them a try. Use ; to show the stack.

The ABC2 examples in this chapter showed repeating patterns of code. This happens in all languages—think of the design patterns often used in software development. The *multiply.abc2* example, in particular, used several repeating patterns of code to push a constant on the stack, get a digit from the user, and multiply by 10. As each command in ABC2 is itself a single character, the patterns become words. Space is not an ABC2 command, meaning we could write code with the patterns as words, words that, with time, "experienced" ABC2 coders (keep your eye on the Help Wanted ads) would learn to recognize.

For example, one pattern in *multiply.abc2* is kc!^!^-+, which gets a character and adds its digit value to the number already on the stack. This pattern (a sentence?) could be written as k c ! ^!^ - + to separate the commands into words with meaning. Another pattern stored a constant in accumulator B. In one instance, the constant was −7 to use with g for branching in a loop. The other was 48, which is the number we needed to subtract from the ASCII character code for a digit. Using accumulator B as a constant argues in favor of a language like ABC3, where we'd have as many variables as we need.

In the end, ABC and ABC2 are toy languages, as esolangs often are. They are fun to think about, fun to implement, and fun to experiment with. They also help us appreciate the careful thought that went into designing the programming languages we use daily.

Summary

This chapter introduced an exceedingly simple esolang called ABC. We took its language description, all that implementors generally have to work with, and built a Python implementation. We quickly understood the language's limitations and extended it to make ABC2, a language with more capabilities that maintained backward compatibility with the original ABC.

We developed a few examples in ABC2 and had some fun with them. We learned how to estimate the value of π by using random numbers. We then paid tribute to an early computer pioneer, Leonardo Torres y Quevedo, with a program mimicking his electromechanical arithmometer from 1920. During that exercise, we learned that ABC2 lends itself to coding patterns we might call words (with apologies to Forth), and that ABC2 programs could be written as a series of words, that is, sentences.

ABC and ABC2 were perfect introductions to our esolang exploration. Let's move on now to FRACTRAN, perhaps the most intellectually interesting esolang we'll encounter.

8

FRACTRAN

John Conway (1937–2020) was a British
mathematician, most famous to the general public for his Game of Life (see *https://
playgameoflife.com/*), but equally famous to his
fellow mathematicians for his many contributions to a
wide variety of mathematical disciplines. In this chapter, we'll examine another of Conway's contributions,
one that isn't as well known as his Game of Life, but
is perfect for our purposes: FRACTRAN. We'll start
with the specification of FRACTRAN, build it, and,
lastly, use it to implement basic programs for addition,
subtraction, and multiplication, among other tasks.
After that, we'll end with a discussion, like always.

Be warned that there's math ahead, at the level of fractions, prime numbers, and big integers. FRACTRAN is the most mathematical esolang we'll
encounter. If you wish, skip this chapter and move on to the remaining esolangs. However, if you do, please don't forget to come back. FRACTRAN
is worth the struggle.

The FRACTRAN Specification

FRACTRAN's specification is straightforward. In fact, it's almost as straight-forward as ABC's. Here's the full specification for FRACTRAN:

```
FRACTRAN

Input:
    A sequence of fractions
    An integer

Operation:
    1. Multiply the integer by the fractions in turn:
    2.   If the product is an integer, use that as the new integer
         and repeat from Step 1.
    3.   If the product is not an integer, move to the following fraction.
    4. If all fractions are exhausted, stop.

Output:
    The final integer
    Optionally: all intermediate integers, if desired

Assumption:
    The implementation must use arbitrary precision fractions.
```

FRACTRAN programs are a sequence of integers and nothing more. An initial integer is tested against each fraction in the program, in order. If the product of the integer and the fraction is itself an integer, that product becomes the new integer and the program loops from the beginning. If the program ever reaches the state where no product results in a new integer, the program ends. That's it.

As the specification is simple, so are the implementations. Let's write two FRACTRAN interpreters because it's fun and it will expose us to another programming language, one that is well suited to this particular task.

A Tale of Two Implementations

The specification above includes the phrase *arbitrary precision*. A FRACTRAN implementation must use fractions where the numerator and denominator are integers of any size, even if that size has thousands of digits.

Most programming languages don't natively support arbitrary-precision integers, let alone fractions (rationals). However, Scheme does. Scheme is a dialect of Lisp, which we first mentioned in Chapter 1. Not only does Scheme support arbitrary-precision integers, it also natively supports rationals. Therefore, Scheme is ideally suited to implementing FRACTRAN.

We've used Python fairly often throughout the book. Python also supports arbitrary-precision integers natively and has a rational arithmetic library module. So we'll implement FRACTRAN in Python as well. The juxtaposition between the two implementations will be illustrative, and allow us to test each against the other to ensure our implementations are correct.

A Scheme Implementation

The version of Scheme we'll use is called Racket (*https://racket-lang.org/*). It's easy to install on Linux:

```
> sudo apt-get install racket
```

See the Racket website to install macOS and Windows versions. Once installed, run Racket by entering **racket** at the command line:

```
Welcome to Racket v6.11.
>
```

Your version should be at least 6.11 or greater. Like Python and Forth, Racket enters an interactive mode if no file is given to it. For now, just quit by entering **(exit)**; note that the parentheses are required.

We certainly don't have the space here to give even a short tutorial on Scheme (Racket). The genuinely motivated will find all they need on the Racket website. Instead, we'll walk through our implementation. Listing 8-1 shows the code.

```
(define argv (current-command-line-arguments))
(define prog (file->list (vector-ref argv 0)))
(define num (string->number (vector-ref argv 1)))
(define trace (string->number (vector-ref argv 2)))

❶ (define (FRACTRAN)
  ❷ (do ((i 0 (+ i 1))) (#f)
    ❸ (when (= i (length prog))
          (when (= trace 0) (display num)(newline))
          (exit))
    ❹ (let ((n (* num (list-ref prog i))))
        ❺ (when (exact-integer? n)
              (set! num n)
              (set! i -1)
              (when (= trace 1) (display num)(newline))) ) ))
❻ (FRACTRAN)
```

Listing 8-1: FRACTRAN in Racket

The Racket implementation of FRACTRAN is compact. The first four lines do nothing more than parse the command line. In Racket, define assigns a value. We use argv to avoid duplicating the call to current-command-line -arguments. Racket returns the command line arguments as a vector, so (vector -ref argv 0) is equivalent to argv[0] in other languages. Racket is a prefix language, meaning that function names come first, followed by the arguments with parentheses around everything. We'll see below how FRACTRAN code is stored. We chose a format friendly to Racket so we can add comments easily. The file->list function reads the code and returns a list of the fractions. The next argument is the starting integer, which Racket puts in num. The last argument, trace, is a 0 or 1 flag indicating whether to output only the final integer or all intermediate integers. We'll learn what that means in a bit.

All of FRACTRAN is a single function that takes no arguments ❶. It consists of a do loop, which is similar to a for loop in other languages, but is configured to run forever ❷. The loop counter is i, which we use to get the ith fraction from prog.

The body of the do loop has two main parts: a when function ❸ and a let function ❹. A when function checks whether a given condition is true, and if so, executes all the code in the body. This when checks to see if the loop counter matches the length of the program, that is, the number of fractions. If so, the program ends, outputting the final value of num if trace is 0.

The let function creates a local environment assigning (* num (list-ref prog i)) to n. What is (* num (list-ref prog i))? It's the current integer times the current fraction: num*prog[i]. The body of let is a single when ❺ function. The function exact-integer? is true when its argument, n, is an integer rather than a rational or a float. Recall that the fractions in prog are native Racket rational numbers. This is the condition we need to check. If true, we have a new integer, so the body of the when destructively sets num to the new value in n and modifies the loop counter by setting it to −1 so that the next iteration of the do begins again with 0. Additionally, if trace is 1, the new integer is output. The program starts by calling FRACTRAN ❻.

Now, let's implement FRACTRAN in Python.

A Python Implementation

The Racket version of FRACTRAN was straightforward, at least after learning to interpret Racket's prefix approach to everything. Our Python implementation is longer, but it's likely more familiar. Racket gave us arbitrary-precision integers, and Python gives us those, too. Racket also gave us rational arithmetic, which is something Python does not have out of the box, but does support via the fractions library module.

Our Python implementation mimics the Racket code in Listing 8-1. The code we'll use is shown in Listing 8-2.

```
❶ n = Fraction(int(sys.argv[2]))
❷ p = LoadProgram(sys.argv[1])
  m = int(sys.argv[3]) if (len(sys.argv) >= 4) else 0
  k = 0
❸ while (k < len(p)):
    ❹ v = n * p[k]
      if (v.denominator == 1):
          if (m):
              print(v)
          n = Fraction(v)
          k = -1
```

```
    k += 1
if (not m):
    print(n)
```

Listing 8-2: FRACTRAN in Python

Listing 8-2 shows the body of `main`. *FRACTRAN.py* uses the expected Python convention of running from `main` if not imported.

FRACTRAN in Python expects the same arguments as the Racket version: the name of the FRACTRAN program, the initial integer value, and whether to output every integer change. Unlike the Racket version, the final argument is optional and defaults to 0 if not present.

The code operates like the Racket version. The command line is parsed to set the initial integer as a rational ❶, followed by loading the FRACTRAN code via `LoadProgram` ❷. We won't show `LoadProgram` here, but it loads the file and returns the fractions as a list of `Fraction` objects. Do read through it.

The `while` loop runs until all fractions in `p` are exhausted ❸. The current integer (`n`) is multiplied by the current fraction (`p[k]`) ❹. If the result is an integer, meaning the denominator is 1, we have a new `n`. Thus, `n` is updated and printed if `m = 1`. Lastly, as in the Racket version, the loop counter is reset so the fractions are scanned from the beginning again (`k = -1`). When the loop ends, the final value of `n` is printed if it has not already been printed above.

We now have two implementations of FRACTRAN ready to go. Why two? To illustrate that different programming languages require different thought processes to arrive at the same endpoint. This is a book on programming languages, after all. Now, lets put them through their paces.

Using FRACTRAN

The simplest FRACTRAN program is the single fraction, 3/2. It's in the file *add.frac*. Let's run it. We won't understand the output just yet, but it will make sense eventually. Try the following:

```
> python3 FRACTRAN.py add.frac 72
243
> python3 FRACTRAN.py add.frac 3888
19683
> python3 FRACTRAN.py add.frac 2519424
43046721
> python3 FRACTRAN.py add.frac 4760622968832
617673396283947
```

To test the Racket version, create a shell script named *FRACTRAN* with the following line, which wraps the command line Racket expects:

```
racket -f FRACTRAN.scm $1 $2 $3
```

Lastly, make *FRACTRAN* executable by typing `chmod a+x FRACTRAN`. Let's test the Racket version using *add.frac*. The output should match the Python version just shown.

```
> ./FRACTRAN add.frac 72 0
243
> ./FRACTRAN add.frac 3888 0
19683
> ./FRACTRAN add.frac 2519424 0
43046721
> ./FRACTRAN add.frac 4760622968832 0
617673396283947
```

The output matches the Python version, so our FRACTRAN implementations are working; however, we don't yet understand what the output means. Let's remedy that situation.

Understanding FRACTRAN

FRACTRAN is perhaps the most elegant of all esolangs. It's subtle, brilliant, strangely beautiful, and difficult. In this section, we'll finally dive into the operation of FRACTRAN. We'll start with *add.frac*, the version included with the book's code. That version contains the following:

```
;   Add two integers
;
;   Input:  (2**a)(3**b)
;   Output: 3**(a+b)
;
3/2
```

It appears that *add.frac* adds two integers. Before learning how, we must make sense of the input and output comments. To do that, we must understand how FRACTRAN represents state.

FRACTRAN is a *register machine*, which is a hypothetical machine that manipulates an infinite set of registers. FRACTRAN uses Gödel numbering to represent its state, the value of the registers. So to understand FRACTRAN, we first must understand Gödel numbering.

Kurt Gödel was a German-Austrian-American mathematician most famous for his *incompleteness theorem*, by which he proved that in any system of axioms capable of describing mathematics with natural numbers, there are true statements that cannot be proved from the axioms. The incompleteness theorem sounded the death knell of early 20th-century attempts to put all of mathematics on rigorous footing.

As part of his incompleteness theorem, Gödel made use of *Gödel numbering*, which itself makes use of the fact that all integers can be expressed as the product of a unique set of prime numbers: *prime factorization*. For example, the prime factorization of 88 is $2^3 11^1$, whereas the prime factorization of 68,600 is $2^3 5^2 7^3$.

Gödel used his numbering scheme to represent the expressions and theorems of mathematics. FRACTRAN uses Gödel numbering to represent its state—the value of all registers—which must be positive or 0. For example, if the state is $88 = 2^3 11^1$, the v2 register is 3, the v11 register is 1, and all other registers are 0. It's customary to refer to the registers by their associated primes. Similarly, the state $68,600 = 2^3 5^2 7^3$ means v2 = 3, v5 = 2, and v7 = 3. As there are an infinite number of primes, there are an infinite number of FRACTRAN registers with all possible states representable by a single integer. This single integer is the integer multiplied by each fraction.

Let's review a bit before proceeding. We must follow the link between the integer FRACTRAN manipulates, prime factorization of a number, and state represented by registers holding specific values.

Let's start with registers holding values. At some point in a program, we may want register v17 to hold the value 12, that is, v17 = 12. Again, registers are identified by their prime, and 17 is a prime. In FRACTRAN, setting v17 to 12 means raising 17 to the 12th power: 17^{12}. Likewise, if we want v3 = 7, we use 3^7. So to set a FRACTRAN register to a value, we raise the corresponding prime to that power.

The state of a FRACTRAN program is the current value of all of its registers. This is because FRACTRAN can manipulate only register values. To continue the example above, if v3 and v17 are the only nonzero registers, then the entire state of the FRACTRAN program is the product of 3^7 and 17^{12}, which is $3^7 17^{12} = 1,274,194,832,821,487,307$. This number is the integer FRACTRAN implementations use to represent the state.

Conway's insight was that all positive integers can be written as the product of a series of primes in only one way, that is, prime factorization. Therefore, the large integer in the previous paragraph represents the state where v3 = 7 and v17 = 12 and all other registers are 0, and that is the *only* integer representing that state.

The fractions of a FRACTRAN program attempt to alter the state in two ways: by decrementing register values via canceling with the denominator and by incrementing register values via multiplying by the numerator. Only fractions where the denominator cancels completely "fire" are allowed to alter the program state.

We're now able to understand the input and output comments from *add.frac*. The expected input sets register v2 = *a* and v3 = *b*. When the program ends, register v3 = *a* + *b*. Therefore, if we want to add *a* + *b* = 3 + 2, the input given to FRACTRAN is

$$2^a 3^b = 2^3 3^2 = 8(9) = 72$$

which is the first test input above. If the input is $2^3 3^2$, then the output is, according to the comments in *add.frac*, $3^{a+b} = 3^{3+2} = 3^5 = 243$, which is the first test output.

Let's work through *add.frac* for the input $2^3 3^2 = 72$ to see each step leading to the output. First, let's run the code with trace on.

```
> ./FRACTRAN add.frac 72 1
108
162
243
```

Trace tells us the program looped three times, changing the state from $72 \to 108 \to 162 \to 243$. Stepping through by hand gives

$$\text{Input} \to 2^3 3^2 \left(\frac{3}{2} \right) = 2^2 3^3 = 108$$

$$2^2 3^3 \left(\frac{3}{2} \right) = 2^1 3^4 = 162$$

$$2^1 3^4 \left(\frac{3}{2} \right) = 2^0 3^5 = 243$$

$$3^5 \left(\frac{3}{2} \right) = \text{not an integer, end, output} \to 3^5 = 243$$

Or, tracking the state: $2^3 3^2 \to 2^2 3^3 \to 2^1 3^4 \to 2^0 3^5 = 3^5$.

Following how the state changes, especially when writing the prime factorization of the state, shows us what FRACTRAN is doing. The add program is a single instruction: 3/2. Every time the state is multiplied by 3/2, the 2 in the denominator decrements v2, and the 3 in the numerator increments v3. This is a general rule: the denominators are gatekeepers, so they decide whether the fraction "fires" or not. If the current integer contains factors of each prime factor of the denominator, to at least the power specified by the factor, then the denominator will be completely canceled and a new integer will be the result. This is what is meant by a fraction "firing." When a fraction fires, it also decrements register values. Numerators, on the other hand, increment register values because they multiply the state integer. A FRACTRAN program is a sequence of operations applied to the state of the register machine.

For addition, every multiplication of the state by 3/2 increments v3 and decrements v2 until v2 = 0, making the state no longer evenly divisible by 2. According to the processing rule, the state should be multiplied by the next fraction in the list; however, there is no next fraction, so the program halts and outputs its state.

It's clever enough to realize that repeated multiplications by 3/2 when an integer has the form $2^a 3^b$ will result in 3^{a+b}, thereby adding a and b, but realizing that this is a general form of computation is brilliant. We'll explore other FRACTRAN programs, but before we do, notice that 3/2 isn't the only add program in FRACTRAN—2/3 works as well. Instead of decrementing v2 and incrementing v3, 2/3 decrements v3 and increments v2, leaving the sum in v2. Let's see that this is so.

```
> python3 FRACTRAN.py add2.frac 72 1
48
32
```

The file *add2.frac* contains 2/3. The input is $2^3 3^2 = 72$ as before. The state transitions are

$$2^3 3^2 = 72 \rightarrow 2^4 3^1 = 48 \rightarrow 2^5 3^0 = 32 \rightarrow \text{end} \rightarrow 2^5 = 32$$

proving that the sum is in v2.

Let's make sure we follow how FRACTRAN manipulates state. These examples are not full programs, but they show the way fractions operate on the state. For example, see Equations 8.1 through 8.5.

$$2^3 5^7 17^2 \left(\frac{7^2 11^1}{5^4 17^1} \right) \rightarrow \text{fires, new state} = 2^3 5^3 7^2 11^1 17^1 \qquad (8.1)$$

$$2^3 5^7 17^2 \left(\frac{3^3}{13^2} \right) \rightarrow \text{does not fire} \qquad (8.2)$$

$$2^3 5^7 17^2 \left(\frac{1}{2^3} \right) \rightarrow \text{fires, new state} = 5^7 17^2 \qquad (8.3)$$

$$2^3 5^7 17^2 \left(\frac{1}{2^5} \right) \rightarrow \text{does not fire} \qquad (8.4)$$

$$2^3 5^7 17^2 \left(\frac{3^2}{1} \right) \rightarrow \text{always fires, new state} = 2^3 3^2 5^7 17^2 \qquad (8.5)$$

Equation 8.1 fires because the denominator contains v5 and v17, which are also present in the state. Notice that several things happen when the fraction fires: v5 goes down by 4, v17 goes down by o1ne, v7 goes up by 2 (from 0), and v11 goes up by 1. Thus, the new state is v2 = 3, v5 = 3, v7 = 2, v11 = 1, and v17 = 1.

For Equation 8.2, there is no factor of 13 in the state (v13 = 0), so the result of multiplying the state by the fraction is not an integer. Therefore, the fraction does not fire, and FRACTRAN proceeds to the next fraction in the list.

Equation 8.3 fires and sets v2 = 0 without changing v5 or v17.

Equation 8.4 does not fire, because even though v2 = 3, attempting to subtract five from its state would make v2 negative, which is not allowed. The rules of FRACTRAN account for this by requiring the product of the state and a fraction to be an integer. The denominator of the fraction must be canceled completely by the prime factors of the state.

The addition example manipulated v2 and v3. These are often used because they are the smallest primes, but there is no reason they must be used. Any two primes will work. For example, 8,675,309 and 8,675,311 are both prime. To show they work just as well, create *add3.frac*, containing

---

8675311/8675309

Then add 3 and 2 as before using v8675309 and v8675311 to set the initial state:

$$8675309^3 8675311^2 = 491388471389499790773480221811755509$$

Run it to get

```
> ./FRACTRAN add3.frac 491388471389499790773480221811755509 0
491388811242697877814581892433975511
```

which is 8675311^5.

```
> python3
>>> 8675311**5
491388811242697877814581892433975511
```

This proves once again that 3 + 2 = 5 and that any pair of FRACTRAN registers work.

More FRACTRAN Examples

Let's examine more FRACTRAN examples. Specifically, let's work through subtraction, the maximum of two values, duplicating registers, and multiplication. We'll conclude by exploring Conway's prime number example, PRIMEGAME, and the Collatz conjecture.

Subtraction

Addition in FRACTRAN is a single fraction, and it turns out that subtraction is as well (see *sub.frac*).

```
;  Input:  (2**a)(3**b)
;  Output: 2**(a-b)
;
1/6
```

Let's run a test to work out 17 − 4 = 13. The input is $2^{17}3^4 = 10{,}616{,}832$, with intermediate values corresponding to states:

$$2^{16}3^3 \rightarrow 2^{15}3^2 \rightarrow 2^{14}3^1 \rightarrow 2^{13}$$

```
> python3 FRACTRAN.py sub.frac 10616832 1
1769472
294912
49152
8192
```

The fraction $1/6 = 1/(2^1 3^1)$, so every multiplication decrements both v2 and v3 by 1.

$$2^{17}3^4 \left(\frac{1}{2^13^1} \right) = 2^{16}3^3$$

$$2^{16}3^3 \left(\frac{1}{2^13^1} \right) = 2^{15}3^2$$

$$2^{15}3^2 \left(\frac{1}{2^13^1} \right) = 2^{14}3^1$$

$$2^{14}3^1 \left(\frac{1}{2^13^1} \right) = 2^{13}$$

It decrements both v2 and v3 by 1 until v3 = 0 and multiplication by 1/6 no longer produces an integer, causing the program to stop. By assumption, the input is of the form 2^a3^b, $a > b$, so continually decrementing v2 and v3 together until v3 is 0 will necessarily leave the difference in v2. If $b > a$, *sub.frac* still works, but the difference is in v3, not v2.

Maximum of Two Integers

FRACTRAN adds and subtracts using single fractions, but to do anything more requires additional fractions. The file *max.frac* contains

```
;  Input:  (2**a)(3**b)
;  Output: 5**max(a b)
;
5/6 5/2 5/3
```

This is our first FRACTRAN program to use more than one fraction. The claim is that *max.frac* finds the largest of two integers, a and b. The input state looks familiar: register v2 = a and v3 = b with v5 holding the larger of the two when the program ends. Let's try it and see.

```
> ./FRACTRAN max.frac 3359232 1
2799360
2332800
1944000
1620000
1350000
1125000
937500
781250
1953125
```

Listing 8-3: Finding the maximum of two integers

The input state is $2^9 3^8 = 3{,}359{,}232$ and the output state is $5^9 = 1{,}953{,}125$, which is correct, as $9 > 8$. Let's follow the state step by step.

$$2^9 3^8 \rightarrow 2^8 3^7 5^1 \rightarrow 2^7 3^6 5^2 \rightarrow 2^6 3^5 5^3 \rightarrow 2^5 3^4 5^4 \rightarrow$$
$$\rightarrow 2^4 3^3 5^5 \rightarrow 2^3 3^2 5^6 \rightarrow 2^2 3^1 5^7 \rightarrow 2^1 3^0 5^8 \rightarrow 5^9$$

Each state is the prime factorization of the sequence of integers shown in Listing 8-3.

The state sequence shows us how the program progresses, but as we have multiple fractions, it doesn't show us exactly what is happening. Therefore, let's trace the program's actual execution.

$$2^9 3^8 \left(\frac{5}{2^1 3^1} \right) = 2^8 3^7 5^1 \text{ new state, loop}$$

$$2^8 3^7 5^1 \left(\frac{5}{2^1 3^1} \right) = 2^7 3^6 5^2 \text{ new state, loop}$$

$$2^7 3^6 5^2 \left(\frac{5}{2^1 3^1} \right) = 2^6 3^5 5^3 \text{ new state, loop}$$

$$2^6 3^5 5^3 \left(\frac{5}{2^1 3^1} \right) = 2^5 3^4 5^4 \text{ new state, loop}$$

$$2^5 3^4 5^4 \left(\frac{5}{2^1 3^1} \right) = 2^4 3^3 5^5 \text{ new state, loop}$$

$$2^4 3^3 5^5 \left(\frac{5}{2^1 3^1} \right) = 2^3 3^2 5^6 \text{ new state, loop}$$

$$2^3 3^2 5^6 \left(\frac{5}{2^1 3^1} \right) = 2^2 3^1 5^7 \text{ new state, loop}$$

$$2^2 3^1 5^7 \left(\frac{5}{2^1 3^1} \right) = 2^1 3^0 5^8 \text{ new state, loop}$$

$$2^1 3^0 5^8 \left(\frac{5}{2^1 3^1} \right) = \text{ does not fire}$$

$$2^1 3^0 5^8 \left(\frac{5}{2^1} \right) = 2^0 3^0 5^9 \text{ new state, loop}$$

$$2^0 3^0 5^9 \left(\frac{5}{2^1 3^1} \right) = \text{ does not fire}$$

$$2^0 3^0 5^9 \left(\frac{5}{2^1} \right) = \text{ does not fire}$$

$$2^0 3^0 5^9 \left(\frac{5}{3^1} \right) = \text{ does not fire}$$

$$\text{end, state is } 5^9$$

Note that $5/6$ is written as $5/(2^1 3^1)$ to make it clear that $5/6$ decrements v2 and v3 when both are greater than 0, and 0 exponents are used to emphasize that a particular register has 0 value.

From the sequence of steps, we see that 5/6 starts a loop, decrementing v2 and v3 for as long as both of them are greater than 0. At the same time, the loop increments v5. Once v2 or v3 are 0, 5/6 does not fire, so the next fraction, 5/2, is tested. In this case, v3 = 0 and v2 > 0, so 5/2 fires, incrementing v5 and decrementing v2. Then, and this is important, as there is a new state, the program loops *from the beginning* so both 5/6 and 5/2 are tested again. As v3 is 0, 5/6 doesn't fire. Additionally, v2 is now 0, so 5/2 doesn't fire, either. That leaves 5/3, but v3 is 0 already, so 5/3 does not fire. There are no more fractions, so the program ends with v2 = 0, v3 = 0, and v5 = 9, as it should in this case. If the program were run with v2=8 and v3 = 9, then after 5/6 stops firing, 5/2 would not fire, but 5/3 would count v3 to 0 while still incrementing v5.

Let's write *max.frac* in a more familiar way. Listing 8-4 presents a Python implementation of the algorithm implied by *max.frac* using register names (see *max.py*).

```
while not ((v2 == 0) and (v3 == 0)):
    if (v2>0) and (v3>0):
        v2 = v2 - 1
        v3 = v3 - 1
        v5 = v5 + 1
        continue
    if (v2>0) and (v3==0):
        v2 = v2 - 1
        v5 = v5 + 1
        continue
    if (v2==0) and (v3>0):
        v3 = v3 - 1
        v5 = v5 + 1
        continue
```

Listing 8-4: The FRACTRAN max program in Python

The outer while loop runs until both v2 and v3 are 0. This is equivalent to restarting the scan of fractions from the beginning every time the state changes. The first if acts like 5/6, looping for as long as both v2 and v3 are greater than 0. Notice that because of the continue, the following if statements are not even considered until at least one of v2 or v3 are 0.

The second if acts like 5/2. It loops if v3 is 0 but v2 is not. The continue here starts the outer while loop again, meaning the first if is evaluated yet again; however, as v3 must be 0 for the second if to fire, the first if does not execute.

Lastly, if v2 is decremented to 0 first by the first if, then the last if fires to decrement v3 until 0. Notice that each if statement increments v5 every time it fires.

The first if decrements both v2 and v3 while incrementing v5. This removes the value in common between v2 and v3. The following two if statements provide clean up. One or the other will fire until whichever register that isn't yet 0, either v2 or v3, becomes 0. As v5 is always incremented regardless of which `if` fires, v5 will ultimately contain v2 or v3, whichever is larger. Note also that this program is destructive; both v2 and v3 will be lost.

Copying a Register

FRACTRAN fractions fire when all of the prime factors of the denominator, to at least the power present in the denominator, are likewise present in the current state. In other words, the registers corresponding to the prime factors of the fraction's denominator must have a value at least as large as the exponent of the denominator's prime factors. Additionally, the act of firing necessarily decrements a register's value. This is exactly how 3/2 operates in *add.frac*.

Therefore, to move the value of register v2 to, say, v7, we need a single fraction, 7/2. This is because every time it fires, v2 is decremented and v7 is incremented until v2 is 0. The value of v2 is now in v7 and is no longer in v2. What if instead we want to copy the value in v2 to v7 while leaving it in v2? Learning how to do this in FRACTRAN will teach us what we need to know to understand our next example, multiplication.

Our copying-a-register code is based on an example found on Chris Lomont's blog (see *http://lomont.org/posts/2017/fractran/*). In this example, he not only gives detailed descriptions of various FRACTRAN programs, but presents a FRACTRAN interpreter written in FRACTRAN. Do take a look.

There is no getting around decrementing our source register, as that's the only way we'll get the fraction to fire. The trick, according to Chris, is to move the register's value to *two* other registers: the desired target register and an auxiliary register. Then, when the move is complete, copy the auxiliary register back to the source.

Listing 8-5 shows *copy.frac*, which copies the contents of v2 to v3.

```
;  Input: 2^a 7
;  Output: 2^a 3^a
;
165/14 7/11 13/7 34/65 13/17 1/13
```

Listing 8-5: Copying v2 to v3

Our plan of attack is to define what each register will do, show the code again using prime factors, and, lastly, walk through the steps to copy v2 = 3 to v3.

To copy v2 to v3, we clearly need at least those two registers. The source is v2 and the target is v3. We'll use v5 as the second copy of v2. The copy algorithm is as follows:

1. Decrement v2; increment v3 and v5.
2. Repeat Step 1 until v2 is 0.
3. Decrement v5; increment v2.
4. Repeat Step 3 until v5 is 0.

We need two loops, one to increment v3 and v5 running v2 times and another incrementing v2 running v5 times. FRACTRAN always scans fractions from the first onward, so loops are implemented by flags triggering the next scan of the code. Two loops imply that we need two additional registers to act as flags. However, to fire a fraction, we must always decrement at least one register, so using a single register to cause a loop destroys the flag value. Two registers are needed—one to trigger the loop and another to restore the flag after it was decremented. We'll use v7 and v11 as flags for the first loop. Registers v13 and v17 will handle the second loop.

We now have our registers. Let's review the code again, but this time using prime factors with labels and comments.

Label	Fraction	Comment
A	$\dfrac{3^1 5^1 11^1}{2^1 7^1}$	Inc v3,v5; Dec v2,v7
B	$\dfrac{7}{11}$	Reset v7
C	$\dfrac{13}{7}$	Clear v7; Set v13
D	$\dfrac{2^1 17^1}{5^1 13^1}$	Inc v2; Dec v5
E	$\dfrac{13}{17}$	Reset v13
F	$\dfrac{1}{13}$	Clear v13

Let's take a walk through the code. We set the initial state to $2^3 7 = 56$ to set v2 = 3 and v7, the flag for the first loop. The program then runs like so:

$$2^3 7 \xrightarrow{A} 2^2 3^1 5^1 11 \xrightarrow{B} 2^2 3^1 5^1 7 \xrightarrow{A} 2^1 3^2 5^2 11 \xrightarrow{B} 2^1 3^2 5^2 7$$
$$\xrightarrow{A} 3^3 5^3 11 \xrightarrow{B} 3^3 5^3 7 \xrightarrow{C} 3^3 5^3 13 \xrightarrow{D} 2^1 3^3 5^2 17$$
$$\xrightarrow{E} 2^1 3^3 5^2 13 \xrightarrow{D} 2^2 3^3 5^1 17 \xrightarrow{E} 2^2 3^3 5^1 13 \xrightarrow{D} 2^3 3^3 17$$
$$\xrightarrow{E} 2^3 3^3 13 \xrightarrow{F} 2^3 3^3$$

The numbers represent the state after each fraction fires. The label above the arrow shows which fraction fired. The loops are evident: fractions A and B repeat three times. This decrements v2 and increments v3 and v5. Then fraction C fires to clear v7 and set v13. Doing this initiates the second loop. The second loop runs three times, with fractions D and E firing to decrement v5 and increment v2, thereby restoring its initial value. The very last fraction, F, then fires to clear v13. After this, no other fractions fire, so the program ends with v2 = v3 = 3, as intended.

Let's look a bit more closely at the paired flags. The program begins with v7 set. Fraction A fires because both v2 and v7 are greater than 0. Register v2 is decremented along with v7. The numerator of fraction A increments v3 and v5 and sets v11. To continue the loop, we must set v7 again.

That's what fraction B does: it fires when v11 is set (>0) and resets v7. The loop then continues firing fraction A again because v2 and v7 are both greater than 0, that is, the state contains factors of 2 and 7. When v2 is drained, v3 and v5 are both set to what v2 was initially. Fraction C then fires to clear v7 and set v13 to begin the second loop to move v5 back to v2 using fractions D and E. To end the program with no flags set, fraction F clears v13.

Now, let's see how this double-move loop structure can be used to implement multiplication.

Multiplication

Multiplication of two integers is repeated addition. To find the product of $a \times b$, we either add a to itself b times or add b to itself a times. This is likely the origin of using the word *times* for multiplication. The copy example given earlier showed us how to use flags to set up independent loops and how to increment a register a set number of times while preserving the source register's value. Let's use repeated addition along with copying to implement multiplication.

Specifically, we want a FRACTRAN program that takes an input state of $2^a 3^b$ and generates a final state of 5^{ab} by adding v2 to v5 v3 times. We'll implement the following algorithm:

1. While v2 > 0, increment v5 and v7.
2. While v7 > 0, increment v2.
3. While v3 > 0, repeat from Step 1.

The first loop is Step 1, which decrements v2 while incrementing v5 and v7. Register v5 holds the product, so we'll only increment it. Register v7 is used to hold v2 as v2 is drained while adding it to v5. Step 2 restores v2 by moving v7 back to v2 just as we did in *copy.frac*. Steps 1 and 2 repeat until v3 is 0, thereby adding v2 to v5 v3 times.

There are three loops, but we can combine Steps 2 and 3 into a single loop. For Step 1, we need a pair of registers for the flag; we'll use v11 and v13. The initial version of this program added v17 for the other loop, but that would only be necessary if there were code after the multiplication.

Listing 8-6 shows the end result (see *mult.frac*).

```
;  Input:  2^a 3^b
;  Output: 5^{ab}
;

455/22 11/13 1/11 2/7 11/3 1/2
```

Listing 8-6: Multiplication by repeated addition

Let's label the fractions A through F as we did earlier. Doing this gives us:

Label	Fraction	Comment
A	$\dfrac{5^1 7^1 13^1}{2^1 11^1}$	Inc v5, v7; Set v13; Dec v2; Clear v11
B	$\dfrac{11}{13}$	Reset v11
C	$\dfrac{1}{11}$	Clear v11
D	$\dfrac{2}{7}$	Inc v2; Dec v7
E	$\dfrac{11}{3}$	Dec v3; Set v11
F	$\dfrac{1}{2}$	Dec v2

With this table, we can walk through a trace of $3 \times 2 = 6$. The input state is $2^3 3^2 = 72$ and the expected output state is $5^6 = 15625$. First, let's see that *mult.frac* actually works:

```
> ./FRACTRAN mult.frac 72 0
15625
```

The output is as expected. Now, let's trace the evolution of the state:

$$2^3 3^2 \xrightarrow{E} 2^3 3^1 11 \xrightarrow{A} 2^2 3^1 5^1 7^1 13 \xrightarrow{B} 2^2 3^1 5^1 7^1 11 \xrightarrow{A} 2^1 3^1 5^2 7^2 13$$
$$\xrightarrow{B} 2^1 3^1 5^2 7^2 11 \xrightarrow{A} 3^1 5^3 7^3 13 \xrightarrow{B} 3^1 5^3 7^3 11 \xrightarrow{C} 3^1 5^3 7^3$$
$$\xrightarrow{D} 2^1 3^1 5^3 7^2 \xrightarrow{D} 2^2 3^1 5^3 7 \xrightarrow{D} 2^3 3^1 5^3 \xrightarrow{E} 2^3 5^3 11$$
$$\xrightarrow{A} 2^2 5^4 7^1 13 \xrightarrow{B} 2^2 5^4 7^1 11 \xrightarrow{A} 2^1 5^5 7^2 13 \xrightarrow{B} 2^1 5^5 7^2 11$$
$$\xrightarrow{A} 5^6 7^3 13 \xrightarrow{B} 5^6 7^3 11 \xrightarrow{C} 5^6 7^3 \xrightarrow{D} 2^1 5^6 7^2$$
$$\xrightarrow{D} 2^2 5^6 7 \xrightarrow{D} 2^3 5^6 \xrightarrow{F} 2^2 5^6 \xrightarrow{F} 2^1 5^6$$
$$\xrightarrow{F} 5^6$$

The first fraction to fire is E, which decrements v3 and sets v11 to cause the add-v2-to-v5 loop to execute. The add loop, fractions A and B, repeats three times to increment v5 and v7. After the third iteration, there is no longer a factor of 2 in the state (v2 = 0), so fraction C fires next to clear v11 and begin the outer loop.

The first part of the outer loop uses D to decrement v7 and increment v2, thereby restoring v2 to its original value. After the third time through that loop, v7 is 0 and 7 is no longer a factor of the state, so fraction E fires to decrement v3 and set v11 to add v2 to v5 again.

The add loop of fractions A and B runs another three times. At this point, we have our answer in v5, and v2 and v3 are both 0, but fraction C fires again because v7 is not 0. Fraction C fires three times to make v7 0 and v2 = 3. However, v3 is now 0, so v11 is never set. Register v7 is now also 0 and the state is only v2 = 3 and v5 = 6. Therefore, no fraction fires until F, which fires three times to decrement v2 to 0. Lastly, the state is only v5 = 6, and no fraction has a factor of 5 in its denominator, so no fractions fire and the program ends. Listing 8-6 multiplies, but cleaning up after calculating the answer requires many additional operations.

Let's change gears now and explore the first FRACTRAN program Conway presented: PRIMEGAME.

Conway's *PRIMEGAME*

When Conway first presented PRIMEGAME, he did so by writing the fractions in Listing 8-7 and claiming that not only does every power of two generated by the program have a prime exponent, the primes are in order. Let's explore in this section what he meant.

```
;  Input:  2
;

17/91 78/85 19/51 23/38 29/33 77/29 95/23 77/19 1/17
11/13 13/11 15/14 15/2 55/1
```

Listing 8-7: Conway's PRIMEGAME

Unlike the copy and multiply examples above, we won't step through Listing 8-7. Conway does so in lectures available on the internet (for example, see *https://www.youtube.com/watch?v=548BH-YFT1E/*). Instead, we'll capture the output of Listing 8-7 to see, empirically, that Conway's claim is true. I leave it as an exercise for the motivated reader to work through the operation of Listing 8-7.

The primes program never halts, so we need to tell the interpreter to display every new state. If you run *primes.frac* with an initial state of 2

```
> python3 FRACTRAN.py primes.frac 2 1
```

your screen would immediately fill with large numbers. Some of these numbers are powers of two. Those are the numbers we want to display. We could modify *FRACTRAN.py* to display only the powers of two, but why alter the code for the interpreter when we can instead feed the output of *primes.frac* to the input of a second program that takes the output and, if it is a power of two, displays it?

The script *power_of_two.py* does what we want. It uses input to read the number FRACTRAN displays and checks whether it is a power of two. Listing 8-8 contains the code.

```
❶ def isPowerOfTwo(d):
      s = "{0:b}".format(d)
      n = s.count("1")
      p = len(s)-1
      return (n == 1), p
```

```
❷ while (True):
    try:
        ❸ d = int(input())
    except:
        exit(0)
    ok, p = isPowerOfTwo(d)
    if (ok):
        print("2**%d = %d" % (p, 2**p))
```

Listing 8-8: A Python script to check for powers of two

The script accepts the input from FRACTRAN as an integer ❸, passes it to isPowerOfTwo, which returns True if the input (d) is a power of two and then prints it along with the exponent (p). This process repeats forever because of the while loop ❷.

The function isPowerOfTwo ❶ must check whether its argument is a power of two. We could call a log base-2 function here, but we'll quickly encounter integers too large for any function expecting a floating-point argument. If an integer is a power of two, that means there is only one digit in its binary representation that is a 1. So d is converted to binary and stored as a string in s. Then we set n to the number of 1s by using count. If d is a power of two, the exponent is the number of digits in d minus one (p). Lastly, any power of two is displayed along with its exponent.

To link the output of FRACTRAN to the input expected by Listing 8-8, we use a Unix pipe character, |:

```
> python3 FRACTRAN.py primes.frac 2 1 | python3 power_of_two.py
```

which feeds the output of FRACTRAN to the input of *power_of_two.py* to display powers of two. For example, the output begins as follows:

```
2**2 = 4
2**3 = 8
2**5 = 32
2**7 = 128
2**11 = 2048
2**13 = 8192
2**17 = 131072
2**19 = 524288
2**23 = 8388608
2**29 = 536870912
2**31 = 2147483648
2**37 = 137438953472
2**41 = 2199023255552
2**43 = 8796093022208
2**47 = 140737488355328
2**53 = 9007199254740992
```

Here the exponents are all primes and, more than that, primes in the correct order with no gaps, just like Conway promised. The rate at which new primes are generated slows as the primes get larger. For example, the file *powers_of_two.txt* contains the output generated by letting the code run overnight. The largest prime found was 953.

Devin Kilminster made a nine fraction version of PRIMEGAME that outputs the primes as powers of 10 instead of two. See Listing 8-9 (*prime10.frac*).

```
;  Input:  10
;
3/11 847/45 143/6 7/3 10/91 3/7 36/325 1/2 36/5
```

Listing 8-9: Kilminster's primes

Run *prime10.frac* with *power_of_ten.py* as we did for Conway's game above.

```
> ./FRACTRAN prime10.frac 10 1 | python3 power_of_ten.py
```

The output sequence using powers of 10 generates the primes, in order.

We might wonder which prime generator is faster. I modified *power_of_two.py* and *power_of_ten.py* to stop after the 100th prime, 541, and timed how long each program took using the Racket version of the FRACTRAN interpreter.

Program	Runtime(s)
Conway	3317
Kilminster	783

Not only is Kilminster's program shorter than Conway's original PRIME-GAME, it's also significantly faster.

Our next example generates the Collatz sequence for an integer. Don't worry, I'll explain what that means.

The Collatz Conjecture

Lothar Collatz was a German mathematician. In 1937, he speculated that the following sequence, for any initial integer, $x_0 = n$, will always end with 1 (see Equation 8.6):

$$x_{i+1} = \begin{cases} \dfrac{x_i}{2} & x_i \text{ even} \\ 3x_i + 1 & x_i \text{ odd} \end{cases} \qquad (8.6)$$

For example, the sequence for $n = 10$ is

$$10 \to 5 \to 16 \to 8 \to 4 \to 2 \to 1$$

Once the output is 4, the sequence $4 \to 2 \to 1$ will repeat forever because $3(1) + 1 = 4$.

To date, no one has succeeded in proving the Collatz conjecture, and all empirical tests have always ended in 1. There is a deep connection between

FRACTRAN and the Collatz conjecture that we'll get to in the discussion below. For now, let's run Conway's FRACTRAN program to generate the Collatz sequence for any integer, n. (It's highly likely Conway wrote this code, but solid proof has not been forthcoming.) The code is in *collatz.frac* and Listing 8-10.

```
165/14 11/63 38/21 13/7 34/325 1/13 184/95 1/19
7/11 13/17 19/23 1575/4
```

Listing 8-10: FRACTRAN code to generate the Collatz sequence

The input is 2^n and the final output is 2^1. All states that are powers of two represent a number in the Collatz sequence. So we must filter the output using *power_of_two.py* as we did for PRIMEGAME above. Let's try a few runs beginning with $n = 128$.

```
> ./FRACTRAN collatz.frac 340282366920938463463374607431768211456 1
    | python3 power_of_two.py
2**64 = 18446744073709551616
2**32 = 4294967296
2**16 = 65536
2**8 = 256
2**4 = 16
2**2 = 4
2**1 = 2
```

The large starting state is 2^{128}. The Collatz sequence ends after seven steps. Not all sequences are so short. For example, changing from $n = 128$ to $n = 129$ generates

```
 388,   194,   97,  292,  146,   73,  220,  110,   55,  166,
  83,   250,  125,  376,  188,   94,   47,  142,   71,  214,
 107,   322,  161,  484,  242,  121,  364,  182,   91,  274,
 137,   412,  206,  103,  310,  155,  466,  233,  700,  350,
 175,   526,  263,  790,  395, 1186,  593, 1780,  890,  445,
1336,   668,  334,  167,  502,  251,  754,  377, 1132,  566,
 283,   850,  425, 1276,  638,  319,  958,  479, 1438,  719,
2158,  1079, 3238, 1619, 4858, 2429, 7288, 3644, 1822,  911,
2734,  1367, 4102, 2051, 6154, 3077, 9232, 4616, 2308, 1154,
 577,  1732,  866,  433, 1300,  650,  325,  976,  488,  244,
 122,    61,  184,   92,   46,   23,   70,   35,  106,   53,
 160,    80,   40,   20,   10,    5,   16,    8,    4,    2,   1
```

for a total of 121 steps. As with PRIMEGAME, parsing the algorithm in *collatz.frac* is left as an exercise for the ambitious reader.

Note that the sequence for 129 included values as large as 9,232. This means the state contained a factor of 2^{9232}, a number with 2,780 digits. Although *collatz.frac* will work for any integer, the intermediate values become quite large. Play around with *collatz.frac* or, if you are impatient, the much faster Python version, *collatz.py*. Do you notice anything interesting about the largest value in each sequence for *n* from 5 to 200?

A FRACTRAN Greeting

We'll end with an example more cute than it is useful. However, it does one interesting thing: the program's goal is not a specific set of register values, per se, but the decimal value of the single integer representing the final state. The code is in *hello.frac* and Listing 8-11.

```
;  Input:   2^3 5^1 7^1 11^1 == 3080
;  Output:  7269767679443287798276833

3/2 41/5 6701021/7 9800132160937639/11
```

Listing 8-11: A FRACTRAN greeting

First, run the program to verify that it produces the claimed output.

```
> ./FRACTRAN hello.frac 3080 0
7269767679443287798276833
```

Next, pipe the output to *hello.py*.

```
> ./FRACTRAN hello.frac 3080 0 | python3 hello.py
HELLO, WORLD!
```

The *hello.py* script is

```
d = input()
while (d != ""):
    print(chr(int(d[:2])), end="")
    d = d[2:]
print()
```

This reads the FRACTRAN output as a string, breaking it up into pairs of digits and outputting the ASCII character corresponding to that pair of digits.

Let's walk through *hello.frac*. The starting state is $2^3 5^1 7^1 11^1$. The denominators of the fractions are also 2, 5, 7, and 11. Therefore, the initial state will match each fraction, but the fractions' order means it matches $3/2$ first. The product of the state and $3/2$ decrements v2 and increments v3, then starts again from the beginning, matching $3/2$ a second time. Now v2 = 1 and v3 = 2. Looping again sets v2 to 0 and v3 to 3. Now the state has no factor of 2, so $3/2$ does not fire, and FRACTRAN moves to $41/5$. The state is $3^3 5^1 7^1 11^1$, which does have a factor of 5, so v5 is decremented, v41 is incremented, and the program loops. There are only factors of 7 and 11 left to match fractions. First, the fraction with a denominator of 7 matches and fires followed by the fraction with a denominator of 11.

The final state of the system is

$$3^3 41^1 6701021^1 9800132160937639^1 = 7269767679443287798276833$$

which is precisely what we want it to be: a string of ASCII character codes.

We wanted *hello.frac* to produce the integer corresponding to the sentence HELLO, WORLD!. That determined the printed output. The prime factorization of that output determined the final registers and their values. The included *primeFactors.py* searches for prime factors, but it is too slow to factor a large integer like the output of *hello.frac*. For that, I used WolframAlpha (see *https://www.wolframalpha.com/*). Prime factors in hand, the program itself was straightforward: set the initial state to v2 = 3, v5 = 1, v7 = 1, and v11 = 1. Then, use the prime factors as the numerators to increment v3, v41, and so on for the necessary number of times: 3, 1, 1, and 1.

Of course, we could initialize the program with the desired output state and, using a fraction with no factor in the denominator matching the state, produce the desired output immediately, but that would be boring.

Discussion

Let's discuss two aspects of FRACTRAN: Turing completeness and its relation to the Collatz conjecture. After that, we'll conclude with some final thoughts.

Is FRACTRAN Turing Complete?

Is FRACTRAN Turing complete? Yes, it is. FRACTRAN has looping and an infinite number of registers as there are an infinite number of primes. Additionally, FRACTRAN can implement FRACTRAN, as Chris Lomont's blog post mentioned previously demonstrates. Also, FRACTRAN is a Minsky-style register machine, a machine that has been proven to be Turing complete, so FRACTRAN is also Turing complete.

Conway himself included a universal FRACTRAN program in his description of FRACTRAN: POLYGAME. See "FRACTRAN: A Simple Universal Programming Language for Arithmetic" in *Open Problems in Communication and Computation* (Springer, 1987).

POLYGAME is a FRACTRAN program capable of computing any function when given the proper "catalogue number" as Conway called it. We'll use the British spelling henceforth. Here is POLYGAME:

$$\frac{583}{559}, \frac{629}{551}, \frac{437}{527}, \frac{82}{517}, \frac{615}{329}, \frac{371}{129}, \frac{1}{115}, \frac{53}{86}, \frac{43}{53}, \frac{23}{47}, \frac{341}{46}, \frac{41}{43}$$

$$\frac{47}{41}, \frac{29}{37}, \frac{37}{31}, \frac{37}{31}, \frac{299}{29}, \frac{47}{23}, \frac{161}{15}, \frac{527}{19}, \frac{159}{7}, \frac{1}{17}, \frac{1}{13}, \frac{1}{3}$$

The input is $c2^{2^n}$, with n the argument and c the catalogue number. The output is 2^{2^m} to implement $f_c(n) = m$. For example, the increment function $n \rightarrow n + 1$ has catalogue number 2,268,945. Therefore, to increment 4, the input to FRACTRAN is

$$(2{,}268{,}945)2^{2^4} = 148{,}697{,}579{,}520$$

to produce the output

$$2^{2^5} = 4{,}294{,}967{,}296$$

which is exactly what we get if we run POLYGAME.

```
> ./FRACTRAN polygame.frac 148697579520 0
4294967296
```

POLYGAME can implement *all* functions given the proper c. Another example is $c = 255$, the identity function: $n \rightarrow n$. The most interesting example Conway gives is c_π. It's an integer, but good luck calculating

$$c_\pi = 3^A \cdot 5^{2^{89 \cdot 101!} + 2^{90 \cdot 101!}} \cdot 17^{101! - 1} \cdot 23$$

with

$$A = 2^{100!} + \sum_{i=1}^{38} 2^{f_i \cdot 101^i \cdot 100!} + 2^{101^{39} \cdot 100!}$$

and the 38 f_i fractions, in order:

$$\frac{365}{46}, \frac{29}{161}, \frac{79}{575}, \frac{7}{451}, \frac{3159}{413}, \frac{83}{497}, \frac{473}{371}, \frac{638}{355}, \frac{434}{335}, \frac{89}{235},$$

$$\frac{17}{209}, \frac{79}{122}, \frac{31}{183}, \frac{41}{115}, \frac{517}{89}, \frac{111}{83}, \frac{305}{79}, \frac{23}{73}, \frac{73}{71}, \frac{61}{67}, \frac{37}{61},$$

$$\frac{19}{59}, \frac{89}{57}, \frac{41}{53}, \frac{883}{47}, \frac{53}{43}, \frac{86}{41}, \frac{13}{38}, \frac{23}{37}, \frac{67}{31}, \frac{71}{29}, \frac{83}{19}, \frac{475}{17},$$

$$\frac{59}{13}, \frac{41}{3}, \frac{1}{7}, \frac{1}{11}, \frac{1}{1024}$$

Yes, that is a 5 raised to the power of two raised to the factorial of 101. Given the insane size of c_π, we'll take Conway's word for it that c_π is the catalogue number for a function, $\pi(n)$, returning the nth digit of π.

FRACTRAN and the Collatz Conjecture

Equation 8.6 defined the Collatz sequence for an integer, n. The equation describes how to generate the next number in the sequence based on whether the current number is even or odd. Another way to formulate Equation 8.6 is shown in Equation 8.7.

$$x_{i+1} = \begin{cases} \dfrac{x_i}{2} & \text{if } \dfrac{x_i}{2} \text{ an integer} \\ 3x_i + 1 & \text{otherwise} \end{cases} \tag{8.7}$$

meaning $x_{i+1} = x_i/2$ if $x_i/2$ is an integer; otherwise, $x_{i+1} = 3x_i + 1$, which is always an integer.

The Collatz sequence is what Conway terms a *bipartite linear function*, meaning a function that can be written as

$$g(n) = g_1(n) \mid g_2(n)$$

with $g(n)$ returning whichever of $g_1(n)$ or $g_2(n)$ returns an integer first when evaluating left to right. Each $g_i(n)$ is of the form

$$g_i(n) = a_i n + b_i$$

which is a linear function (a line). For the Collatz sequence, $a_1 = 1/2$ and $b_1 = 0$. Similarly, $a_2 = 3$ and $b_2 = 1$.

There is no reason why $g(n)$ should be limited to only two parts. A k-partite linear function is

$$g(n) = g_1(n) \mid g_2(n) \mid g_3(n) \mid \ldots \mid g_k(n)$$

Conway calls k-partite functions with $g_i(n) = a_i n + b_i$ *Collatzian games*. The rule for evaluating $g(n)$ is to calculate $g_1(n)$ followed by $g_2(n)$ and so on until one of them returns an integer. If none of them return an integer, or if the integer returned is some specified value, like 1, stop.

This rule sounds familiar. If we set all the b_is to 0 and all the a_is to rationals, then $g(n)$ is a FRACTRAN program. Therefore, FRACTRAN programs are Collatzian games. However, note that the Collatz conjecture is not a FRACTRAN program, as $b_2 = 1$.

Gödel's incompleteness theorem states that arithmetic contains true statements it cannot prove using the axioms of arithmetic. Alan Turing translated this concept into the *halting problem*, which states that it is impossible to find an algorithm that will correctly decide in all cases whether a program (a Turing machine) with a finite input will eventually stop or run forever. The term to describe these cases is *undecidable*. An undecidable problem has been *proven* to be so; there is no algorithm that will correctly decide in all cases.

FRACTRAN programs are undecidable, and FRACTRAN programs are a type of Collatzian game. Therefore, there are Collatzian games that are undecidable, games for which it is impossible to prove that the game ends as desired for all inputs, n. This fact does not solve the question of the Collatz conjecture, as the conjecture applies to a Collatzian game that is not a FRACTRAN program. However, showing there are undecidable Collatzian games is an important result all the same. It may be that the Collatz conjecture is undecidable, too.

Final Thoughts on FRACTRAN

When first encountered, FRACTRAN might appear to be a cute but useless esolang, much like the original form of ABC from Chapter 7. The trick of using Gödel numbering to hold the state of the program makes FRACTRAN more interesting, but still, it's just another esolang, though now a clever one.

The universality of FRACTRAN adds to its intellectual attractiveness. However, the fact that FRACTRAN links Gödel's incompleteness theorem with Turing's halting problem and Conway's Collatzian games is brilliant. FRACTRAN is set apart from the other languages we'll explore. I hope it causes you to ponder deeper issues related to programming, computation, what can and cannot be known, and what it even means to know that you cannot know.

Summary

In this chapter, we explored FRACTRAN, an esolang that at first glance seems like nothing more than a clever game. After implementing the language in both Racket and Python, we tested it and struggled to understand how it worked. Next, we explored multiple examples of FRACTRAN programs to help build our intuition about what coding in FRACTRAN entails. Along the way, we learned about the Collatz conjecture, itself an interesting intellectual exercise.

We closed the chapter by discussing the connections between FRACTRAN, Gödel's incompleteness theorem, Turing's halting problem, and Collatzian games, all of which provide much food for thought.

FRACTRAN forced us to think mathematically. Now, let's mix things up with Piet, a language that forces us to think visually.

9

PIET

Piet (pronounced "Pete") is a visual esolang. It's a perfect example of what an esolang aims to be: a novel way to embody the
process of coding. Piet programs are executable
pictures. The language is named after Dutch artist Piet
Mondrian (1872–1944) because Piet programs often
appear similar to his abstract, rectangular paintings.
In Piet, art meets code. People talk about elegance
in source code, and Piet takes this idea to an entirely
new level.

Piet is a stack-based language with a minimal instruction set. In Piet,
blocks of the same color represent positive integers, and transitions from
one color to another specify the executed instruction. Piet programs are 2D,
with code running whichever way is desired: left, right, up, or down.

In this chapter, we'll first walk through the language to understand how
to turn a picture into code. Next, we'll go finger painting and get messy with
some example programs. Along the way, we'll learn how to use the interpreter and its visual tracing abilities.

After that, we'll explore the npiet visual editor to create a simple tribute
to Mondrian by turning one of his iconic paintings into code.

Piet's popularity has created many implementations, associated tools, and even assemblers to generate Piet pictures from more traditional, text-based assembly code. We'll take a quick look at the Piet universe to point you toward the resources you'll need if you want to spend more time with Piet. Lastly, as always, we'll conclude the chapter with a brief discussion.

Installation

Piet's creator, David Morgan-Mar, has a helpful page at *https://www.danger mouse.net/esoteric/piet.html*. The page includes background information and an explanation of Piet's operation. There's also a nice collection of example programs and a link to third-party tools. Do take a look.

To work with Piet, we need an interpreter. We'll use Erik Schoenfelder's npiet. It's written in C and is fast enough for our purposes.

To install and build npiet, first go to *http://www.bertnase.de/npiet/* and download *npiet-1.3f.tar.gz* (or any later version you see). The site includes a compiled executable for Windows users. The command sequence below, if libgd is available, should be (largely) appropriate for macOS.

Once you have *npiet-1.3f.tar.gz* enter the following commands:

```
> tar xzf npiet-1.3f.tar.gz
> cd npiet-1.3f/
> sudo apt-get install libgd-dev
> ./configure
> make
```

After a few warnings, there should be three executable files in the *npiet-1.3f* directory: npiet, npietedit, and npiet-foogol. The first is the interpreter. The second is a simple editor we'll use to make our example programs. The third translates foogol programs into Piet. Foogol is an ALGOL-like language.

You may need to install additional packages like groff and tk. If so, this should be close to what you need:

```
> sudo apt-get install groff
> sudo apt-get install tk
```

The book's GitHub repo includes a *Piet* directory with example programs. I suggest copying npiet to the *examples* directory, or one level up, to simplify execution.

To test npiet, try

```
> npiet examples/hi.png
Hi
```

If you see our favorite greeting, npiet is working correctly.

Understanding Piet

Piet is unlike any of the languages we've previously encountered. Of course, we should expect a language using pictures as programs to be unusual. This section seeks to understand Piet, meaning how Piet represents numbers, programs, commands, and program flow. As a language, Piet is relatively simple. There are only 17 commands, four of which are solely for input and output. However, program flow in Piet is more complex than in traditional languages.

We'll begin with colors, as Piet programs are all about colors. Then we'll learn how to represent numbers and programs. Next, we'll discuss the command set and the unique way Piet implies commands using transitions between colors. Color transitions lead naturally to program flow.

Piet Colors

We have a problem at the start. Piet uses color images to represent programs, but this book is printed in grayscale. Therefore, referring to the GitHub examples is essential. That said, we'll do what we can without color. For instance, Figure 9-1 presents the specific colors Piet uses as shades of gray along with HTML-style hex codes representing the color. A color version of this chart is in the file *piet_colors.png*. Lack of color won't stop us, but be aware that color is critical to Piet and how it functions.

#FFC0C0 light red	#FFFFC0 light yellow	#C0FFC0 light green	#C0FFFF light cyan	#C0C0FF light blue	#FFC0FF light magenta
#FF0000 red	#FFFF00 yellow	#00FF00 green	#00FFFF cyan	#0000FF blue	#FF00FF magenta
#C00000 dark red	#C0C000 dark yellow	#00C000 dark green	#00C0C0 dark cyan	#0000C0 dark blue	#C000C0 dark magenta

Figure 9-1: Piet color chart

Our Piet programs use only the colors in Figure 9-1 along with black (#000000) and white (#FFFFFF). Some interpreters treat unknown colors as white, but we'll restrict ourselves to only approved colors. The hex color codes specify the mix of red, green, and blue that make up the color.

Representing Numbers

Piet is stack based, like Forth. Numbers are represented as blocks of the same color and the number of pixels in the block specifies the color. Therefore, a 3×5 pixel block represents $3 \times 5 = 15$, whereas a square with 5 pixel sides is 25. Note that the blocks need not be rectangular or square, but only connected on the edges. A block may even contain holes. If that sounds very abstract, don't worry. We'll see examples below.

Representing Programs

Each pixel of the program is significant. However, if we attempt to look at the program at the pixel level, we'll be hard-pressed to see anything. Therefore, we'll present programs as magnified images. When images are magnified, each pixel becomes a square of pixels. The square of pixels mapping to the original pixel is called a *codel*. For example, if the image is magnified by a factor of 10, each pixel becomes a 10×10 square; therefore, the codels are each a 10×10 pixel region.

Consider the example program *add.png*, shown in grayscale in Figure 9-2.

Figure 9-2: Adding two numbers, 2 + 2 = 4

The original image is 9 pixels wide and 4 pixels high. The version shown in Figure 9-2 is magnified by 200, so each pixel becomes a 200×200 pixel square, a codel. For this example, I added grid lines to explicitly mark the codel boundaries.

Typesetting alters the codel to pixel mapping, but knowing that *add.png* is 4 pixels high helps us look at Figure 9-2 and understand the codels. For example, from bottom to top, the leftmost column is two black codels and two light red codels. Piet treats black as a wall, so the two light red codels form a 2×1 rectangle, that is, the number 2. We'll walk through *add.png* below. For now, just focus on the mapping between blocks, pixels, and codels.

Piet Commands

Look again at Figure 9-1. Beginning with the upper-left corner and moving to the right transitions the colors from red to yellow to green to cyan to blue, and, wrapping around from the right to the left, back to red. Moving along the rows in Figure 9-1, we see a change in the hue (that is, the color) without a change in lightness. Each move along the top row of Figure 9-1 changes a single $C0_{16}$ to FF_{16} or vice versa. Similarly, for the middle row, values change from 00_{16} to FF_{16}, and for the bottom row, from 00_{16} to $C0_{16}$.

Moving up and down the columns changes the lightness of the color while preserving the hue. From top to middle, $C0_{16}$ becomes 00_{16}, whereas from middle to bottom, FF_{16} becomes $C0_{16}$. As with rows, moving from the darkest color in a column to the lightest is also a single transition step. This all means that movement along the color table is cyclic.

Why all this concern about hue and lightness? It's because Piet does not represent commands uniquely. There isn't a single color that means "push a number" or "add." Instead, it's the number of hue or lightness steps taken between regions that specifies the command. The colors themselves do not matter. The color table is cyclic, so it's possible to move from any initial color to any ending color. This means that any command can be specified from any starting color.

Table 9-1 lists Piet's commands according to the hue and lightness change that causes the command to execute. Here, the rows represent a change in hue by that many steps and the columns a similar change in lightness.

Table 9-1: Piet Commands as Specified by Transitions in Hue (Row) and Lightness (Column) Between Blocks

	0	1	2
0	none	push	pop
1	+	−	×
2	÷	mod	not
3	>	pointer	switch
4	dup	roll	inN
5	inC	outN	outC

For example, to push a number on the stack, the transition between blocks must involve a lightness change of one step but no change in hue. Therefore, any block transition from a particular row of Figure 9-1 to the row below that keeps the column constant results in a push command. The number pushed on the stack is the number of codels (pixels) in the block just exited. Recall that moving from the darkest to the lightest for any color is also a lightness transition of one.

Similarly, to execute an outC instruction to output the top stack item as an ASCII character, the block transition must change lightness by two and hue by five. For example, moving from a block that is light red to one that is dark magenta will execute outC. Likewise, moving from a cyan block to a light green block will also execute outC. Count the hue and lightness changes necessary using Figure 9-1 to convince yourself that moving from a cyan block to a light green block will indeed specify an outC command.

Many of the commands in Table 9-1 are familiar to us after our investigation of Forth in Chapter 4. This is especially true of the math operators, greater-than, and dup, which duplicates the top stack item. Also, push was described in the previous paragraph. Lastly, pop is intuitive: drop the top stack item (this is DROP in Forth).

Using Forth-style stack effect comments helps to illuminate this set of Piet commands.

```
pop    ( a   -- )
  +    ( a b -- a+b )
  −    ( a b -- a-b )
  ×    ( a b -- a*b )
  ÷    ( a b -- a/b )
mod    ( a b -- a%b )
  >    ( a b -- a>b )
```

The input and output commands, inN, inC, outN, and outC, are similarly straightforward. The N versions accept a number or output a number. The C versions accept a character or output the top stack item as an ASCII character. For example, outC prints A if the top stack item is 65—the ASCII code for capital *A*.

The remaining instructions, not, pointer, switch, and roll, need some explanation. The simplest of these is not. In this instruction we pop the top stack item, and push a 1 on the stack if the item is not 0 and push 0 on the stack otherwise. The net effect is to toggle the truth value where 0 is false, and anything else is true, as in C. The npiet interpreter is written in C, so this behavior is natural.

The pointer command rotates the direction pointer (DP) clockwise the number of times specified by the top stack item. The switch command pops the stack and toggles the codel chooser (CC) that many times, ignoring the sign. We'll cover the DP and CC in detail in the next section. For now, just know that pointer affects the DP and switch affects the CC.

Piet's most complex command is roll, which is used to manipulate the stack by rolling a set number of items a given number of times. Let's look at an example to see what this means.

The file *roll32.png* contains a program that places the numbers 1 through 5 on the stack and sets up a call to roll to rotate the top three items two times. Visually, *roll32.png* looks like this:

The program flows from left to right, column by column, to push 1, then 2, 3, 4, and 5 on the stack. The following two columns push 3 and then 2. The remainder of the code calls roll to rotate the top three stack items two times and dump the stack by repeated calls to outN.

Before the call to roll, the stack, from left to right, is

1 2 3 4 5 3 2

The call to roll first pops 2, then 3. The 2 is the number of times to roll the top 3 items. A roll rotates the items so that 3 4 5 becomes 5 3 4. Therefore, two rolls are

$$3\ 4\ 5 \rightarrow 5\ 3\ 4 \rightarrow 4\ 5\ 3$$

and the final stack is

$$1\ 2\ 4\ 5\ 3$$

The stack being popped from right to left implies that the output of *roll32 .png* should be 35421, as no spaces are printed. Indeed, this is the output, so roll behaves as we think it should.

Program Flow

Program flow in most languages is straightforward. Unless a branch, goto, or equivalent happens, statements are executed sequentially. Thinking now of low-level machine code, there is a single program counter, something that points to the next instruction. In Piet, program flow is more complex. Flow moves from a block of the same color to the next block, beginning with the top leftmost block. The direction is controlled by the *direction pointer (DP)*. When a Piet program begins, the DP is to the right.

At first, we might think we need only a DP; however, there is a minor issue. Piet moves from block to block, but to determine the next block, it needs to know how far to move along which edge of the current block. This introduces the *codel chooser (CC)*. The CC is initially to the left, but it can also be to the right. Whose left or right? The DP's left or right. Therefore, when a Piet program begins, the DP is to the right and the CC is to the left, meaning the next block is the one to the topmost right edge of the current block. In fact, it is to the furthest right extent of the block. Thus, Piet selects the next block by going as far as possible in the current block in the direction of the DP and then respecting the current value of CC.

For example, consider the image below.

The program is currently in the left block, 2×1 codels, and the DP is pointing to the right. Which block should be considered next? The top or the bottom of the second column? If the CC is to the left, Piet moves to the right from the top of the 2×1 block to select the top block of the right column, which is the darker block. If the CC were to the right, we would choose the lower block instead.

Figure 9-3 presents the relationship between the DP and CC in two different ways.

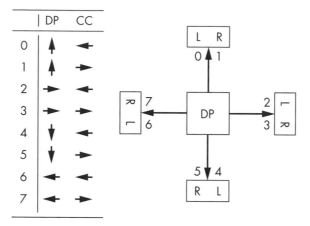

Figure 9-3: The relationship between the direction pointer (DP) and the codel chooser (CC)

The diagram on the right shows the DP as arrows leading up, down, left, or right, with the CC for each direction marked as *L* or *R*. The numbers correspond to the rows of the table on the left of the figure. The table shows DP and CC with arrows. The two complementary presentations should clarify how to use DP and CC to control program flow.

Piet moves from colored block to colored block based on DP and CC, but there are two special colors we must also consider: black and white. Black, as stated above, acts like a wall or the edge of the image. When Piet encounters black or an edge, it begins adjusting the DP and CC to try to find an escape, that is, a way out to continue the program. If it can't find an escape, the program ends. Specifically, Piet uses the following steps to move through the image:

1. From the current position, move as far as possible in the direction of the DP until you encounter either a color change or the edge of the image.

2. From the position found in Step 1, move as far as possible to the left or right depending on the CC direction. This selects the first codel of the next block.

3. If the steps above encounter a black block or image edge, we toggle the CC from left to right or right to left and repeat the steps above. If this process fails, the DP is rotated clockwise and CC toggling repeats. This process continues until a path is found to a new block or all moves fail.

4. If all DP and CC adjustments fail, the program terminates.

The steps above handle colored blocks, black blocks, and image edges. To further complicate matters, Piet also allows white blocks. White blocks are no-operation blocks called *no-ops*. The interpreter passes through white blocks like any other block, but the transition does not imply a command. This allows the programmer to change from one colored block to another without executing a command, and, as we'll see below, the arrangement of black and white blocks can act as a control structure to enforce desired program flow.

Piet in Action

In this section, we'll get our hands dirty and work through four examples: *add.png*, *hi.png*, *countdown.png*, and *random.png*. The first prints the sum of 2 + 2; the second, which we saw above, prints Hi; the third is a countdown loop; and the fourth is a simple pseudorandom number generator.

Proving 2 + 2 = 4

Our first example, *add.png* has a direct analog in the following Forth code:

```
2 2 + .
```

The number 2 is pushed on the stack, followed by another 2, then + pops the top two stack items, adds them, and pushes the sum onto the stack which is then printed as a number. Let's walk through the execution of *add.png* to understand how it works.

First, run *add.png* using npiet.

```
> npiet examples/add.png
4
```

If all npiet did was run the program given, we'd be hard-pressed to understand program flow, let alone debug it if necessary. Fortunately for us, npiet can dump an output image and show an execution trace. For example, the following command produces an output file, *npiet-trace.png*, as shown in Figure 9-4.

```
> npiet -tpic -tpf 80 examples/add.png
```

The -tpic option produces the trace and -tpf 80 scales the output so the text is easier to read, at least in the output image file if not on the printed page.

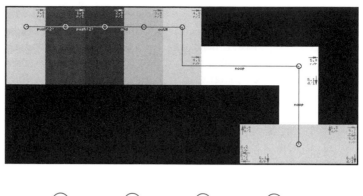

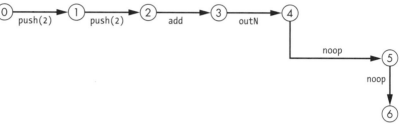

Figure 9-4: Tracing add.png

The top part of Figure 9-4 is npiet's output in grayscale. The bottom part of the figure traces the program flow to make it easier to follow in the book. The file *add.png* consists of five blocks, each 2×1 codels, corresponding to the first five circles marked 0 through 4. Recall that Piet commands are specified by hue and lightness transitions, so the commands are printed above the arrows moving from block to block.

The Forth code above is duplicated by the Piet code:

$$\text{push(2)} \rightarrow \text{push(2)} \rightarrow \text{add} \rightarrow \text{outN}$$

After outN is a white region, which represents a no-op, so Piet flows through the white area following the flow rules above. First, as DP is to the right, Piet moves to the end of the first part of the block and encounters a black codel. The CC is right, and Piet can't move further to the right because of the black block, so DP rotates to face downward and moves into the light colored block at the lower right. This block is surrounded by black or the edge of the image. As it moves to the edges of the current block, Piet can find no way out even after rotating DP all the way around, so the interpreter gives up and the program ends.

If you look at the *npiet-trace.png* image npiet created via the -tpic option, you'll see color and small substeps showing how CC changes as DP changes. Please do look at the trace image, as it is too hard to read the substep indications in Figure 9-4.

Saying Hi

We tested our Piet installation with *hi.png*. Now let's walk through the code to learn more about how Piet applies flow control rules to select where to move next. Unlike *add.png*, *hi.png* doesn't use simple blocks, so some thought is required to understand why the Piet interpreter does what it does.

Figure 9-5 shows us a trace of *hi.png* with the program flow below it.

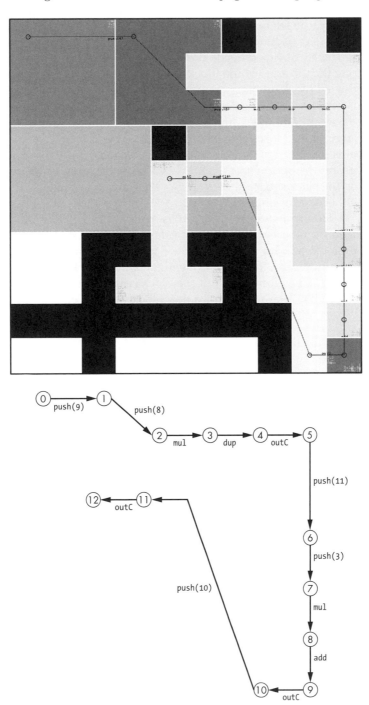

Figure 9-5: Tracing hi.png

In this case, the blocks have irregular shapes, and it might not be obvious why the interpreter selects the path it does. The irregular blocks in Figure 9-5 have been outlined in white to make them easier to see.

The transition from Step 0 to Step 1 is simple enough: Block 0 is a square, the DP begins to the right, and CC is to the left (top), so the only place to go is Block 1. However, the transition from Step 1 to Step 2 isn't immediately obvious. Inside Block 1 we expect the flow to move to the right along the top edge of the block. Although it is not clearly visible in Figure 9-5, the top block is black and acts as a barrier. Therefore, according to Piet's flow rules, CC is toggled to be to the right or bottom of the block as DP is to the right. This alone might imply rotating DP to face down and selecting the large, light-colored irregular block. However, Piet's flow rules apply to the maximum extent of a block in the direction DP is facing. For Block 1, this means the bottom of the block, as it is furthest to the right and not stopped by the black square at the top. So, Piet moves from Block 1 to the small, light-colored square of Step 2.

Flow from Step 2 to Step 10 is straightforward. To go from Step 10 to Step 11, we use the same set of rules as going from Step 1 to Step 2, but this time DP is facing to the left, so we select the leftmost edge of Block 10 and flow moves to Block 12, the terminal block. Block 12 is a trap. DP is to the left and the leftmost part of the block is at the bottom, but once there, Piet will find no way to move to a new block, thereby ending the program.

As for the code implied by *hi.png*, it's quite simple:

```
push(9)
push(8)
mul
dup
outC        -- "H"
push(11)
push(3)
mul
add
outC        -- "i"
push(10)
outC        -- "\n"
```

with $9 \times 8 = 72$, the ASCII code for *H*, and $72 + 11 \times 3 = 105$, the code for *i*, followed by ASCII 10 for the final newline character.

Countdown

The file *countdown.png* contains a program to count down from 10 to 1. To make our lives easier, as far as tracing goes, we'll work with the slightly edited version in *countdown3.png*, which counts down from 3.

Running *countdown3.png* produces the following:

```
> npiet -tpic -tpf 80 examples/countdown3.png
3
2
1
```

I admit the output of *countdown3.png* is not particularly interesting, but this example shows us how to work with loops in Piet, which is. The top part of Figure 9-6 is a trace of *countdown3.png*. As printed, it won't be possible to see the flow properly. So as with Figure 9-4, refer instead to the flow diagram at the bottom of Figure 9-6 and review the file *npiet-trace.png* that npiet made for us when executing *countdown3.png*.

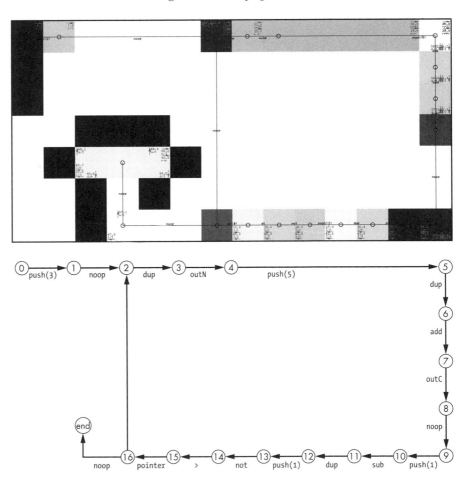

Figure 9-6: Tracing countdown3.png

We might write *countdown3.png* as in Listing 9-1.

```
        push(3)
❶ loop  dup
        outN
    ❷   push(5)
        dup
        add
        outC
    ❸   push(1)
        sub
        dup
    ❹   push(1)
        not
        if (tos > 0) goto loop
        end
```

Listing 9-1: countdown3.png *as text*

The code pushes the limit, 3, onto the stack, and then the loop begins by duplicating the top stack item so it can be printed as a number ❶. The next block of code pushes 10 on the stack and outputs it as a character. For Unix systems, ASCII 10 is newline ❷.

The counter value is still on the stack, so it's decremented by 1 ❸. The final dup in this section of the code sets up for the comparison to see whether the countdown is 0.

Piet uses the number of pixels in a block to represent numbers. Therefore, it isn't possible to directly represent 0 and push it on the stack. However, ❹ shows us a useful Piet idiom: get a 0 on the stack by pushing a 1 and calling not. The stack is now set up with two copies of the counter value and a 0. The top two stack items are consumed by >, leaving a 0 or 1 on the stack.

Here's where things get interesting. Piet has no explicit branch instruction, that is, no direct analog of the if statement shown in Listing 9-1. Instead, Piet uses the pointer instruction to rotate the DP, which at this point in *countdown3.png* is facing left. The pointer instruction uses the top stack value to rotate DP clockwise by that many steps. The result from > is a 0 or 1. If 1, it means that the counter value is greater than 0, so we want the loop to continue. In that case, pointer will rotate DP one position clockwise so that it is now facing up. Moving directly up from this part of *countdown3.png* puts us right at the beginning of the loop, ❶ in Listing 9-1. The direction pointer is facing up, but there is nowhere to go, so Piet, following the flow rules, rotates DP clockwise, so it is now facing right, and the loop continues.

If > leaves 0 on the stack, the DP is unaffected by pointer, and flow continues to the left, ultimately landing in the trap where Piet is unable to find an exit, so the program ends.

A Pseudorandom Number Generator

The final example in this section is *random.png*, a simple pseudorandom number generator. The program implements a *linear congruential* pseudorandom number generator, which is a simple way to generate a sequence of integers that appears random. We'll work with this type of generator again in Chapter 13.

The generator itself is the single equation

$$s_{i+1} \leftarrow as_i \bmod m$$

for some initial seed value, s_0. Both a and m are integer constants. If a and m are properly selected, then the sequence of s_i values generated by taking the output and using it as the new input will pass statistical tests for randomness, or so we hope.

We can break the equation down into steps: first, multiply the current seed value (s_i) by the multiplier, a. Then, calculate the remainder when dividing that product by m and set that as the new seed value (s_{i+1}). The modulo operation (mod) gives the remainder and, fortunately for us, is one of the math operations Piet supports.

Of course, we need to select a and m. Good values are large, but we don't want to work with large integers, as they correspond to large uniform blocks in the program image. Linear congruential generators have been studied for decades, and many sets of constants have been found. We'll use $a = 209$ and $m = 2^{12} - 3 = 4093$ because they are small values.

Okay, we now need a program to take an initial seed value, apply the equation, output the new seed value, and repeat. Piet's stack will hold the current seed value. The initial seed value will be pushed onto the stack, after which we'll calculate the new seed, print it, and leave it on the stack for the next pass through the loop. We'll want to capture the sequence of integers, so we'll loop forever and use CTRL-C to stop the program when we've generated all the numbers we care to output.

In text, we might write the program as

```
       push(1)
loop   push(209)
       mul
       push(4093)
       mod
       dup
       outN
       push(10)
       outC
       goto loop
```

where goto loop will be achieved by arranging a sequence of white and black regions to force program flow back to the top of the loop.

We could make an image like the program, but notice the push(4093). That's a rather large block by Piet standards, so let's replace both push(209) and push(4093) with a set of calculations that end with the proper number on the stack. For example, push(209) is the same as

---

push(10), dup, mul, push(2), mul, push(9), add

---

and push(4093) is

---

push(10), dup, dup, mul, mul, push(4),
mul, push(10), push(9), mul, push(3),
add, add

It's not pretty as text, but it is easy to implement as a picture. Figure 9-7 shows the resulting program (see *random.png*). The program flow is below, where adjacent labeled circles are connected in a clockwise direction.

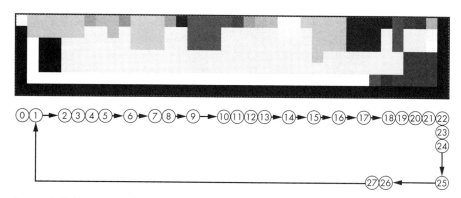

Figure 9-7: Tracing random.png

The transition from Step 0 to Step 1 pushes the initial seed (1) on the stack. Steps 2 through Step 24 generate the next seed value and display it as an integer. Steps 25 through 27 print the newline. The white region causes the program to flow back to Step 2 to generate the next seed. The loop runs until we press CTRL-C to quit the interpreter.

Let's run *random.png* and capture the output so we can analyze it.

```
> npiet examples/random.png >examples/random.txt
```

Let the code run for 10 to 20 seconds and then stop it with CTRL-C. My run produced 2,333,347 values, which is quite sufficient for our purposes.

The sequence begins with the following numbers:

209
2751
1939
44

```
1010
2347
```

This seems "random," but how can we know? Of course, we know the sequence cannot possibly be random, as it was generated deterministically. However, suppose we didn't know that. In that case, we could perform tests to help us decide if the sequence is or isn't worth calling "random." The entire point of developing high-quality pseudorandom number generators is to create deterministic sequences that pass all known randomness tests.

Before we can apply randomness tests, we must convert the text file of integers into a binary file of double-precision floating-point numbers in the range $[0, 1)$, meaning from 0 up to, but not including, 1. For that, we'll use *random_double.py*.

```
import struct
v = [float(i[:-1])/4093.0 for i in open("random.txt")]
s = struct.pack('d'*len(v), *v)
with open("random.dat","wb") as f:
    f.write(s)
```

Here, *random_double.py* produces *random.dat* from *random.txt* by dividing each value by 4,093, which is one more than the largest possible integer the generator outputs.

One way to check for randomness is to build a *histogram*. A histogram partitions the range of possible integers—in this case, $[1, 4092]$—into several equal-sized bins, say 10. Then we locate the bin each number falls into and increment the count for the bin. When all the random values have been tallied, the histogram shows us how many have fallen into each bin. If we divide the count per bin by the number of values tallied, which in this case is 2,333,347, the counts become frequencies telling us the fraction of numbers we can expect in each bin. If we want, we can interpret the frequencies as the probability a random value will land in that bin.

If the values are randomly distributed, each bin is equally likely, so we expect the fraction in each bin to be roughly the same. So, for example, if we have 10 bins, we expect about 10 percent of the values to fall into each of them.

To perform the tallies, we need a bit of Python code and access to the NumPy library. The actual code is in the file *random_histogram.py*, but you need not install NumPy to run it. The histogram gives us the following:

```
10.019,9.996,9.996,9.995,9.995,9.996,9.995,9.995,9.995,10.019
```

Here I've rounded the percentages to three decimals. The first number tells us the percent of samples in the range $[0, 0.1)$, the second the percent in $[0.1, 0.2)$, and so on. The percentages are virtually identical. So that's a good sign that *random.png* is giving us well-distributed values.

Does that mean *random.png* is a good pseudorandom number generator? Not quite. If *random.png* were generating 1, 2, 3, 4, and so on modulo 4093, we'd still get the histogram above with enough samples. To be a good pseudorandom generator, the ith value and the $i + 1$th value must not be correlated. In other words, there should be no easy way to predict the next value generated from the previous.

To check if there is a correlation between one value and the next, we can use the code in *corr_test.c*. This program reads *random.dat* and calculates the *correlation coefficient*, a single number. If the values are not correlated one to the next, the correlation coefficient will be very close to 0 to indicate there is no relationship between them.

Compile *corr_test.c* using the following command:

```
> gcc corr_test.c -o corr_test -lm
```

Then run it on *random.dat*.

```
> corr_test 3 random.dat
corr = 0.00047 (n=2333347), expected 95% CI=[-0.00131, 0.00131],
      test PASSED
```

The 3 in the command line tells corr_test that *random.dat* is a binary file of double precision floating-point values.

The output has the word PASSED in it, in all caps to boot. So *corr_test* believes *random.dat* is not correlated. The correlation coefficient is close to 0. The CI part of the output is a *confidence interval*. We can read the confidence interval as meaning there's a 95 percent chance the true correlation coefficient is between the given limits. Notice that the range includes 0, another good sign.

Therefore, *random.png* is a good pseudorandom generator, right? Still, not quite. We only checked for correlations between one value and the next. There might be correlations between a value and some other, later value. You begin to see the issue with testing pseudorandom generators. Real generators are tested against large test suites that include many different kinds of tests, all of which only the best pseudorandom generators pass.

We'll do one more straightforward test of the output in *random.dat*. Let's take successive pairs of values and plot them as a point. Then, we'll look at the resulting plot to see if any pattern jumps out at us. For example, the first two values in *random.dat* are 0.05106279 and 0.67212314. So we'll plot a point at (0.05106279, 0.67212314), then do the same for the next pair. We'll stop after plotting 1,000 points to avoid cluttering the plot.

Take a look at Figure 9-8. Does anything jump out at you?

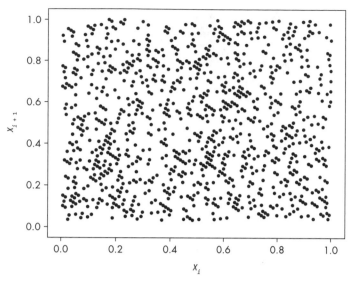

Figure 9-8: Plotting pairs of pseudorandom values

The points often lie along a diagonal from upper left to lower right. This is a strong indication of longer-range correlations in the sequence. At last we can now make a statement about the output of *random.dat*: it's a lousy pseudorandom generator. However, it does fill the space. There are no obvious regions in Figure 9-8 where there are no points. So the output of *random.png* is sufficient for a simple video game, but don't make policy decisions related to climate change based on simulations using it.

Pseudorandom number generation will show up again later in the book. For now, let's return to Piet's artistic roots and create a small tribute to Piet Mondrian.

A Tribute to Piet Mondrian

Piet Mondrian was an important member of a group of Dutch artists and architects who developed what has come to be known as the *De Stijl* movement. De Stijl, literally "the style," uses abstract forms with basic elements. One of Mondrian's most widely recognized works is his unexpectedly satisfying *Composition II in Red, Blue, and Yellow*. The painting is an excellent example of the De Stijl movement. As a tribute to Mondrian, let's make an executable copy of *Composition II*. In the process, we'll learn how to use npiet's editor, npietedit.

Duplicating the original painting with a modern graphics program is straightforward. Figure 9-9 shows the result.

Figure 9-9: A re-creation of Mondrian's Composition II

The largest block is red, the smaller block on the left is blue, and the smallest block on the right is yellow. The remainder of the painting is black and white.

The original painting is signed on the lower left with *P M 30* for Piet Mondrian, 1930. We'll make the copy executable by embedding a simple program to output PM30 in place of the signature. The code that we need isn't particularly challenging, but it is helpful as an exercise in learning to use npietedit.

One of the immediate challenges in writing code for Piet is working with colors and transitions to get the desired commands. Although we might work with pencil and paper, counting from color to new color to get the correct number of hue and lightness changes to cause the desired command to execute, we need not be so primitive. Instead, the clever npietedit program lets us color the program image as needed while also calculating the proper color transitions.

To output PM30, we need to push the ASCII values for each character on the stack before calling outC. We'll add a final newline as well to put PM30 on its own line. Therefore, we need a program to output five characters. However, we must embed the program in the larger *Composition II* image in a way that isn't too conspicuous. Fortunately for us, the way Piet runs and the structure of *Composition II* match nicely. For example, Piet begins in the upper leftmost pixel of the image with the DP to the right and CC to the left. As that portion of the image is white, Piet will run across to the first black pixel, the beginning of the large vertical black bar. We'll embed our code in this bar, knowing Piet will find it. Additionally, we'll orient the program vertically, with DP moving down.

Of course, we must have a program to embed, so let's use npietedit to create it. Launch npietedit with no arguments.

```
> npietedit
```

The interface is in Figure 9-10.

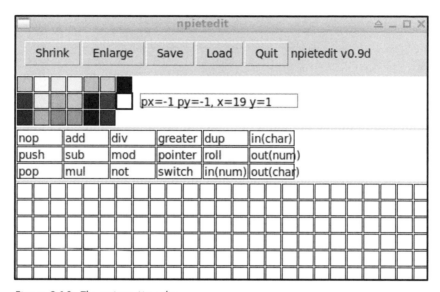

Figure 9-10: The npietedit editor

The interface consists of a color selector, a command selector, and a drawing area showing individual pixels. Select a color and click in the drawing area to set that pixel. The command selector is the most valuable part of the editor. For example, to push the number 5 on the stack, select any desired color, say light red, the top leftmost color. Then, fill in five pixels to make a block, say five rows tall and one column wide. Then, as DP will be to the right, select the topmost pixel of the block and then select **Push**. The editor, knowing the current color is light red, switches the color to red, one lightness level darker.

Changing the lightness by 1 is how Piet specifies push, so this is the correct color. Click the top pixel to the immediate right of the light red block to place a single red pixel. Given how DP is pointed, Piet will correctly push 5 on the stack. In this way, it is possible to draw any sequence of commands, with a little practice and attention paid to selecting the proper color before clicking the command to arrive at the necessary hue and lightness change.

Use the buttons at the top of the interface to control npietedit. They are largely self explanatory. However, Save and Load will not bring up the usual file selection dialog. Instead, they write and read a fixed filename, npietedit-filename.ppm. So, use Save to dump the drawing and then rename npietedit-filename.ppm to something else to preserve the program. Likewise, copy a saved version of a program to the same filename to then load it into npietedit. The .ppm file format is a portable pixmap image. The npiet interpreter will use these files as they are. Most graphics programs will load and display portable pixmap images as well. If you wish to change to another filetype, use something like gimp or convert, a command line tool that is part of ImageMagick (*https://imagemagick.org/index.php*). ImageMagick is included in the base Ubuntu installation.

Our program needs to push ASCII values on the stack and then call outC. The Forth equivalent of this is as follows:

```
8 10 * emit 11 7 * emit 10 5 * 1 + emit 6 8 * emit 5 5 + emit
```

The Forth word emit has the same effect as Piet's outC command, and multiplication of smaller numbers is used to prevent large blocks of one color.

Let's translate the Forth code into Piet using npietedit. The only twist is that we want the code to run vertically so we can embed it in the black part of the larger *Composition II* image. To do this, we must rotate DP downward from the right. This is easily done by a white region with a 90-degree turn.

The file *composition.ppm* contains the necessary Piet code as a direct translation of the Forth above. If you run it, you'll see that it produces the desired output.

```
> npiet examples/composition.ppm
PM30
```

To see the code in npietedit, copy *composition.ppm* to *npietedit-filename.ppm* in the same directory as npietedit, launch the editor, and click **Load**. The result is Figure 9-11. The code runs from top to bottom.

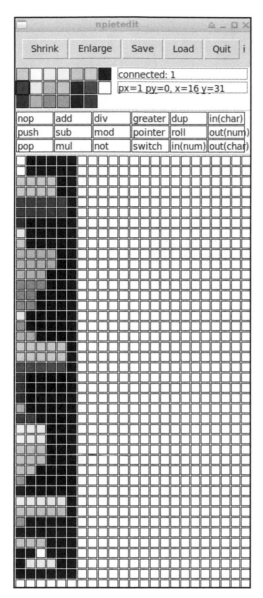

Figure 9-11: Code to output PM30

We're almost finished with our tribute. All that remains is to embed *composition.ppm* in the redrawn *Composition II*, which is in the file *mondrian .png*. To do the embedding, I use gimp to load both images, select the actual image portion of *composition.ppm*, copy it, and paste it into *mondrian.png*, moving it over to the central vertical black region.

The Piet interpreter will pass over the white region on the upper left, so we need to add a single white pixel after positioning the code so that the vertical bar is now

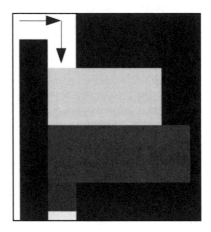

with arrows showing how DP changes direction to execute the code vertically.

The resulting combined image is in *compositionII_pm30.png*. If you run it with npiet, you get the expected PM30 output. Take a look at the image itself. It looks like *Composition II* with a splash of color toward the top.

The Piet Universe

A successful esolang engenders a following. People use it, share it, modify it, build tools for it, and create websites about it. By this measure, Piet is successful. What follows are links to excellent Piet code examples, tools, and generally anything else worth noting about Piet. The list is by no means exhaustive, and worthy entries have doubtless been missed.

About Piet

Piet has generated a collection of blog posts and many online discussions. The short list here explores more about the language itself and includes some interesting (unusual) Piet experiments.

Main Piet site   The main Piet page by creator David Morgan-Mar. Start here to learn more about the language. (*https://www.dangermouse.net/esoteric/piet.html*)

Piet tutorial   This is a nice, basic tutorial to programming in Piet and works well as an adjunct to what we've discussed in this chapter. (*https://www.youtube.com/watch?v=4kH4T8uwHMw/*)

Piet in the literature   Piet is an example in this paper about code visualization. Alex McLean's dissertation is also online and similarly mentions Piet. See "Visualisation of live code," Electronic Visualisation and the Arts (EVA 2010), 26–30.

Running classic paintings as Piet programs   This is an experiment in mixing Piet and classic works of art. Piet fans are nothing if not creative. (*http://omnigatherum.ca/wp/?p=57/*)

Piet meets poetry   An experiment with Piet and poetry. The final product, *bark.png*, generates a haiku. (*http://theorangeduck.com/page/making-poetry-piet/*)

Code

The best way to learn a language is to review examples in that language. Therefore, should Piet draw you further in, the examples here will help you improve your Piet prowess.

Main Piet examples page   The best place for Piet examples is off the main Piet site. Not all of these examples work with npiet, but most do. The works of the great masters are here; check them out. (*https://www.dangermouse.net/esoteric/piet/samples.html*)

FizzBuzz   Historically, a common programming interview question was to write code to generate the numbers from 1 to 100 but replace multiples of 3 with "Fizz," multiples of 5 with "Buzz," and multiples of 3 and 5 with "FizzBuzz." FizzBuzz is a simple program and therefore a favorite target for esolangs. A Piet version of FizzBuzz is at *http://www.toothycat.net/~sham/fizzbuzz.png*, and, should you feel like diving into far too much detail about FizzBuzz, you can read Tom Dalling's blog post at *https://www.tomdalling.com/blog/software-design/fizzbuzz-in-too-much-detail/*.

Tic-tac-toe   A fully interactive, unbeatable Piet version of tic-tac-toe (naughts and crosses) is worth a bit of your time. (*https://freesoft.dev/program/9705871/*)

Implementations and Tools

Computer people love to build things. The description of Piet on the main page mentioned earlier is begging to be written up in some language or another. The implementations here are in many different languages, like C++, Python, Rust, and even Haskell. Not every implementation can run every example program, but most perform reasonably well.

A Python interpreter, *https://www.dangermouse.net/esoteric/piet/Piet_py.txt*

Another Python interpreter, *https://github.com/JensBouman/Piet_interpreter/*

An interpreter in Haskell,*https://hackage.haskell.org/package/piet-0.1/docs/Language-Piet-Interpreter.html*

An interpreter in C++, *https://www.matthias-ernst.eu/fpiet.html*

An interpreter in Rust, *https://github.com/dfockler/rustpiet/*

A browser-based interpreter and IDE in TypeScript, *https://gitlab.hrsw.eu/thomas.richter/piet-ide/*

Several projects have gone the other way to produce assemblers or compilers from a text-based language to Piet. That is, the output is an image implementing the program in Piet. Again, computer people are a creative bunch.

GitHub repositories devoted to Piet, *https://github.com/topics/piet/*

An assembler and compiler producing Piet code, *https://www.toothycat .net/wiki/wiki.pl?MoonShadow/Piet/*

The PietC compiler, which produces Piet code as output, *https://github .com/cjayross/pietc/*

Another assembler generating Piet output, *https://github.com/sl236/Piet/*

Discussion

Piet is a procedural language with arbitrary-sized programs. There are no variables, but the stack is unlimited. So we might suspect that Piet is Turing complete. In fact, Piet is definitely Turing complete because a clever individual has written a Brainfuck (BF) interpreter in Piet and BF is known to be Turing complete as we'll see next in Chapter 10. The BF interpreter (*https://lutter.cc/piet/*) is worth a look, perhaps after reading Chapter 10. To test it, don't forget to add a pipe (|) at the end of the BF code even if the code itself does not accept any input. I tried it with "Hello, world!" and npiet and it works. Don't forget to add the -q command line option to suppress the input prompt.

Okay, Piet is a Turing complete language. What else can we say about it? Programming in Piet is quite a challenge, perhaps because it is so alien to standard text-based programming or even standard visual programming languages that ty the drag-and-drop of components.

I find it fascinating that loops in Piet are, literally, loops—the image structure itself controls the flow of the program, so a loop really does find its way back to the starting point. For example, the loop in *random.png* is implemented by a long white block along the bottom of the program image followed by a 90-degree turn to force DP to point in the right direction to encounter the beginning of the loop. Also, Piet's flow control rules make it such that the DP will rotate again to the right to be pointing in the proper direction to repeat the loop endlessly, all without a single bit of standard syntax. In a way, Piet has no syntax, just flow rules; the image itself becomes the syntax. In that sense, Piet programs are not unique, as multiple, nearly infinite, ways to draw the required flow exist.

Piet's method for implying commands using hue and lightness changes, as opposed to assigning specific colors to the commands, is equally clever and again magnifies the number of possible Piet programs considerably. Even if we choose the same layout, sequence of blocks, and image size, we get many options simply by selecting a different starting color. Piet's instruction set is small, so learning the necessary transitions for each command isn't too difficult. If you experiment with Piet for any length of time, you'll begin to pick up on these transitions. For example, changing lightness by 1 is push, which is a command you'll learn quickly.

It's also interesting that Piet separates block size and commands. For example, if we want to execute push(4) and know that the next instruction is push(3), we might make the first block 2×2 pixels, say light red, and make the second block three vertical pixels of red. The transition from light red to red implies push with the argument, 4, from the size of the light red block. The push command does not care about the size of the new block, only that it is red, one lightness level darker. The fact that the new block is of size 3 is useful to push 3 when transitioning to the next block, which must be dark red, so we combine a number with a color transition, thereby making the code more compact. Of course, color transitions are commands, so it might sometimes be necessary to use a white block to change color without executing a command.

In the end, Piet is a fun esolang and an excellent example of a novel way to think about coding. Some forethought is necessary when designing a program, as it isn't easy, even with tools like npietedit, to suddenly add new code by moving an existing block to make room, but editors capable of such actions are certainly possible.

Piet is Turing complete, but extensions to the language might be of interest. For example, the ability to access the stack as an array adds variables. Also, some kind of subroutine ability would make coding easier. All of these are exercises for the ambitious reader.

Summary

This chapter introduced us to Piet, the language where pictures are programs. First, we walked through the elements of the language to understand how it works and how to code with colors. Next, we went finger painting and got messy learning how specific programs worked, step by step. This led us to a simple tribute to Piet Mondrian, whose style and name inspired Piet's creation. Piet has grown in popularity, at least as far as esolangs go, to the point where many program examples, implementations, and ancillary tools are now available. We cataloged several of them should you wish to explore further. Then, as always, we ended the chapter with some thoughts on the language and its capabilities.

Our next esolang is perhaps the best known of all. We're simply calling it *BF*. If Piet is a local celebrity, BF is a superstar.

10

BRAINFUCK

Brainfuck, or *BF* as we'll call it, is more or less the grandfather of all esolangs. It's one of the earliest and probably the most extended, modified, discussed, and parodied esolang in existence. In this chapter, we'll see what all the fuss is about it—there's more to it than just the name!

WTF Is BF?

BF is the brainchild of Urban Müller, who loosed it upon an unsuspecting world in 1993. His goal was to create a tiny language leading to a tiny compiler for the Amiga computer. His compiler was 296 bytes long. Later in the chapter, we'll encounter a BF compiler that's only 166 bytes long.

How can BF compilers be so tiny? Because BF itself is tiny (see Table 10-1, which describes all *eight* commands). As a certain pig might say, "Th-th-that's all, folks!"

Table 10-1: BF in All Its Glory

Command	Action
>	Increment memory pointer
<	Decrement memory pointer
.	Print memory as a character
,	Input a character to memory
+	Increment memory
-	Decrement memory
[	Begin loop if memory not 0
]	Continue loop if memory not 0

The machine BF expects is quite similar to a Turing machine. The BF machine is a vector of cells, each of which holds a single value. Originally, there were 30,000 cells, each capable of holding a single byte [0, 255]. The interpreters we'll use in this chapter have 32-bit cells. BF is analogous to what's called a *Harvard architecture*, a hardware architecture in which the program space and memory are distinct. There's no self-modifying code here, though I wouldn't be surprised if someone has created a von Neumann version of BF just to explore what self-modifying BF code might be able to accomplish. Recall that a von Neumann architecture combines program space and memory. Modern PCs are von Neumann machines.

A Turing machine has a tape head that moves along a tape to read and write symbols. BF does the same, but in this case we'll call the "tape head" a memory or cell pointer. The > and < instructions move the memory pointer from cell to cell and the remaining BF instructions operate on the current memory cell. When a BF program starts, it assumes each memory cell has a value of 0 and the pointer is looking at cell 0.

We now know what two of BF's eight instructions do. The comma (,) and period (.) are input and output, respectively. The + increments the cell and - decrements it.

What makes BF interesting as a language are the [and] loop instructions. Loops begin with [and end with], but both are commands. When BF executes the [instruction, it looks at the current cell and asks: "Is the value 0?" If the answer is "yes," BF skips ahead to the] instruction and continues with the instruction after it. If the answer is "no," BF moves to the next instruction to begin the loop.

When BF encounters a] instruction, it doesn't automatically jump to the corresponding [. Instead, it examines the *current* memory cell and jumps back if that cell *isn't* 0. Otherwise, the loop ends and BF continues with the next instruction.

Think about this for a bit. The [command is a gatekeeper that decides whether a loop begins, but it doesn't check anything after that. The decision about continuing a loop falls to the matching] instruction. Also, the cell that initiated the loop need not be the cell that decides whether the loop continues. BF is very flexible when it comes to looping, as we might expect from such a provocatively named language—it's messing with our brains. BF loops are neither top-tested nor bottom-tested, but rather are a mix of both. There is a top test to decide whether the loop even begins, but from then on, the loop is bottom-tested. In C, we can accomplish something similar by nesting loops:

```
int cond1=1, cond2=1;
while (cond1) {
    cond1 = 0;
    do {

    } while(cond2);
}
```

To begin the loop, cond1 must be true. However, after cond1 begins the loop, it isn't examined again; the loop runs until cond2 is no longer true. To get the desired effect in C, cond1 must be made false (cond1 = 0), so the entire structure exits when cond2 becomes false.

BF code isn't particularly easy to write, but it is complete enough to implement interesting, nontrivial programs. BF is more than ABC. We need an interpreter to see that's the case; we'll leave compiler design for another day.

The Two Implementations

BF implementations abound. Let's investigate two in this section. The first is a slightly updated version of Urban Müller's original 1993 C code for the Amiga computer. The second we'll build from scratch in SNOBOL because an unusual, minimalist esoteric language deserves an equally unusual implementation. If you skipped Chapter 5 on SNOBOL, now's a good time to go back and read it.

The Original

The original Amiga LHA archive with the first version of BF is in the file *brainf-2.lha*. Müller's implementation is in plain C. To work with the code on a modern Linux system, I took the liberty of updating it to compile without warnings, changed the cell size from 8 bits (unsigned char) to 32 bits (int), and increased the program space to 70,000 cells. Using 32-bit cells matches the SNOBOL implementation we'll develop in the next section.

Listing 10-1 shows the interpreter in its entirety.

```c
#include <stdio.h>
#include <stdlib.h>
#define MAXPROG 70000
#define MAXMEM 30000
int   p, r, q;
int a[MAXMEM];
char f[MAXPROG], b, o, *s=f;

void interpret(char *c) {
    char *d;
    r++;
    while( *c ) {
        switch(o=1,*c++) {
        case '<': p--;        break;
        case '>': p++;        break;
        case '+': a[p]++;     break;
        case '-': a[p]--;     break;
        case '.': putchar(a[p]); fflush(stdout); break;
        case ',': a[p]=getchar();fflush(stdout); break;
        case '[':
            for( b=1,d=c; b && *c; c++ )
                b+=*c=='[', b-=*c==']';
            if(!b) {
                c[-1]=0;
                while( a[p] )
                  ❶ interpret(d);
                c[-1]=']';
                break;
            }
        case ']':
            puts("UNBALANCED BRACKETS"), exit(0);
        case '#':
            if(q>2)
                printf("%2d %2d %2d %2d %2d %2d %2d %2d %2d %2d\n%*s\n",
                        *a,a[1],a[2],a[3],a[4],a[5],a[6],a[7],a[8],a[9],
                        3*p+2,"^");
            break;
        default: o=0;
        }
        if( p<0 || p>(MAXMEM-1))
            puts("RANGE ERROR"), exit(0);
    }
    r--;
}

int main(int argc,char *argv[]) {
    FILE *z;
```

```
    q=argc;
    if(z=fopen(argv[1],"r")) {
        while( (b=getc(z))>0 )
            *s++=b;
        *s=0;
        interpret(f);
    }
}
```

Listing 10-1: Urban Müller's original BF interpreter (updated)

This implementation is quite compact and handles loops via recursion (notice the recursive call to interpret ❶). Our SNOBOL implementation will process loops without recursion. Also, notice that # is a supported command. It prints basic debugging information if the interpreter is called with a second command line argument. The # command was dropped from later versions of BF. My modifications introduce MAXMEM and MAXPROG and the addition of int before main to avoid a gcc warning.

The interpreter processes the input BF program loaded into f. The interpret function loops over the characters in f, or the characters of the nested loop enclosed in brackets via the recursive call. If the character is a BF command, the command is performed; otherwise, it is ignored.

Building the interpreter is straightforward:

```
> gcc bfi.c -o bfi
```

So is testing it:

```
> bfi examples/hello.b
Hello World!
```

All the BF examples in the book's GitHub repository work with this interpreter. However, not every BF example you'll find on the web does. Take a look at the *README* file in the *examples* directory, as it contains attribution and license information. Credit is given to code authors where authorship is known. I'll leave working through the operation of *hello.b* as an exercise, as there are explanatory comments in the file. As you might expect, it involves generating and printing the required sequence of ASCII values.

SNOBOL Meets BF

The seductive elegance of BF requires, indeed, almost demands that we make our own interpreter. We'll use SNOBOL because SNOBOL provides all the facilities we need. Besides, it's fun. The full interpreter is in *bf.sno*. Let's begin with the parser:

```
        MAXPROG = 70000
        MAXMEM = 30000
        prog = array('0:' MAXPROG)
❶ mem = array('0:' MAXMEM, 0)
```

```
              jump = table()

              define('parse(name)c,n,pat')        :(eparse)
parse         pat = break('><+-.,[]')
              input('reader', 10, 'B,1', name)
parse_l0      c = reader                          :f(parse_l1)
              c pat                               :f(parse_l0)
              prog[n] = c
              n = ne(n,MAXPROG) n + 1             :s(parse_l0)
parse_l1      endfile(10)
              parse = n                           :(return)
eparse
```

Listing 10-2: Parsing the input file

Listing 10-2 presents global memory definitions and the parse function to read the input file and keep only actual program commands. Code is stored in the array prog with memory in mem, a second array. BF expects memory to be initialized to 0, which SNOBOL does for us via the second argument to array ❶. We'll discuss the jump table momentarily.

The parse function accepts the name of the input text file, defines a pattern to match valid program characters (pat), and opens the file for input, reading one character at a time.

The loop (parse_l0) reads a character into c and applies the pattern. If the pattern succeeds, then c contains one of the allowed command characters; therefore, prog is set and its index is incremented. Notice the SNOBOL idiom of embedding the ne predicate to test for maximum program length. If the predicate fails, the increment to n does not happen and execution falls through to endfile.

When parse finishes processing the input file, prog contains the valid commands and only the valid commands. The number of commands read is returned by assigning n to parse.

A BF program is executed sequentially until the interpreter encounters a loop. The original BF interpreter used recursion to handle loops; however, we'll take a more literal approach. Every time we see an opening bracket ([), we'll scan the program text forward to find the corresponding closing bracket (]). Similarly, for a closing bracket, we'll scan backward to find the matching opening bracket. We could do this while interpreting the code, but that's hideously inefficient—imagine a loop running tens of thousands of times.

A moment's thought makes it clear that a single pass through the code before starting the interpreter is sufficient to locate each opening bracket and its corresponding closing bracket. This is where the jump table comes into play. Recall that a SNOBOL table is like a Python dictionary; it's an associative array. The index into the table is the index of an opening bracket in prog. Closing brackets also go in jump, as their index values are unique. With jump built ahead of time, a single reference to jump during program execution returns the proper index into prog for both the opening and closing brackets.

Listing 10-3 shows buildtable and its helper function, closing.

```
          define('closing(pc,plen)n,p')    :(eclosing)
closing   n = 1
          p = pc
closing_lo p = p + 1
          eq(p,plen)                       :s(bad0)
          ident(prog[p],']')               :s(closing_l1)
          ident(prog[p],'[')               :s(closing_l2)
closing_l3 eq(n,0)                          :f(closing_lo)
          closing = p                       :(return)
closing_l1 n = n - 1                        :(closing_l3)
closing_l2 n = n + 1                        :(closing_l3)
eclosing


          define('buildtable(plen)n,m')    :(ebuildtable)
buildtable n = 0
build_lo  ident(prog[n],'[')               :s(build_l1)
build_l2  n = n + 1
          eq(n,plen)                       :f(build_lo)s(return)
build_l1  m = closing(n,plen)
          jump[m] = n
          jump[n] = m                       :(build_l2)
ebuildtable
```

Listing 10-3: Building the jump table

Here, buildtable scans the program text looking for an opening bracket. When it finds one, it calls closing to return the index of the corresponding closing bracket. Next, buildtable sets the jump table to the opening and closing locations for rapid lookup during program execution.

The closing function locates the matching closing bracket by scanning forward and incrementing n each time a new opening bracket is found. When a closing bracket is found, n is decremented. When n is zero, the closing bracket matching the initial opening bracket has been found, so its index is returned.

BF accepts single-character input that it stores in memory as an ASCII value. SNOBOL has a char function to return the character associated with a given ASCII value; however, it lacks what many languages call ord, a function to return the ASCII value of a given character. No matter; we'll make our own:

```
      define('ord(c)v')          :(eord)
ord   &alphabet break(c) . v
      ord = size(v)              :(return)
eord
```

SNOBOL includes a special variable, &alphabet, which is the full range of ASCII characters, [0, 255]. The ord function uses pattern matching to locate all the characters of this special variable up to the given character, c. The pattern stores this substring in v and the length of the substring is the ASCII code for the character.

We're now ready to run the BF program in prog. Let's walk through the main portion of the interpreter. We'll add some debugging abilities to help us later. BF is hard, so we'll take all the help we can get.

The main portion of the interpreter is in Listing 10-4.

```
        plen = parse(host(2,2))
        buildtable(plen)
        input('cin', 10, 'B,1', '-')
        output('cout', 11, 'WB,1', '-')
        pc = 0
        mp = 0
        gmp = 0
loop    ident(prog[pc],'-')              :s(dec)
        ident(prog[pc],'+')              :s(inc)
        ident(prog[pc],'<')              :s(decp)
        ident(prog[pc],'>')              :s(incp)
        ident(prog[pc],',')              :s(gchar)
        ident(prog[pc],'.')              :s(pchar)
        ident(prog[pc],'[')              :s(begin)
        ident(prog[pc],']')              :s(again)
cont    pc = pc + 1
        ne(pc,plen)                      :f(pend)s(loop)
dec     mem[mp] = mem[mp] - 1            :s(cont)f(bad1)
inc     mem[mp] = mem[mp] + 1            :s(cont)f(bad1)
decp    mp = mp - 1                      :(cont)
incp    mp = mp + 1
        gmp = gt(mp,gmp) mp              :(cont)
gchar   ch = ord(cin)                    :f(pend)
      ❶ eq(ch,13)                        :f(gchar0)
        ch = 10
        cout = char(ch)
gchar0  mem[mp] = ch                     :s(cont)f(bad1)
pchar   cout = char(mem[mp])             :s(cont)f(bad1)
❷ begin pc = eq(mem[mp],0) jump[pc]      :(cont)
  again pc = ne(mem[mp],0) jump[pc]      :(cont)
```

Listing 10-4: The main BF interpreter loop

Listing 10-4 consists of some preliminaries followed by a loop that moves through the program in prog. The preliminaries call parse to process the input file and buildtable to configure the jump table. BF expects single-character input and output with the console, which SNOBOL supports using the given input and output incantations.

The current program counter is pc and the memory pointer is mp. We'll use gmp to track the highest memory cell accessed by the program. Doing this simplifies dumping relevant memory when the program ends.

The loop executes the current instruction depending on its character. Recall that ident is the SNOBOL predicate to compare two strings. Executing an instruction is a jump to the relevant line. Most instructions are a single statement. For example, > moves the cell pointer to the right (mp=mp+1). When incrementing the cell pointer, there's an extra check to see if gmp should be updated.

SNOBOL has one quirk requiring a bit of extra code. Take a look at gchar, which reads a single character of input. The cin variable reads the character and places its ASCII value in ch. The problem occurs when the user presses ENTER. On Unix systems, this should return the ASCII value 10; however, the SNOBOL interpreter returns the ASCII value 13. So a quick check converts ASCII 13 to ASCII 10 before assigning the character to the current memory location (gchar0) ❶. Notice that each instruction ends with a jump to cont to continue processing the next instruction.

Additionally, observe how opening and closing brackets are handled as begin and again, respectively ❷. Even though there is a single statement for each, a bit of explanation is in order. For example, the code for an opening bracket is

```
pc = eq(mem[mp],0) jump[pc]      :(cont)
```

The BF standard says to begin a loop if the currently active memory cell is not 0; otherwise, skip the loop. Here, the SNOBOL predicate eq will succeed if the current memory cell is 0. In that case, the assignment happens and pc is set to jump[pc], which is the *end* of the loop that we're currently considering. In contrast, if the memory cell is not 0, eq fails and the assignment does not happen. Therefore, the interpreter enters the loop as it should. The test in again is much the same, only the logic is reversed, so we jump to the beginning of the loop if the memory cell is not 0.

Take another look at the statement to decrement the current cell:

```
dec  mem[mp] = mem[mp] - 1    :s(cont)f(bad1)
```

If the decrement succeeds, flow continues with the next instruction, s(cont). However, if mp is negative or too large, the statement fails and the interpreter jumps to bad1:

```
bad1  output = 'memory access error, mp = ' mp  :(end)
```

This prints an error message and exits. A similar error happens if an opening bracket has no matching closing bracket.

If the second command line argument is dump, the interpreter will dump the final value of all memory locations accessed by the program before exiting. The code for this is in Listing 10-5.

```
pend   ident(host(2,3),'dump')              :f(end)
       output =
```

```
          output = 'Memory: (mp = ' mp ')'
          n = 0
ploop  ascii = ''
          gt(mem[n],31)                              :f(print)
          lt(mem[n],127)                             :f(print)
          ascii = ' ' char(mem[n])
print  s = dupl(' ', 6 - size(n)) n
          s = s ':' dupl(' ', 6 - size(mem[n])) mem[n]
          output = s ascii
          n = n + 1
          gt(n,gmp)                                  :f(ploop)
          output =                                   :(end)
```

Listing 10-5: Dumping memory

Memory values are dumped, one per line. If the value is in the range $31 < v < 127$, the corresponding character is displayed.

The BF interpreter is now complete. Let's test it.

```
> snobol4 bf.sno examples/hello.b dump
Hello World!

Memory: (mp = 6)
    0:      0
    1:      0
    2:     72   H
    3:    100   d
    4:     87   W
    5:     33   !
    6:     10
```

The memory dump shows that cells 0 through 6 were used at some point in the program, and that the program ended with the memory pointer looking at cell 6. Knowing which memory cell is active is critical to successful BF programming.

Our implementation appears to work. Now, let's do stuff with it.

BF in Action

Let's explore BF with worked examples. I encourage you to consider the other examples included on the GitHub site. However, the more complex ones like *mandelbrot.b* and *hanoi.b* are the output of programs that generate BF code. They were not written by hand.

We'll start with some basic examples and then develop more advanced examples that require a bit of thought. For example, we'll end with a program to multiply two numbers.

Baby Steps

Consider the following code:

```
+++++[-]
```

It increments cell 0 five times, then starts a loop: [-]. Incrementing five times is obvious, so let's work through the loop to see what it does. The first command is [. It checks to see whether the current cell is 0. In this case, the cell is 5 and not 0, so [succeeds and the loop begins.

The next instruction, -, decrements the value in the current memory cell (cell 0), so the value is now 4. The closing bracket,], asks if cell 0 is 0, which it isn't, so it jumps to the beginning of the loop. Note that the beginning of the loop isn't [, but the first instruction after it (-). Cell 0 is decremented again and] runs again. When the value of cell 0 is 0,] will fail and the program will end. Therefore, the snippet of code above zeroes a cell. You'll see [-] in many BF programs.

Now that we have a basic loop under our belt, let's contemplate the following bit of code:

```
,+[-.,+]
```

What do you think it might be doing? The code itself is in *cat.b*. Let's run it and see what it produces. To run it, use this command line:

```
> snobol4 bf.sno examples/cat.b <bf.sno
```

Do you see the text of *bf.sno*? The filename is a clue, of course, but this simple program acts like the Unix cat command to display the contents of a file. Let's add comments to the code to explain what is happening.

```
,    read a character; mem(0) = ch
+    inc mem(0)
[    loop if mem(0) is not zero
  -  dec mem(0)
  .  print mem(0) as a character
  ,  read another character to mem(0)
  +  inc mem(0)
]    loop if mem(0) is not zero
```

Reading a character, printing, and looping until there are no more characters to read is a good idea in this case, but what's with + and -? These extra commands handle the case where a 0 character has been read. They are present to deal with how different systems process end-of-file (EOF). For example, this version of the program works nicely with our SNOBOL interpreter

```
,[.,]
```

but hangs at EOF when using the C interpreter.

Let's look at another loop example. Honestly, all our examples will be loop examples, as that's all BF has to offer that isn't quickly boring. This example is in *countdown0.b*:

```
++++++++++[-.]
```

It's only slightly more interesting than our first example. Beyond counting down, we also print the value of cell 0. However, BF's print (.) expects an ASCII character, so this example won't print anything visible, only a set of control characters. We can see this by using the Unix xxd command to dump binary files:

```
> snobol4 bf.sno examples/countdown0.b | xxd
00000000: 0908 0706 0504 0302 0100  .........
```

The xxd command dumps binary data as hexadecimal values. Looking at the output you'll see the countdown (09, 08, 07, . . . , 00). To get a countdown we must convert the current value of cell 0 to a digit. The offset between a digit value and the ASCII code for the digit is 48, so we must add 48 before printing and subtract 48 afterward.

Listing 10-6 shows us *countdown1.b*. We've included comments to explain the code.

```
++++++++++    mem(0) = 10
>             look at mem(1)
++++++++++    mem(1) = 10
[             enter loop if mem(1) not zero
 -            decrement mem(1)
 ++++++++++
 ++++++++++
 ++++++++++
 ++++++++++
 ++++++++      add 48
 .             print
 ----------
 ----------
 ----------
 ----------
 --------      sub 48
 <             look at mem(0)
 .             print it
 >             look at mem(1)
]             loop if mem(1) is not zero
```

Listing 10-6: Countdown with ASCII output

Running Listing 10-6 produces a countdown as output (9, 8, 7, . . . , 0). To output newline repeatedly, it's easiest to store it somewhere, so we set cell 0 to 10. Next, > moves the cell pointer to look at cell 1. As you write BF code, pay very close attention to where the cell pointer is looking. Cell 1 is set to 10 as well, but in this case, it is the value to count down.

The loop begins by incrementing the value in cell 0 with 48 + commands. This is boring but quick to implement. The current loop count is now a valid ASCII digit, so we print it and subtract 48 to get back to the actual count. The bottom of the loop looks at cell 0, which is always 10, and prints it to get the newline character. The code then looks again at cell 1, where our count lives, and loops until 0.

Bunches O'Bits

Bit twiddling, meaning fiddling around with the bits of a byte, is the goal of this section. Here we'll implement two examples. The first calculates the ones' complement of a byte. The second calculates the even parity bit. Don't be concerned if these terms are new to you; I'll clarify as we go.

A Complimentary Complement

Internally, computers represent integers as a set number of bits, that is, as a base-2 number. One method for encoding negative numbers is to use the *ones' complement*, where each bit is the opposite of what it would be for a positive value. For example, if a number is 00001101_2 = 11, then 11110010_2 = −11 where each 1 is now a 0 and vice versa. In this encoding, the leading bit will be one when the number should be interpreted as a negative value. Our goal is to write a BF program to calculate the ones' complement of an input byte. The byte will be entered as a string of eight characters (each 0 or 1).

Let's think about this task for a bit (or eight). We know we'll likely want a loop to read eight bits. After reading a bit, we need to subtract 48 to map the ASCII value read to its actual value (0 or 1). Once we have the actual value, we then output a 0 if the value is 1 or a 1 if the value is 0. In typical languages, a simple if statement would do the trick. Of course, we're not working with an ordinary language, but rather in the strange world of BF.

A loop to read a byte's worth of bits could be written as

```
++++++++[->,<]
```

In this code, we first set cell 0 to 8 and then start a loop. The loop decrements cell 0, moves to cell 1, and inputs something. It then moves the memory pointer back to cell 0 and loops if the count isn't 0. This reads eight characters and then exits. Adding a period after the comma echoes the input. Of course, we need a 0 or 1 in memory, not the ASCII code for 0 or 5, so somewhere we'll have to subtract 48. We'll use a sequence of 48 - instructions.

All right, we have the input bit, but how do we decide whether we should output a 0 or a 1? If the bit is 1, we could enter a loop that is otherwise skipped if the bit is 0. How can we use that? Well, we might be able to set another memory location to 1, read the input bit, and if it is 1, decrement the preset memory location. If we do that, we'll be in business. However, before we go too far, it's a good idea to make a map of how we are using BF memory. So far, we have the setup

```
cell    :   0   1   2
value   :   8  0|1  1
pointer:        ^
```

where our loop counter is in cell 0, the bit entered by the user is in cell 1, cell 2 holds a 1, and the memory pointer is looking at cell 1.

If the user's bit is 1, we want to enter a loop to decrement cell 2. If the bit is 0, the loop will be skipped and cell 2 will remain 1. Then, we print cell 2 and we have it: a 1 is changed into a 0, and a 0 is changed into a 1. We then move the memory pointer back to cell 0 to decrement the bit counter and repeat until we're done.

Listing 10-7 shows *ones.b*, which implements our algorithm. Let's walk through the code to see that it does what I claim.

```
++++++++[
    ->          decrement mem(0); look at mem(1)
    >+<,        look at mem(2); inc; mem(1); input
    ----------
    ----------
    ----------
    ----------
    --------    sub 48
    [->-<]      if one then dec mem(2)
    >           look at mem(2)
    ++++++++++
    ++++++++++
    ++++++++++
    ++++++++++
    ++++++++.   add 48; print
    [-]<        zero mem(2); look at mem(1)
    <           look at mem(0)
]
++++++++++.     mem(0) = 10; print newline
```

Listing 10-7: Ones' complement

First, the outermost loop uses cell 0 to count down from 8. Inside this loop, after decrementing the count, the memory pointer is moved to cell 2, which is then incremented. We know that cell 2 was initially 0, so it must be 1 now. We then move back to cell 1 to get the user's input, which we'll assume is a 0 or 1. This much is ->>+<, if the comments are removed. Look at the commands until you are sure you follow what's going on.

The next block of code is an uninspired sequence of 48 - commands to change the user's input into either a 0 or 1. Recall that we're looking at cell 1. At this point, we have memory as we want it: cell 1 is 0 or 1 and cell 2 is 1. The next set of commands are key to the entire program: [->-<]>. The small loop ([->-<]) executes if the user's bit is 1 because we are looking at cell 1 and it isn't 0; therefore, [enters the loop. Cell 1 is immediately decremented to make it 0 because we only want the code in the loop to execute once. Next, > looks at cell 2 and - decrements it to change it from 1 to 0. Lastly, < looks again at cell 1, which is now 0, so the loop exits, and the final > executes to look at cell 2. If the user's bit is a 0, then [fails, skipping the entire loop and moving directly to the final > to also look at cell 2. At this point, cell 2 is the focus, and it contains a 1 if the input bit was a 0 or a 0 if the input bit was a 1. The next block of 48 + commands increments the value in cell 2 to get the corresponding ASCII code and . prints it.

What does [-] do? As we saw above, [-] is the BF idiom to zero a memory location. This is necessary to make sure cell 2 is 0 when the outer loop comes around for the next input bit. Right now, cell 2 is either 48 or 49. The final two << instructions move focus back to cell 0, the loop counter. The outer] then loops if cell 0 isn't 0. When it is, the final line, ++++++++++., outputs ASCII 10, a newline, and the program exits.

Whew! Let's see Listing 10-7 in action. Run *ones.b* like so:

```
> echo 00001101 | snobol4 bf.sno examples/ones.b dump
11110010

Memory: (mp = 0)
    0:    10
    1:     0
    2:     0
```

The echo command is a convenient way to send input to a program without typing it directly. Notice that the input is 11 as we saw it earlier, 00001101_2. The output is 11110010_2, which is −11 in ones' complement, as we wanted. The memory dump tells us we end the program looking at cell 0, which contains 10 for the final newline. The other two cells used by the program are both 0.

One note before moving on. Listing 10-7 excludes a comment block at the top of *ones.b*. The BF interpreter ignores non-command characters; however, the comments must not include any command characters. That gets a bit annoying at times. The comments at the top of *ones.b* are enclosed in brackets ([and]). This means the entire comment block (at least the characters that are valid BF commands) is a loop. But this doesn't matter. The comment block is the first loop in the program, and we know cell 0 is always 0, so the loop will never execute and we are free to enter whatever text we want in the comments. This was not my idea, but it is another illustration of the creativity present in the esolang community.

Achieving Parity

Serial communication protocols sometimes use a *parity bit*, an extra bit transmitted with the data that makes it easier to detect transmission errors. For example, if the data fits in seven bits, as standard ASCII characters do, then an eighth bit can be added to make the number of one bits (bits with a value of 1) in the 8-bit byte even. This is known as even parity. If the received byte does not have an even number of one bits, the receiver immediately knows there is an error and can request the byte again. A single parity bit can capture a single-bit error, which is sufficient in most cases.

Our mission is to write a BF program to accept seven input bits and output the proper even parity bit. We'll input bits as a sequence of seven ASCII characters as before and then output either ASCII 0 or ASCII 1 to make the number of one bits even. The following are some examples of bytes with parity bits:

$$
\begin{array}{ccc}
0000000 & \rightarrow & 0000000\mathbf{0} \\
0000010 & \rightarrow & 0000010\mathbf{1} \\
0011001 & \rightarrow & 0011001\mathbf{1} \\
1111111 & \rightarrow & 1111111\mathbf{1}
\end{array}
$$

The bold output bit ensures that every byte has an even number of 1s.

How should we go about getting BF to do this for us? There are likely multiple approaches, but the approach we'll use here is first to tally the number of 1s present in the seven inputs. Then we'll decide which bit to output based on this tally. As with *ones.b* above, we need an outer loop to read the ASCII bits and subtract 48. To tally the one bits, we'll increment a memory cell each time the bit is a 1.

Listing 10-8 presents a loop to read seven bits and tally the number of one bits.

```
+++++++[        mem(0) = 7
    >,.         mem(1) = input; echo
    --------------------
    --------------------
    --------    sub 48
    [           inner loop if bit is one
        -       subtract the bit from mem(1)
        >+      look at mem(2); increment mem(2)
        <       look at mem(1)
    ]           exit loop because mem(1) is zero
    <-          look at mem(0); decrement mem(0)
]               loop if mem(0) not zero
```

Listing 10-8: Adding the input bits

As always, tracking memory use is essential. In this case, cell 0 holds the bits read counter, cell 1 is the input bit, and cell 2 the tally of one bits. The first part of the loop is >,., which moves to cell 1, reads the input bit, and echoes it. Next comes a block of 48 - commands to turn the ASCII character code into a 0 or 1.

If the bit is a 1, [begins the inner loop. The loop body, ->+<, decrements cell 1, looks at cell 2 and increments it, and looks again at cell 1. Because cell 1 is now 0,] fails and the loop ends. If the input bit is 0, [skips ahead to <-. In both cases, the memory pointer is looking at cell 1, so < looks at cell 0, which - then decrements. The final] fires to repeat the loop six more times.

When the loop ends, cell 2 contains a tally of the number of one bits read and the memory pointer is looking at cell 0. It's important to note that cell 0 and cell 1 are both 0 when the outer loop exits.

Cell 2 contains the number of one bits in the input. If this number is odd, the output bit should be 1. Otherwise, it should be 0. How do we tell if cell 2 is even or odd? Here's where things get a bit tricky. Our solution is in Listing 10-9, but we must walk through it to understand it.

```
>>              look at mem(2)
[               loop if mem(2) not zero
    [           if mem(2) not zero
        -       subtract one
        >       look at mem(3)
        +       increment it
        >       look at mem(4); which is zero
    ]           do not loop
❶ <<            look back to mem(2)
    [           if mem(2) not zero
        -       subtract one
        >       look at mem(3)
        -       decrement
        >       look at mem(4); which is zero
    ]           do not loop
    <<          look at mem(2) or mem(0) if sum exhausted
]               loop if not zero
```

Listing 10-9: Using the ones tally to decide the parity bit

In essence, when the outer loop of Listing 10-9 ends, the memory pointer will be looking at cell 0 if the output bit should be 1 or cell 2 if the output bit should be 0. Additionally, cell 3 will be 1 if we end at cell 0 and cell 5 will be its default value of 0.

The code before the main loop of Listing 10-9 is simple enough. Move the memory pointer twice to look at cell 2, which has the one bits tally. If this tally is 0, the loop is skipped by [and we move to the final bit of code with the memory pointer looking at cell 2. We'll get to the final bit of code soon.

If the tally in cell 2 isn't 0, we enter the main loop of Listing 10-9. The body of this loop has two inner loops, one after the other. The body of the first inner loop is ->+>. It subtracts 1 from cell 2, looks at and increments cell 3, and then looks at cell 4, which is always 0. Because cell 4 is 0,] exits the loop, meaning the loop never actually loops. Notice that when the loop exits, the memory pointer is looking at cell 4 and cell 3 is 1.

If we assume that cell 2 was initially 1 ❶, cell 2 is now 0, cell 3 is 1, and we are looking at cell 4, which is also 0. The << between the inner loops moves back to cell 2, which, as it is 0, skips the second inner loop and hits the final << to move back from cell 2 to cell 0. Because cell 0 is 0, the outer loop exits, meaning we are looking at cell 0 and cell 3 is still 1.

This situation happens every time cell 2 contains an odd value. What if cell 2 contains 2? After the first inner loop of Listing 10-9, cell 2 contains 1, cell 3 contains 1, and we are looking at cell 2. Therefore, the second inner loop fires to decrement cell 2 and cell 3, making them both 0. The loop then moves to cell 4, which is always 0, exits, and moves back to cell 2, which is now also 0. The outer loop then exits, and we are looking at cell 2 this time, not cell 0. Whenever cell 2 is initially even, both inner loops will repeatedly fire to make cell 2 0. Cell 3 is also decremented by the second inner loop to make sure it only ever contains a 1.

We're almost done. The code in Listing 10-9 ends, leaving BF in one of two states. If the tally in cell 2 was even, we're looking at cell 2. If the tally is odd, we're looking at cell 0 and cell 3 is 1. To output the proper bit, we need the code in Listing 10-10.

```
>>>                       look at mem(3) or mem(5)
+++++++++++++++++++++
+++++++++++++++++++++
++++++++.                 add 48 and print
>                         look at the next location which is zero
++++++++++.               set to 10 and print the newline
```

Listing 10-10: Printing the proper parity bit

We use >>> to move to either cell 3 or cell 5. Cell 3 would be 1 if we ended at cell 0 and that's the value we want to output. If we ended at cell 2, we move to cell 5, which is initialized to be 0 and is also the value we want. All that remains is to add 48 to convert the value to the ASCII character code for either 1 or 0, print it, and then move to either cell 4 or cell 6, both of which are initially 0, to output the final newline character.

Let's try *parity.b* with the example inputs above:

```
> echo 0000000 | bfi examples/parity.b
00000000
> echo 0000010 | bfi examples/parity.b
00000101
> echo 0011001 | bfi examples/parity.b
00110011
> echo 1111111 | bfi examples/parity.b
11111111
```

The output is as expected, meaning that *parity.b* works. You'll get the same results if you use the SNOBOL interpreter as well.

Now, let's work on our final BF example: multiplication.

Multiplicative Multiplicity

Multiplication is repeated addition. Let's use that fact to write a BF program to accept two single-digit numbers and compute their product. We'll write two versions. The first version implements multiplication but leaves the product in memory. This is unsatisfying, so the second version uses freely available code from *https://esolangs.org/* to output the product as ASCII characters. The full source code for both examples is in *mult.b* and *mult2.b*, respectively.

We require two inputs, which we'll store in cells 0 and 1. We'll use cells 2 and 3 while multiplying and place the final product in cell 3. Reading the input characters is straightforward; see Listing 10-11.

```
,--------------------
--------------------    mem(0) = input
--------                sub 48
>+++++++++++++++++      mem(1) = 32 (space)
+++++++++++++++++.      print
++++++++++.             add 10; print *
----------.             sub 10; print space
,--------------------   mem(1) = input
--------------------
--------                sub 48
```

Listing 10-11: Reading and printing the inputs

The first character is read and converted to its numeric value. Then cell 1 is used to output * before reading the second digit.

To multiply, we must increment a memory location as many times as the value in cell 1 dictates (that is, increment it cell 1 times), and repeat until cell 0 is 0. For example, if cell 0 is 5 and cell 1 is 4, the algorithm is to calculate

$$5 \times 4 = 4 + 4 + 4 + 4 + 4 = 20$$

which we might write in a language like Python as

```
ans = 0
for i in range(5):
    for j in range(4):
        ans += 1
```

Let's duplicate this code in BF. However, we have a minor issue. We need two loops, an outer loop running until cell 0 is 0, and an inner loop to increment cell 3 by cell 1 times. Recall that BF loops are destructive. For example, if we write ++++[.-], we'll print the current value of cell 0 four times, from 4 down to 1. When the loop exits, cell 0 is 0, meaning its original value has been lost. Thus, we must preserve the value of cell 1 to use it again on the next pass.

Listing 10-12 shows us the multiplication algorithm. Let's see how it preserves the inner loop counter.

```
<[-         dec mem(0)
  >[-       look at mem(1); dec
    >+>+<<  inc mem(2); inc mem(3); look at mem(1)
  ]         continue until mem(1) is zero
```

```
>[-<+>]             look at mem(2); copy back to mem(1)
   <<               look at mem(0)
]                   loop until mem(0) is zero
```

Listing 10-12: Multiplying the two digits

The first < moves us back to cell 0 as the code in Listing 10-11 ends with the memory pointer looking at cell 1. Cell 0 isn't 0, generally, so the outer loop begins, and cell 0 is immediately decremented. Next, > moves to cell 1, and the first inner loop begins if cell 1 isn't 0. Cell 1 is also immediately decremented.

The body of the first inner loop is >+>+<<. The >+ instructions move to cell 2 and increment it. The following >+ does the same to cell 3. Lastly, << moves back to cell 1 so] can decide whether to continue the loop or not. When the loop exits, memory looks like this, assuming the user entered 5 and 4:

```
cell    :   0    1    2    3
value   :   4    0    4    4
pointer:         ^
```

Recall that cell 3 holds our product. It's currently 4 because the first inner loop ran four times. We now must restore cell 1. That's why the loop incremented both cell 2 and cell 3. We use cell 3 for the product and we can use cell 2 to restore the inner loop counter. That's what >[-<+>] does; it decrements cell 2 while incrementing cell 1. The final << ensures that the outer loop's] instruction is looking at cell 0.

Each pass through the outer loop adds cell 1 to cell 3, using cell 2 to restore cell 1 for the next pass. When cell 0 is finally 0, cell 3 holds the product. Note that we entered single digits, but this multiplication routine is generic and will work for any two values. Also, the trick of double incrementing memory to have a place to restore from is another BF idiom. We saw similar code in Chapter 8 when we implemented multiplication in FRACTRAN.

Let's take *mult.b* out for a test drive. We'll use our interpreter's ability to dump memory to see if it is working. For example:

```
> snobol4 bf.sno examples/mult.b dump
3 * 5

Memory: (mp = 0)
    0:     10
    1:      5
    2:      0
    3:     15

> snobol4 bf.sno examples/mult.b dump
9 * 8
```

```
Memory: (mp = 0)
    0:     10
    1:      8
    2:      0
    3:     72   H
```

In both cases, we see that cell 3 contains the correct product.

To print the product as a number, we add the code in Listing 10-13 to the end of the multiplication routine in Listing 10-12 (see *mult2.b*).

`>>>`	move to mem(3)
`>[-]>[-]+>[-]+<`	set n and d to one to start loop
`[`	loop on 'n'
`    >[-<-`	on the first loop
`        <<[->+>+<<]`	copy V into N (and Z)
`        >[-<+>]>>`	restore V from Z
`    ]`	
`    ++++++++++>[-]+>[-]>[-]>[-]<<<<<`	init for the division by 10
`    [->-[>+>>]>[[-<+>]+>+>>]<<<<<]`	full division
`    >>-[-<<+>>]`	store remainder into n
`    <[-]++++++++[-<++++++>]`	make it an ASCII digit; clear d
`    >>[-<<+>>]`	move quotient into d
`    <<`	shuffle; new n is where d was and
	old n is a digit
`]`	end loop when n is zero
`<[.[-]<]`	move to where Z should be and
	output the digits til we find Z
`<`	back to V
`<++++++++++.`	newline

Listing 10-13: The print routine

As mentioned, this routine comes from *https://esolangs.org/*. What is particularly nice about this routine is that it works with any memory location, so we move from cell 0 to cell 3 prior to running it. The provided comments give some indication of what the routine is doing. Notice that the second line of Listing 10-13 uses the "clear a cell" idiom three times to initialize memory. We won't walk through Listing 10-13 in any detail, as it is quite challenging. Motivated readers will find the code, with some additional details, at *https://esolangs.org/wiki/Brainfuck_algorithms* under the heading beginning with "Print value of cell x as number."

Let's review some examples to see that the routine works as advertised.

```
> snobol4 bf.sno examples/mult2.b
3 * 5 = 15
> snobol4 bf.sno examples/mult2.b
9 * 8 = 72
```

The examples of this section, *ones.b*, *parity.b*, *mult.b*, and *mult2.b*, serve as our introduction to BF. There's much more we might say, but we covered the essentials. Let's turn now to outside resources to see additional examples, learn more about BF programming, and gain insight on how BF has influenced esolangs as a whole, to say nothing of genuine academic research involving BF.

The BF Multiverse

If Piet generated a universe, then to be fair, we must say that BF has created a multiverse. Let's briefly investigate some of those universes in this section: examples, tutorials, implementations, inspirations, and academic BF. Enjoy!

Examples

The best way to learn a language is to use it. We did that in the previous section. The next best way to learn a language is to see how others have used it. Let's take a cursory look at the BF examples included with this book. I did not write these examples. See the *README* file for attribution information.

The most impressive set of BF programs written by hand and not generated by another system producing BF code as output I've found are by Daniel B. Cristofani. You'll find them at *http://brainfuck.org/*, which alone tells you Cristofani's a serious BF coder—he registered the domain name. I suspect you'll learn much from the examples and even more from the tutorial information on his site.

The book repository contains the following, all of which run with both the C and SNOBOL interpreters:

squares.b   Print n^2 for [0, 100].

fib.b   Generate an endless stream of Fibonacci numbers. We encountered the Fibonacci sequence in Chapter 1 and will again in Chapter 13. This version does not use a single cell to hold the number, but rather handles arbitrary-sized numbers. This is a good example of how compact BF code can be while still doing something interesting.

factorial2.b   Another gem. This one calculates an endless stream of factorials.

sierpinski.b   The Sierpiński triangle is a common fractal, one that a straightforward algorithm can generate. This version produces ASCII output. We'll work with the Sierpiński triangle again in Chapter 13. Consider this example a preview.

random.b   Implements Wolfram's Rule 30, a 1D cellular automaton. This automaton, especially the center bit, passes many tests for randomness and formed the basis for Mathematica's first pseudorandom generator. To experiment more with Rule 30 and other 1D automatons, see Chapter 7 of my book *Random Numbers and Computers* (Springer, 2018).

golden.b   Calculates the decimal expansion of $\phi = \frac{1+\sqrt{5}}{2}$.

e.b Calculates the decimal expansion of *e*, the base of the natural logarithm. The natural log can be defined via an integral, $\ln x = \int_1^x \frac{1}{t} dt$ with *e* the limit such that the log is 1, $1 = \int_1^e \frac{1}{t} dt$.

tictactoe.b Tic-tac-toe in BF. You against the computer. Good luck.

The remaining examples, beyond *cat.b* and *hello.b*, which we saw earlier, include the following:

prime.b Calculate prime numbers less than the given number. This commented example was written by hand, but I have not succeeded in identifying the author.

hanoi.b An animated Tower of Hanoi. This example is the output of Claire Wolf's BF compiler suite (see below). It's fun to watch, but run it with the C interpreter or you'll be waiting a very long time indeed.

mandelbrot.b Creates an ASCII version of the Mandelbrot set. The *README* file gives the URL of the code. It appears to be the output of Wolf's BF compiler as well. If you use the SNOBOL interpreter, you'll eventually finish, but it runs about 100 times slower than the C interpreter.

Tutorials

The tutorials here offer plenty of good BF programming insights, idioms, and explanations.

Daniel B Cristofani's BF pages Mentioned earlier but worth mentioning again because of the helpful programming advice. You'll even find advice on how to write a "compliant" interpreter. Our SNOBOL interpreter is not compliant, but we're happy with it. (*http://brainfuck.org/*)

Frans Faase's BF pages You'll find many good reference/tutorial pages here. Some are Faase's, whereas others are links to still more information about BF. The World Wide Web is a web, after all. (*https://www.iwriteiam.nl/Ha_BF.html*)

Katie Ball's BF tutorial Ball's tutorial is another good reference. (*https://gist.github.com/roachhd/dce54bec8ba55fb17d3a/*)

Implementations

The implementations of BF are legion, which is somehow fitting. Only a tiny selection is referenced here, and I'm completely ignoring all the hardware implementations.

Compilers

The phrase *BF compiler* has multiple meanings. For example, a BF compiler might be a program that takes a higher-level language and produces BF code. In that case, BF is the machine code for the compiler. Alternatively, a BF compiler might be just that: a program that takes BF as input and produces executable code from it. I offer an example of each kind here.

Brian Raiter's native BF compiler   As promised above, here's Brian Raiter's 166-byte BF compiler. It's written in assembly language (install nasm on Linux) and produces standalone executables. Not every example in the repository works with this compiler, but many do, and the results are significantly faster than even the C interpreter. Try *e.b*, *golden.b*, and *tictactoe.b*. There are many comments in the source code, *bf.asm*. Hopefully, your x86 assembly is much stronger than mine. (*http://www.muppet labs.com/~breadbox/software/tiny/bf.asm.txt*)

Claire Wolf's compiler to BF   This compiler takes a higher-level macro language and produces executable BF code. It produced two of our examples: *hanoi.b* and *mandelbrot.b*. (*http://bygone.clairexen.net/bfcpu/bfcomp.html*)

Interpreters

We saw how easy it is to write a BF interpreter, even in SNOBOL. The two links here point to large lists of BF interpreters in all kinds of languages.

esolangs.org's BF implementations   This page has a long list of BF and BF-related goods and services, er, implementations. (*https://esolangs.org/wiki/Brainfuck_implementations*)

Rosetta Code's BF implementations   BF interpreters in a plethora of languages. Neither Jefe nor I are responsible for time or bits lost due to incomplete or erroneous code. (*http://rosettacode.org/wiki/Execute_Brain*****)

Inspirations

Perhaps the greatest tribute to BF is that it has inspired many other esolangs. Some are serious, genuine extensions to core BF. Others are less serious or even outright jokes. If you browse the (long) language list at *https://esolangs.org/wiki/Language_list*, you'll recognize many BF-related languages from nothing more than the colorful, if not sometimes offensive, names.

Academic BF

BF isn't all just fun and games. The language is elementary, yet Turing complete. This makes it attractive to researchers looking for a target or other language to use in their systems. The references here are to academic papers that use BF, either actively or as an example. What's particularly interesting is that not all of the references are from traditional computer science journals. BF is useful even in relation to more traditional human pursuits, like poetry. This list is by no means exhaustive, merely illustrative, and favors more recent references to BF.

BF++: A Language for General-purpose Program Synthesis, Vadim Liventsev, Aki Härmä, and Milan Petković (2021).

Neural Program Synthesis with Priority Queue Training, Daniel A. Abolafia, Mohammad Norouzi, Jonathan Shen, Rui Zhao, and Quoc V Le (2018).

Resisting Clarity/Highlighting Form: Comparing Vanguard Approaches in Poetry and Programming, Irina Lyubchenko (2020).

Fully Human, Fully Machine: Rhetorics of Digital Disembodiment in Programming, Brandee Easter (2020).

50,000,000,000 Instructions per Second: Design and Implementation of a 256-Core BrainFuck Computer, Sang-Woo Jun (2016).

A Box, Darkly: Obfuscation, Weird Languages, and Code Aesthetics, Michael Mateas and Nick Montfort (2005).

The first two references use BF with reinforcement learning, thereby combining esolangs and deep machine learning. Advanced neural networks generate BF programs to solve problems.

Discussion

BF is Turing complete. It is imperative, has the requisite control structures (brackets), and, ignoring the self-imposed 30,000-cell memory limit, uses arbitrary memory. Additionally, and impressively, Daniel Cristofani implemented a universal Turing machine in BF, thereby directly demonstrating Turing completeness. The machine is in *utm.b* in the BF examples directory. Comments in the file explain, in detail, what the program is and what it means.

There's a certain enticing nature to BF due to its simplicity. Yes, it's challenging to work with, which might have been intentional, like a gauntlet thrown down to see who might pick it up. But I don't view BF that way. Life is built from the combinatorial mixing of a multitude of smaller components. Might it be possible to view something like BF as the DNA of programming? We already know from Chapter 3 that a Turing machine captures the essence of what an algorithm is. BF is more advanced than a Turing machine, but just barely, so it can serve the same purpose as an encapsulation of the idea of an "algorithm."

In his famous *Epigrams on Programming*, Alan Perlis wrote

> 19. A language that doesn't affect the way you think about programming, is not worth knowing.

This is true for every language in this book, but I hope it is especially so for the esolangs, with BF chief among them. Struggling to write code in BF, especially when decades of experience make the necessary code almost instantly present itself in more familiar languages, does affect the way you think about programming. I found myself trying, with varying levels of success, to think in a new way to understand how to fit what BF offers to what

I would instinctively do in a language like Python or C. Perhaps that's the most enduring effect of learning BF. It requires you to think in new ways instead of relying on what is already familiar. BF is a way out of the Python (or C or Java or . . .) echo chamber, as it were.

Perlis offers more wisdom directly applicable to BF:

> 23. To understand a program you must become both the machine and the program.

For modern, high-level languages, we need not think about the machine too much. Indeed, modern languages go to great lengths to abstract themselves from the machine. With BF, as with a Turing machine, we must consider both the machine and the program if we hope to be successful.

As we're quoting Perlis, I'd be remiss not to include this epigram:

> 54. Beware of the Turing tar-pit in which everything is possible but nothing of interest is easy.

Turing tar-pits might be a bit like beauty—in the eye of the beholder. The following that has grown around BF and, by extension, esolangs in general, argues against Perlis in this case, at least to me. Perlis's first epigram is "One man's constant is another man's variable." I'm tempted to rephrase it: "One man's Turing tar-pit is another man's inspiration."

Summary

This chapter introduced us to the strangely attractive, if frustratingly difficult, multiverse of BF. We explored what BF is and then implemented it twice: once in C using the original implementation and again in SNOBOL. After this, we wrote a few example programs to get a feel for thinking in BF. With a basic grasp of the language in hand, we then turned our gaze upward to examine some of the brighter lights in the BF multiverse. As with every language, we closed the chapter with a brief discussion.

In Chapter 9 we painted pretty pictures with Piet, a 2D language. Let's close our survey of existing esolangs by returning to the world of 2D programming, but this time using text instead of pixels. Next stop: Befunge.

11

BEFUNGE

Like Piet, Befunge is a 2D programming language. Befunge is fun, is not particularly difficult to work with, and produces some of the most aesthetically pleasing source code I've ever seen. I think you'll agree by the end of this chapter.

Our goal is to learn and experiment with Befunge. After BF, it's perhaps the most influential esolang, and is usually included in lists with titles like "Ten of the weirdest programming languages you've never heard of." We'll learn why Befunge exists and why it's called Befunge. We'll then follow our usual pattern of exploring the gist of the language with examples. We'll conclude with a discussion. I hope this marks only the beginning of your Befunge experiments.

Befunge-93 World Tour

In 1993, the movie *Jurassic Park* brought dinosaurs to the big screen, Mulder and Scully were chasing aliens on TV, and Bill Clinton was beginning his first term as president. In 1993, a typical home computer cost about $1,800 in 2022 dollars, had around 4MB of RAM, a 16 MHz clock speed, a 20MB hard drive, and a "high-density" 1.44MB floppy drive. And, most notably for us, in 1993, Chris Pressey gifted Befunge to the world.

Depending on how you view things, Befunge was the world's first 2D programming language. One might argue that Konrad Zuse's *Plankalkül* was the first because its source code included stacked commands, but I think Befunge's approach is sufficiently different to claim the honor. Pressey's intention for Befunge was to create a language that was as difficult to compile as possible. The "Befunge" name is a misspelling of "before" as typed on a BBS in the wee hours of the morning. If the term BBS is unfamiliar, it stands for "bulletin board system," which was how early personal computer enthusiasts communicated with each other over slow modems before the internet became accessible to the general public.

Let's dive into the world of Befunge to learn how it works and how to write code for it. We'll begin by installing and building the canonical interpreter for Befunge-93, after which we'll take it for a ride with some simple examples. Along the way, we'll learn how to use BEdit, a Befunge-93 editor. You don't need to use BEdit to write Befunge code—any text editor will do—but I found BEdit handy. Then again, I wrote it, so I'm biased.

Building Befunge-93

Run the following command to obtain Befunge-93 from creator Chris Pressey's GitHub site.

```
> git clone https://github.com/catseye/Befunge-93.git
```

This will get you the latest version, most likely the Silver Jubilee version from 2018. That's the version we'll work with.

Building the Befunge interpreter is straightforward. However, before you build it, if you wish, I suggest making a small code change to initialize the pseudorandom number seed using /dev/urandom instead of using time, which is how it's written. That way, if you run the interpreter many times within a second, which we'll do later in the chapter, the pseudorandom generator will not produce the same sequence repeatedly.

I suggest the following steps to build bef, the Befunge interpreter:

```
> cd Befunge-93
> vi src/bef.c
```

The second command starts a text editor with *bef.c* open. If you don't use vi or vim, make the appropriate substitution for your typical editor (then learn vim). Look for srand, which should be around line 252. Then replace

```
srand((unsigned)time(0));
```

with

```
unsigned int seed;
f = fopen("/dev/urandom","rb");
fread(&seed,4,1,f);
fclose(f);
srand(seed);
```

Lastly, use make to build the interpreter.

```
> make
```

We want the *bef* executable in the *bin* directory. I encountered no issues using gcc and suspect you won't, either. Change to the *bin* directory and test the build by typing

```
> ./bef
USAGE: bef [-d] [-o] [-u] [-q] [-i] [-=] [-l] [-t]
           [-r input] [-w output] [-s stack] [-y delay] foo.bf
```

Befunge is simple to use. We'll explore its visual debugger, -d, later. You'll probably want to use -q to suppress the startup message. I defined an alias:

```
> alias bef="bef -q"
```

Befunge is ready. Let's see how to use it.

Printing Text

Befunge programs live on a playfield that is 80 characters across and 25 lines tall. All Befunge commands are a single character. For data, Befunge uses a stack, like Forth. Befunge even supports a few Forth primitives to manipulate the stack: DUP, DROP, and SWAP. Of all the esolangs we've explored, Befunge has the richest command set.

The best way to get into Befunge is to see it in action. Let's start with *cow.bf*. First, we'll run it:

```
> bef examples/cow.bf
How now brown cow?
```

I agree, nothing too impressive. Let's look at the code.

```
<v"How now brown cow?"0
 >:v
 ^,_91+,@
```

Okay, now things are a little more interesting. What are we to make of this jumble of characters? Befunge programs, like Piet programs, run in all directions, beginning in the upper-left corner (row 0, column 0), with the instruction pointer to the right, meaning instructions are evaluated from left to right running along the row.

The first row of *cow.bf* is <v"How now brown cow?"0. The first instruction is <, which tells Befunge to change the instruction pointer to move to the left. The playfield wraps at the edges and ignores spaces. Therefore, the first instruction of *cow.bf* moves flow to the left, which wraps around, ignores spaces, and encounters 0 moving right to left. Befunge pushes digits onto the stack, so 0 pushes a 0 on the stack. The next instruction is the double quote ("), which begins string mode. The interpreter then pushes ASCII values of the characters onto the stack until it encounters the next double quote. Therefore, the string How now brown cow? is pushed on the stack in ASCII, one character at a time. However, program flow in Befunge moves right to left, so the string is pushed on the stack *backward*, starting with the question mark first and ending with H. But this is exactly what we want because stacks are LIFO data structures. We now have our first Befunge idiom: push strings on the stack from right to left so the string can be read in code from left to right.

The character after the leftmost double quote is v, which changes program flow to down. The very next instruction is >, which changes the flow to the right again. Then comes :, which duplicates the top stack value, the ASCII code for H.

Program flow is again directed down by v to hit underscore (_), the first of Befunge's two conditional commands. The _ command pops the top stack item and, if it is 0, changes program flow to the right; otherwise, it goes left. If the top stack item is 0, we want to end, as the string has been printed. Recall that the first instruction after < in the upper left pushed 0 on the stack.

If the top stack item isn't 0, the string hasn't been entirely printed yet. Therefore, moving to the left from _ uses a comma (,) to print the character and change the program flow to up. Going up hits > on the second line to start the loop again.

The _ command encounters the 0 initially pushed on the stack at the beginning of the program. This will direct flow to the right to execute 91+,@. The first three commands push the digits 9 and 1 onto the stack and add the digits so the stack contains 10. Even though only single digits can be pushed onto the stack in code, the stack itself supports a signed 64-bit integer. With 10 on the stack, we hit , to print the top stack item as an ASCII character—in this case, a newline. To end a Befunge program, execute @.

We now understand how *cow.bf* works. With all this flowing left, right, up, and down, it would be nice to *see cow.bf* working. Thankfully, Befunge is cleverly made, and by using the -d command line option, we can, literally, watch program flow happen. This works best when any output is directed to a file. Similarly, if there is input from the user, it's best read from a file. Naturally, a static book cannot show you the flow of the program, but the following command will:

```
> bef -d -w ttt examples/cow.bf
```

Once you press ENTER you'll see the source code at the top of the screen with a cursor flowing over each instruction as it is executed. You can watch the loop repeat to print each character on the stack before ending. The output is then written to the temporary file, *ttt*.

Using BEdit

How was *cow.bf* created? You could use a normal text editor, but I used *bedit.py*, a simple Befunge editor created in Python. We won't discuss the code, but do take a look if you are curious. Note that the terminal window in which you run *bedit.py* must be at least 120 characters wide and 26 lines tall. If not, *bedit.py* will happily remind you.

Executing `python3 bedit.py examples/cow.bf` produces Figure 11-1.

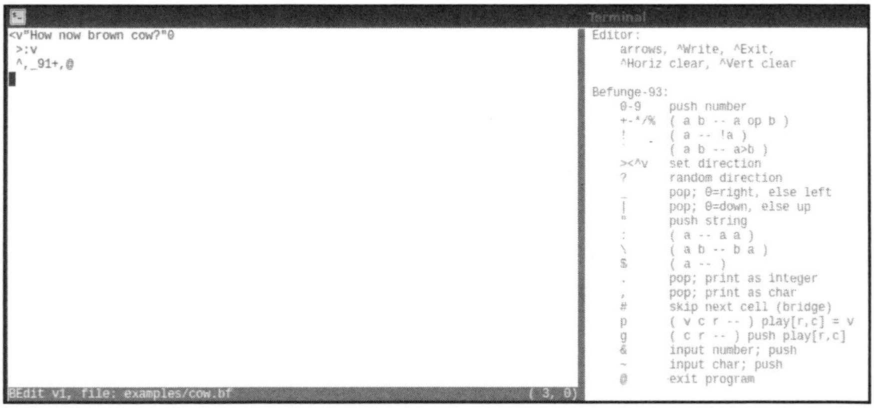

Figure 11-1: Editing cow.bf

The editor has two panes. On the left is a pane of 80×25 characters. This is the Befunge playfield where code goes. On the right is a summary of the editor and Befunge commands for reference. To move around the code, use the arrow keys. Any character you enter will go where the cursor currently is. To make entering code easier, typing characters moves in the direction of the last arrow key. Therefore, to type from right to left, move the cursor to the left with the left arrow key and begin typing. A bit of experimentation is all it takes to get the hang of it.

Use CTRL-W to write the file and CTRL-E to exit, which will also write the file if it has been modified. You must supply the name of the file on the command line, whether new or not. Pressing CTRL-H clears the current row from the cursor to the right edge. Likewise, CTRL-V clears the current column from the cursor down. That's it; the editor is simple, but I used it to create all the examples in this chapter.

Befunge Says Hello

Before we get to genuinely interesting, or at least illustrative, Befunge programs, we must look at our obligatory example. Run *hello.bf* to see our favorite greeting. Then, bring it up in BEdit to look at the code.

```
v>v
8-8    Print "Hello, world!"
479
*:*
1:,
+-,
:3,
3:,
*+,
12,
++,
:*,
83,
+7,
:*,
62,
+:,
:+9
3*1
-2+
:6,
8:@
+*
84
>^
```

This is one of the more unusual examples of "Hello, world!" we've yet seen. Note that anywhere the program doesn't go is fair game for comments, like the one on the second line (line 1, counting from 0). We'll count lines from 0 because that's how computer people count. See if you can figure out how this version works (hint: think characters, not strings). It's not tricky, just unusual because of Befunge's 2D program flow. Because Befunge can't directly push numbers larger than 9 on the stack, larger values must be calculated piece by piece.

Table 11-1 lists Befunge's commands.

Table 11-1: The Befunge-93 Command Set

Command	Description
0–9	Push a digit
+-*/%	(a b -- a op b)
!	(a -- !a)
`	(a b -- a>b)
><^v	Set instruction pointer direction
?	Pointer to random direction
_	Pop; 0 = right, else left
|	Pop; 0 = down, else up
"	Push string
:	(a -- a a)
\	(a b -- b a)
$	(a --)
.	Pop; print as integer
,	Pop; print as char
#	Skip next cell (bridge)
p	(v c r --) play[r,c] = v
g	(c r --) push play[r,c]
&	Input number; push
~	Input char; push
@	Exit program

Most commands are easy to understand, but a few, like #, ?, p, and g, are less clear and are the focus of the examples that follow. Note the use of Forth-style stack effect comments where appropriate.

Befunge in Action

The Befunge-93 repository includes many examples in the *eg* directory. That said, with one exception mentioned in the discussion, we'll roll our own examples in this chapter.

Specifically, we'll explore what makes Befunge unique. Naturally, a 2D language is unusual, but I find other parts of the language even more interesting in terms of thinking about coding.

However, first we must explore flow control and, at the same time, how input works. Doing this leaves us well situated to explore other language features. After flow control, we'll explore Befunge's # bridge command, which might seem unnecessary at first, but it is really quite clever. After that comes ?, Befunge's version of a pseudorandom number generator. We close the section with p and g, which enable both data storage in program space and self-modifying code.

Going with the Flow

Flow control in Piet (Chapter 9) was accomplished by setting up barriers. Befunge makes life easier by explicitly selecting new directions through the playfield, as we saw above with *cow.bf* and *hello.bf*.

Let's work through two examples to improve our understanding of flow in Befunge. The first example converts a string of binary digits to decimal. The second converts text files using DOS line endings to Unix format.

Binary to Decimal

One approach to converting a binary number to decimal is to add the binary digit, from left to right, to a running total initialized to 0, then multiply by 2. When all the digits have been processed, divide by 2 to get the final value. Division by 2 is necessary because multiplying by 2 sets up for the next digit; however, there is no next digit after the last digit is read.

For example, if the input is 1101_2, we get the decimal equivalent as

$$(((((((((0 + 1) \times 2) + 1) \times 2) + 0) \times 2) + 1) \times 2) \div 2 = 13$$

We'll use the stack to hold the running total; therefore, the first thing we need on the stack is a 0. Then, we'll begin a loop to read a character, subtract 48 to make it a 0 or 1, add it to the running total, and then multiply by 2. When all binary digits are read, divide by 2, print the top stack item as a decimal, and exit. Simple.

Well, not quite. How do we know all the binary digits have been read? One of two things will happen, both of which affect the value of the input character read. If the character is a newline, ASCII 10, then we know input is complete. Also, if reading from a file, the input might be end-of-file (EOF), which Befunge reports as −1. Therefore, we'll need to check for both cases.

Listing 11-1 presents *bin2dec.bf*.

```
0v          >68*-+2*  v
        >:1+|
 >~:55+-|   >$2/.55+,@>
        >$2/.55+,@
```

Listing 11-1: Converting binary strings to decimal

This code is fairly compact with only four lines of code. The first line begins with 0v to push 0 on the stack and move down. The next instruction is > to move again to the right. At this point, we want to read a binary digit and check if it's a newline: ~:55+-|. The first character (tilde) reads the binary digit as a character and places it on the stack. The second character (colon) duplicates the character value so we can subtract 10 from it without losing it.

To get 10 on the stack, we use 55+, and we use - to subtract. The stack now contains the running total, which is still 0, the first character, and whatever we get from subtracting 10 from the character. If the character is a newline, the stack contains 0 and pipe (|) will change program flow to down, thereby executing >$2/.55+,@ to drop the extra copy of the final input character, divide the running total by 2, print it as a number, output a newline, and exit. Notice that | is the down/up equivalent of _. It moves program flow down if the top stack item is 0 and moves it up otherwise.

If the character isn't a newline, flow moves up from | to >:1+|. This block of code checks if EOF was read by adding 1 and asking if the top stack item is 0 or not. If it is, flow goes down from the second pipe to execute the second copy of >$2/.55+,@, thereby printing the decimal answer.

Lastly, if the character isn't newline or EOF, we move to the rest of line 0, >68*-+2*, to subtract 48, add the 0 or 1 to the running total, and multiply by 2. The final character of line 0 is v to direct flow to the final character of line 2, >, which wraps back around to the beginning of line 2 to get the next input character.

There are several ways to run *bin2dec.bf*. We could just run it and manually type the binary number. Or we might use echo to send the number to bef. Lastly, we might use file redirection. For example:

```
> bef examples/bin2dec.bf
1101
13
> echo 11010 | bef examples/bin2dec.bf
26
> bef examples/bin2dec.bf <ttt
52
> cat ttt
110100
```

To watch a trace of *bin2dec.bf*, we can use ttt as above, but we need to use Befunge's command line arguments. For example:

```
> bef -d -r ttt -w qqq examples/bin2dec.bf
```

If you watch the trace, you'll see that the program ends when newline is read. We can see the newline explicitly with xxd.

```
> xxd ttt
00000000: 3131 3031 3030 0a
```

However, the input file need not have a final newline. In that case, the program does not exit by the first pipe, which checks for newline, but by the second pipe, which reads EOF (that is, −1). The following snippet of Python creates a new input file without a final newline.

```
with open("zzz","r") as f:
    f.write("110100")
```

Now run *bef* with -d as above, substituting zzz for ttt, and watch carefully. The program ends by taking the second pipe. The moral of the story is: care is required when deciding whether the input to a Befunge program is complete.

DOS to Unix

A common issue when moving files from one computer system to another is a mismatch in end-of-line conventions. Unix systems end each line of a text file with ASCII 10. This is a linefeed and is sometimes called newline. However, Windows systems, which are built on MS-DOS, use two characters at the end of each line: ASCII 13 and ASCII 10. ASCII 13 is a carriage return. Besides being an unnecessary waste of disk space, the carriage return causes trouble with systems that expect only a linefeed. ASCII 13 is CTRL-M, so some Unix editors show an extraneous ^M when manipulating files with DOS line endings. Thus, it would be nice to convert such files to Unix format. To complicate matters still further, older Macintosh text files use only ASCII 13 as the line ending. Thankfully, such text files are becoming rare.

Naturally, there are utilities to convert text file line endings, to say nothing of modern text editors that handle DOS files without trouble. But just for a moment, let's pretend it's still 1993 and our Amiga computer isn't that influenced by DOS. We need a conversion utility, and we happen to have this nifty new language called Befunge to play with. Surely it can do what we want.

Listing 11-2 contains *dos2unix.bf*, a program to convert text files with DOS line endings to Unix (and Amiga). Structurally, it's rather similar to Listing 11-1, but there are some differences.

```
v          >        >>,
    >:85+-|
>~:1+|        >$~:55+-|
     @                 >^
```

Listing 11-2: Converting DOS line endings to Unix

The overall flow of the program is left to right, from column 0 of line 2 on over. The first block of code, ~:1+|, reads a character and ascertains whether it is EOF. If so, we're done and @ calls it a day. If not, we need to check if the character read is ASCII 13, which is precisely what >:85+-| does. If we subtract 13 and get 0, then the character is ASCII 13. In that case, take the branch on line 2, >$~:55+-|, which drops the extra ASCII 13, reads the next input character, and checks if it's ASCII 10. If it is, we want to keep it, so >^ moves up to >>, to print it. If the second character read isn't ASCII 10, we have an embedded ASCII 13, which is weird, but whatever, we'll keep it. That's the top branch of the second pipe on line 2. Lastly, if the pipe in line 1 does not move down, it moves up to print the input character. This is the path taken for most of the characters read.

Now let's test *dos2unix.bf*. To run it with redirection, use the following commands:

```
> bef examples/dos2unix.bf <ttt.dos >ttt.unix
> xxd ttt.dos
00000000: 4142 430d 0a44 4546 0d0a 4142 430d 0a44  ABC..DEF..ABC..D
00000010: 4546 0d0a                                EF..
```

```
> xxd ttt.unix
00000000: 4142 430a 4445 460a 4142 430a 4445 460a  ABC.DEF.ABC.DEF.
```

The input file, *ttt.dos*, uses DOS line endings. The output of xxd shows the carriage return and linefeed characters as 0d0a. The output, *ttt.unix*, has only 0a, as it should.

I admit that the two examples in this section are not the most beguiling. However, they help check your understanding of how Befunge works. Writing programs is more fun than reading them, so I encourage you to give something similar a go. Perhaps a utility to take a Unix text file and spit out a DOS version? When you are ready, move on to the next section.

Building Bridges

The command that likely made the least sense at first blush when you read through Table 11-1 was # (hash mark), the bridge command. This command skips the next instruction, acting as a bridge to move over it.

For example, a Befunge program consisting of only 88*1+#., will print the letter *A* forever. The first part, 88*1+, puts 65 on the stack. Then, # skips the next instruction, which is a period to print 65, and instead hits the comma to print ASCII 65, which is A. That is all the text on the first line, so the instruction pointer will wrap around to repeat it, over and over (Listing 11-3).

```
<v"xyzzy"0
 >:#v_82+,@
 ^ ,<
```

Listing 11-3: One use for the bridge instruction

The # skips the next instruction—why on earth would we want to do that? One reason for # is found in *bridge.bf* (Listing 11-3), which does nothing more than print the word xyxxy. If you hear a hollow voice saying "fool," fear not. (And if you don't understand that reference, fear not as well.)

As with the *cow.bf* example above, *bridge.bf* moves from right to left and loops to print character after character. However, in this case, consider line 1, >:#v_82+,@. From left to right, the commands are to move right, duplicate the character at the top of the stack, and then skip the v command but execute the underscore (_), which moves to the right if the top stack item is 0 and moves to the left otherwise.

Here's where we see the utility of bridge. If the character is 0, go right to push 10 on the stack, print the newline character, and exit. Otherwise, move left. The first instruction moving left from _ is v, the very instruction # skipped when moving from left to right.

Executing v moves down, then left, to print the character and ultimately loop around to process the next character. So the bridge command is essential in this case as it allows one set of commands when the program flows to the right while executing a different set of commands when it flows to the left. Keep this behavior in mind because we'll see it again in the next section.

Fun with Dice

Befunge's ? command randomly changes the instruction pointer's direction. It might be up, down, left, or right. Let's have some fun with this unusual instruction. At first blush, we might think it useless: who wants a program that isn't deterministic? Then again, random numbers are frequently used in everything from games to simulations. Can we press ? into similar service?

As ? selects a new instruction pointer direction, it seems reasonable we might use it to simulate dice. In particular, ? selects from four possible directions, so we might simulate what gamers call a D4, which is a die with four sides instead of the usual six.

How can ? help us here? Well, if we encounter ?, there are four possible directions to go, so if we push a 1, 2, 3, or 4 depending on which direction is selected, we'll get our four-sided die.

Listing 11-4 shows one approach to simulating a four-sided die.

```
v  > v
>#v?v
  1234
  >>>>.91+,@
```

Listing 11-4: Simulating a four-sided die

In this case, we move to ? by moving down to line 1, then right. Notice the bridge instruction in line 1. When moving to the right, we want to skip the v instruction to reach ?. If ? selects to move to the left, we hit the v to move to line 2 and push 1 on the stack. Likewise, the other three directions away from ? end up pushing 2, 3, or 4 before hitting line 3, which moves to the right to print the selected value.

If we run *die4.bf* 10,000 times, we expect each outcome value to appear with roughly equal frequency. One such experiment of 10,000 runs produced [2472, 2577, 2452, 2499] as the respective number of 1s, 2s, 3s, and 4s. The values are similar, so it's fair to say our four-sided die program works.

Listing 11-5 shows a first attempt at simulating a standard six-sided die.

```
      v
v  .2?1.  v
      v
v .4?3. v
      v
 v.6?5.v
      ^
>>>  v  <<<
      5
      5
      +
      ,
      @
```

Listing 11-5: Attempting to simulate a six-sided die

If nothing else, Listing 11-5 is nice and symmetric. I toyed with putting it on a t-shirt. Flow moves down the center from top to bottom. When the interpreter encounters a ?, moving back up forces flow back into ?, leaving only three exits: to either side or down. If to the side, a number from 1 to 6 is pushed on the stack and printed, and arrows move flow to the bottom to print a newline before exiting.

There are six numbers, so surely this arrangement is appropriate. If you run this version 10,000 times, you might get a distribution similar to [3337, 3333, 1072, 1109, 543, 606], which is not at all uniform. Listing 11-5 can be found in *die6_biased.bf*, and as you might expect from the name, it is a loaded die that strongly favors 1s and 2s.

From the counts, the ratio between 1s and 2s to 3s and 4s then 5s and 6s is 6:2:1, meaning one is six times as frequent as six. If we look at the structure of Listing 11-5, we can calculate the probabilities associated with each outcome. The first ? has a 1 out of 3 chance of selecting 1, 2, or moving on to other numbers. Therefore, the probability of choosing a 1 or a 2 is $1/3 + 1/3 = 2/3$. That means the sum of the remaining probabilities, those for selecting 3 through 6, must total $1/3$. Selecting 3 or 4 is similar to 1 or 2—there is a 1 out of 3 chance—but it's 1 out of 3 from what is already a 1 out of 3 chance. Therefore, there is a 1 in 9 chance of selecting 3 and the same for selecting 4. The final 1 in 9 chance is split evenly between choosing 5 or 6, or 1 in 18 each.

If the probabilities above are correct, they must add up to 1. Let's use Scheme to check that they do.

```
> racket
Welcome to Racket v6.11.
> (+ 1/3 1/3 1/9 1/9 1/18 1/18)
1
```

Our calculations are correct. Clearly, we don't want Listing 11-5, aesthetics aside. So how can we use something that selects 1 in 4 to get something that selects 1 in 6 with equal probabilities?

If we restrict ? to select one of two options only, we can use each of those outputs to choose another pair, thereby changing two options into four. Do the same for each of the four, and we have eight outputs, each equally likely to be selected. We only want six of the eight, so if either of the remaining two are selected, we repeat until one of the six is chosen.

There are different ways to write such an algorithm. The file *die6.bf* holds one of them (see Listing 11-6). Take a moment to look at the code to absorb what it means. Then linger a little longer to appreciate the code's ethereal beauty.

```
v                     >
           >          ?<
                      >6  v   v
      >         ?<
                      >5  v
```

```
        >      ?<
               >4  v
>        ?<           >.91+,@
               >3  ^
        >      ?<
               >2  ^
     >      ?<
               >1  ^
        >      ?<
^               >
```

Listing 11-6: Simulating a six-sided die with equal probabilities

The rightmost instructions push 1 through 6 on the stack. However, if flow reaches the top or bottom, it continues to the right to wrap around and move back to the beginning until one of the six desired paths is selected.

Running the code in Listing 11-6 10,000 times gives us frequencies of [1678, 1638, 1705, 1660, 1637, 1682], which is exactly what we want; each outcome is now equally likely. As an exercise, see if you can come up with arrangements of ? to simulate an 8-sided die, 12-sided die, or even 20-sided die.

Wandering Around

The file *brownian.bf* contains a program where the entire playfield is filled with ? and nothing else. Running this program on its own is boring; it produces no output and never ends. However, running it with Befunge's debugger is mesmerizing:

```
> bef -d examples/brownian.bf
```

The cursor wanders over the playfield in a way that is reminiscent of Brownian motion, the random motion of particles in some medium.

Before we move on, take a look at *zero.bf*. It consists of an entire playfield of ? commands with a single period (.) in the middle.

Befunge never throws an error because of the stack. If you attempt to pop the stack when it is empty, Befunge returns 0. The print command pops the stack, so printing when the stack is empty outputs 0. If you run *zero.bf* with the debugger, you might think you're in for a long wait to hit the one print instruction. However, if you run *zero.bf* without the debugger, your screen will quickly fill with 0s. Human perception of how fast computers operate is orders of magnitude too slow. Computers are so much quicker than we can appreciate that even a simple interpreter like Befunge randomly hits that one print command at a tremendous rate. In fact, dumping the output to the screen is slow. Direct the output to a file instead, and even my old system has Befunge printing nearly 15,000 0s per second.

However, it turns out my statement about Befunge not throwing stack errors is incorrect. Run this program: 00/.@. I consider it an Easter egg.

Updating the Playfield on the Fly

Befunge programs live in the playfield and memory is restricted to the stack. Or is it? The p instruction lets the programmer write to the playfield as the program runs. If the altered cell happens to be part of the running program, and the value written is the ASCII code for a valid command, then Befunge will use that command. This means that Befunge allows self-modifying code, which, under normal circumstances, is taboo. But we're working with eso-langs, so what was forbidden may be permitted. Use p to write to the playfield and g to read from it.

Let's explore p and g with two examples. The first converts an integer less than 65,536 (= 2^{16}) to a four-digit hexadecimal number. The second is a simple calculator.

What the Hex?

Old-school BASIC used DATA and READ to store data in source code. These were usually instructions for small machine language routines that were POKEd into memory and later CALLed from BASIC. We can use g similarly to read data from the playfield.

Suppose we have a number, v, on the stack. We'll assume it's positive and less than 65,536. Our task is to convert this number to four hex digits and print them. One way to do this is to split v in two by replacing it with $v/256$ and $v \bmod 256$. Then, if we do the same with the split values using 16 in place of 256, we'll extract the four hexadecimal digit values.

For example, if the user enters 1234, the sequence of operations leads to

$$1234 \rightarrow 1234/256 = 4$$
$$\rightarrow 1234 \bmod 256 = 210$$
$$4 \rightarrow 4/16 = \mathbf{0}$$
$$\rightarrow 4 \bmod 16 = \mathbf{4}$$
$$210 \rightarrow 210/16 = \mathbf{13}$$
$$\rightarrow 210 \bmod 16 = \mathbf{2}$$

or $(0, 4, 13, 2) = 04D2_{16} = 1234$.

Let's put this algorithm to the test and, at the same time, use p and g because we can. The code we need is in *dec2hex.bf* and is shown in Listing 11-7.

```
v     0123456789ABCDEF
>&:55*55+*6+/\55*55+*6+%              v
v                   p01%*28p02/*28:<
>:82*%30p82*/40p                     v
v                         ,g0+5g04<
>30g5+0g,                            v
v                         ,g0+5g02<
>10g5+0g,55+,@
```

Listing 11-7: Converting decimal to hex

The program flows in a zig-zag pattern, row by row, beginning with line 1. First, the user is asked for a number (&), after which comes the division and modulo by 256. At the end of the line, $v/256$ and $v \bmod 256$ are on the stack.

Line 2 runs from right to left. Flipping the instructions, the interpreter executes `:82*/20p82*%10p`. Let's break this down a bit. The first instruction duplicates the top stack item, $v \bmod 256$. Next, `82*/` divides the top stack item by 16, thereby calculating the second digit of the answer. To store it in the playfield, we use `20p`.

Table 11-1 says the `p` instruction expects three values on the stack: the value to store, the playfield column, and the playfield row. Therefore, `20p` stores the second digit value in row 0, column 2. The remainder of line 2 uses modulo to get the value of the first digit and places it in `10p`, row 0, column 1. Line 3, running left to right, repeats the calculation to find the values of digits 3 and 4.

When line 4 begins, again running right to left, we have the digit values in row 0 of the playfield. We now need to print them as ASCII characters. You've likely noticed the string `0123456789ABCDEF` in line 0. We'll use this string to get the characters we need. This is the Befunge equivalent of DATA in BASIC or FORTRAN. The digit value serves as an index into this string.

Flipped, line 4 is `40g5+0g,`. The first part, `40g`, reads the value of digit 4, which is the most significant digit. To index the proper character, we must add 5, then another `g` pulls the proper character, placing its ASCII value on the stack for `,` to print. The remainder of Listing 11-7 prints the rest of the answer and a newline and then ends.

Running *dec2hex.bf* shows that the program works.

```
> bef examples/dec2hex.bf
1234
04D2
```

It's more interesting to run this example with the debugger. For example, if the temporary file *ttt* contains an integer, say 6,502, we might run the code with the following:

```
> bef -d -r ttt -w qqq examples/dec2hex.bf
```

While the code executes, watch the top row carefully. You'll see four lights, er, dots appear. These are the specific digits placed in the playfield by the `p` instructions. When the program ends, the output is in another temporary file, *qqq*, which contains $1966_{16} = 6502$.

Using the playfield to store program data is a handy option. Using the playfield to alter program execution is the next step. Let's see how.

Program Transmogrification

Self-modifying code, or, as I like to call it, *program transmogrification*, is seldom used and with good reason. However, Befunge supports it, and there are times it's more handy than not. For example, a calculator program needs to accept a number, an operator, and another number. The code is much the same regardless of the operator, as long as the operator is binary. Befunge supports five binary arithmetic operators: +, -, *, /, and %. Let's make a simple calculator that lets users enter a single digit, the desired operator, and a second digit before calculating and printing the answer.

In Python, we might implement such a calculator with

```
a = int(getch())
op= getch()
b = int(getch())
if op == "+":
    ans = a + b
elif op == "-":
    ans = a - b
elif op == "*":
    ans = a * b
elif op == "/":
    ans = a / b
elif op == "%":
    ans = a % b
print(ans)
```

We're assuming the existence of a function, getch, that returns a single character from the keyboard.

The Python code would do the trick, but its highly repetitive if statement isn't particularly attractive. If we know the operation is addition, the code becomes simpler.

```
a = int(getch())
b = int(getch())
print(a+b)
```

If the operation is division, the code is the same; just replace + with /.

The key to our Befunge calculator is in the phrase, "just replace X with Y." That is exactly what we'll do: we'll write the program as if the operator were always addition, but modify the program source in the playfield during program execution to use the user's actual operator.

Algorithmically, then, we need to do the following:

1. Get a single digit character from the user and convert it to a number on the stack.

2. Get a single operator character from the user and place it in the proper location in the playfield so Befunge uses it when calculating the answer.

3. Get a second digit from the user on the stack.

4. Perform the operation and print the answer.

Listing 11-8 shows *calc.bf*. It's even shorter than the description of what it does.

```
~68*-~61p~68*-84*,88*3-,84*,v
@,+82.+                        <
```

Listing 11-8: Program transmogrification in action

The first part reads a character, assumed to be a digit, and subtracts 48 to convert it to an integer. That's ~68*-. The program then asks for the operator, which it places in row 1, column 6 (~61p). If you look at row 1, column 6, you'll see it contains a +, which is overwritten by the operator character the user enters—program transmogrification!

The rest of line 0 gets the second digit, prints a space, an equals sign, and another space. Line 1 applies the updated operation, prints the result and a newline, and exits. Let's see Listing 11-8 in action.

```
> bef examples/calc.bf
8*5
 = 40
> bef examples/calc.bf
9%4
 = 1
> bef examples/calc.bf
2+2
 = 4
> bef examples/calc.bf
2-9
 = -7
```

The stated goal of Befunge was to make a language that is too hard to compile, so it makes sense to allow self-modifying code. In this particular case, especially given how Befunge works as a programming language, a bit of self-modification was the more elegant solution. Without it, *calc.bf* would have to be much larger: it would need to enable comparing the operator character with each of the five possible operators along with a different code path for each operator. This would definitely not be as elegant.

Discussion

Befunge-93 is imperative, and the stack is of arbitrary size, limited only by the computer's RAM, so we might think it's Turing complete. However, it isn't. What keeps it from being Turing complete is a limitation many other languages do not have: the program *must* fit in the playfield, as that's all the room there is. Therefore, programs cannot be arbitrarily complex and Befunge-93 is not Turing complete.

You may notice that in the previous paragraph, I was careful to type "Befunge-93." A later version of Befunge, Befunge-98, removes the limitation on playfield size and therefore *is* Turing complete. However, I felt an affinity for the original, which is why we worked with it here.

The web has many additional resources for Befunge, though not at the scale of BF or even Piet. The best resources for Befunge are *https://esolang .org/* and Chris Pressey's site (*https://git.catseye.tc/Befunge-93/*). I also found this interview with Pressey interesting: *https://esoteric.codes/blog/interview-with -chris-pressey/*. Befunge figures prominently. Last of all, if you're like me, you'll find plenty to explore and think about by examining all of Pressey's site, including the many other programming languages he's developed over the years (*https://catseye.tc/*).

Befunge has been written in Befunge—see the included *befunge.bf* file. It's from the esolang wiki. To use it, run *befunge.bf*, passing in the Befunge program you want to run from standard in. If the program has input, separate the program text from the input with a semicolon (;). For example:

```
> bef examples/befunge.bf <examples/cow.bf  2>/dev/null
How now brown cow?
```

This is quite impressive and reinforces the argument that Befunge-93 would be Turing complete if there were enough program space. The 2> redirection ignores the Befunge error messages that you'll see if you don't use it.

It just happens that the Befunge interpreter in Befunge fits in the playfield. The esolang wiki does not provide authorship information for *befunge .bf*, so I'm not sure who we should thank for such a clever implementation.

2D programming is cute and much in line with what a "good" esolang is—something outside the box. The clever bits, to me, are seeing the utility of an instruction like #, the bridge instruction, and with it the recognition that programs running in multiple directions might want to do slightly different things when running left to right or right to left, even for the same line of code. Using single-digit numbers, knowing any number can be built on the stack as needed, is also quite clever.

Good esolangs inspire other esolangs. Befunge is no different. For example, if there is a 2D language, then why not a 3D language? Interested? If so, take a look at Suzy (*https://github.com/gvx/suzy/*). However, be aware that it hasn't been updated for more than a decade, so use Python 2.*X* to run its examples.

What about other 2D languages? Befunge has inspired so many esolangs that a term has evolved just to describe them: *fungeoids*. The esolang wiki lists pages of fungeoids at *https://esolangs.org/wiki/Category:Two-dimensional _languages*. If imitation is the sincerest form of flattery, then Befunge should feel abundantly flattered, provided Befunge can feel anything, of course.

Summary

Befunge was the target of this chapter. We learned that Befunge is the first 2D programming language, has been around long enough to have a silver jubilee, and is fun to program in. We also learned that Befunge has inspired a swarm of related esolangs: the fungeoids.

And, with that, our exploration of existing esolangs draws to a close. Part I of the book discussed the essentials of programming languages. Part II prepped us for esolangs by studying atypical programming languages, and Part III explored existing esolangs. Now we move to Part IV to implement two homegrown esolangs: Filska and Firefly.

PART IV

HOMEGROWN ESOLANGS

12

FILSKA

It's time to design our first esolang, Filska. Filska, pronounced "full-ska," is a word in the dialect of the Shetland Islands. It means "high-spirited fun." Whether a programming language can embody such a thing is up for reasonable debate, but, as with most esolangs, fun is an ingredient, so the name seems appropriate. (As an aside, if you happen to enjoy Scottish fiddle music, as I do, you might look for music by a band from Shetland with the same name. The convergence of names is pure chance, I assure you.)

In this chapter, we'll outline Filska's philosophy and design. Then, we'll create an interpreter for it in Python. We'll experiment with Filska itself in Chapter 13.

Philosophy and Design

Filska is an answer to this question: what is it like to program in a language where each subprogram can manipulate only a single memory location?

Filska works with floating-point numbers and the language itself is simple to make implementing the interpreter easy. As we've seen, this is often the case with esolangs. So superficially, Filska looks a bit like assembly language. We're interested in the experience of trying to code in a restricted language, one where each subprogram is allowed to manipulate only a single memory location; therefore, we might be excused for making the syntax simple.

Of course, if each subprogram manipulates only its own memory location, there is no way to share information between subprograms. A typical solution to such a problem is to use a stack, á la Forth, but we'll be even more restrictive and emulate simple microprocessors. Therefore, Filska supports three floating-point registers, X, Y, and Z, which any subprogram can manipulate along with its memory location. And, as with many simple microprocessors, the registers are somewhat limited in their abilities. We might think of each Filska subprogram as having its own accumulator along with access to the three index registers.

Conceptually, a Filska program looks like Figure 12-1.

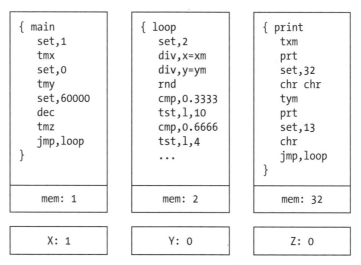

Figure 12-1: The conceptual structure of a Filska program

The code in Figure 12-1 is part of the example program outputting the points of the Sierpiński triangle. There are three subprograms: main, loop, and print. All Filska programs have at least a main subprogram where execution begins. The similarity to assembly language is clear.

Each subprogram is responsible for a single memory location. In Figure 12-1, the values in the memory location represent a possible state of the program. The set,1 instruction in main sets main's memory location to 1.

Also indicated are the three general purpose registers, X, Y, and Z. In the figure, X is set to 1 because of the tmx instruction in main, which transfers the current subprogram's memory value (1) to X.

There's more to say about what's happening in Figure 12-1, but we need a better understanding of Filska first. Therefore, let's detail Filska so we can implement it in Python.

Program Structure and Syntax

A Filska program is a set of one or more subprograms. Execution begins with the main subprogram, which must exist. Filska's syntax is especially simple: tokens are separated by whitespace. Each token is either part of a subprogram declaration or an instruction associated with a subprogram. Comments are allowed; they begin with a double quote (") and run to the end of the line.

Listing 12-1 shows the complete source code to a simple program counting from 10 down to 1.

```
"  Loop and decrement (ex1)
{ main
    set,10     " set mem to 10
    prt        " print it
    tmx        " mem -> X
    set,13     " 13 -> mem
    chr        " newline
    txm        " X -> mem, restore count
    dec        " decrement mem
    tst,n,-6   " if mem != 0, go back six instructions
    hlt        " end
}
```

Listing 12-1: Counting down from 10 to 1

The first items to notice are the comment lines beginning with double quotes. As you expect, comments are ignored by the interpreter. Next, a single subprogram, the required main, is defined. Syntactically, a subprogram is an opening brace ({), a name, one or more instructions, and a closing brace (}). All tokens are separated by whitespace, implying that a complete instruction, even if it consists of several parts, must not have spaces within it. Again, we do this to make our implementation easier so we can focus on the language itself. Lastly, Filska is not case sensitive, so hlt and HLT are the same instruction. We'll use hlt in the text, but in code, any combination of case is fine.

If you run the program in Listing 12-1 with

```
> python3 filska.py examples/ex1.filska
```

you'll get output counting down from 10 to 1 with one number per line. We'll walk through this example later in the chapter.

If this were all there is to the idea of Filska, I wouldn't waste time with it. However, there are some interesting constraints that make working with the language a bit of a challenge. It's also fun: Filska requires alternative thinking to do things that might be second nature to you if you are used to standard programming languages.

We already mentioned how each Filska subprogram manipulates its own memory. That's one constraint. The other constraint has to do with program flow between subprograms. Filska does not have a call stack. There is no idea of a subroutine or function. Instead, a subprogram runs and, if instructed, transfers flow to another subprogram. Filska only runs one subprogram at a time, so we aren't talking about concurrency here.

All subprograms run forever unless instructed otherwise. If the last instruction in a subprogram is executed, flow starts again at the top of the subprogram. Thus, a single Filska subprogram acts as a loop on its own. However, the example above ended with a call to hlt (halt). If you remove the hlt instruction, the countdown will repeat forever. Try it. Use CTRL-C to quit the interpreter when you get tired of watching the numbers flash by.

So infinite loops are implicit in Filska. What else is there to know? Each Filska subprogram maintains its own program counter, which is its own pointer to the instruction that should be executed next. In some fashion, all the programming languages we used do this. If we have a function like the following in Python

```
def f(x):
    y = 2*x**2 + 3*x - 4
    return y
```

we would expect to call f(3) and get a return value of 23. If we call f a second time with a different value, say f(4), we would expect it to begin again from the first instruction and run through the return to give us 40 as the output. The program counter for f resets to 0 after the first call.

In Filska, unless we are explicit about resetting them, program counters persist when transferring to another subprogram. We'll see how this works in the next section, but for now, it means if subprogram *A* moves to subprogram *B* and, after some sequence of instructions, subprogram *B* moves back to subprogram *A*, execution of *A* will begin *with the next instruction* and not with the first instruction. Therefore, it is incorrect to think of Filska subprograms as subroutines, as they don't reset themselves, but rather persist in their current state between transfers to and from them.

We can express the environment in which Filska operates with the following statements:

- Filska programs are collections of independent subprograms.
- Filska subprograms manipulate a single floating-point memory location, M.
- Filska subprograms have access to three floating-point registers shared between them: X, Y, and Z.
- Filska subprograms loop when the last instruction is executed.

- Transfers between subprograms do not automatically reset the caller's program counter.

This environment is nonstandard, that is, it's different from what we are used to in traditional programming languages. We might think of Filska as some sort of weird machine from the early days of computers, but that, of course, would be grossly unfair to those early machines. Perhaps we can agree that Filska is just a bit weird, but in a good way, because working with it forces us to expand our thinking—the usual approach to even basic programs doesn't always work, as we'll see in Chapter 13.

Flow Control

Filska supports five instructions affecting program flow. We'll talk about four of them here and defer the fifth until we discuss comparisons. The four instructions are: jpr, jmp, gto, and hlt. We'll discuss them in reverse order beginning with hlt, which, as we've already seen, stops the Filska program and exits.

To control flow within a subprogram, use gto, which is a three-letter mnemonic for "goto," the bane of early computer programming. In Filska, gto accepts an offset in terms of instructions. An offset of 1 would move to the next instruction, an offset of 2 would move to the instruction after that, and so forth. To go backward, make the offset values negative. Primitive, yes, but doing this helps simplify the implementation and adds another small twist to the language. If you find yourself writing large Filska programs, feel free to add labels to the implementation.

Use gto to execute an unconditional jump *within* a subprogram. For example, this little block of code will set the subprogram's memory location to 0 then loop forever, adding 1.

```
set,0
inc
gto,-1
```

We use gto,-1 to go back to the instruction immediately before the gto. Note the syntax gto,*<offset>*, where no spaces are allowed, the comma is required, and *<offset>* is an integer, that is, the number of instructions to skip. Note that Filska does not insist on a single instruction per line, so

```
set,0 inc gto,-1
```

works just as well.

To move program flow from one subprogram to another, use jmp or jpr followed by the new subprogram's name. For example, in Figure 12-1, the main subprogram transfers to loop with jmp,loop. Note that the name of the target subprogram is fixed. Filska does not support any form of indirection.

We said before that Filska does not reset the program counter for a subprogram when transferring to a new subprogram. This is true if jmp is used.

However, if you use jpr instead, then the current subprogram's counter *is* reset to 0, so the next time the subprogram is started, it will start from the beginning.

Let's set up an example. First, let's write a small program to output some numbers to the console, one number per line. The code is shown in Listing 12-2.

```
{ main
    set,1 prt
    jmp,newline
    set,2 prt
    jmp,newline
    set,3 prt
    jmp,newline
    hlt
}


{ newline set,10 chr jmp,main }
```

Listing 12-2: jmp example

There are a few things to note in Listing 12-2. First, there are two subprograms, main and newline. Second, we stated already that set,1 sets main's memory to one. Also, prt will display the current subprogram's memory as a floating-point number. So the first line of main will display 1 at the console.

The next line transfers control from main to newline. This subprogram sets its memory to 10 and calls chr. Recall that ASCII 10 is the character code for a newline character on Linux. For Windows, it's ASCII 13. The Filska interpreter is happy with either character. It's the same as using "\n" in Python. The chr instruction displays the subprogram's memory as a character. So the point of newline is to move output to the next line.

The last instruction in newline is jmp,main to transfer control back to main. But *where* in main will execution start? Because main called newline with jmp, main's program counter was not reset, so the next instruction executed is set,2 followed by another transfer of control to newline.

Where will newline pick up? Previously, it transferred control back to main with a jmp instruction as well, so it will pick up at the next instruction. However, that was the last instruction in newline, so, according to our design, program flow will loop back to the beginning, making set,13 the next instruction executed.

Therefore, each jmp to newline will effectively run the entire subprogram again. Good. This is what we want. Similarly, each transfer to newline from main uses jmp, so when newline transfers back to main, the next instruction is executed.

Listing 12-2 will output 1, then 2, followed by 3, and then stop because of the hlt instruction. The jumps to newline ensure each number is on its own line in the output.

Note that because newline transfers to main via its final instruction, it has the effect and feel of a subroutine or function. But don't be fooled. If another subprogram were to transfer control to newline, the result wouldn't be to transfer back to that subprogram when done. Instead, newline would transfer control to main.

Listing 12-2 shows us how to use jmp to transfer control between subprograms and how to pick up where we left off if we return to the transferring subprogram. Now, let's mess things up a bit. We'll keep the code of Listing 12-2, but replace the first instance of jmp,newline with jpr,newline, using jpr in the place of jmp.

If you make this change and run the code, you won't see 1, 2, 3 at the console. Instead, you'll see 1 repeating forever until you hit CTRL-C. Why? Because jpr transfers control to a new subprogram, just like jmp, but it also resets the caller's program counter to 0. So when main transfers control to newline, main's program counter is set to 0, causing it to pick up at set,1 again when newline transfers back to main. This sets up an endless loop that outputs 1 repeatedly.

As an exercise, restore the jmp,newline instruction in main, replace jmp,main in newline with jpr,main, and run the code. Is there any difference in the output compared to our earlier output? If not, why?

The answer is no, there is no difference; both versions output 1, 2, and 3 at the console. This is because the transfer back to main from newline is the *last* instruction, so resetting newline's program counter is irrelevant in this case. If the program counter is reset, newline starts from its first instruction. If the program counter isn't reset, it will loop back around to the beginning and start with the first instruction anyway.

Table 12-1 summarizes Filska's flow control instructions.

Table 12-1: Flow Control Instructions

Instruction	Description
jmp	Transfer to a new subprogram and preserve the caller's program counter.
jpr	Transfer to a new subprogram and reset the caller's program counter.
gto	Jump forward or backward within the current subprogram.
hlt	Halt. Stop the program immediately and exit.

Let's move on now to see how Filska handles its little bit of memory.

Memory

We already know that each Filska subprogram manages a single floating-point number. We also know subprograms share access to three floating-point index registers. Let's look at the instructions that manipulate these data values.

To set a subprogram's memory, use set.

```
set,42
set,-6502
set,0.007
set,6.62607015e-34
```

The only way to directly set a memory value to a constant is via set.

Several instructions transfer subprogram memory to or from an index register. The form of the instruction is straightforward: the source of the data comes before the destination. So to transfer a memory value to the X register, use tmx. Similarly, to transfer memory to the Z register, use tmz. To move data from an index register to memory, reverse the letters. Therefore, tym moves the current value of the Y register to memory.

The transfer instructions are destructive, meaning that the destination value is overwritten. The swp instruction swaps two data values instead. The instruction takes a two-letter argument representing the two data sources to swap. The current subprogram's memory is denoted as M. For example,

```
swp,mx
swp,yz
```

will first swap memory and the X register and then swap the Y and Z register values.

Filska does not support arrays or any form of heap memory, so that immediately precludes many possible programs. However, there is no practical upper bound on the number of subprograms allowed, so creative programming might mimic some larger memory operations. Listing 12-3 shows how to use a subprogram as a set-once, read-many memory location.

```
{ main
  ❶ set,123
    tmx jmp,mem
  ❷ set,1 prt
    set,13 chr
  ❸ jmp,mem txm
    prt set,13 chr
    jmp,mem txm
    prt set,13 chr
    jmp,mem txm
    prt set,13 chr
    hlt
}

{ mem
    txm
    inc
    jmp,main
    tmx
    gto,-2
}
```

Listing 12-3: Using a subprogram as ROM

The main program of Listing 12-3 loads the X register with 123 by first setting main's memory to 123 followed by a transfer to the X register ❶. Then, a jmp to mem moves the 123 from X to mem's memory. Just to show we can, we increment the memory before returning to main via jmp.

This first call to mem sets the local data value to 124 (as we incremented it). Subsequent calls to mem from main will start mem at the tmx instruction to transfer the 124 to the X register. In main, we set its memory to 1 and print it at the console along with a newline character to show that main's memory is now changed ❷.

Next, we make three calls to mem. After each call, the X register will contain mem's local data value (124). Back in main, we transfer the X value to main's memory and print it at the console ❸. It is not hard to imagine using a second index register, say Y, as an argument of sorts to tell mem to set its local memory to whatever is in X instead of setting X to the local memory.

Arithmetic

By *arithmetic* we mean binary math operations like addition and multiplication. The full list of supported binary operations is in Table 12-2. The general format of the instruction is

---

<op>,<dst> = <op1><op2>

---

with *<op>* being the command, *<dst>* the destination, and *<op1>* and *<op2>* the operands. The infix version is *<dst>* = *<op1><op><op2>* as in $c = a - b$.

Table 12-2: Binary Arithmetic Instructions

Instruction	Example	Operation
add	add,m=xy	Addition, $M \leftarrow X + Y$
sub	sub,x=yz	Subtraction, $X \leftarrow Y - Z$
mul	mul,z=xy	Multiplication, $Z \leftarrow X \times Y$
div	div,m=zx	Division, $M \leftarrow Z \div X$
mod	mod,y=mz	Modulo, $Y \leftarrow M \bmod Z$
pow	pow,z=xy	Power, $Z \leftarrow X^Y$

You'll notice from the examples in Table 12-2 that the operands and the destination must be subprogram memory or one of the index registers. No constants are allowed. However, any combination of memory and registers is permitted. And as usual, to simplify the implementation, no spaces are allowed in the command.

Comparisons

Filska handles logical comparisons via a flags register and two instructions. The flags register is a list of Boolean values indicating the result of the most recent comparison instruction (cmp). The flags are zero (Z), equal (E), less than (L), and greater than (G). The cmp instruction accepts a single argument and compares it to the subprogram's memory, setting the appropriate flags as needed. The argument is a constant or one of the index registers.

For example, these instructions first set memory and then call cmp.

```
set,3
cmp,x
```

The comparison asks about the relationship between memory and the current value of the X index register. Let's say X is 4. The comparison code is

```
flags = [False, False, False, False]
if (mem < n):
    flags[2] = True  # L
if (mem > n):
    flags[3] = True  # G
if (n == mem):
    flags[1] = True  # E
if (mem == 0):
    flags[0] = True  # Z
```

with mem being the current subprogram's memory and n being the value of the X register.

Which flags are set depends on the values, but for this example, 3 < 4, so the L flag will be set and the others will remain unset. If X were 3, the E flag would be set instead. Now, consider these instructions:

```
set,0
cmp,5
```

In this case, cmp will set two flags. First, it will set the L flag because 0 < 5. Second, cmp will also set the zero flag (Z) because memory is 0.

The code above actually sets the zero flag twice. Checking whether a value is 0 is so common that all of Filska's instructions that modify subprogram memory check if the result is 0 and if so, set the zero flag. So the set,0 instruction set the zero flag even before the cmp instruction, which sets it a second time. We'll often use this fact in our example programs to branch on memory becoming 0 without an explicit call to cmp. Note that even the transfer instructions affect the zero flag when moving values from the index registers to subprogram memory.

If cmp performs tests and sets flags, how do we act on the results? That's where the test instruction, tst, comes into play. The tst instruction branches within the current subprogram based on the value of a flag. The syntax of the instruction is tst,<flag>,<offset>. For example, consider this sequence of instructions:

```
set,1
tst,z,10
dec
tst,z,8
```

We first set memory to 1 and then execute tst to branch forward 10 instructions if the zero flag is set. Assigning a 1 to memory does not set the zero flag, so the tst instruction does not branch and execution continues with the next instruction. The dec instruction decrements memory, making it 0. This operation *does* set the zero flag, so the next tst instruction will branch eight instructions forward. Note that branching eight instructions forward from the second tst instruction sets the program counter to the same instruction that the first tst instruction was targeting.

To test for conditions other than memory is 0, use cmp followed by the tst instruction. For example:

```
cmp,x
tst,l,-15
tst,e,-16
```

These instructions compare memory to X and branch backward if memory is less than or equal to X. Note that for the equal test to branch to the same location as the less-than test, we must account for the presence of the less-than tst instruction, which explains using −15 and −16, respectively.

The tst instruction's first argument is the flag to test: Z, L, G, or E. However, tst accepts one more flag, N, which means "not zero." We saw this version of tst in Listing 12-1 earlier.

Mathematical Functions

Filska's intended use is to crunch numbers. That's why it manipulates floating-point values. To that end, Filska supports a set of mathematical functions, all of which operate on the current subprogram's memory. Table 12-3 has the complete set of supported functions.

Table 12-3: Filska's Mathematical Functions

Instruction	Operation	Description
inc	$M \leftarrow M + 1$	Increment memory by one
dec	$M \leftarrow M - 1$	Decrement memory by one
sin	$M \leftarrow \sin(M)$	Sine of M (radians)
cos	$M \leftarrow \cos(M)$	Cosine of M (radians)
tan	$M \leftarrow \tan(M)$	Tangent of M (radians)
asn	$M \leftarrow \sin^{-1}(M)$	Inverse sine of M (radians)
acs	$M \leftarrow \cos^{-1}(M)$	Inverse cosine of M (radians)
atn	$M \leftarrow \tan^{-1}(M)$	Inverse tangent of M (radians)
log	$M \leftarrow \log(M)$	Natural log
exp	$M \leftarrow e^M$	Exponential
flr	$M \leftarrow \lfloor M \rfloor$	Floor of M
cel	$M \leftarrow \lceil M \rceil$	Ceiling of M
rnd	$M \leftarrow U[0, 1)$	Uniform random number, $[0, 1)$
neg	$M \leftarrow -M$	Negation of M
sqr	$M \leftarrow \sqrt{M}$	Square root of M

The set of functions in Table 12-3 are the minimal set supported by most programming languages. With these, it's possible to implement many mathematical expressions, at least in pieces.

Internally, our implementation of Filska will use Python floats, meaning IEEE 754 *binary64* values (C double). We have a good range available numerically, but if our algorithm naturally uses integers, we might be limited a bit, as we will not take advantage of Python's abilities with arbitrary-sized integers. We'll see this effect in Chapter 13 when we develop a Filska program to output the Fibonacci sequence.

Input and Output

Filska supports three input/output instructions: prt, chr, and ipt. The first two we've seen several times already in the examples above. Use prt to output subprogram memory as a floating-point number. Filska's implementation does check to see if memory is actually an integer and outputs it with an integer format if so. Otherwise, the format is explicitly for floating-point with 10 digits after the decimal.

The chr instruction interprets memory as an ASCII code. This casts memory to an integer and then keeps only the lowest eight bits to ensure it is in the range $[0, 255]$. Then, it outputs the character associated with the resulting ASCII value.

The final instruction, ipt, accepts input from the user as a floating-point number. If the input received cannot be properly interpreted as a floating-point number, ipt unceremoniously returns 0. The ipt instruction sets the zero flag as well.

Listing 12-4 is a simple program that asks the user for a number and multiplies it by 2.

```
{ main
    set,63
    chr
    ipt
    tmx
    set,2
    mul,m=mx
    prt
    set,13
    chr
    hlt
}
```

Listing 12-4: Getting input from the user

The program first prints a ? and then uses ipt to set memory to whatever number the user enters. Filska does not allow constants in arithmetic operations, so to multiply memory by 2, the user's value is moved to the X register and memory is set to 2. The mul instruction multiplies memory and

X stores the result in memory. Next, the program prints the product (prt) with a newline character and then halts.

Input and output to the console are as straightforward as can be; however, when combined with input/output redirection, Filska can operate on a file and produce a new file as output. A simple modification to Listing 12-4 makes it possible to multiply a file of numbers by 2 (see Listing 12-5).

```
{ main
    ipt
    tmx
    set,2
    mul,m=mx
    prt
    set,13
    chr
}
```

Listing 12-5: Multiplying a file by 2

Listing 12-5 removes the question mark prompt and hlt instruction to make main loop forever. By design, Filska exits if the call to ipt fails for some reason, including if reading from a redirected file fails.

To try Listing 12-5, first create a file of numbers, one per line. I used 1 through 10. Ensure the final number does not have an empty line after it, as empty lines are read as 0. With the file of numbers in place, run the program.

```
python3 filska.py example_input_file.filska <input.txt
```

Assuming you stored the code in *example_input_file.filska* and your table of numbers in *input.txt*, you should see your table output at the console with each number multiplied by 2. Naturally, you can redirect Filska output to a different file.

Now that we know what Filska is as a language and the instructions it supports, let's implement it in Python.

Implementating Filska

In this section, we'll implement portions of Filska. I won't be so pedantic as to dump every line of Python code on you here. The code for Filska is in the file *Filska.py*. Please read through it. All told, *Filska.py* is less than 700 lines, including comments and blanks.

Here, we'll detail the essential parts of the implementation. For example, a single instance of a particular class of instruction is all you need to understand the implementation of the entire class.

Therefore, we'll present the implementation in a top-down fashion, starting with the code's overall structure and operation. Then we'll discuss parsing, which is especially easy given Filska's design, and the execution loop.

Next comes an example of an instruction without arguments, followed by instructions that accept arguments. Lastly, we'll end with flow control within and between subprograms. Again, I assume that you'll look at *Filska.py* yourself. After all, at this point in the book we've gained enough experience with source code to learn directly from it most of the time.

Overall Structure and Operation

Conceptually, a Filska interpreter parses the input source code into tokens, ignoring comments, and sorts those tokens into a dictionary of subprograms indexed by the subprogram name. Each subprogram has an associated local memory value, local flags, and a local program counter, an index into the subprogram's token list. Tokens, memory, flags, and program counters are stored in Python dictionaries, each indexed by the subprogram name. Execution happens one token at a time for the current subprogram, looping at the end of the subprogram, and persisting the program counter between transfers to and from other subprograms, unless the jpr instruction is used, in which case the subprogram's counter is set to 0.

The Filska interpreter itself is a single Python class, Filska. The constructor expects a string, the text of the code to be run, and, optionally, a Boolean flag to turn on runtime execution tracing. We'll get to tracing later on when we start working with our example programs. We won't look at how tracing is implemented here. Review the Filska source code to see how it's done.

Using a class to implement a Filska interpreter enables the easy embedding of Filska into another program. Why you'd want to embed a Filska interpreter is a reasonable question, but you can if you want a quirky scripting language for your larger application. Modifications to Filska's input/output instructions might make embedding more attractive. Imagine a version of the Run method (see below) that accepts a list of inputs and returns the program output as a list of tokens, and so on.

When run from the command line, Filska expects the program's name and an optional -t flag to turn on execution tracing. On startup, Filska runs main, the traditional name for a Python program's startup function (see Listing 12-6).

```
def main():
    trace = False if (len(sys.argv) < 3) else True
    app = Filska(open(sys.argv[1]).read(), trace=trace)
    app.Run()


if (__name__ == "__main__"):
    main()
```

Listing 12-6: Creating a Filska interpreter from the command line

If no arguments are given, Filska displays a short usage message (not shown in the listing). Otherwise, main looks to see if a second command line argument is present and sets trace appropriately. The following line creates an instance of a Filska interpreter passing in the actual text of the program to run. Next, execution begins with a call to Run.

The constructor defines state member variables, including the index registers, a dictionary holding per subprogram memory (mem), a dictionary of subprogram instructions (prog), the per subprogram program counter (PC), and the name of the currently running subprogram (CP) initialized to main. The status flags come next (flags), also defined as a dictionary. Dictionaries are used for memory, program text, program counters, and status flags to isolate subprogram state. The only link between subprograms is the ability for each subprogram to interact with the shared index registers.

Filska programs are tokenized; therefore, running a subprogram means interpreting token by token. When instructions are encountered as tokens, the instruction is parsed if there are arguments. Then the instruction is looked up in a table, exe, which holds references to Python methods implementing the function.

Parsing

Parsing a Filska program means splitting the source code string into tokens, ignoring comments, and separating the subprogram tokens and storing them in the prog dictionary. The Parse method tokenizes a program string to return a list of tokens. Next, InitializeProg sorts the subprograms and places them in the prog dictionary.

Listing 12-7 shows how to split a source code string into tokens separated by whitespace.

```
def Parse(self, src):
    eoln = False
    t = ""
    for c in src:
        if (eoln) and (c == '\n'):
            eoln = False
        elif (c == '"') and (not eoln):
            eoln = True
        elif (not eoln):
            t += c
    return " ".join(t.split()).upper().split()
```

Listing 12-7: Tokenizing the source code

Filska comments begin with a double quote (") and run to the end of the line. The Parse method scans the input source code character by character, keeping all characters that are not part of a comment line. This means a double quote is not allowed as part of a token.

With comments removed, the return statement uses standard Python functionality to first split on whitespace and then join again with a single space between tokens. The new string is made uppercase, thereby requiring Filska to be case insensitive, so main and MAIN refer to the same subprogram. Lastly, the last call to split tokenizes the program text returning a Python list of tokens.

Listing 12-8 scans the list of tokens looking for opening braces ({).

```python
def InitializeProg(self, tokens):
    idx = 0
    k = 0
    while (k < len(tokens)):
        if (tokens[k] == "{"):
            k = self.ExtractProg(tokens,k)
        else:
            k += 1

def ExtractProg(self, tokens, ks):
    k = ks + 1
    p = []
    while (k < len(tokens)) and (tokens[k] != "}"):
        p.append(tokens[k])
        k += 1
    self.prog[p[0]] = p[1:]
    self.PC[p[0]] = 0
    self.mem[p[0]] = 0.0
    self.flags[p[0]] = [False, False, False, False]
    return k
```

Listing 12-8: Separating subprogram text

When the parser encounters an opening brace, a new subprogram starts. The ExtractProg method captures the subprogram's tokens using the first token as the new subprogram name. Subprogram state, meaning memory, program counter, and flags, is also defined at the same time.

When InitializeProg exits, all subprograms have been defined and all their states initialized. The Filska program is then ready to execute with a call to Run.

The Execution Loop

The Run method starts the execution loop (see Listing 12-9).

```python
def Run(self):
    if (self.trace):
        self.Trace()
```

```
while (True):
    self.Execute()
    if (self.trace):
        self.Trace()
    time.sleep(self.naptime)
```

Listing 12-9: The execution loop

The execution loop is quite short. If not in trace mode, Run is nothing more than an endless loop that executes instruction after instruction until hlt quits inside Execute or the user hits CTRL-C. The value of naptime controls the overall speed of a Filska program. The default sleep time is 0.00001 seconds, which basically means "run as fast as possible."

The Execute method in Listing 12-10 executes a single instruction of the current subprogram.

```
def Execute(self):
    prog = self.prog[self.CP]
    pc = self.PC[self.CP]
    flags = self.flags[self.CP]
    mem = self.mem[self.CP]
    inst = prog[pc]

    cp, pc, mem, flags = self.Exec(inst, len(prog), mem, pc, flags)

    self.mem[self.CP] = mem
    self.PC[self.CP] = pc
    self.flags[self.CP] = flags

    if (self.CP != cp):
        self.CP = cp
        self.flags[cp] = [False, False, False, False]
```

Listing 12-10: Executing a single instruction

First, the current program (prog), program counter (pc), flags, and local memory (mem) are loaded for the current subprogram (CP). Next, the instruction executes by calling Exec, which we'll detail shortly. When Exec returns, it passes back updated values for the current subprogram, program counter, local memory, and local flags. The state of the current subprogram is updated along with the name of the current subprogram if a jmp or jpr instruction was executed. Notice that mem, pc, and flags are updated first before the current subprogram name, as they refer to the subprogram whose instruction was just executed. If transferring to a new subprogram, the new subprogram's flags are reset.

The Exec method in Listing 12-11 is responsible for processing a single instruction.

```
def Exec(self, inst, proglen, mem, pc, flags):
    cp = self.CP
    if (inst[:3] == "JMP"):
        pc, cp = self.JMP(inst, pc, proglen)
    elif (inst[:3] == "JPR"):
        pc, cp = self.JPR(inst, pc)
    elif (inst[:3] == "GTO"):
        pc = self.GTO(inst, pc, proglen)
    elif (inst[:3] == "TST"):
        pc = self.TST(inst, pc, proglen, flags)
    else:
        if (inst[:3] not in self.exe):
            raise ValueError("Illegal instruction: %s" % inst)
    ❶ rest = inst[4:]
    ❷ mem, flags = self.exe[inst[:3]](rest, mem, flags)
    ❸ pc = (pc+1) % proglen

    return cp, pc, mem, flags
```

Listing 12-11: Evaluating a single instruction

Exec receives the token representing the instruction (inst), the number of instructions in the current subprogram (proglen), the current value of subprogram memory (mem), the program counter (pc), and the flags (flags). Exec returns the name of the subprogram to execute next (cp), which is usually unchanged, and the updated state for the subprogram whose instruction was just executed.

Each Filska instruction is processed by a method with the same name as the instruction. If the instruction affects flow control, like jmp, jpr, gto, or tst, it is processed with a varying set of arguments and return values. We'll return to these instructions shortly. All other instructions follow the same format: they accept any remaining instruction text (rest ❶), memory, and flags as input, and return updated memory and flags ❷. Because most Filska instructions do not affect program flow, the program counter is updated by adding 1 and rolling over to 0 if the subprogram's length is exceeded ❸.

Instructions Without Arguments

Non-flow control instructions come in two varieties: with arguments and without arguments. Let's see how Filska instructions without arguments are implemented.

Listing 12-12 implements the cos instruction.

```
def COS(self, rest, mem, flags):
    mem = cos(mem)
    flags[0] = False
```

```
    if (mem == 0.0):
        flags[0] = True
    return mem, flags
```

Listing 12-12: A representative no-argument instruction

The arguments are any remaining portion of the instruction token after the three-character instruction has been removed, the current subprogram's memory value, and the associated flags. For no-argument instructions, rest is an empty string. No-argument instructions operate on the subprogram's memory or one of the index registers. Here, the cosine of memory is used to update it. As with almost all Filska instructions, a 0 result sets the zero flag. All instruction implementations return any new value of the memory and any updated flags.

Instructions with Arguments

Filska instructions with arguments include set, swp, and all binary math operators. Of the latter, we'll only detail add, as the others operate similarly.

Let's begin with SET (see Listing 12-13). The swp instruction is similar.

```
def SET(self, rest, mem, flags):
    try:
        n = float(rest)
    except:
        n = 0.0
    mem = n
    flags[0] = False
    if (mem == 0):
        flags[0] = True
    return mem, flags
```

Listing 12-13: Implementation of SET

The single argument passed to SET, meaning the text of the token beyond the string SET, is in rest. Filska attempts to interpret rest as a floating-point number and uses 0 if the conversion fails. Naturally, a more sophisticated approach would issue an error message, but we can live with the simplification. If n is 0, the zero flag is set, and the updated memory value and flags returned (see Listing 12-14).

```
def ADD(self, rest, mem, flags):
    op0,op1,dst = self.ops(rest,mem)
    ans = op0 + op1
    return self.assign(ans, dst, mem, flags)
```

Listing 12-14: Implementation of ADD

Binary math operations like ADD use a four-character argument of the form *<dst>* = *<op1><op2>*. where *<dst>* is a destination, either memory or an index register, and *<op1>* and *<op2>* are sources. Memory is denoted as M and index registers by their names.

Listing 12-14 implements addition. The text of the argument is in rest, as with SET. Interpretation of the argument happens in the ops method, which returns the operand values and the destination register's name (or memory). The operation ADD adds the two operands (ans) and updates memory or index registers based on the destination by calling the assign method. The other binary operations are similarly implemented, differing only in the line defining ans.

The ops method parses the four-character argument returning numeric values pulled from memory, or the index registers for the operands and the single character indicating the destination. The assign method takes the result, destination, current memory value, and flags, and updates the proper destination with the result. If the destination is memory and 0, the zero flag is also updated. Lastly, memory and flags are returned.

Flow Control Instructions

Instructions controlling program flow are implemented separately, as their inputs and outputs vary depending on the instruction. We'll begin with the jump instructions (JMP and JPR, which transfer program flow between subprograms (see Listing 12-15).

```
def JMP(self, inst, pc, proglen):
    pc = (pc+1) % proglen
    cp = inst[4:]
    return pc, cp

def JPR(self, inst, pc):
    pc = 0
    cp = inst[4:]
    return pc, cp
```

Listing 12-15: The JMP and JPR instructions

The only implementation difference between JMP and JPR is how the program counter of the current subprogram is modified. For JMP, the program counter is incremented, rolling over if necessary, so the next transfer to the current subprogram begins with the instruction following JMP. For JPR, the program counter is set to 0 instead. Both instructions return the name of the subprogram to which execution is transferred.

The remaining flow control instructions, GTO and TST, operate within the current subprogram. Listing 12-16 presents the GTO instruction.

```
def GTO(self, inst, pc, proglen):
    try:
        offset = int(inst[4:])
        if (offset == 0):
            offset = 1
    except:
        offset = 1
    pc += offset
    if (pc < 0):
        pc = 0
    if (pc >= proglen):
        pc = proglen-1
    return pc
```

Listing 12-16: Unconditional jump within a subprogram

The GTO instruction's argument is an integer offset to the current program counter value, that is, a relative number of instructions to branch from the current instruction. First, GTO extracts the offset from the instruction text and converts it to an integer. If the conversion fails, the offset is silently set to 1 to move to the next instruction. Updating the program counter comes next. The instruction adds the offset, which may be positive or negative, to the program counter, with suitable checks for jumping too far back or forward. The updated program counter value is then returned.

The most complex Filska instruction is TST (see Listing 12-17).

```
def TST(self, inst, pc, proglen, flags):
❶   if (inst[4] == "Z"):
        v = flags[0]
    elif (inst[4] == "E"):
        v = flags[1]
    elif (inst[4] == "L"):
        v = flags[2]
    elif (inst[4] == "G"):
        v = flags[3]
    elif (inst[4] == "N"):
        v = (flags[0] == False)
    if (v):
    ❷   try:
            offset = int(inst[6:])
            if (offset == 0):
                offset = 1
        except:
            offset = 1
        pc += offset
```

```
        if (pc < 0):
            pc = 0
        if (pc >= proglen):
            pc = proglen-1
    else:
    ❸ pc = (pc+1) % proglen
    return pc
```

Listing 12-17: Conditional branching within a subprogram

The first part of the TST instruction examines the first argument, the flag to test ❶. The current value of the flag is put into v. Notice how checking for "not zero" asks if the zero flag is currently false. The second part of the instruction interprets the offset argument if the desired flag is set ❷. This code matches GTO in that the offset is extracted and added to the program counter. If the flag is not set, the program counter is incremented as usual ❸.

The core of Filska is in the code above, but not all of it. Again, please spend some time reading through *filska.py* to familiarize yourself with the entire implementation.

Summary

This chapter introduced Filska by discussing its design and the thinking behind it. We then detailed key portions of the Python implementation to see an embodiment of the design.

Now that Filska exists, let's try to write some programs with it.

13

USING FILSKA

In Chapter 12, we designed and implemented Filska. Now, let's use it to write some programs. We'll develop six Filska programs of increasing complexity to gain experience thinking in the restricted world Filska offers us.

To be more specific, this rather long chapter comprises disconnected sections, each implementing a particular Filska example. You need not read straight through because no section builds necessarily upon any previous section. Instead, the goal of the chapter is to present case studies in using Filska, all with the hope of helping you think about how to code in Filska and, more importantly, how to think in new ways to help you be more creative in your own coding tasks, regardless of the language. So put on your dancing shoes, turn the fiddle music up to 11, and get ready to have some (possibly) high-spirited fun.

Hello, World!

We'd be remiss if we didn't start with the expected "Hello, world!" example. The most obvious way to write it in Filska is to load the respective ASCII codes for each character into subprogram memory and call chr to output the string one character at a time. However, this is also quite boring and not the least bit mathematical, so we'll forgo the obvious and instead embrace the obfuscated.

Hello, Math!

Let's develop the necessary sequence of characters as a series of simple math operations. We'll use the X register and output it as a character when needed. Therefore, we need a subprogram to output the X register as a character.

```
{ dump  txm chr jmp,main }
```

The above fits the bill. The first instruction moves X to the subprogram memory, and the second dumps the ASCII character it represents to the console. The final instruction returns to main and, as it is the final instruction, the next call from main to dump will loop around and begin again with txm, as we desire.

We can now dump ASCII characters in X to the console. Next we need our sequence of operations on X. The ASCII code for H is 72, so we'll start there and move from the current character to the next via additions of positive and negative offsets. The sequence we need is

$$X \leftarrow 8$$
$$X \leftarrow X \times 9$$
$$X \leftarrow X - 3$$
$$X \leftarrow X + 7$$
$$X \leftarrow X + 0$$
$$X \leftarrow X + 3$$
$$X \leftarrow X - 35$$
$$X \leftarrow X - 12$$
$$X \leftarrow X + 55$$
$$X \leftarrow X - 8$$
$$X \leftarrow X + 3$$
$$X \leftarrow X - 6$$
$$X \leftarrow X - 8$$
$$X \leftarrow X - 35$$

Note that here we output X with dump after each operation except the first.

We have an assignment, a multiplication, and a bunch of additions. So we need set, mul, and add along with jmp to call dump. Translating the sequence into code gives us Listing 13-1.

```
{ main
    set,8
    tmx
    set,9      mul,x=mx    jmp,dump
    set,-3     add,x=mx    jmp,dump
```

```
set,7        add,x=mx    jmp,dump
set,0        add,x=mx    jmp,dump
set,3        add,x=mx    jmp,dump
set,-35      add,x=mx    jmp,dump
set,-12      add,x=mx    jmp,dump
set,55       add,x=mx    jmp,dump
set,-8       add,x=mx    jmp,dump
set,3        add,x=mx    jmp,dump
set,-6       add,x=mx    jmp,dump
set,-8       add,x=mx    jmp,dump
set,-35      add,x=mx    jmp,dump
set,10
chr
hlt
}
```

```
{ dump  txm chr jmp,main }
```

Listing 13-1: A first version of "Hello, world!" in Filska

Listing 13-1 is in the file *hello.filska*. The code uses main's memory to hold the offset and X to hold the running total. Each operation on X is followed by a call to dump. The final three instructions output a newline character and then halt. As we might expect, removing hlt makes the code dump HELLO, WORLD! forever.

Hello, Poly!

Listing 13-1 is indeed obfuscated, but we can do better while still dumping HELLO, WORLD! to the console. The ASCII values we need to dump as characters are

```
72, 69, 76, 76, 79, 44, 32, 87, 79, 82, 76, 68, 33
```

Can we create a mathematical function, $y = f(x)$, to generate this sequence for $x \in [0, 12]$? If we had such a function, we could generate HELLO, WORLD! character by character with repeated calls to $f(x)$ for $x = 0, 1, \ldots, 12$.

A good candidate for such a function is a polynomial. We remember these from our high school algebra days as sums of terms where each term is a coefficient multiplying some power of x. Let's use a polynomial for $f(x)$. The degree of the polynomial is the highest power of x present. We need to pick a degree for the polynomial and then find the set of coefficients. For example, if we decide to use a third-degree polynomial, we get

$$y = p_0 x^3 + p_1 x^2 + p_2 x + p_3$$

Remember that $x^1 = x$ and $x^0 = 1$. The ps are the coefficients, and we need to find them somehow after picking the degree.

What we are talking about here is known as *curve fitting*, which is the process of finding the equation of a curve that best fits a set of data. For us, our dataset is the sequence of ASCII characters we want to generate along with the input x value, a sequence of points, (x, y), so that $72 = f(0)$, $69 = f(1)$, and so on.

```
(0,72) (1,69) (2,76) (3,76) (4,79) (5,44) (6,32)
(7,87) (8,79) (9,82) (10,76) (11,68) (12,33)
```

We'll use a polynomial for $f(x)$, but we still need to pick a degree and then learn how to fit a polynomial of that degree to the dataset. It's known that an $n - 1$ degree polynomial can perfectly fit a dataset with n points. Generally, this isn't what is wanted. The point of fitting the function is to explain the trend of the data using the function to make meaningful predictions at points not measured. However, we actually *do* want to hit each data point exactly. Therefore, let's use a 12th degree polynomial to fit our 13 points (see Equation 13.1). We now need to find the coefficients of

$$y = p_0 x^{12} + p_1 x^{11} + p_2 x^{10} + p_3 x^9 + p_4 x^8 + p_5 x^7 + p_6 x^6 +$$
$$p_7 x^5 + p_8 x^4 + p_9 x^3 + p_{10} x^2 + p_{11} x + p_{12} \quad (13.1)$$

Great! How do we find the coefficients? The answer is to use *least-squares fitting*, a method for finding the values for p that minimize the square of the difference between the data points and the function value at those data points. Implementing a routine to do least-squares fitting to a polynomial is beyond the scope of this book. Fortunately, we can use the power of NumPy to do it for us. Incidentally, we'll encounter least-squares fitting of data later in this chapter when we write a Filska program to fit data to a line.

Consider the Python program in *hello.py*. We won't show the code here, but please do review it. The code uses NumPy, specifically the `np.polyfit` routine, to fit the dataset and generate the coefficients we need. The same code also calculates the difference between the dataset and the polynomial values at the given x values, and generates a plot of the resulting polynomial. NumPy found the following coefficients:

```
X**12, P = -4.6431994663395692e-05
X**11, P = 3.2633752799095354e-03
X**10, P = -1.0079445322316360e-01
X** 9, P = 1.7997278464174311e+00
X** 8, P = -2.0561041293073888e+01
X** 7, P = 1.5712412821126304e+02
X** 6, P = -8.1556740929381863e+02
X** 5, P = 2.8598281210109303e+03
X** 4, P = -6.5979225156803523e+03
X** 3, P = 9.4649124982355879e+03
X** 2, P = -7.5173478664143449e+03
X** 1, P = 2.4648319340174303e+03
X** 0, P = 7.2000000563347072e+01
```

Here, each P is the coefficient for the corresponding power of *x*. The polynomial is sensitive enough that all digits displayed are necessary. Our Filska program will use these constants in all their glory.

Figure 13-1 shows us what the polynomial looks like. The circles are the actual data points we want the polynomial to output, and the curve is the polynomial itself (Equation 13.1).

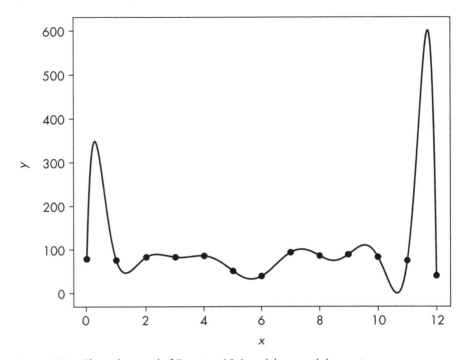

Figure 13-1: The polynomial of Equation 13.1 and the actual data points to output

A glance at Figure 13-1 shows that the 12th degree polynomial fit is hitting all the points we want it to hit, but the function itself acts wildly outside of those points, so it wouldn't be a good fit to the dataset if we were looking to learn something about the general trend of the data. Thankfully, we aren't. Instead, we're looking to build a needlessly complicated implementation of HELLO, WORLD! so we are doing just fine with our 12th degree polynomial.

Hello, Poly Implementation!

Let's start designing the Filska code. We need the equivalent of the Python code in Listing 13-2.

```
from math import floor

def f(x):
    return -4.6431994663395692e-05*x**12 + \
            3.2633752799095354e-03*x**11 + \
```

```
        -1.0079445322316360e-01*x**10  +  \
         1.7997278464174311e+00*x**9   +  \
        -2.0561041293073888e+01*x**8   +  \
         1.5712412821126304e+02*x**7   +  \
        -8.1556740929381863e+02*x**6   +  \
         2.8598281210109303e+03*x**5   +  \
        -6.5979225156803523e+03*x**4   +  \
         9.4649124982355879e+03*x**3   +  \
        -7.5173478664143449e+03*x**2   +  \
         2.4648319340174303e+03*x**1   +  \
         7.2000000563347072e+01*x**0

for x in range(13):
    y = f(x)
    d = int(floor(y+0.5))
    print("%s" % chr(d), end="")
print()
```

Listing 13-2: Python code to generate HELLO, WORLD! *with a polynomial*

The function f(x) implements the polynomial returning the *y* for any given *x*. The *x* values we need are the numbers from 0 through 12. Looking at the for loop, each *x* is given to *f(x)* to create a *y* output, which is a floating-point number we need to round to the nearest integer. Rounding means *y* = 72.04 leads to *d* = 72 and *y* = 72.54 produces *d* = 73. It's *d* we'll treat as the ASCII character code to output, which is precisely what the print statement is doing via chr. To round *y* to get integer *d*, we use the standard trick of adding 0.5 followed by floor to arrive at *d*. Without this rounding, the output will not be HELLO, WORLD! but HDKKN+VNQLD!

To generate Filska code equivalent to Listing 13-2, we need a subprogram implementing *f(x)* and a main loop over the integers from 0 through 12. After passing each integer to *f(x)* and rounding, we emit the result as a character. The complete code is in *hello2.filska*. We'll present the important parts in Listing 13-3, but please review the entire file to see all the source code.

```
{ main
❶ set,0        " M = 0
  tmx          " X = M
❷ jmp,calc     " Y = f(X)
  jmp,dump     " dump Y as character
❸ inc          " M = M + 1
❹ cmp,13       " M == 13?
  tst,e,2      " yes, done
  gto,-6       " no, loop
  set,10       " done
  chr
  hlt
```

```
}
```

```
{ dump tym chr jmp,main }
```

Listing 13-3: The main loop of hello2.filska

Listing 13-3 presents main and dump. Let's begin with dump. We've seen this subprogram before in Listing 13-1. It takes the contents of a register, here Y, and dumps it as a character to the console before returning to main.

The main subprogram of Listing 13-3 implements the loop over x values. In this case, we'll use the X register as x, so we initialize it to 0 ❶. Next, we transfer control to the calc subprogram ❷. This subprogram implements $y = f(x)$ and returns y in the Y register. We'll get to calc's implementation momentarily. With Y, the ASCII value we want for the current X, we call dump to display the character at the console.

We want x from 0 through 12, so we increment memory, which holds our counter ❸, and check to see if we've hit 13 characters ❹. If memory equals 13, the tst returns true and we jump ahead two instructions. Otherwise, $x < 13$ and we go back to the tmx instruction to move the new x value from memory to the X register. The program ends when $x = 13$ by outputting a newline character and calling hlt.

All we have left to implement is calc, the subprogram mapping X to Y via the polynomial. Listing 13-2 points the way for us. We need something like f(x), which calculates the polynomial term by term. If we create a sequence of Filska instructions that find px^n for some power, n, and some coefficient, p, we need only accumulate the terms for all powers and coefficients to arrive at y. We also need to round y, but that comes after we calculate it.

Rather than show all of calc, we'll show how we start accumulating the proper terms of the polynomial, how we end, and how we round before returning to main. See Listing 13-4.

```
{ calc
    " Y = P0*X**12
❶ set,12
    tmz
    pow,z=xz
    set,-4.6431994663395692e-05
    mul,y=mz

    " Y += P1*X**11
❷ set,11
    tmz
    pow,z=xz
    set,3.2633752799095354e-03
    mul,m=mz
    add,y=my
--snip--
```

```
    "  Y = floor(Y+0.5)
❸  set,0.5
   add,m=my
   flr
   tmy
   jmp,main
}
```

Listing 13-4: The calc *subprogram of* hello2.filska

The code is sectioned into blocks that each raise X to some power, multiply it by the proper coefficient, and add the product to the total in Y. The first block starts the chain, and the last block concludes it. Let's start with the highest power of X, which is 12 ❶.

To calculate $y = f(x)$, we'll use subprogram memory and Z as scratch space and accumulate the value of the polynomial term by term in Y. To start, we move 12 into M then to Z. Recall that set applies to only the current subprogram's memory. Next, we calculate x^{12} by raising X to the Z power, putting the result back into Z. This is the pow instruction. Now we need to multiply x^{12} by the proper coefficient, so we set M to the necessary value, multiply by Z, and store the result in Y as the first term of the polynomial.

The next term of the polynomial is calculated similarly ❷. The difference here is using 11 as the exponent, multiplying by the proper coefficient for x^{11}, and adding the product to Y via the mul,m=mz and add,y=my instructions. The polynomial's remaining terms are found in precisely the same way, by replacing the exponent with 10, then 9, and so on down to 0, multiplying by the appropriate coefficients each time.

At this point, Y holds the answer. All that remains is to round it to the nearest integer ❸. We add 0.5 to Y, leaving the answer in M. Then, we call flr, move the result back to Y, and jump back to main to output Y as a character.

In this section, we developed two obfuscated ways to dump the string HELLO, WORLD! to the console. How many more can you think of? If you create a novel approach, please share it with me, and I'll put it on the book's GitHub site.

Let's move on to our next example: one that introduces us to execution tracing with Filska.

Fibonacci, Anyone?

In the previous section, we spent far too much energy developing cute ways to output the string HELLO, WORLD!. This section will work with a more straightforward example and use it to explore execution tracing. Our goal is to generate as many terms of the Fibonacci sequence as can fit properly in a Python float.

The Fibonacci sequence uses the recurrence relation

$$F_1 = 1, \quad F_2 = 1$$
$$F_n = F_{n-1} + F_{n-2}$$

so that $F_3 = F_2 + F_1 = 1 + 1 = 2$, and $F_4 = F_3 + F_2 = 2 + 1 = 3$, and so on. The first few terms of the Fibonacci sequence are

$$1, 1, 2, 3, 5, 8, 13, 21, 34, 55, 89, 144, \ldots$$

The Fibonacci sequence is named after Leonardo Bonacci, sometimes referred to as Leonardo of Pisa or, most commonly, as Fibonacci. The sequence was known outside of Europe for well over a millennia when Fibonacci used it as an idealized example of rabbit population growth in his 1202 text *Liber Abaci* (*The Book of Calculation*).

Many books have been written about the Fibonacci sequence and all the places it appears in mathematics. There is even an academic publication, *The Fibonacci Quarterly*, with issues going back to 1963 (see *https://www.fq.math .ca/*). Here we'll relate only a few interesting observations about the sequence.

The Fibonacci sequence is intimately related to ϕ (phi), also known as the golden ratio

$$\phi = \frac{1 + \sqrt{5}}{2} \approx 1.618033988749895$$

where the golden ratio is a solution to

$$\frac{x + y}{y} = \frac{x}{y}, \; x > y > 0$$

For example, if we set $y = 1$, we get

$$\frac{x + 1}{x} = x$$

or

$$x^2 - x - 1 = 0$$

with the positive solution, via the quadratic formula, as

$$x = \frac{-b + \sqrt{b^2 - 4ac}}{2a} = \frac{1 + \sqrt{1^2 - 4(1)(-1)}}{2} = \frac{1 + \sqrt{5}}{2}$$

which is ϕ. Like the Fibonacci sequence, ϕ shows up everywhere in mathematics and nature. A link to the Fibonacci sequence comes from the fact that as $n \rightarrow \infty$, the ratio of the $n + 1$th Fibonacci number to the nth approaches ϕ

$$\frac{F_4}{F_3} = \frac{3}{2} = 1.5$$

$$\frac{F_7}{F_6} = \frac{13}{8} = 1.625$$

$$\frac{F_9}{F_8} = \frac{34}{21} = 1.619047619047619$$

$$\frac{F_{78}}{F_{77}} = \frac{8944394323791464}{5527939700884757} = 1.618033988749895$$

where the last ratio is ϕ to the precision of a Python float.

With ϕ in hand, we can calculate the nth Fibonacci number directly via

$$F_n = \left\lfloor \frac{\phi^n}{\sqrt{5}} + \frac{1}{2} \right\rfloor$$

which works in code for small values of n, but fails when n gets large because of precision issues.

We could fill the remainder of this book with fascinating facts and observations about the Fibonacci sequence, but we'll bring things back to coding and implement the sequence in Filska (see Listing 13-5). The code itself is in *fib.filska*.

```
{ main
  ❶ set,78      " number to generate
    dec          " dec twice, just printing the first two
    dec
    tmz          " Z is the counter
    set,1        " print '1' and '1'
    tmx          " X holds the i-2 value
    prt
    jmp,nl
    tmy          " Y holds the i-1 value
    prt
    jmp,nl
  ❷ add,m=xy     " find i-th value
    swp,xy       " X <-- Y, new i-2 value
    tmy          " Y <-- M, new i-1 value
    prt          " print ith value
    jmp,nl
    tzm          " decrement Z
    dec
    tst,z,3      " if zero, done
    tmz          " Z <-- M
    gto,-9       " loop
    hlt          " quit
}

{ nl  set,10 chr jpr,main }
```

Listing 13-5: Generating the Fibonacci sequence

In Listing 13-5 we initialize a counter in Z set to 78 ❶. Therefore, we'll output 78 Fibonacci numbers, counting Z down by 1 each time until it is 0. Why 78? Because $F_{78} = 8{,}944{,}394{,}323{,}791{,}464$ is the largest Fibonacci number that fits in a 64-bit float. Were Filska extended to operate on integers as Python integers instead of Python floats, we could generate Fibonacci numbers until we run out of memory.

To get the first two numbers, we decrement Z twice and print the constant 1 twice. Boring, but effective. Then, we use the X and Y registers to hold the previous two Fibonacci numbers and their sum to generate the next. The recurrence loop begins by calculating the next Fibonacci number ❷. X and Y are updated by shifting the current value of Y to X and the new Fibonacci value in M to Y. We then decrement Z and branch forward to hlt if it is 0; otherwise, the loop repeats ❸. Listing 13-5 is straightforward; therefore, it's a good example for execution tracing.

To run *fib.filska* with tracing, use a command line like this:

```
> python3 filska.py fib.filska -t
```

The -t flag is the signal to trace execution, one instruction at a time. Doing this presents us with

```
CP:MAIN,PC:000,X:0.000000,Y:0.000000,Z:0.000000,M:0.000000,
   Z:0,E:0,L:0,G:0,   SET,78
<enter> or 'q' to quit:
```

and a prompt waiting for us to hit ENTER or q to quit. Let's break down the status line:

Displayed Text	Description
CP:MAIN	Current subprogram name
PC:000	Current program counter
X:0.000000 Y:0.000000 Z:0.000000	Register values
M:0.000000	Local memory value
Z:0	"Zero" flag
E:0	"Equal" flag
L:0	"Less than" flag
G:0	"Greater than" flag

The next instruction is set,78. Hitting ENTER gives us

```
CP:MAIN,PC:001,X:0.000000,Y:0.000000,Z:0.000000,M:78.000000,
   Z:0,E:0,L:0,G:0,     DEC
<enter> or 'q' to quit:
```

showing us that local memory is now 78 and that the next instruction is dec. If we press ENTER exactly seven times from this instruction, we pass through to the jmp,nl instruction

```
CP:NL,PC:000,X:1.000000,Y:0.000000,Z:76.000000,M:0.000000,
   Z:0,E:0,L:0,G:0,   SET,10
<enter> or 'q' to quit:
```

telling us that we are about to execute the first instruction of subprogram nl. How do we know it's the first instruction? Because the program counter,

PC, is 0. Note also that the X register is 1, set previously by the tmx instruction in main.

After three more presses of ENTER, we get

```
CP:MAIN,PC:008,X:1.000000,Y:0.000000,Z:76.000000,M:1.000000,
    Z:0,E:0,L:0,G:0,    TMY
<enter> or 'q' to quit:
```

which shows us back in main and about to execute instruction 8 to move the 1 from memory to Y.

Six more presses of ENTER later, and the one after that gives

```
CP:MAIN,PC:011,X:1.000000,Y:1.000000,Z:76.000000,M:1.000000,
    Z:0,E:0,L:0,G:0, ADD,M=XY
<enter> or 'q' to quit:
CP:MAIN,PC:012,X:1.000000,Y:1.000000,Z:76.000000,M:2.000000,
    Z:0,E:0,L:0,G:0,  SWP,XY
<enter> or 'q' to quit:
```

The add instruction has set local memory to 2: $M \leftarrow X + Y$.

Repeated ENTER keypresses trace through the remainder of the recurrence loop to tst on Z equal to 0 and then follow gto back to add, looping until Z is eventually 0.

The tracing functionality is quite useful when developing Filska programs. Also helpful is working with code in small pieces—usually individual subprograms—to get them running as they should.

The remainder of this chapter presents several other Filska programs for fun and learning. Let's see how Filska generates random numbers.

Random Numbers

Filska's rnd instruction sets subprogram memory to a random floating-point number, [0, 1). In reality, of course, this number isn't random, but a pseudorandom approximation. Also, it's cheating because rnd is using Python's random module under the hood. Python's random module uses the Mersenne Twister pseudorandom number generator, a pretty good generator that is sufficient for all but the most demanding of tasks. One measure of a pseudorandom generator's quality is its *period*, that is, how many numbers it can generate before the sequence begins to repeat. For the Mersenne Twister, the period is $2^{19937} - 1$, which should be good enough for most anyone.

In this section, we'll develop code to generate pseudorandom numbers with Filska *without* cheating, that is, without the rnd instruction. Instead, we'll implement the Park and Miller linear congruential generator, also known as MINSTD. This linear congruential generator is a simple algorithm with a period of about 2^{31}. Far less than the Mersenne Twister period, but still quite sufficient for many noncritical tasks like games.

Implementing MINSTD

Most pseudorandom number generators are iterative, meaning the previous pseudorandom value is used to generate the next. The first value in the sequence is generated from a user-supplied seed value. Fixing the seed value fixes the sequence of values generated. In this way, it's possible to create a deterministic sequence of values that pass randomness tests, as strange as that sounds.

NOTE *There exist pseudorandom generators capable of generating the nth value of the sequence for a specified seed without generating the* n − *1 values before it. To find such a generator, search for "counter-based random number generator."*

The Park and Miller algorithm runs as follows:

1. Select a seed value and call it x_0.

2. Generate the next seed value: $x_{i+1} \leftarrow 48271 x_i \mod (2^{31} - 1)$.

3. Return the floating-point version: $x_{i+1}/(2^{31} - 1)$.

4. Use x_{i+1} as x_i for the next pseudorandom value.

The algorithm is a recurrence relation similar to what we used above for generating Fibonacci numbers. Therefore, we expect an initialization section followed by a loop that spits out the next number in the sequence as a float. For the seed, x_0, we are free to pick any integer in $[1, 2^{31} - 1]$. We'll use 8,675,309, but you can replace it with any number you wish to get a different sequence of values. The code we need is in *random.filska* (see Listing 13-6).

```
{ main
    set,8675309     " the seed
    tmx
    set,48271
    mul,x=mx
    set,2147483647  " 2^31 - 1
    mod,x=xm
    jmp,make_float
    gto,-5
}

{ make_float
    set,2147483647
    div,m=xm
    prt
    set,10
    chr
    jmp,main
}
```

Listing 13-6: Park and Miller LCG in Filska

Listing 13-6 initializes X with the desired seed, stores the multiplier (48,271) in memory, and starts the loop to calculate the next seed value. The recurrence relation is implemented in stages. First, the seed in X is multiplied by 48,271, with the result back in X. Then $2^{31} - 1$ is loaded into memory, followed by the modulo operation, again with the result in X. X is now the next value in the sequence. The floating-point version is output by make_float, which divides X by $2^{31} - 1$, dumping the result to the console along with a newline to get one pseudorandom float per line. Back in main, the loop continues, so the program dumps floats forever.

Run the program and direct output to a file, say *numbers.txt*.

```
> python3 filska.py random.filska >numbers.txt
```

Allow the program to run for maybe 15 minutes, or until there are more than 1 million lines in the file. We need many values to get meaningful statistics on the quality of the output, and the more the merrier. When you get tired of waiting, use CTRL-C to exit the program.

Evaluating MINSTD

We now have a large text file of floating-point values. They certainly look random enough, but are they? How can we tell? The honest answer is that we can't. We cannot *prove* these are random values, and in fact, we know that they aren't because we used a deterministic method to generate them. John von Neumann, one of the founders of computer science, famously quipped that anyone considering deterministic methods for generating random numbers is "in a state of sin." Still, we'd like to think the sequence we just generated is at least random-ish, meaning knowing one value doesn't help us much in guessing the next value.

As it happens, there are many highly sophisticated ways to test for randomness. None are conclusive, but as a group, they lend credence to a belief that a sequence of values is random for all practical purposes. The tests are extensive, far beyond what we need, but fortunately for us, there is one that is simple, easy to evaluate, and included with standard Linux distributions. To boot, it has a cool, Tolkienesque name: ent.

However, ent only works with random *bytes*, not floating-point numbers. That's okay; a snippet of Python converts our file of random floats into a file of random bytes.

```
import numpy as np
d = np.loadtxt("numbers.txt")
b = []
for i in range(len(d)):
    b.append(int(np.floor(256*d[i])))
open("random.dat","wb").write(bytearray(b))
```

We assume the captured floats are in the file *numbers.txt*. The byte version is stored in *random.dat*. The array d contains the floats read from *numbers.txt*. The loop generates a list, b, of integers found by multiplying the float value by 256 and dropping any fractional part via floor. Lastly, the list of integers is formed into a byte array and dumped into the output file.

Let's run ent on *random.dat*

```
> ent random.dat
```

producing

```
Entropy = 7.999803 bits per byte.

Optimum compression would reduce the size
of this 1044919 byte file by 0 percent.

Chi square distribution for 1044919 samples is 285.53, and randomly
would exceed this value 9.16 percent of the times.

Arithmetic mean value of data bytes is 127.5722 (127.5 = random).
Monte Carlo value for Pi is 3.138619490 (error 0.09 percent).
Serial correlation coefficient is -0.001688 (totally uncorrelated = 0.0).
```

The values you see when you run the code will be slightly different because the number of randoms generated before hitting CTRL-C will be different, or if you change the seed value.

What to make of ent's output? We'll skip the chi-square part and consider the other metrics: entropy/compression, arithmetic mean value, estimate of π, and the serial correlation.

The *entropy* is a measure of the information content, in this case as bits per byte. There are eight bits in a byte, so the maximum possible entropy is 8.0. This means there is no way to simplify the file's representatio, as there is no redundancy. Our file has an entropy of 7.999803 bits per byte, meaning it's close to maximum randomness. This is essentially what the statement about optimum compression is saying.

If the file consists of purely random bytes, we expect as many bytes to be above the median value of 127.5 / 2 as below, so the arithmetic mean should be 127.5. Our file has a mean value of 127.5722, which, again, is pretty close to what we'd expect from a random sequence.

A Monte Carlo process simulates something. In this case, it's using the random bytes to simulate dart throws then asking how many darts land inside a circle of radius 1 and how many land inside a square of side 1 circumscribed over the circle. The ratio of darts landing within the circle to those landing within the square leads to an estimate of π. Here, the estimate is in the ballpark but not too impressive. Also, there are only 1 million or so values in the file. Most randomness tests want hundreds of millions to billions of examples before making a statement, so we are doing well here, too.

The final test is a serial correlation test. The earlier tests looked at the values without caring about their ordering in the file. The serial test pays attention to the order. It's looking to see if knowing the value of one byte gives you knowledge about the value of the next byte. For a random sequence, there should be no such correlation. Here we get a slight negative correlation, which, again, is a reasonable statement that we've generated a (mostly) random sequence.

The results above give us confidence that our Filska pseudorandom number generator is working correctly. Let's move on to our next example, one that also generates data to be captured in a file.

A Simple Fractal

In Chapter 10 we briefly encountered the Sierpiński triangle. Let's see how to generate the points of this fractal in Filska. The algorithm is

1. Define three triangle vertices: (x_0, y_0), (x_1, y_1), and (x_2, y_2).

2. Choose one vertex at random, say $(x, y) = (x_0, y_0)$.

3. Select another vertex at random, say (x_1, y_1).

4. Update $x, y \leftarrow \frac{1}{2}(x + x_1), \frac{1}{2}(y + y_1)$.

5. Output (x, y) to be plotted later.

6. Repeat from Step 3 for the desired number of points.

In essence, we plot the midpoint between the current point and a randomly selected vertex of the triangle and repeat until we generate as many points as we wish to plot. Once again, this is a recurrence relation where the $n + 1$th point is constructed from the nth point, only now we are working in two dimensions, not one (see Listing 13-7).

```
x,y = 1,0
repeat for N points:
    r = RND
    if (r < 0.333333):
        x = 0.5*(x + 0) = 0.5*x
        y = 0.5*(y + 0) = 0.5*y
    elif (r < 0.666666):
        x = 0.5*(x + 0.5) = 0.5*x + 0.25
        y = 0.5*(y + 1) = 0.5*y + 0.5
    else:
        x = 0.5*(x + 1) = 0.5*x + 0.5
        y = 0.5*(y + 0) = 0.5*y
    print x,y
```

Listing 13-7: Pseudocode for the Sierpiński triangle

Let's make the algorithm explicit with pseudocode. First, we'll pick the vertices of the triangle: (0,0); (0.5,1); (1,0). Then, we need to code Listing 13-7 where rnd returns a random float, [0, 1). We initialize x and y to the point (1,0). Any of the three points would do.

Next, we start a loop for the desired number of points, N. The three cases select one of the three vertex points with equal probability. If the random value in r is below one-third, we've selected the first point, (0,0), so the midpoint is the average of both the x and y values plus 0 and 0. Similarly, if r is $0.333333 \leq r < 0.666666$, we select the vertex at (0.5,1). Lastly, if r is ≥ 0.666666, we use the vertex at (1,0). After updating x and y, we print them as a pair and repeat the loop.

The midpoint formulas simplify as shown in Listing 13-7. Observe that each pass through the loop updates x and y by first dividing by 2 (multiplying by 0.5) and then adding an offset depending upon the selected vertex. If the vertex is (0,0), the offset is 0 for both x and y. If the vertex is (0.5,1), the offset is 0.25 in x and 0.5 in y. Lastly, for (1,0), the offset is 0.5 in x and 0 for y.

This observation means the loop can be rewritten first to divide x and y by 2, and then we can add the offset—there is no need to have code that calculates the repeated instances of 0.5*x and 0.5*y as shown in Listing 13-7. This simplification helps considerably when writing the Filska implementation.

Our implementation uses three subprograms: main, loop, and print. Also, we'll store the current x value in the X register and, not surprisingly, the current y value in the Y register. We'll use main to initialize X and Y, set up the counter for the desired number of output points, which we'll store in Z, and then transfer execution to loop (see Listing 13-8).

```
{ main
    set,1        " start at 1,0
    tmx
    set,0
    tmy
    set,60000    " number of points to output
    dec
    tmz
    jmp,loop
}
```

Listing 13-8: The main loop of sierpinski.filska

Next, we'll use print to display the X and Y registers as an (x,y) pair on the same line (see Listing 13-9).

```
{ print
    txm
    prt
    set,32
    chr chr
    tym
```

```
    prt
    set,10
    chr
    jmp,loop
}
```

Listing 13-9: The print subprogram of sierpinski.filska

Listing 13-9 first moves X to local memory to print it. Then it prints two spaces (character 32) before printing Y and a newline.

Listing 13-10 contains the bulk of the program. It's the body of the loop in Listing 13-7.

```
{ loop
❶ set,2
    div,x=xm
    div,y=ym
❷ rnd
    cmp,0.333333
❸ tst,1,10
    cmp,0.666666
❹ tst,1,4

❺ set,0.5
    add,x=xm
    gto,5

❻ set,0.25
    add,x=xm
    set,0.5
    add,y=ym

❼ jmp,print

❽ tzm
    dec
    tst,z,3
    tmz
    jpr,loop
    hlt
}
```

Listing 13-10: The loop subprogram of sierpinski.filska

First, we divide the X and Y registers by 2 ❶. Then, we use loop's memory to hold a random value ❷.

If the random value is less than 0.333333, the tst,1,10 instruction ❸ is true and execution moves to the jmp to print ❼. This is the (0,0) vertex where there is no offset to add. If memory is less than 0.666666 ❹, execution moves to adding an offset of 0.25 to X and 0.5 to Y ❻. This is the (0.5,1) vertex case. Lastly, if memory is greater than or equal to 0.666666, we have the (1,0) case so we need only add an offset of 0.5 to X ❺. After printing the new X and Y values ❼, the Z register is decremented and tested for 0 ❽. If Z is 0, hlt stops the program. If not, the loop subprogram is run from the beginning courtesy of the jpr instruction.

Let's run the program and capture the output.

```
> python3 filska.py sierpinski.filska >points.txt
```

Here, *points.txt* becomes a collection of 60,000 (x, y) pairs.

To see the fractal, we need to plot the points. A few lines of Python will do the trick.

```
>>> import numpy as np
>>> import matplotlib.pylab as plt
>>> d = np.loadtxt("points.txt")
>>> plt.plot(d[:,0],d[:,1], linestyle='none', marker=',')
>>> plt.show()
```

The result should look very much like Figure 13-2. Note that Figure 13-2 uses 600,000 points, 10 times as many as *sierpinski.filska* generates by default.

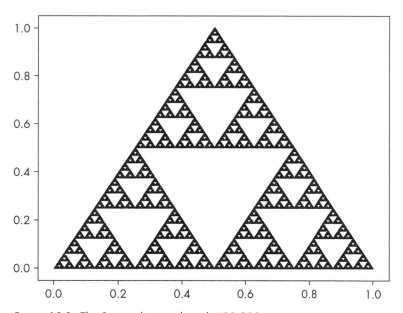

Figure 13-2: The Sierpiński triangle with 600,000 points

Getting to the Roots of the Problem

In algebra class, we all spent far too much time factoring quadratic equations of the form $ax^2 + bx + c$ to find the roots, that is, the values of x such that $ax^2 + bx + c = 0$. After much consternation and many practice problems, we were told of the formula to find the roots directly. This is the quadratic formula, which we used above to find the value of ϕ, the golden ratio.

$$x = \frac{-b \pm \sqrt{b^2 - 4ac}}{2a}$$

The value under the square root is known as the *discriminant*, $\Delta = b^2 - 4ac$. The sign of the discriminant tells us something useful about the roots.

$$\Delta \begin{cases} < 0, & \text{two imaginary roots} \\ = 0, & \text{one real root} \\ > 0, & \text{two real roots} \end{cases}$$

For the first case, the discriminant is negative, and the square root of a negative number is imaginary. For the second case, the square root is 0, and the single root is $x = -b/(2a)$. For the third case, the discriminant is positive, the square root exists, and there are two distinct real roots.

The file *roots.filska* contains a complete program to calculate the roots of an arbitrary quadratic polynomial. Let's run it a few times to see what it outputs. Then, we'll examine the portions of the code related to the discriminant and the roots themselves. The remainder of the code handles text output. It is primarily a series of set and chr instructions, which are essential to the nice formatting of the program, but not helpful in learning how to implement the calculations in Filska.

Listing 13-11 shows the output for three separate runs of *roots.filska*.

```
A? 1
B? 2
C? 4

Complex roots: -1+1.732050808i
               -1-1.732050808i
-------------------------------
A? 1
B? 4
C? 2

1st root: -0.5857864376
2nd root: -3.414213562
-------------------------------
A? -4
B? 12
C? -9

One root: 1.5
```

Listing 13-11: Three runs of roots.filska

The prompts ask the user to enter the coefficients of the quadratic, the *a*, *b*, and *c* values. In the first case, we are asking for the roots of $x^2 + 2x + 4$ and are told they are complex because the discriminant is negative. In the second case, we want the roots of $x^2 + 4x + 2$, which are real. The last case is asking about $-4x^2 + 12x - 9$, which leads to a zero discriminant and only one root.

The flow of this program is quite linear: the user enters the coefficients, the discriminant is calculated, and, based on the value of the discriminant, the proper roots are calculated. If you look at *roots.filska*, you'll see that the key subprograms are main, positive, equal, and negative, along with three subprograms to get the coefficients: getA, getB, and getC.

Listing 13-12 presents the main subprogram.

```
{ main
    "  Get a, b, and c
❶ jmp,getA
   jmp,getB
   jmp,getC

   "  Calculate D
❷ jmp,getA        " X=a
   set,4           " M=4
   mul,m=mx        " M = M*X  (4a)
   jmp,getC        " X=c
   mul,m=mx        " M = M*X  (4ac)
   neg             " M = -M   (-4ac)
   tmz             " Z = M    (-4ac)
   jmp,getB        " X=b
   txm             " M=b
   mul,m=mx        " M = M*X  (b*b)
   add,m=mz        " M = M+Z  (b*b - 4ac)
   tmy             " Y = D    (disc)
   jmp,getA        " X = a
   txm             " M = X
   tmz             " Z = M    (a)
   jmp,getB        " X = b    (b)
   tym             " M = Y    (disc)
❸ cmp,0           " compare(M,0)
   tst,g,3         " D > 0  --> positive
   tst,e,3         " D == 0 --> equal
   tst,l,3         " D < 0  --> negative
   jmp,positive
   jmp,equal
   jmp,negative
}
```

Listing 13-12: The main subprogram

From the comments, we see that main asks for *a*, *b*, and *c* and then calculates the discriminant (D) before using its value to jump to either positive, equal, or negative.

Let's begin with the last three instructions in main. At first glance, it seems odd to put them one after the other, but that's merely an illusion caused by thinking in terms of functions. We need to consider them in relation to the cmp and tst instructions above.

The cmp instruction compares main's memory, the discriminant, to 0 ❸. If the discriminant is greater than 0, we transfer control to the positive subprogram by branching three instructions forward using tst,g,3. Similarly, we transfer control to equal if the discriminant is 0 and negative if the discriminant is less than 0. All three of these subprograms eventually execute hlt and none return control to main.

Filska is quite limited in the data it can track, an intentional design goal to make us think more about how to arrange our programs, so we need to consider which values must be stored and when. We should ask the user for the coefficients of the quadratic. We also need to keep them somewhere and get them back on demand. We have the three registers, but if we store the coefficients in them, we have only the single memory location of each subprogram to use for calculations. We need the registers to transfer data between subprograms and to participate in calculations.

The solution is to create a subprogram that acts as a small object. The subprogram can store a value passed to it and then return the value on demand. Think of the subprogram as an instance of a simple class that we might express in Python as follows:

```python
class Store:
    def __init__(self, v):
        self.v = v
    def Get(self):
        return self.v
```

Instances of this class are given a value to store when they are created, and later return that value when asked using the Get method. This is what we need: to assign a value once and then retrieve it multiple times later on.

In Filska, we get the same effect with a subprogram using its memory to store the value. Consider getA.

```
{ getA
    set,65 chr
    set,63 chr
    set,32 chr
    ipt
    jmp,main
    tmx
    jmp,main
    gto,-2
}
```

The first three lines of getA print A? and then ask for a number from the user with ipt. Whatever number the user enters is stored in local memory. Then, control is transferred back to main via jmp. The next transfer from main back to getA begins with the tmx instruction to put the user's value in the X register and then transfer back to main. However, any future transfer back to getA will begin with the gto instruction jumping back 2 to start again at tmx. This loop repeats indefinitely: getA will now only load X with the user's value. We have a "write once, read many" place to hold a number—precisely what we need.

Looking again at Listing 13-12, we see the first three transfers to get the coefficients ❶. This is followed later, during the calculation of the discriminant, by transfers to getA, getB, and getC when those values are needed.

Calculation of the discriminant is an exercise in juggling data values so that we do not run out of places to put them (see Listing 13-12 ❷). Let's walk through the code. We need to calculate b^2-4ac and begin by calculating $-4ac$.

```
jmp,getA      " X=a
set,4         " M=4
mul,m=mx      " M = M*X   (4a)
jmp,getC      " X=c
mul,m=mx      " M = M*X   (4ac)
neg           " M = -M    (-4ac)
tmz           " Z = M     (-4ac)
```

We store $-4ac$ temporarily in Z. Now we need to find b^2 and add $-4ac$ to it.

```
jmp,getB      " X=b
txm           " M=b
mul,m=mx      " M = M*X   (b*b)
add,m=mz      " M = M+Z   (b*b - 4ac)
tmy           " Y = D     (disc)
```

We now have the discriminant in Y. To calculate the roots, let's rewrite the quadratic equation using the discriminant, Δ.

$$x = \frac{-b \pm \sqrt{\Delta}}{2a}$$

Writing the equation in this form buys us something: we need only a, b, and Δ to calculate the roots. Good! We have three registers available, so let's use Z for a, X for b, and Y for Δ.

```
jmp,getA      " X = a
txm           " M = X
tmz           " Z = M     (a)
jmp,getB      " X = b     (b)
tym           " M = Y     (disc)
```

Here, the last instruction moves the discriminant to main's memory for the cmp instruction of Listing 13-12 ❸.

The remaining subprograms, positive, equal, and negative, and the subprograms used by them, calculate and output the specific roots. As mentioned, many of the instructions relate to formatting the output. You can review those instructions on your own, but let's conclude by stepping through positive to see how the calculation is done for two real roots.

```
{ positive
 ❶ set,2          " M = 2
    mul,m=mz       " M = 2a
    div,m=xm       " M = b/(2a)
    neg            " M = -b/(2a)
    jmp,rest       " X = sqr(Y)/(2a)
    jmp,?double
    add,y=mx       " Y = M + X    (-b/(2a)+sqr(D)/(2a))
    jmp,?double
    sub,y=mx       " Y = M - X    (-b/(2a)-sqrt(D)/(2a))
    jmp,?double
}

{ rest
    set,2
    mul,x=mz
    tym
    sqr
    div,x=mx
    jmp,positive
}
```

Rewriting the quadratic equation one last time, we see that the two roots for a positive discriminant are

$$x = \frac{-b}{2a} \pm \frac{\sqrt{\Delta}}{2a}$$

implying we need both $-b/(2a)$ and $\sqrt{\Delta}/(2a)$ so we can add and subtract them. The first term is built piece by piece, as indicated in the comments ❶. It's left in positive's memory. Then, transfer to rest builds $\sqrt{\Delta}/(2a)$ in X. Notice that doing this destroys b, which was previously in X. That's okay; we no longer need it. When rest transfers execution back to positive, X has the other term we need, so we first add the terms and call ?double (read "print double") to output what is in Y, subtract the terms, and call ?double to get the other root. Notice also that using Y destroys the discriminant, but we no longer need it, either.

Whew! That was a lot of steps for something that a more powerful language could implement quickly. Still, the challenge, and fun, is in getting a constrained language to do something useful.

Linear Least-Squares Fit to a Line

Previously, we fit a polynomial to a set of points to arrive at a silly way of printing HELLO, WORLD!. In this section, we'll again use least-squares fitting, but this time to a line, which is far simpler. Specifically, we have a collection of (x, y) points, and we want to find the equation of a line that best fits them:

$$y = bx + a$$

for some a and b we need to calculate from the data.

Unlike least-squares fitting to a polynomial or other function, fitting a line to a dataset has a closed-form solution; this means we can write the equations that give us a and b (see Equation 13.2)

$$a = \frac{\sum x_i^2 \sum y_i - \sum x_i \sum x_i y_i}{\Delta}$$

$$b = \frac{N \sum x_i y_i - \sum x_i \sum y_i}{\Delta}$$

$$\Delta = N \sum x_i^2 - \left(\sum x_i \right)^2 \tag{13.2}$$

for N, the number of points in the dataset.

Equation 13.2 appears a bit daunting at first. Don't let it throw you. It says we must accumulate sums of all the x values and all y values along with the sums of x^2 and x times y. Once we have these sums, calculating b (the slope) and a (the intercept) is straightforward because the $\sum$ terms become simple numbers.

The code for this example is in *linfit.filska*. From a programming perspective, we'll see a new kind of Filska subprogram, one that expands on the "write once, read many" idea we used in the previous section. However, before we write code, we must decide how we'll get Filska to read the datafile. Normally, we'd store the data points as (x, y) pairs, one pair per line. However, if we use redirection to send the data to the Filska program, the ipt instruction will read only one value per line of the input file. Also, we need to tell Filska to stop reading the file so we can complete our calculations.

The solution is to put the data in the file with one value per line, first the *x* value and then the associated *y* value on the next line. To tell Filska we are done, we'll end the file with a flag value, one that won't show up in our dataset. We'll use −999999, an unlikely data value.

For example, if our dataset is

$$(0, 0.5), \ (1, 1.1), \ (2, 2.4), \ (3, 3.6)$$

we'll format it for input as

```
0
0.5
1
1.1
2
2.4
3
3.6
-999999
```

so each *x* is followed by its *y*, and the last value, `-999999`, tells us there's no more data to read.

As far as Equation 13.2 is concerned, we get the following sums for our example dataset:

$$N = 4$$

$$\sum x_i = 0 + 1 + 2 + 3 = 6$$

$$\sum y_i = 0.5 + 1.1 + 2.4 + 3.6 = 7.6$$

$$\sum x_i^2 = 0^2 + 1^2 + 2^2 + 3^2 = 14$$

$$\sum x_i y_i = (0)(0.5) + (1)(1.1) + (2)(2.4) + (3)(3.6) = 16.7$$

Meaning the best fit line is

$$\Delta = N \sum x_i^2 - \left(\sum x_i \right)^2 = (4)(14) - (6)^2 = 20$$

$$a = \frac{\sum x_i^2 \sum y_i - \sum x_i \sum x_i y_i}{\Delta} = \frac{(14)(7.6) - (6)(16.7)}{20} = 0.31$$

$$b = \frac{N \sum x_i y_i - \sum x_i \sum y_i}{\Delta} = \frac{(4)(16.7) - (6)(7.6)}{20} = 1.06$$

or *y* = *bx* + *a* = 1.06*x* + 0.31.

Let's see the code in action; then we'll dive into it. I've included a sample dataset, *linfit_dataset.txt*. If you run *linfit.filska* using *linfit_dataset.txt* as the input you get

```
> python3 filska.py linfit.filska <linfit_dataset.txt
A=10.46698813
B=2.272733952
```

which tells us that the best-fit line is $y = Bx + A$ (see Figure 13-3). The fit looks pretty good, so we have confidence that the code is working.

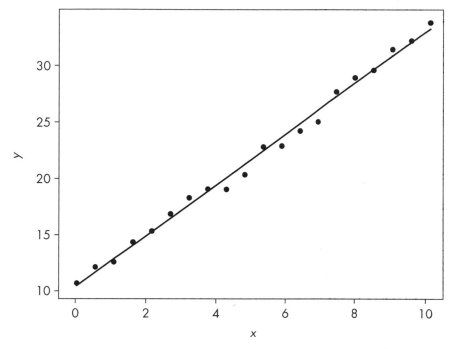

Figure 13-3: Best-fit line to the sample dataset

If we were using a high-level language to code this example, we'd likely store the dataset in some kind of array or list. Then we'd run through the list to generate the necessary sums. However, Filska has no arrays. So how can we do it? The solution comes from observing that all we need is a single pass through the dataset and some way of accumulating each point as we read it. There is no need to store all the data first and then process it, because we can process each point as it is read. In algorithm form, we need to code the following:

1. Read a point from the input file, (x, y).
2. Add the x value to the running total of x values.
3. Add x^2 to the running total of x^2 values.
4. Add y to the running total of y values.
5. Add xy to the running total of xy values.
6. Repeat from Step 1 until all points have been read.
7. Calculate a and b using the running totals.

We need to track the sums of x, y, x^2, and xy, along with the total number of points read, N. That's too many values to depend solely upon memory and the registers. Thus, we need something much like the subprograms of the previous section, which can be initialized, sum, and finally report their totals. Using the analogy of a class, as we did previously, we need something like the following.

```
class Adder:
    def __init__(self):
        self.s = 0
    def Add(self, v):
        self.s += v
    def Get(self):
        return self.s
```

This class sets its internal state to 0 when instantiated, and then adds values passed to Add and reports its current sum when Get is called.

We can build this structure in Filska using subprogram memory to store the sum and registers to provide values or return values. We'll keep the current point's *x* value in the X register and the *y* value in the Y register. We'll use the Z register to tell the subprogram whether to accumulate (Z = 0) or return the sum (Z ≠ 0) in Y.

Now take a look at Listing 13-13, which shows the sumxy subprogram from *linfit.filska*.

```
{ sumxy
  ❶ set,0        " first call: zero sum
    jmp,main     " and back to main
  ❷ swp,mz       " look at Z stashing M
    tst,n,8      " return value in Y
  ❸ swp,mz       " restore total
    mul,z=xy     " Z <-- X*Y
    add,z=mz     " Z <-- M + X*Y
    set,0        " M <-- 0
    swp,mz       " M <--> Z, restore Z and M
    jmp,main     " return to main
    gto,-8       " test again
  ❹ swp,mz       " Z=1, return M in Y
    tmy          " and put it in Y
    jmp,main     " and back to main
    gto,-2       " put sum in Y and return to main
}
```

Listing 13-13: The sumxy subprogram

When sumxy is called the first time, it sets its local memory to 0 and returns to main ❶. Subsequent calls begin with ❷ and branch depending upon Z. At this point, X and Y contain the respective *x* and *y* values of the current point. If Z is not 0, the tst instruction branches forward to ❹ to move local memory, the sum of the products of *x* and *y*, to Y.

Note two things about the code so far. First, at ❷, to test that Z is not 0, we have to swap memory and Z, so Z's value is in memory, but the memory value is stashed in Z. After all, losing the sum in memory would make the entire subprogram useless. Therefore, at ❹ the swap must happen again to restore the actual sum of the *xy* pairs and ensure that Z is also unchanged. Second, when $Z \neq 0$, the subprogram is in a permanent state of simply reporting its sum in Y. That means it no longer pays attention to Z's state. This works for our program and frees Z for other uses, if necessary. The gto jumping back to tmy makes this happen.

If Z is 0, the tst fails, and execution continues ❸. First, Z and memory are swapped, as at ❹ to restore the sum. Then Z is used to hold the product of *x* and *y* and added to memory, thereby accumulating the product for the current point. Of course, using Z in this way changes its value, so before transferring back to main, we must reset Z to 0. The jmp to main is followed by a gto to branch back the beginning of the test on Z for the next transfer to sumxy from main.

The pattern set up in sumxy is repeated for sumx, sumy, sumx2, and sum, where the second to last accumulates x^2 and the last counts the number of points processed. By controlling the state of Z, main moves from accumulating to calculating. The trigger to change state is reading the flag value of -999999 for *x*.

The main subprogram of *linfit.filska* is rather long, so we'll only examine pieces of it. Listing 13-14 covers the first part, which initializes the sums and processes the data points.

```
{ main
❶ jmp,sum
   jmp,sumx
   jmp,sumy
   jmp,sumxy
   jmp,sumx2

   set,0         " Z=0, accumulate mode
   tmz           "
   ipt           " read X
   cmp,-999999   " data done?
   tst,e,10      " yes, calculate
   tmx           " no, move to X register
   ipt           " read Y
   tmy           " move to Y register

❷ jmp,sum        " accumulate the x,y data
   jmp,sumx
   jmp,sumy
   jmp,sumxy
   jmp,sumx2

   gto,-11       " continue the loop
```

Listing 13-14: Accumulating sums in main

The first block of code calls each of the accumulator subprograms to initialize them ❶. Next, the main loop starts by setting Z = 0 to put each subprogram in accumulator mode. The first ipt instruction reads an *x* value, checks to see if it is -999999, and if so, branches forward to exit the loop. The code then places *x* in the X register. The second ipt reads the *y* value and puts it in Y.

The second block of jmp instructions accumulates each of the totals ❷. Lastly, the gto branches back to the beginning of the main loop, the first ipt instruction.

When the flag value of -999999 is read, the input file has been processed, and execution moves to calculation mode, so it's time for Equation 13.2. If we look at Equation 13.2, we see that both *a* and *b* depend on Δ. Therefore, we split the calculation into finding the numerators for *a* and *b* and then dividing by Δ.

Listing 13-15 calculates the numerator for *a*.

```
set,1          " Z = 1, return sums in Y mode
tmz
jmp,sumx2      " Y = sumx2
tym            " M = sumx2
jmp,sumy       " Y = sumy
mul,z=my       " Z = sumx2*sumy
jmp,sumx       " Y = sumx
tym            " M = sumx
jmp,sumxy      " Y = sumxy
mul,m=my       " M = sumx*sumxy
sub,z=zm       " Z = sumx2*sumy - sumx*sumxy
jmp,numA       " store in numA
```

Listing 13-15: Calculations in main

First, Z is set to 1 to cause the subprograms to return their sums in Y, and then the sequence of steps calculates what we need for *a*'s numerator in Equation 13.2. The numA subprogram, not shown, stores what's in Z on the first call, returning it in Y on all future calls. A similar sequence of steps calculates the numerator for *b*, stored in numB, and Δ itself in delta. The final instructions of main calculate numA divided by delta and print it as *a*. Then the same is done for *b* using numB. The program ends with hlt.

Discussion

It's clear Filska is a limited language, though useful for specific tasks. Many programming languages develop idioms, which are snippets of code that show up frequently. We developed a Filska idiom above by using a subprogram as a memory location with additional functionality, something we showed was similar to a simple class in other languages. We used this idiom as a "write once, read many" memory, with or without additional processing, or, via a flag in a register, as a read/write memory, as we did for the linear least-squares fit example.

Filska does not support arrays, but it is possible to emulate them using subprograms as the array elements. We won't list the code here, but do take a look at *array.filska*, an example that creates an array of 10 values. The demo stores values in the array by index and then dumps the array in order.

In the end, what should we make of Filska? We've seen it implement certain algorithms, even ones leading to useful outcomes. Is Filska Turing complete? Although it's true that most imperative programming languages are very likely Turing complete, Filska is perhaps not because of its severe memory constraints. Three general-purpose registers and one memory location per subprogram might be the limiting factor. However, there is no limit to the number of subprograms we can define, and the array demo shows how to use that feature to emulate an array that is, in theory, as large as we would care to make it. Therefore, we might argue we do have an arbitrary amount of data available. In the end, deciding whether Filska is Turing complete is beyond what we can reasonably address in this book. Perhaps a theoretical computer scientist will take up the challenge and share their results with us. If so, check the GitHub site for the book.

Summary

This chapter used Filska to implement a set of (hopefully) fun math-related examples. We got geeky and used curve fitting to produce HELLO, WORLD!. We explored the Fibonacci sequence, pseudorandom number generation, fractals, roots of equations, and fitting a data to a line. In each case, we needed to think carefully about the structure of our data and code to make the best use possible of Filska's severe programming constraints.

Filska was designed to calculate, and all of our examples involved math in some way. Let's relax a bit now and consider our second esolang, one designed purely for fun, and one that's considerably simpler in every way. Let's leave math behind, step outside, and watch the fireflies.

14

FIREFLY

Firefly is a minimalist programming language for animation and sound. Firefly targets the BBC micro:bit, but you don't need one to have fun with the language—the console version will work just fine. The inspiration for the language comes from the 5×5 grid of LEDs that form the display of the micro:bit. The language manipulates a "firefly" that lives on the grid. As it flies, it leaves a luminous trail of light behind it. Oh, the firefly also sings, because why not?

This chapter introduces the philosophy and design of the language, followed by its implementation. The chapter ends with a section on configuring a micro:bit, should you wish to use one for the experiments of Chapter 15. Again, you don't need a micro:bit; you can run everything just fine at the command line using the console version of the interpreter. However, the micro:bit isn't too expensive, and it's a fun little device that itself runs Python. Also, console fireflies don't know how to sing.

Philosophy and Design

Our environment is this: a small firefly is flying around a tiny 5×5 grid. As it flies, it leaves behind a luminous trail and sometimes sings.

To be more specific, a Firefly program manipulates a 5×5 grid of single digits. On the micro:bit, these become intensities of the 5×5 grid of LEDs. The firefly can sing by making the micro:bit sound a note of a particular pitch and duration.

A Firefly program is a series of single-character instructions that either move the firefly around the grid, set the way its luminous trail acts, or make the firefly sing a note. The Firefly language also supports what is known as *double buffering*, meaning instead of one 5×5 grid of digits, there are two 5×5 grids. The program controls which grid is shown to the user and which grid the firefly is making a trail on (drawing to). Double buffering is a common computer animation technique in which the user sees one display while the program is updating the other and then the view switches. Doing this prevents the user from watching the display draw and makes for smooth animation. Don't worry if double buffering is a new concept; we'll detail it in Chapter 15 when we use it.

A Firefly program instructs the firefly by directing its movements and when and how it should sing. If you've never heard a singing firefly, you're in good company because I haven't either. Still, it's fun to pretend.

The firefly is constrained to move on a 5×5 grid. The upper-left corner of the grid is position (0,0), and the lower-right corner is position (4,4). Positions are given as the row number before the column number. The firefly moves one position at a time, either north (N), south (S), east (E), or west (W). When it moves off one edge of the grid, it wraps around to the other side. For instance, moving east from position (1,4) puts the firefly at position (1,0). Likewise, a firefly moving south from (4,2) arrives at position (0,2).

When the firefly moves, it leaves behind a trail, meaning it sets the position it *just left* to some value. On the micro:bit, the value is the LED's intensity at that position where 0 is off and 9 is maximum brightness. The console interpreter shows 0 as space and anything else as the numeric value of the position, but if desired, the console will show 0 as 0.

Therefore, if the firefly is currently at position (2,2) and the intensity is set to 3, an instruction telling the firefly to move one position to the west, that is, to (2,1), will set position (2,2) to intensity 3. There is also an instruction telling the firefly to stay put, so it is possible to update a position value in place.

The 5×5 grid is all the memory we have. It's also the display: we see the value of each grid cell as a number (console) or brightness of the LED (micro:bit). Therefore, a Firefly program has no variables.

Using memory as the display isn't novel, but it puts us in good company. The Manchester Baby, the world's first stored-program computer with random access memory, circa 1948, also used memory as its display (see Figure 14-1).

Figure 14-1: The memory/display of the Manchester Baby

The Baby's memory is literally the cathode-ray tube shown in the photograph. If a bit was on, one pattern was displayed, and if the bit was off, a slightly different pattern was shown. Figure 14-1 shows a working replica of the original Baby built at the University of Manchester in 1998 in celebration of the original Baby's 50th anniversary.

The Baby had memory for 32 instructions of 32 bits each. It was a von Neumann machine, meaning program memory and data storage were mixed as they are in a modern desktop computer. Firefly is more like a Harvard architecture machine, as memory for data and program instructions is separate. Many microcontrollers use a Harvard architecture. In our case, the display is the data memory and a Python string represents program memory.

We have two versions of the Firefly interpreter to work with. The console version is intended for program creation. It knows how to parse input text to remove whitespace and comments. It also supports program tracing. When the program is working as it should, a utility converts the source code to a form we can load onto the micro:bit. The micro:bit runs a single Python program. For Firefly, the program is the interpreter with the source code we want to execute embedded in it as a string constant.

Perhaps the simplest way to understand Firefly is to detail its instructions. Knowing what the instructions do tells us how to use them. Firefly instructions are single characters and case insensitive. The instructions fall into distinct groups: movement, display, music, and whatever's left. Most instructions relate to movement, so we'll begin with those.

Movement

Firefly move instructions fall into two groups: those that move the firefly and those that define what happens to the position the firefly leaves when it moves. We'll refer to these latter instructions as setting the *mode*. Movement is north, south, east, or west, with the option to stay put (see Table 14-1).

Table 14-1: Firefly Movement Commands

Instruction	Effect
N	Move north
S	Move south
E	Move east
W	Move west
T	Stay put ("tick" of the clock)

What happens to the position after the firefly moves is the mode given in Table 14-2. Note that when the program begins, the firefly is in move-only mode at position (2,2).

Table 14-2: Firefly Intensity (Mode) Commands

Instruction	Effect
0–9	Constant intensity value
I	Increment the current value
D	Decrement the current value
M	Move only; no change in value
R	Random value 1 through 9

Let's consider a program that begins with the following instructions:

```
SS5NNNNN
```

Here, the firefly will move south twice to be at position (4,2), set the intensity to 5, and then move north five times to arrive back at position (4,2) with a vertical trail of five 5s behind it so that the display looks like this:

```
0   0   5   0   0
0   0   5   0   0
0   0   5   0   0
0   0   5   0   0
0   0   5   0   0
```

Figure 14-2 illustrates the process.

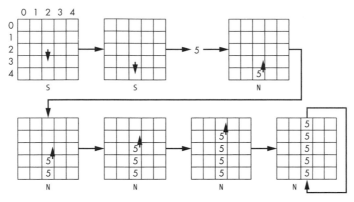

Figure 14-2: How the firefly moves

The first command, S, moves the firefly south from (2,2) to (3,2), as shown with the arrow. The next S moves the firefly to (4,2). The 5 sets the trail to intensity 5. Lastly, the five N commands move the firefly as shown, leaving a trail behind it and finishing at position (4,2).

Note that there is no way to ask what the current value of a position is. When the program starts, all positions are 0. If the move mode is increment, adding 1 to the current position's value wraps around, so 9 becomes 0. Similarly, if the mode is decrement, 0 wraps around to become 9. Use mode R to set the value to a random integer between 1 and 9.

Display

Double buffering maintains two 5×5 memory grids. Only one grid is shown at a time, and it's possible to create any combination of the grid shown and the grid the firefly is making a trail on. We'll call our two grids A and B. When the program starts, grid A is shown and the firefly draws on grid A. The display instructions are in Table 14-3.

Table 14-3: Firefly Display Commands

Instruction	Effect
X	Show grid A
Y	Show grid B
A	Draw on grid A
B	Draw on grid B
C	Clear active grid
V	Clear grid A
Z	Clear grid B

The instruction C clears the grid currently being displayed, but V and Z clear their respective grids regardless of which one is currently displayed. Therefore, to show grid A but make the firefly draw on grid B, execute XB, and then, when the firefly is done drawing, show grid B with Y. We'll explore animation more in Chapter 15.

Music

To make the firefly sing, we need the three instructions in Table 14-4.

Table 14-4: Firefly Music Commands

Instruction	Effect
J	Set note duration
G	Set octave
F	Play a note

Each instruction uses the value of the firefly's current position for the duration, octave, or note.

Under the hood, these instructions use the play function in the Micro-Python music module. The easiest instructions to understand are duration and octave. The micro:bit range is such that octave 4 includes middle C, which is the default value. So, to set the octave to 4, we first need to set the firefly's current position and then the octave: 4TG. The 4 sets the mode to 4, meaning the firefly's trail uses intensity 4. Next, we keep the firefly in place with T. Lastly, we set the octave with G.

Note that durations are relative, with a duration of 4 being a reasonable value for a quarter note. Therefore, a duration of 2 implies an eighth note and 8 a half note. Durations, and octaves, are persistent, meaning that once set, their value will stay until changed. To set the duration to quarter notes, use something like 4TJ.

To play a note, we need F. The firefly's current position indicates the actual note according to Table 14-5.

Table 14-5: Firefly Note Commands

Value	Note
0	Rest
1	C
2	D
3	E
4	F
5	G
6	A
7	B
8	Rest (same as 0)
9	C (same as 1)

As an example, to play middle C as a quarter note, we would need something like 1TF to set the move mode, or intensity, to 1 ("move" by staying in place); this sets the current position to 1, and F to play the note. This assumes that the octave and duration are both their default values of 4. As Firefly memory holds only a single digit at a time, we are limited to the C major scale with no sharps or flats.

Our singing firefly will have several opportunities to serenade us in Chapter 15.

What's Left

Only three instructions remain. The first is H, which stops the program. Similar to H is L, which enters an eternal loop (that is, sleeps the program). The difference between the two is most noticeable with the micro:bit. If H is executed, the program stops and Python clears the display. If we execute L instead, the program sleeps "forever" and the display remains active.

The final instruction is P, which pauses for 0.1 seconds before continuing. Use P to add timing effects. We'll see P in Chapter 15 when we implement a tea timer and a counter.

Table 14-6 serves as a reference for all Firefly instructions.

Table 14-6: The Firefly Instruction Set

Instruction	Effect
N	Move north
S	Move south
E	Move east
W	Move west
T	Stay put ("tick" of the clock)
0–9	Constant intensity value
I	Increment the current value
D	Decrement the current value
M	Move only, no change in value
R	Random value 1 through 9
X	Show grid A
Y	Show grid B
A	Draw on grid A
B	Draw on grid B
C	Clear active grid
V	Clear grid A
Z	Clear grid B
J	Set note duration
G	Set octave
F	Play a note
P	Pause for 0.1 seconds
L	Loop forever
H	Halt

Now, let's get down to business and actually implement the language.

Implementation

Firefly is written in Python, both for simplicity and because the micro:bit runs only a single Python program. We'll list Python code for the micro:bit version here, but show example Firefly code for the console version in Chapter 15. Doing this lets us use whitespace and comments. In Chapter 15, we'll walk through the development process, which typically involves both the console and micro:bit interpreters.

Firefly programs are ultimately a string of uppercase letters and digits. For the micro:bit, the string is literally embedded within the Python code for the interpreter after all whitespace has been removed. The micro:bit does have a flat file system, but it's simpler to embed the Firefly code at the top of the interpreter.

The console interpreter allows whitespace and comments beginning with an exclamation point (!) and running to the end of the current line. The console interpreter also supports execution tracing, which we'll see in Chapter 15.

Interpreter Structure and Main Loop

The Firefly interpreter consists of a set of global variables, including the displays, a few functions to handle specific Firefly instructions, and the main loop that executes character after character of the program string. The implementation is deliberately not object oriented, in part to possibly reduce overhead and preserve room on the micro:bit for Firefly code, and in part to be old-school about things as a change of pace. Therefore, the interpreter begins with a series of declarations and necessary imports (see Listing 14-1).

```
PRG = """
1TJ0TITFTFTFTFTFTFTF5TG8TJ1TFH
"""

from microbit import display
from music import play
from time import sleep
from random import randint

DIGITS = ["0","1","2","3","4","5","6","7","8","9"]
MOVES = ["N","E","W","T","S","L"]
BUFS = ["A","B","X","Y"]

A = bytearray(25)
B = bytearray(25)
C = A
D = A
M = "M"
I = 12
```

```
dur = 4
oc = 4
display.clear()
```

Listing 14-1: Firefly interpreter preamble

The global variable PRG holds the Firefly program to execute. The example program in Listing 14-1 plays a simple scale.

Necessary Python imports come next. The first two functions are exclusive to MicroPython, which runs on the micro:bit; they handle the LED display and playing musical notes, respectively. The time and random modules are standard Python fare. We use sleep to implement the P instruction and randint for the R movement mode.

The Firefly display, a 5×5 grid of single-digit values, is stored in a Python bytearray. There are two of them, A and B. The display currently shown is the array assigned to D, with A being the default. Likewise, the array currently drawn to by the moving firefly is in C, which is also A by default. M holds the current movement mode with "M", which is the default value and means "move with no trail."

The display is in A or B with I as the index or current position of the firefly. When needed, this index is converted into row and column. The default note duration is in dur and the default note octave is in oc. When the program starts, the actual micro:bit display is cleared (display.clear()).

After the preamble in Listing 14-1 come seven function definitions. We'll get to these in the following sections. The main loop comes last. Note that there is no main function, as the interpreter runs as a script. The main loop is in Listing 14-2.

```
R = True
while R:
    for c in PRG:
        if c == "I":
            M = "I"
        elif c == "D":
            M = "D"
        elif c == "M":
            M = "M"
        elif c == "R":
            M = "R"
        elif c in DIGITS:
            M = c
        elif c == "H":
            R = False
            break
        elif c in MOVES:
            Move(c)
        elif c == "P":
            sleep(0.1)
```

```
        elif c == "C":
            Clear()
        elif c == "V":
            ClearA()
        elif c == "Z":
            ClearB()
        elif c in BUFS:
            Display(c)
        elif c == "J":
            dur = C[I]
        elif c == "F":
            Play()
        elif c == "G":
            oc = C[I]
        Update()

C = A
D = A
M = "M"
I = 12
display.clear()
```

Listing 14-2: Firefly interpreter main loop

The main loop runs as long as R is True. This means that a Firefly program will begin again after the last instruction. It also means that memory will not be erased. This is the only looping supported by Firefly. We'll see how to use it in Chapter 15 when we implement a counter.

The inner for loop is over the characters representing the Firefly program (PRG). Interpretation is a straightforward nested if statement. Certain instructions are handled directly in the for loop, like setting the movement mode to increment (I) or decrement (D). If the current character, c, is a digit (in DIGITS), the move mode is set to that digit value, M=c.

The only way to exit a Firefly program completely is to execute H, which sets R to False and then uses break to exit the inner for loop.

Movement instructions (MOVES), display instructions (BUFS), and playing a note (F) all call out to external functions to perform actions.

Notice the note duration (J) and note octave (G) instructions. They set the dur or oc global variables to C[I]. The index, I, represents the firefly's current position in the range $[0, 24]$, and C is assigned the bytearray for the memory the firefly is currently drawing to, either A or B.

A call to Update happens after each instruction is executed to update the micro:bit display. This is what the Update function looks like:

```
def Update():
    i = 0
    while i < 25:
        display.set_pixel(i%5, i//5, D[i])
        i += 1
```

A simple loop over the 25 elements of the bytearray assigned to global variable D determines the brightness of each of the LEDs in the 5×5 display. Note the conversion from a linear index (i) to display column (i%5) and row (i//5) for the currently active memory (D).

The final set of instructions—the bottom of the main loop shown in Listing 14-2—resets the display at the end of the program and then executes again from the beginning. Note that the default firefly position of (2,2) is set, as is showing and drawing on the first memory, A. However, the memories themselves are *not* reset to 0.

Movement

Memory is not updated unless the firefly "moves." What happens when the firefly moves is determined by the value of global variable M, which holds the current move mode. Listing 14-3 shows how movement is processed.

```
def Move(c):
    global I,C

❶   if M == "M":
        pass
    elif M == "I":
        C[I] += 1
        if C[I] > 9:
            C[I] = 0
    elif M == "D":
        if (C[I] == 0):
            C[I] = 9
        else:
            C[I] -= 1
    elif M == "R":
        C[I] = randint(1,9)
    else:
        C[I] = int(M)

❷   i = I//5
    j = I%5

❸   if c == "N":
        i -= 1
        if i < 0:
            i = 4
    elif c == "S":
        i += 1
        if i > 4:
            i = 0
    elif c == "E":
        j += 1
```

```
            if j > 4:
                j = 0
        elif c == "W":
            j -= 1
            if j < 0:
                j = 4
        elif c == "T":
            pass
        elif c == "L":
            while True:
                sleep(1000)

    I = 5*i + j
```

Listing 14-3: Firefly interpreter movement

First, the current mode is applied to the *current* firefly position ❶. Incrementing the position wraps around after 9 while decrementing wraps the other way if below 0. If the mode is R, a random integer is assigned to the current memory location, C[I]. Lastly, if the mode is a digit, that value is used to update memory.

Next, the interpreter converts the linear index into memory, I, to a row (i) and column (j) format so that we can apply the actual movement command ❷. Integer division by 5 maps I to 0 through 4 to give us the row. The modulo, that is, what's left over after integer division by 5, gives us the remainder representing the column.

The current move is now applied ❸. Note that Move is called only if the instruction is a move instruction. The cardinal directions update the row and column position accordingly, wrapping around as needed so that moving east when in column 4 moves back around to column 0, and so on.

There are two special move commands, T and L. The former acts like a tick of a clock. The firefly doesn't actually move to a new position, hence pass, but the interpreter does update the current position. The latter instruction, L, is specifically for the micro:bit. It enters an infinite loop that sleeps for 1,000 seconds before waking up briefly, only to sleep again. As stated above, a Firefly program executes H to halt the program and the interpreter exits. On the micro:bit, when a program exits, the display is cleared. Calling L instead of H preserves the display.

After the move command is executed, i and/or j have been updated. Before returning to the main loop, a new value for I is calculated by multiplying the row number (i) by 5, which is the number of elements per row, and adding the column number (j).

Display

Four functions control the display, as shown in Listing 14-4.

```
def Clear():
    global C
```

```
    k = 0
    while k < 25:
        C[k] = 0
        k += 1

def ClearA():
    global A
    k = 0
    while k < 25:
        A[k] = 0
        k += 1

def ClearB():
    global B
    k = 0
    while k < 25:
        B[k] = 0
        k += 1

def Display(c):
    global C,D
    if c == "A":
        C = A
    elif c == "B":
        C = B
    elif c == "X":
        D = A
    elif c == "Y":
        D = B
```

Listing 14-4: Firefly interpreter display

Three of the functions in Listing 14-4, Clear, ClearA, and ClearB, simply zero the display memory. The first function zeroes the current display, and the last two zero a given display, that is, A or B. Simply assigning a new bytearray to these global variables will not work because that would break the link with A and B, which are bytearray objects, while C and D act more like pointers that reference A or B. Recall that C references the memory the firefly is updating and D references the memory currently displayed.

The Display function updates the displayed or drawn-to memory based on the argument, c. Specifying "A" as the argument makes C reference A. Likewise, passing "B" points C at B. Passing "X" changes the displayed memory to A and passing "Y" points the display to B. Note that the global statements used by these functions to update the global variables properly. Most Python programs use objects, so the global keyword is seldom used. We decided on a strictly imperative implementation of Firefly, thereby requiring global statements.

Music

We've surveyed the main interpreter loop, movement, and display. Now let's finish Firefly by implementing the music instructions.

The J and G instructions, which set the note duration and octave, respectively, are in the main loop (see Listing 14-1). The play instruction, F, calls Play.

```
def Play():
    note = ["R","C","D","E","F","G","A","B"][C[I] % 8]
    play("%s%d:%d" % (note,oc,dur))
```

Play translates the current firefly position into a note string and then plays the note using the current octave and duration via the MicroPython music function, play. There are 10 possible values for a memory location, so the note is modulo 8 to handle cases where the memory value is 8 or 9 by wrapping around to 0 and 1 instead.

With Play, our micro:bit implementation of Firefly is complete. As mentioned earlier, the console version has extra code to handle console cursor positioning, execution tracing, and to capture SIGINT via CTRL-C; please do take a look at how those features are implemented by reading through *firefly.py*, which is the name of the console version of the interpreter.

We're almost ready for some Firefly programming. However, if we're using an actual micro:bit, we should become at least familiar enough with it to configure a speaker and power it up. We'll save programming the micro:bit for Chapter 15. For now, let's take a crash course in micro:bit hardware.

Configuring the Micro:bit

The BBC micro:bit (*https://microbit.org/*) is a small, single-board computer. Out of the box, it runs MicroPython (see the documentation at *https://microbit-micropython.readthedocs.io/en/v2-docs/*). The micro:bit is intended to introduce as many people as possible to programming via an inexpensive computer system. There are two versions available: the older v1 which has 16KB of RAM, and the newer v2 with 128KB of RAM. Both versions are geared toward hardware projects, and a plethora of accessories exist (*https://microbit.org/buy/accessories/*). To learn more about the impressive amount of hardware supported by the micro:bit itself, see *https://tech.microbit.org/hardware/*. Lastly, to learn more about implementing hardware projects with the micro:bit, see Simon Monk's excellent book *Micro:bit for Mad Scientists* (No Starch Press, 2019).

Micro:bit Hardware Overview

Figure 14-3 details the micro:bit and its features.

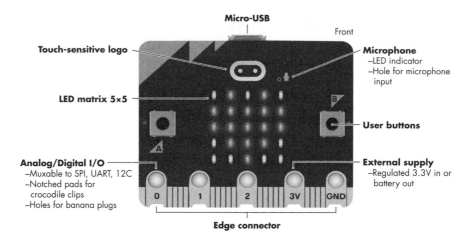

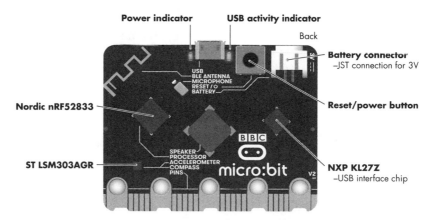

Figure 14-3: A hardware overview of the micro:bit (version 2)

Of primary interest to us is the 5×5 LED display, the speaker, and the Micro-USB connector to program the device. If you have the older version 1 device, there is no built-in speaker. In that case, you'll need to attach an external speaker; see the following section.

The micro:bit comes with a small battery pack for two AAA batteries. However, it runs just fine from the Micro-USB connector when attached to a computer or a 5V power supply. However, early versions of the micro:bit, those before version 1.3B, should not be run from an external 5V supply. If your micro:bit has a speaker, it's good to go. If it doesn't, check the version, which is visible on the back in small print near the right side of the edge connector, to make sure it is at least version 1.3B or 1.5.

Using an External Speaker

Skip this section if your micro:bit is version 2 with a built-in speaker. For version 1 devices, we'll need to add an external speaker, but have no fear: doing so is painless. Let's walk through the process.

First, you need a speaker of some sort. If you have an old speaker from a defunct electronics device, like an old radio, you can use it. In years past, most tinkerers had many such speakers pulled from dead transistor radios. However, in this day and age, it's more likely you don't have a bare speaker lying around. But not all is lost! It turns out that a pair of headphones will work just fine.

The micro:bit edge connector is the interface between the micro:bit and external hardware devices. To connect a speaker, attach one wire to connector 0 (the one with the "0" on it), and the other wire to the connector marked "GND." If using headphones, connect the headphone plug's tip to connector 0 and the part of the plug farthest from the tip to the GND connector. The connections are easiest to make with alligator clips, but if you don't have those handy, bare wires twisted together and wrapped around the connectors going through the holes on the micro:bit will do the trick. Figure 14-4 shows how to connect a generic speaker using alligator clips. The inset shows how to connect headphones.

Figure 14-4: Connecting an external speaker or headphones

Some speakers are marked with plus (+) and minus (−) connections. If so, connect the white wire in Figure 14-4 to the + connection and the red to the − connection. Don't worry if the speaker isn't marked for polarity; it will still work whichever way you connect the wires. For the headphones, the part of the plug farthest from the tip is usually ground, so connect the red wire to it and the white to the tip.

Summary

This chapter introduced us to Firefly, its design, and the rationale behind it. We then walked through the implementation as we'll soon run it on the micro:bit and concluded by configuring the micro:bit for our Firefly experiments. Firefly is about as simple as a programming language gets. Now, let's watch some fireflies and see what they can do.

15

USING FIREFLY

Chapter 14 introduced us to Firefly. Now let's see what we can make it do. First, we'll walk through the environment for building and testing Firefly programs. Then, we'll look at five examples that put Firefly to the test. For the first test, we'll make the firefly count ("Fly Time"). After that, we'll simulate a 1960s sci-fi computer display ("Space Trek"). Then, we'll go high-brow and play some classical music ("Beethoven in Lights"). We'll even experiment with animation effects ("Dance Dance") and end with something useful, a tea timer ("Tea Time"). We'll conclude the chapter with a discussion of Firefly as a programming language.

The Process

There are two versions of the Firefly interpreter: one for the console and one for the micro:bit. Chapter 14 presented the micro:bit version. In this section, we'll walk through developing Firefly programs, testing with the console interpreter, debugging via execution tracing, and deploying code on the micro:bit. The last step is optional for all the examples in the chapter, should you not have a micro:bit handy. However, you won't hear the firefly sing.

The process involves the sequence of steps listed next. Steps 4, 5, and 6 are specific to the micro:bit, so console-only users should stop after Step 3.

1. Write Firefly code, including comments and whitespace, in a text editor.

2. Run the code with the console interpreter, *firefly.py*.

3. Optionally debug the code with execution tracing.

4. Package the debugged program using *fly_dump.py*.

5. Build a micro:bit runtime to bundle the compacted Firefly code with the micro:bit interpreter, *firefly_micro.py*.

6. Transfer the bundled runtime to the micro:bit using the *microbit.org* Python editor, *https://python.microbit.org/v/2/*.

If you plan on using a micro:bit, we'll be using the online Python editor at *https://python.microbit.org/v/2*. It works best with Windows. I used the Microsoft Edge browser and had no trouble at all.

To work with the micro:bit on Linux, I had some success with the Mu editor when using a version 1 micro:bit and the 1.0.2 version of Mu. With later versions of the editor and a version 2 micro:bit, I was only able to get stable functionality from Ubuntu 18.04 when running the editor directly from the GitHub repo at *https://github.com/mu-editor/mu/*. Your mileage may vary.

Figure 15-1 shows the Python editor running on Windows in the Microsoft Edge browser.

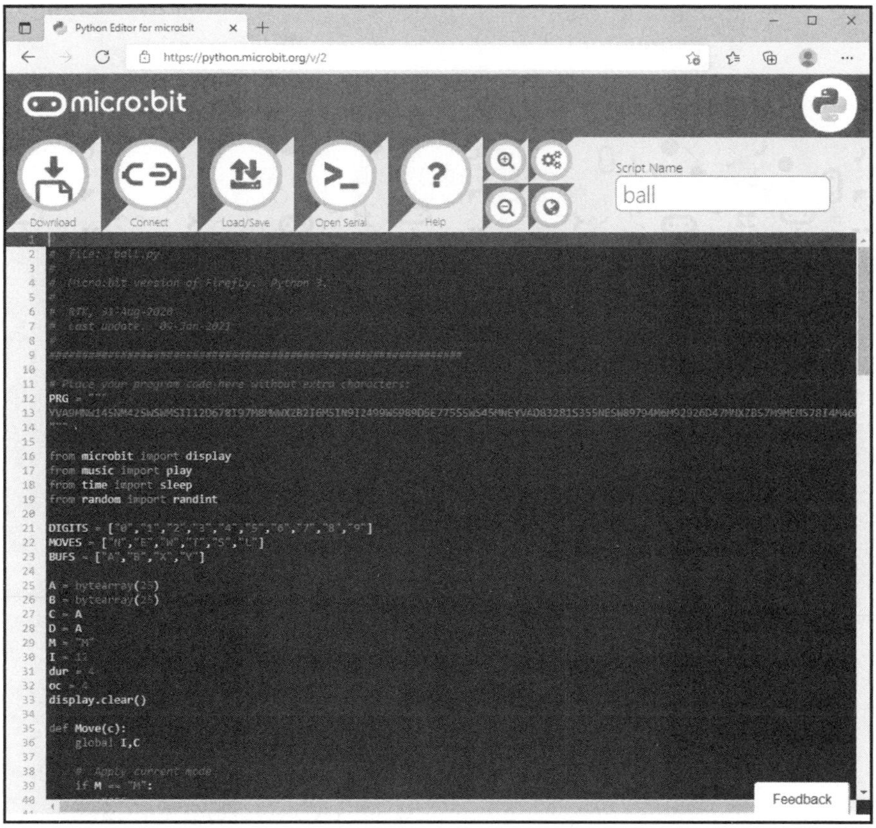

Figure 15-1: The Python editor for micro:bit

Note that the book's GitHub site contains short videos showing the code running on a micro:bit. Please take a look, especially if you do not intend to use the micro:bit yourself.

Writing Firefly Code

Our first example is the Firefly equivalent of "Hello, world!" The program draws the letters HI on the screen. The source code is in *hi.fly* in the *firefly/console/examples* directory (see Listing 15-1).

```
MNNWW5   ! move mode, go to (0,0), intensity 5
SSS      ! left side of the "H"
MNN5     ! up to (1,0)
EEE      ! crossbar of the "H"
MNW      ! move to (0,2)
5SSS     ! right side of the "H"
MEEN     ! move to (0,4)
5NNN     ! "I"
L        ! loop
```

Listing 15-1: "Hello, world!" in Firefly

The first line of *hi.fly* ensures move mode (no trail) and moves the firefly from its initial (2,2) position to the upper-left corner, (0,0). The mode is then set to intensity 5.

The next line moves south three spaces to draw the left side of the H. At this point, the firefly is at position (3,0), so switching to move mode and going north twice puts the firefly at (1,0). Setting the mode to 5 and moving east three times draws the crossbar of the H. The next two lines finish the H and MEEN moves to (2,4). From (2,4), setting the mode to 5 and moving north three times draws the I, ending with the firefly at position (4,4). The L instruction loops forever to preserve the "HI" display on the micro:bit.

Using the Console Interpreter

To execute Listing 15-1, we need the console interpreter. Run the code with

```
> python3 firefly.py examples/hi.fly
```

to produce

```
    5   5   5
    5 5 5   5
    5   5   5
```

The 5×5 display is indented four spaces and one space is printed between each digit. By default, *firefly.py* shows 0 intensity as a space. Adding the -z command line option shows 0 intensity as 0s

```
    5 0 5 0 5
    5 5 5 0 5
    5 0 5 0 5
    0 0 0 0 0
    0 0 0 0 0
```

where we now see the full 5×5 grid.

Next, step through *hi.fly* by adding the -t (trace) command line option:

```
> python3 firefly.py examples/hi.fly -t
```

In trace mode, an instruction is executed and the display is updated; then, before execution of the next instruction, the interpreter shows a status line and waits for the user to press ENTER or Q to quit the program. For example, running *hi.fly* in trace mode presents us with

```
I=(2,2)(12), SHOW=A, DRAW=A, M=M, INST=M
```

which tells us that the last instruction executed was M (set move mode). This is the INST part of the status line. The rest of the status line is described as follows:

Instruction	Explanation
I=(2,2)(12)	The firefly is at (2,2) (index 12)
SHOW=A	Grid A is currently visible
DRAW=A	Grid A is currently drawn to
M=M	Move mode is "M"

The index is into the bytearray of the currently active memory grid.

Pressing ENTER moves us to

```
I=(1,2)( 7), SHOW=A, DRAW=A, M=M, INST=N
```

which informs us that the firefly is now at position (1,2) (index 7) because a "move north" instruction was executed.

Continuing to press ENTER traces through the entire program.

```
I=(0,2)( 2), SHOW=A, DRAW=A, M=M, INST=N
I=(0,1)( 1), SHOW=A, DRAW=A, M=M, INST=W
I=(0,0)( 0), SHOW=A, DRAW=A, M=M, INST=W
I=(0,0)( 0), SHOW=A, DRAW=A, M=5, INST=5
I=(1,0)( 5), SHOW=A, DRAW=A, M=5, INST=S
I=(2,0)(10), SHOW=A, DRAW=A, M=5, INST=S
I=(3,0)(15), SHOW=A, DRAW=A, M=5, INST=S
--snip--
```

We continue to the L instruction, which throws us into an infinite loop. Use CTRL-C to exit the loop.

We have a working program. Let's now bundle it to run on the micro:bit.

Packing a Bundle

We can't use *hi.fly* as-is with the micro:bit version of Firefly because we first need to strip the comments and whitespace. We could do this manually, but why bother when we already have a utility to do it for us? In the same console directory as *firefly.py* is *fly_dump.py*. Let's run it to get a single-string version of *hi.fly*.

```
> python3 fly_dump.py examples/hi.fly ../micro/examples/hi.fly
```

The first argument is the console version of the code with comments and whitespace. The second is the output, which in this case is sent to the *examples* directory of the micro:bit version in *micro*. The output generated is

```
MNNWW5SSSMNN5EEEMNW5SSSMEEN5NNNL
```

This version of the code still runs in the console interpreter. Give it a try and see for yourself.

To make the micro:bit bundle, we'll need to complete the following steps:

1. Copy *firefly_micro.py* to *hi.py*.
2. Edit *hi.py* and update *PRG* to be the text in *micro/examples/hi.fly*.
3. Run the Python editor and load *hi.py*.
4. Attach the micro:bit via USB.
5. Program the micro:bit from the online Python editor.

Steps 1 and 2 mean that bundles are copies of the micro:bit version of the interpreter edited to contain the compacted Firefly code. The default *firefly_micro.py* file begins with

```
PRG = """
1TJ0TITFTFTFTFTFTFTF5TG8TJ1TFH
"""
```

which becomes

```
PRG = """
MNNWW7SSSMNN7EEEMNW7SSSMEEN7NNNL
"""
```

This embeds the code in *hi.py*. The remainder of *hi.py* is the same as the interpreter code of Chapter 15.

To program the micro:bit, first run the editor in Microsoft Edge by opening *https://python.microbit.org/v/2/*. Then, connect the micro:bit's Micro-USB port to the computer's USB port. The micro:bit will likely automount. If so, just close any Explorer window that opens.

Next, connect to the micro:bit by clicking **Connect** and selecting the micro:bit from the resulting dialog. The micro:bit is present and working if you see a string similar to "'BBC micro:bit CMSIS-DAP' – Paired." Select the micro:bit and click **Connect**.

Next, open *hi.py* by clicking **Load/Save** followed by **Download** to program the micro:bit. Programming takes a few seconds. When complete, the program starts immediately producing Figure 15-2.

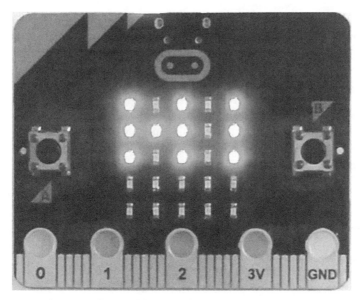

Figure 15-2: "Hello, world!" micro:bit style

Did you notice something when the program ran? Rerun it by pressing the reset button beneath the micro:bit.

If you are using a version 1 micro:bit, you'll see the message draw on the screen from left to right. The *hi.fly* program moves the firefly on grid A while showing grid A, so we see each instruction's effect. Later in the chapter, we'll adjust *hi.fly* to use double buffering (see "Space Trek" below).

The remainder of this chapter walks through each example's code, running it on the console when applicable and then running the code on the micro:bit. In each case, program the micro:bit as we did here: use *fly_dump.py* to strip comments and whitespace, paste the compacted Firefly program text into a suitably renamed copy of *firefly_micro.py*, and load the copy onto the micro:bit via the Python editor. Don't forget to take a look at the micro:bit videos on the book's GitHub site as well.

Let's put our firefly to work.

Fly Time

The P instruction pauses the program for 0.1 seconds. Therefore, PPPPPPPPPP pauses the program for one second. Let's use this as the basis for a counter/timer. Our goal is a Firefly program that counts seconds, up to 1,000, before rolling over and starting again. Firefly lacks any looping mechanism other than starting a program from the beginning after it ends; therefore, we need to design our program so that looping from the beginning starts the counter again from 0.

If 10 P instructions give a one-second pause, then PPPPPPPPPPT pauses for one second before "moving" the firefly by remaining in place. If the mode is I (increment), the net effect is a one-second pause before incrementing the current firefly position. Repeat the one-second pause 10 times with T after each pause, and we have a 10-second timer.

To count, we increment the ones digit until it rolls over back to 0 and then increment the tens digit by 1. We can use this approach with the one-second timer to build a two-digit timer by moving from the current firefly position, the ones position, over to the left and incrementing, and then moving back and repeating for another 10 seconds.

This thought suggests a set of repeated instructions. The program begins with the firefly at position (2,2). Let's use position (0,4) for the ones and position (0,3) for the tens. Consider the sequence of instructions shown in Listing 15-2.

```
NNEE                ! move to (0,4)
I                   ! increment mode
PPPPPPPPPPT         ! 1 second and increment
PPPPPPPPPPT         !
PPPPPPPPPPT         !
PPPPPPPPPPT         !
PPPPPPPPPPT         !
PPPPPPPPPPT         !
PPPPPPPPPPT         !
PPPPPPPPPPT         !
PPPPPPPPPPT         !
PPPPPPPPPPT         !
MWIT                ! move over 1 and increment
MEI                 ! move back, set increment mode
```

Listing 15-2: A 10-second timer

The first line moves the firefly from (2,2) to (0,4), which is the ones position. The second line sets the mode to increment. Next comes a one-second delay followed by a "tick" to increment the ones position. Nine more one-second delays finish the 10-second delay, and the ones position has moved from 0 up through 9 and back to 0.

The line MWIT moves one position to the left, to (0,3), and increments the tens position by 1. Let's break the steps down: M sets move mode (no trail), W moves left one position, I sets increment mode, and T increments position (0,3). The block of steps ends with MEI to move back to (0,4), the ones position, which is currently 0 because it rolled over, followed by I to reassert increment mode.

Listing 15-2 counts for 10 seconds. If Listing 15-2 is repeated nine more times, except for the top two lines, NNEE and I, which set up the initial firefly position and mode, we'll have a 100-second timer.

The file *fly_time.fly* in *console/examples* contains the code we need. Most of the code is repeated blocks like Listing 15-2. However, the 10th block ends with Listing 15-3.

```
PPPPPPPPPPT          ! 1 second and increment
MWIT                 ! move over 1 and increment
MWIT                 ! move over 1 more and increment
MEEI                 ! move back, set increment mode
```

Listing 15-3: End of the 10th timer block

The last one-second pause and an increment happens, followed by `MWIT` to move from (0,4) to (0,3) and increment the tens value. As this is the 10th block, the tens value has rolled over from 9 back to 0. So a second `MWIT` moves from (0,3) to (0,2), the hundreds position, and increments it.

This last step completes a counter from 0 to 100. If the firefly moves back to (0,4) and the program loops by starting over, the display will still read 1 0 0. The final line is `MEEI` to move back to (0,4) and set increment mode. As there is no H or L instruction, the program begins again.

Note that when the program loops, the display memory is preserved, but the firefly is warped back to its initial position of (2,2). However, this is what we want. The first instructions in *fly_time.fly* tell the firefly to move to (0,4), which is just where we need it to be to count another 100 seconds.

The hundreds position, (0,2), is incremented again after another 100 seconds, leaving the display at 2 0 0. Another 100 seconds later, the display is 3 0 0. This continues to 1,000 seconds, after which the display rolls over to all 0s. We don't increment the thousands position, but the program continues to loop until we hit CTRL-C, so the 1,000-second counter begins again, over and over.

Run *fly_time.fly* with the console interpreter using -z to show 0 memory as 0s.

```
> python3 firefly.py examples/fly_time.fly -z
```

The program counts until you hit CTRL-C. By starting the program at the beginning of an interval, and using CTRL-C to stop the program at the end of an interval, we have a primitive stopwatch—geeky to be sure, but functional.

This example makes use of the only looping available to Firefly: restarting the program. It is naturally designed for the console so we can read the time directly as a number, but nothing stops you from running this code on the micro:bit. If you do, you'll see sequences of increasingly bright LEDs. If you are like me, you'll see the LEDs change and understand that the program is counting up, but not be able to reliably tell the difference between an LED that is at, say, brightness 3 versus one at brightness 4.

Of course, *fly_time.fly* is counting in base-10; however, there is no reason why other bases couldn't be used. If we used binary, then the micro:bit would work nicely. Or perhaps we could use base-3, with LED intensities of 0, 5, and 9 to make the distinction between digits clear. Changing the base changes the repeated code block used, but the general idea remains the same. Instead of ones (10^0), tens (10^1), and hundreds positions (10^2), we would use ones (3^0), threes (3^1), nines (3^2), and possibly twenty-sevens positions (3^3).

We'll implement a different sort of timer later in the chapter, but for now, let's learn how to use Firefly's double buffering for animations.

Space Trek

We've mentioned Firefly's double buffering several times now. Let's see it in action. The examples in this section work best on the micro:bit. Depending on your machine's speed, you might see some effect when using the console interpreter; however, it's most noticeable on the micro:bit.

Earlier in the chapter, we played around with *hi.fly* and commented that since we are showing grid A while drawing on grid A, we see the letters as they're drawn. A simple modification uses double buffering to present the letters to us only after being drawn. The code we need is in *hi2.fly* under *console/examples*.

Listing 15-4 presents the updated code. The only difference between Listing 15-4 and Listing 15-1 is the first line, Y, and the second-to-last line, X.

```
Y        ! show grid B, drawing on A
MNNWW5   ! move mode, go to (0,0), intensity to 5
SSS      ! left side of the "H"
MNN5     ! up to (1,0)
EEE      ! crossbar of the "H"
MNW      ! move to (0,2)
5SSS     ! right side of the "H"
MEEN     ! move to (0,4)
5NNN     ! "I"
X        ! now show grid A
L        ! loop
```

Listing 15-4: "HI" with double buffering

We show grid A and draw to it. Executing Y shows grid B, which is empty, while still drawing to grid A. The letters are drawn as before, but the user does not see it because grid B is shown. When the letters are finished, X shows grid A again, and L enters the loop to preserve the micro:bit display.

Bundle *hi2.fly* and load it on the micro:bit. When it runs, instead of watching the letters draw, you'll see nothing until the complete word HI suddenly appears. If you run *hi2.fly* in the console using the -t option, you'll notice HI suddenly appear as well.

Listing 15-4 is a bare-minimum example of double buffering. The core concept of double buffering is to show grid B while updating grid A and then switch and show grid A while updating grid B. We repeat this as necessary so that the user never views a grid as it is being drawn.

Let's see a slightly more interesting example where we simulate the random "computer" displays often seen in the background of 1960s sci-fi shows. First, we'll generate the display live, without double buffering. Then we'll change the code to use double buffering. The difference between the two is visibly clear; however, to be honest, both approaches are pretty cool to watch.

Listing 15-5 generates random displays without double buffering.

WWNN	! move to (0,0)
R	! set random mode
EEEES	! random row 0
WWWWS	! random row 1
EEEES	! random row 2
WWWWS	! random row 3
EEEES	! random row 4

Listing 15-5: Random computer lights

The first line moves to (0,0), the upper-left corner of the display. Recall that not only does the firefly start at position (2,2), it also starts in "move" mode (M) so there is no trail. The second line sets the mode to "random" (R).

The third line moves east from (0,0) four times. Each move sets the previous position to a random intensity. After the last move east, the firefly is at position (0,4), so a move south sets position (0,4) to a random intensity and puts the firefly at position (1,4).

To fill in the second row of the display, we'll need four moves to the west followed by a move south to end up at the beginning of the third row. This zig-zag continues through the remaining rows until the final S moves the firefly to (0,4). A final move then sets the last LED at (4,4).

There is no halt instruction, so the program loops after filling the display. The firefly is reset to (2,2), immediately moved to (0,0), and the grid is drawn again from top to bottom. Therefore, the display is overwritten continuously, row by row, with the previous set of random intensities still present.

The console interpreter is too fast to see the overwriting effect, but running *random.fly* on the micro:bit makes it visible, though just barely. Even on the micro:bit, the code is almost too fast. The effect is mesmerizing. Unfortunately, there is no way to capture the effect in a still image in a book. To see the effect, do view the videos on the GitHub site.

Instead of overwriting the display one row at a time, we can introduce double buffering and display a full grid of random intensities while generating the next grid, then flip and display that grid, and so on.

Listing 15-6 shows us *random2.fly*.

B	! draw on B, showing A
WWNN	! move to (0,0)
R	! set random mode
EEEES	! random row 0
WWWWS	! random row 1
EEEES	! random row 2
WWWWS	! random row 3
EEEES	! random row 4, end at (4,0)
M	! move mode
NNNN	! move to (0,0)
YA	! show B, draw on A

```
R              ! set random mode
EEEES          ! random row 0
WWWWS          ! random row 1
EEEES          ! random row 2
WWWWS          ! random row 3
EEEES          ! random row 4, end at (4,0)
X              ! show A
```

Listing 15-6: Random computer lights with double buffering

The code is in two distinct blocks. The first block is nearly identical to Listing 15-5 except for the addition of a leading B instruction to tell the firefly to make trails on grid B even though grid A is being shown. At the bottom of the first block, after the entirety of grid B is updated, come M and NNNN to set move mode and then move back to (0,0).

The second block of code now takes over. First, YA shows grid B, the grid the first block of code just filled with random intensities, and switches to drawing trails on grid A. The next six lines fill grid A and the final instruction is X to show grid A.

At this point, the program loops and begins again, filling grid B. The final X has us looking at grid A, just as we do when a Firefly program begins, so the sequence repeats: show A, draw on B, show B, draw on A, and repeat forever.

Unlike Listing 15-5, which constantly overwrites the one grid shown, Listing 15-6 ping-pongs between the two grids, so the user only sees the grid that was most recently filled and never the grid actively being drawn to. The effect is perhaps even more like the old sci-fi movies. There is no flow from top to bottom and the intensities change seemingly at once.

Beethoven in Lights

I claimed in Chapter 14 that our firefly knows how to sing. Let's prove it now by writing some music in Firefly. Of course, without an actual micro:bit, console-only runs of the examples in this section will be disappointing. Have no fear! You can always listen to the song via the videos included on the book's GitHub site.

Firefly supports playing notes in the key of C. Middle C (the default) is octave 4, and middle C itself is note 1. Therefore, the simplest way to play a note in Firefly is to execute 1TF, which sets the intensity to 1, "ticks" to update the default firefly position of (2,2), and plays with the default duration of a quarter note. The code loops, of course, and after a brief pause for reset, the note plays again. The result is a dim LED in the middle of the grid followed by buzzing at the pitch of middle C, over and over and over until you cut the power. Still, it's impressive to get sound from a three-character program.

A slightly longer program does sound fun and a bit outer space-ish: 1TJRTF. First, it sets the note duration to 1, which is one-quarter of a quarter note (a sixteenth note). Then it sets the note itself to a random note and plays it. Visually, the higher the pitch, the brighter the LED. The R instruction sets positions to a random value in the range $[1, 9]$. However, you'll notice pauses while the random melody plays. If the random value is 8, it acts as note 0, which is a rest. For fun, experiment with two slightly different versions: RTJRTF and OTJRTF. The first makes the note duration random as well, and the second sets the duration to 0, causing a staccato effect.

We'll get to Beethoven in time, but before we do, Listing 15-7 shows us how to play an actual scale.

```
1TJ     ! set note duration
OTI     ! set first note and increment mode
TF      ! increment and play note
TF      ! increment and play note
TF      ! increment and play note
TF      ! increment and play note
TF      ! increment and play note
TF      ! increment and play note
TF      ! increment and play note
5TG     ! set octave to 5 (default is 4)
8TJ     ! set duration
1TF     ! play note 1 of octave 5
H       ! halt
```

Listing 15-7: A simple C-major scale

The first line sets the duration to 1, as we did with the random melody. Next, we set the note to 0 and the mode to increment. Then, TF increments to 1 and plays the note (middle C). The next TF increments to 2 and plays D. This repeats for notes E through B.

To play the C one octave above middle C, we need to update the octave with 5TG, remembering that middle C is octave 4. Lastly, 8TG sets the duration to a half note (8) and plays the first note of octave 5 before halting.

The scale plays quickly, but there is a distinct pause before the final note plays. In this case, it adds a bit of dramatic effect, but in reality, the pause is an artifact of how slowly the micro:bit interprets Firefly instructions. There are eight instructions between playing the second-to-last note, B, and the last note, C. Interpreting these eight instructions causes the pause you hear.

Let's get classical. We want code to make the firefly "sing" Beethoven's *Ode to Joy* (see Figure 15-3).

$\quad = 120$

Figure 15-3: Beethoven's Ode to Joy

Instead of simply playing the notes in one place, wouldn't it be nice if the firefly displayed the notes as it played them? S- along with singing, we want the firefly to show us the notes in lights on the display.

There are 30 notes in Figure 15-3, split into two musical phrases of 15 notes each. There are five LEDs per row on the micro:bit display. How convenient for us. We'll show the notes, one per position, using the first three rows of LEDs to cover a 15-note phrase. Then, we'll clear the screen and repeat the process for the remaining 15 notes. The code we need is in *ode.fly*.

Let's walk through the code by musical phrase. The first phrase is in Listing 15-8.

```
NNWW      ! move to (0,0)
3TFE      ! E
3TFE      ! E
4TFE      ! F
5TFE      ! G
5TFEMS    ! G
4TFE      ! F
3TFE      ! E
2TFE      ! D
1TFE      ! C
1TFEMS    ! C
2TFE      ! D
3TFE      ! E
3TFE      ! E
2TFE      ! D
B8TJ      ! draw on B, showing A
A2TF      ! draw on A, D8
```

Listing 15-8: Ode to Joy, first phrase

By default, the octave is that of middle C, and the duration matches a quarter note, so we need not change the duration or octave. We want the notes displayed as they play, row by row, so we first move the firefly to position (0,0). The next line sets up a pattern we'll repeat for each note. For example, 3TFE sets the current position to 3 (3T) and plays the note (F) before moving one position to the east (E). This pattern of instructions is used for every note of the piece.

The next four notes, E-F-G-G, finish the first row and leave the firefly back at position (0,0). To get to the next row, we use MS to move south to (1,0) without changing the current value of (0,0). The notes of the second row play next, F-E-D-C-C, before moving to the third row.

The first four notes of row 3 play: D-E-E-D. Then, we change the duration from quarter notes to half notes. If we make the change directly, we'll upset the display, as we need to set a position to 8 for the J instruction. So we tell the firefly to draw on grid B, which is not displayed, and set the duration that way before switching back to drawing on grid A and playing the note: A2TF. The first phrase is now complete.

Listing 15-9 plays the second phrase.

```
CB4TJA  ! clear A, draw on B, set duration, draw on A
MNNE    ! back to (0,0)
3TFE    ! E
3TFE    ! E
4TFE    ! F
5TFE    ! G
5TFEMS  ! G
4TFE    ! F
3TFE    ! E
2TFE    ! D
1TFE    ! C
1TFEMS  ! C
2TFE    ! D
3TFE    ! E
2TFE    ! D
1TFE    ! C
B8TJ    ! draw on B, showing A
A1TF    ! draw on A, C8
H       !
```

Listing 15-9: Ode to Joy, second phrase

Listing 15-9 is much the same as Listing 15-8 except for the first line. That line clears the display, grid A, switches to grid B to reset the duration to 4, and then goes back to drawing on grid A. The next line moves the firefly to (0,0), and the second phrase plays just as the first did. After the final note, the program executes H to end.

Naturally, we must run this program on the micro:bit, but you can play the associated video to see how it goes if you don't have one. It would be straightforward to copy this technique to play other melodies, though we were fortunate that *Ode to Joy* consists of two distinct musical phrases of exactly 15 notes and thus fits perfectly on the 5×5 display.

If you watch the melody play, you'll see how the LED intensity is related to the pitch of the note; higher notes are brighter, at least within the same octave.

Dance Dance

Now let's use Firefly's double-buffering abilities to do a bit of animation with music. We'll begin with the animation and add the music later.

Our goal is to make a simple figure "dance." With a 5×5 display, the emphasis is definitely on the word *simple*. Each stance of the figure is a display. To make the animation, we'll use double buffering and a collection of independent stances. We'll proceed by defining the stances in code, putting them together in an animation, and adding the dance music. Our firefly will be quite the busy flier for this example.

The Stances

We'll make the firefly trace the figure for each stance beginning and ending at position (2,2). This allows us to string the stances together in any order that we wish and be in the proper position when the program loops and begins again.

We will begin with Stance 1. As the figure dances, each move returns to Stance 1 before moving on to the next. Listing 15-10 shows the code for Stance 1 along with the stance itself.

MNN5	!	
SSSMW	!	5
5SS	!	55555
MNNEE	!	5
5SS	!	5 5
MSE	!	5 5
5WWWWW	!	
MWWS	!	

Listing 15-10: Stance 1

With a bit of imagination, you'll see a figure with outstretched arms. To make the figure dance, we'll move the arms and legs in sequence. We can move both arms up or down, or move one up and the other down. Similarly, we can move the right leg out or the left leg out for a total of six possible stances. Table 15-1 gives us the code and the appearance of each stance.

Table 15-1: The Remaining Stances

Stance 2			Stance 3			Stance 4		
MNN5	!		MNN5	!		MNN5	!	
SSSMW	!	5 5	SSSMW	!	5 5	SSSMW	!	5 5 5
5SS	!	555	5SS	!	555	5SS	!	555
MNNEE	!	5 5	MNNEE	!	5 5	MNNEE	!	5
5SS	!	5 5	5SS	!	5 5	5SSME	!	5 5
ME5SMW	!	5 5	MEE5E	!	5 5	5EEMS	!	5 5
5WWW	!		MS5EEE	!		5EEE	!	
MS5E	!		MS5W	!		MSWW	!	
ME	!		MW	!				

Stance 5			Stance 6			Stance 7		
MNN5	!		5NNE	!		5NNE	!	
SSSMW	!	5	MES	!	5	MES	!	5
5SS	!	555	5WWWWS	!	55555	5WWWWS	!	55555
MNNEE	!	5 5 5	MSS	!	5	MSE	!	5
5SSMS	!	5 5	5EMN	!	5 5	5SE	!	5 5
5WWW	!	5 5	5EME	!	5 5	MEE5N	!	5 5
MS5E	!		5SS	!		MW5N	!	
MEEE	!		MWSS	!		MW	!	
5WMW	!							

While developing this example, it was extremely helpful to use the console interpreter in trace mode. I first generated the code for each stance independently of the others. We'll see below how this helps create the desired animation sequence by literally copying and pasting code in the right place.

The Dance

To animate the figure, we start with Stance 1, and after each move go back to Stance 1. The sequence is

$$1 \rightarrow 2 \rightarrow 1 \rightarrow 3 \rightarrow 1 \rightarrow 4 \rightarrow 1 \rightarrow 5 \rightarrow 1 \rightarrow 6 \rightarrow 1 \rightarrow 7$$

where we end with Stance 7 and allow the program to loop to begin again with Stance 1.

Look carefully at the sequence of stances and think of Firefly's double buffers. When the program starts, we're looking at grid A and the firefly is drawing to grid A. We'll draw Stance 1 in grid A, but doing that will let the user see the firefly draw, so we'll show grid B while drawing Stance 1. Likewise, when the firefly has drawn Stance 1 in grid A, we'll show grid A and tell the firefly to draw in grid B. Then, we'll render Stance 2 in grid B.

At this point, we might be tempted to draw Stance 1 in grid A; however, Stance 1 is already in grid A, so we don't need to draw it again. This is why the figure always returns to Stance 1 before moving to another stance—we can leave Stance 1 in grid A and only draw it once. When we need to draw a new stance, we'll do it in grid B while showing Stance 1 in grid A.

Therefore, to animate, we need the following sequence, formatted as (*shown,drawn*):

$$(B, A) \rightarrow (A, B) \rightarrow (B, *) \rightarrow (A, B) \rightarrow (B, *) \rightarrow (A, B) \rightarrow$$
$$(B, *) \rightarrow (A, B) \rightarrow (B, *) \rightarrow (A, B) \rightarrow (B, *) \rightarrow (A, B)$$

Here, $*$ means we don't change the grid drawn to as we're showing Stance 1, which never needs to be redrawn. At each step in the sequence, save the first, the grid shown reveals the most recently drawn stance (or Stance 1).

Listing 15-11 presents the animation code in skeleton form to show the sequence of stances drawn and how the different grids are displayed and drawn to. To generate the actual code, replace instances of "draw Stance 1" and so on with the proper code block from Table 15-1 or Listing 15-10.

```
YVA      ! show B, clear A, draw A
... draw Stance 1 ...
PPPPP
XZB      ! show A, clear B, draw B
... draw Stance 2 ...
PPPPP
Y        ! show B
PPPPP    ! pause
XZB      ! show A, clear B, draw B
... draw Stance 3 ...
```

```
PPPPP
Y        ! show B
PPPPP
XZB      ! show A, clear B, draw B
... draw Stance 4 ...
PPPPP
Y        ! show B
PPPPP
XZB      ! show A, clear B, draw B
... draw Stance 5 ...
PPPPP
Y        ! show B
PPPPP
XZB      ! show A, clear B, draw B
... draw Stance 6 ...
PPPPP
Y        ! show B
PPPPP
XZB      ! show A, clear B, draw B
... draw Stance 7 ...
PPPPP
```

Listing 15-11: Animation sequence code skeleton

The PPPPP blocks delay for 0.5 seconds to control the speed of the animation. These are also the locations where we'll later add music. To watch the animation without music, execute *dance.fly*.

The Music

Let's add some music. The melody we'll use was kindly written for us by film and television composer Paul Kneusel (see Figure 15-4).

Figure 15-4: "Dance dance" by Paul Kneusel (https://www.paulkneusel.com/)

Translating the score into Firefly code leads to Listing 15-12.

```
!  first measure
5TG4TJ1TF 2TJ1TF 4TG1TJ6TF 5TG1TF 2TJ0TF 5TG1TF 1TF4TG2TJ 6TF

!  second measure
4TJ5TF 2TJ5TF 1TJ3TF 5TF 2TJ0TF 5TF6TF 5TF

!  third measure
4TJ4TF 2TJ4TF 1TJ3TF2TF 2TJ0TF 4TF 3TF 2TF
```

```
!  fourth measure
4TJ5TF  3TG1TJ5TF  6TF  0TF  4TG1TF  0TF  2TF  0TF  3TF  2TJ2TF  1TF
```

Listing 15-12: "Dance dance" in Firefly

You can hear the melody by loading *dance_loop.fly* onto the micro:bit or by watching the video on the GitHub site. The music plays in place, so the center LED on the micro:bit fluctuates in brightness as the melody plays.

To complete this section, we'll merge the melody with the animation code. Listing 15-11 has pauses between screens, PPPPP. For the musical version, we'll replace the pauses with successive measures from the melody, so the first instance of PPPPP in Listing 15-11 is replaced by the first measure of Listing 15-12 and so on. The result is *dance_music.fly*. We won't show the code here, but do read through it.

If you run *dance_music.fly*, you'll hear the first measure as a sort of intro before the animation. There are noticeable pauses while successive screens are rendered in the buffer not shown, but the tune and animation still work.

Tea Time

There is no general agreement as to how long one should steep a cup of tea, but a rule of thumb I often use is about three and a half minutes for a cup of black tea. In this section, we'll use Firefly to write a tea timer that runs for about three and a half minutes. Once you see the pattern, you'll be able to adjust the delay to suit your tastes.

The timer counts down a display of LEDs. When the countdown is complete, the program animates the display while playing an alarm sound to let us know our tea is ready. This example is practical enough to make it worth dedicating an entire micro:bit to the task. Just put your teabag in the hot water, start the micro:bit, and wait for the visual and audio alarm to sound—your tea is now ready.

The source code is in *tea_timer.fly*. The program fills the first four rows of the display with maximum intensity. Then, starting with position (0,0), the program dims the LEDs by 1 after a one-second delay. When the LED at the current position is 0, the program moves to the next position and repeats. LED after LED is dimmed to 0 this way until all four rows are 0. After the display is completely 0, a brief animation of star patterns plays along with a rapid scale as the audio alarm.

Filling four rows of the display means we have 20 LEDs to dim. Each LED takes 10 seconds to go from maximum intensity to 0; therefore, dimming the display takes

$$20 \text{ LED} \times 10 \text{ second/LED} = 200 \text{ seconds}$$
$$= 3 \text{ minutes } 20 \text{ seconds}$$

The animation and alarm add a few more seconds to give us an approximate three-and-a-half minute timer.

The timer starts by filling the first four rows of grid A with 9s (see Listing 15-13).

```
Y        ! show B while setting up the screen
WWNN     ! move from (2,2) to (0,0)
9        ! full power
EEEES    ! first row
WWWWS    ! second row
EEEES    ! third row
WWWWS    ! fourth row, at (4,0)
M        ! move mode
NNNN     ! move to (0,0)
XD       ! screen ready, show A, decrement mode
```

Listing 15-13: Filling the display

To avoid watching the display draw, grid B is shown until the first four rows of grid A are full, and then grid A is shown again after moving the firefly to position (0,0).

The countdown now begins. Here's where the simplicity of Firefly pains us a bit. The pattern we need to implement is

```
for r in 0..3:
    for c in 0..4:
        for i in 0..9:
            wait one second
            M[r,c] = M[r,c] - 1
```

Here, M is the micro:bit display, grid A. It would be nice to have some sort of looping construct, but Firefly is too primitive to support looping, so we need to unroll the loops and manually decrement each position to 0 before moving to the next position and then repeat, row by row.

Fortunately, once we have a pattern in place for the current position, we have what we need for virtually all the positions in a row. Once we have all we need for a row, we have what we need for all four rows. So unrolling the loops isn't too bad and is relatively straightforward with the help of some copy-and-paste magic.

For example, to process the first column of the first row, meaning position (0,0), we need

```
PPPPPPPPPPT ! show for one second, decrement
PPPPPPPPPPT
PPPPPPPPPPT
PPPPPPPPPPT
PPPPPPPPPPT
PPPPPPPPPPT
PPPPPPPPPPT
PPPPPPPPPPT
PPPPPPPPPPT
PPPPPPPPPP  ! show for one second
MED         ! move to the next column, restore decrement
```

The first line pauses for one second, then uses T to decrement the current position without moving. This changes intensity 9 to intensity 8. Repeating this process eight more times results in intensity 0 at (0,0). We need to wait one more second for the 0 intensity before moving to the next column with MED. We are now at position (0,1) and ready to repeat this code block. We do the same for positions (0,2), (0,3), and (0,4).

At the end of position (0,4), we need to move to the next row. So instead of executing MED, we execute MESD to arrive at (1,0). The entire process repeats for row 1, row 2, and row 3. However, at the end of row 3, the timer portion is complete and all of grid A is empty. We conclude by moving to (2,2) via MWWN so we are in position to begin the animation and alarm.

The animation is straightforward: two star patterns, with one stored on each grid. We'll toggle between them while playing the alarm. Listing 15-14 shows the code.

```
YA          ! show memory B, draw on A
7EM         ! (2,2) = 7
N5W         ! (1,3) = 5
MW5W        ! (1,1) = 5
MN3EM       ! (0,0) = 3
EEE3S       ! (0,4) = 3
MSSS3W      ! (4,4) = 3
MWWW3N      ! (4,0) = 3
ME5E        ! (3,1) = 5
ME5E        ! (3,3) = 5
MNWW        ! at (2,2)

XB          ! show memory A, draw on B
7E5E3S      ! (2,2)=7, (2,3)=5, (2,4)=3
MWW5W       ! (3,2)=5
MN5W3N      ! (2,1)=5, (2,0)=3
MEE5N       ! (1,2)=5
3E          ! (0,2)=3
MSSSSW      !
3W          ! (4,2)=3
MNNE        ! to (2,2)
1TJI        ! set duration and note
Y           ! show memory B

PTFXPTFYPTFX  ! animate for ~2 seconds
PTFYPTFXPTFY  ! while playing the scale
PTFXPTFYPTFX
PTFXPTFYPTFX
PTFYPTFXPTFY
PTFXPTFYPTFX
AC            ! showing A, work with A, clear
H
```

Listing 15-14: Animation and alarm code

There are three code blocks. The first generates an X shape on grid A and the second displays a + shape on grid B. The last block toggles between grids A and B while playing a scale over and over. Note that the firefly is at position (2,2), so the center pixel on both grids changes as the animation happens. When complete, the program exits, and our tea is ready.

The tea timer concludes our Firefly examples. There is one more, using genetic programming to evolve Firefly programs, but its complexity requires moving it to Appendix 16. Do take a look. The examples of this chapter are fun and whimsical. The example in Appendix 16 demonstrates a more sophisticated way to use even the tiniest of esolangs.

Discussion

Firefly is most definitely *not* Turing complete. We learned in Chapter 3 that a Turing complete imperative programming language requires some form of conditional branching and arbitrary memory. Firefly has no branching, conditional or otherwise, and minimal memory; therefore, Firefly is not Turing complete and not able to implement, even in theory, arbitrary algorithms.

However, as the examples of this chapter demonstrate, Firefly does support useful programs. We created a counter suitable for timing things in the real world. We also created a timer for steeping tea and programs to play music. Even the random sci-fi backgrounds are useful, if desired: imagine a wall of micro:bits each running *random.fly* or *random2.fly* and built into a prop.

Is Firefly all it could be? Definitely not. The micro:bit has two pushbuttons for user input, but Firefly ignores them. And this says nothing about all the many other advanced features the micro:bit supports. One reason for making Firefly primitive was the limited memory of the version 1 micro:bit. Another was the need for simplicity in the presentation via a physical book. Firefly is screaming for enhancement. I genuinely hope a reader or two accepts the challenge and enhances the language. If you do, please share it with us. Part of the fun of esoteric programming languages is how they build upon each other—just witness the many variants of BF. One language's ideas prompt new thoughts about languages and lead to "what if" ideas, which lead to new esolangs.

Summary

In this chapter, we presented many examples of Firefly programs. Some were trivial, like *hi.fly*, and others were visually appealing, like *random.fly*, or musical, like *ode.fly*. Some were cute, like *dance.fly*, and some were perhaps even a bit useful, like *fly_time.fly* and *tea_timer.fly*. Regardless, all were (hopefully) fun. Many more fun Firefly programs doubtless exist, waiting to be extracted from the ether and written down. For example, its display and its compact size makes the thought of embedding the micro:bit in a craft or holiday decoration something to consider.

Firefly also concludes our exploration of esolangs and programming languages in general. Only one chapter remains: where to go from here.

16

GOING FURTHER

We've reached the end, so let's make it a good one. I sincerely hope your adventure with programming languages continues. To aid you on your quest, I offer micro-vignettes of additional esolangs you may wish to investigate, a collection of links to increase your programming language prowess, and a brief postlude.

The Runners-Up

There are too many excellent esolangs out there to include all of them in a single book; choices had to be made. This section presents micro-vignettes of the esolangs that didn't make the cut. Let them inspire you to explore, wonder, design, and code.

Malbolge

How difficult can a programming language be to use but still be Turing complete? In 1998, Malbolge's creator, Ben Olmstead, attempted to answer that question. The resulting language was so difficult to code in that two years passed before Andrew Cooke presented a working "Hello, world!"

example. The name, Malbolge, is a (purposeful?) misspelling of *Malebolge* the eighth circle of hell from Dante's *Inferno*—the level reserved for swindlers and cheats.

Malbolge runs on a virtual machine using base-3 numbers or *trits* (ternary digits). Malbolge's virtual machine is a von Neumann architecture with memory and code sharing the same space, thereby allowing self-modifying code.

To experiment with Malbolge, download the original version and associated files from *http://esoteric.sange.fi/orphaned/malbolge/*, placing the files in the *Malbolge* directory of the book's repo.

Building the interpreter is easy. Just compile the C source file as follows:

```
> malbolge.c -o malbolge
```

"Hello, world!" in Malbolge, which was found by an extensive computer search, is

```
(=<`#9]~6ZY327Uv4-QsqpMn&+Ij"'E%e{Ab~w=_:]Kw%o44UqpO/Q?xNvL:`H%c#DD2^WV>gY;dts76qKJImZkj
```

You'll find it in *hello.mal*. To see that it works, run the following command:

```
> malbolge hello.mal
Hello, world.
```

The virtual machine is described in *malbolge.txt* with an alternative description available at *https://esolangs.org/* on the Malbolge page. The truly daring can satisfy their lust for adventure by working through the "Malbolge Programming" article at *https://esolangs.org/wiki/Malbolge_programming*, which is itself a reworking of Lou Scheffer's original investigations (see *http://www .com/malbolge.shtml*).

It's likely Malbolge *is* the most difficult programming language in the world. Using the eighth circle of hell as the name is clever, though. Is Malbolge really a fraud? To me, it's a classic example of what an esolang encapsulates: it's the result of a specific, pointed question. It does appear that Malbolge is Turing complete, which makes it all the more interesting.

Dante's ninth circle is reserved for the treasonous. It might be interesting to contemplate a successor to Malbolge, that is, one reflecting the ninth circle, a language that breaks trust with the programmer, perhaps by randomly providing wrong answers.

INTERCAL

INTERCAL ("Compiler Language With No Pronounceable Acronym") was developed by Don Woods and James Lyon in 1972. INTERCAL was meant as a joke. For example, if the compiler is given a program that does not use the PLEASE keyword often enough, it is rejected for being impolite. Similarly, if PLEASE appears too frequently, the compiler will reject the program as overly polite. Perhaps the most interesting part of INTERCAL is its humorous documentation.

Humor aside, INTERCAL is Turing complete. To work with it, I suggest using the implementation included in Q. P. Liu's collection of esolang implementations. To install it, use

```
> git clone https://github.com/qpliu/esolang.git
```

Liu's implementation is in Go, which you can install like so:

```
> sudo apt-get install golang-go
```

To build INTERCAL, change to the INTERCAL directory and run make.

```
> cd esolang/intercal
> make
```

Liu's implementation includes a compiler and interpreter plus some examples. We'll use the interpreter. The compiler threw an error on *hello.i* when I tried it.

To run the interpreter, use

```
> ./COMPILAC examples/hello.i
<code listing deleted>
GOOD BYTE, CRUEL WORLD!
```

What's impressive to me is the INTERCAL implementation of *Adventure*. *Adventure*, created in the mid-1970s, was the first interactive fiction text adventure game. It's sometimes known as *The Colossal Cave* and, in parts, became most of Infocom's *Zork* series of games for microcomputers. *Adventure* was written by Will Crowther and Don Woods, the same Don Woods who created INTERCAL. Let's run it.

```
> ./COMPILAC examples/ADVENT.I
WELCOME TO ADVENTURE!!  WOULD YOU LIKE INSTRUCTIONS?
> no
YOU ARE STANDING AT THE END OF A ROAD BEFORE A SMALL BRICK BUILDING.
AROUND YOU IS A FOREST.  A SMALL STREAM FLOWS OUT OF THE BUILDING AND
DOWN A GULLY.
> go building
YOU ARE INSIDE A BUILDING, A WELL HOUSE FOR A LARGE SPRING.
THERE ARE SOME KEYS ON THE GROUND HERE.
THERE IS A SHINY BRASS LAMP NEARBY.
THERE IS FOOD HERE.
THERE IS A BOTTLE OF WATER HERE.
> take keys
OK
> take lamp
OK
> take food
OK
```

```
> score
IF YOU WERE TO QUIT NOW, YOU WOULD SCORE  32 OUT OF A POSSIBLE 350.
DO YOU INDEED WISH TO QUIT NOW?
> yes
OK
YOU SCORED  32 OUT OF A POSSIBLE 350, USING    6 TURNS.
YOU ARE OBVIOUSLY A RANK AMATEUR.  BETTER LUCK NEXT TIME.
TO ACHIEVE THE NEXT HIGHER RATING, YOU NEED  4 MORE POINTS.
```

NOTE *In Chapter 11, we discussed the Befunge program* bridge.bf, *which included the word* xyzzy. *If you continue to play* Adventure, *you'll eventually find a use for* xyzzy.

INTERCAL supports 16-bit and 32-bit integers, which are identified by a prefix and a decimal number in the range [1, 65535]. For example, .123 ("spot") is a 16-bit integer, whereas :123 ("two-spot") is a 32-bit integer. INTERCAL also supports 16-bit and 32-bit arrays that are prefixed with , ("tail") or ; ("hybrid") and a number. Constants are prefixed with # ("mesh").

INTERCAL has five operators, all of which are bit-oriented. This includes two binary, "mingle" and "select," and three unary logical operators: AND, OR, and XOR.

"Select" (~) picks bits from the first operand based on the bits set in the second, building the result bit by bit from right to left. The example from the manual is #179~#201, which returns 9. To see it, first write the arguments in binary: $10110011_2 = 179$ and $11001001_2 = 201$. Then, find all the one bits in 201—bits 7, 6, 3, and 0—and build the result from the corresponding bits of 179, which are 1, 0, 0, and 1, that is, $1001_2 = 9$.

Unary logical operators are atypical. The INTERCAL manual uses the example of #V77 to apply logical-OR to the constant value, 77. Figure 16-1 shows the operation.

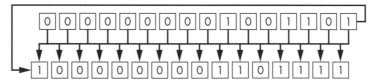

Figure 16-1: Unary OR in INTERCAL

The input, a 16-bit integer, 77, is on the top. The arrows show successive pairs of bits that are ORed together to produce the marked output bit. Notice that the output's most significant bit is the logical-OR of the last and first bit of the input.

INTERCAL's logical operators map to Wolfram's 1D cellular automata. A 1D *cellular automaton* is a rule that maps an input to an output by examining three bits at a time. There are 256 such rules for bytes, one of which, Rule 30, is chaotic enough to serve as a good pseudorandom number generator. The rule names correspond to the integer value of the output bits.

INTERCAL's OR operator implements Rule 238. It may be written as

```
111 110 101 100 011 010 001 000
 1   1   1   0   1   1   1   0  = 238
```

To find the output bit value for a given input, examine the center bit and the two neighbors on either side. Then, match that bit pattern to the rule table to set the output bit as indicated. The output is built bit by bit, that is, it does not modify the input in place. For example, if the input bit is 1 and the neighbors to the left and right are 0 and 1, respectively, then Rule 238 says $011 \rightarrow 1$, meaning the corresponding bit position in the output is set to 1.

Apply the Rule 238 table to the input of Figure 16-1. You'll see that the output matches. Similarly, INTERCAL's AND operator (&) matches Rule 136 and the XOR operator (?) implements Rule 102.

To learn more about INTERCAL, or to simply appreciate the humor, check out the full manual (*http://www.muppetlabs.com/~breadbox/intercal-man/*).

Whitespace

INTERCAL is a joke language that's powerful enough to do useful things. Whitespace is another joke language. And like INTERCAL, it's also Turing complete: Whitespace has sequence, unbounded heap storage, conditional looping, and subroutines.

In Whitespace, the only valid program characters are space, tab, and newline (ASCII 10, linefeed, LF). Everything else is ignored. Therefore, a clever person with too much free time might embed a Whitespace program inside code for another language, perhaps as super-secret spy code or the like. Or perhaps not.

As a programming language, Whitespace is rather typical. There is a stack, like Forth, and a heap for generic storage. Input and output commands work with numbers or characters, like Befunge. In reality, the only exciting part of Whitespace is its chosen symbol set. All the same, it makes most lists of "Try these bizarre programming languages," so it's worth a cursory peek at the very least.

I experimented with the C implementation by GitHub user Koturn. Clone it and build it like so:

```
> git clone https://github.com/koturn/Whitespace.git
> cd Whitespace
> make
```

There are several examples in the *t* directory. Kudos for using a short pathname. For example:

```
> ./whitespace.out t/hworld.ws
Hello, world of spaces!
> ./whitespace.out t/fact.ws
Enter a number: 10
```

```
10! = 3628800
> ./whitespace.out t/hanoi.ws
Enter a number: 3
1 -> 3
1 -> 2
3 -> 2
1 -> 3
2 -> 1
2 -> 3
1 -> 3
```

The difficult part of Whitespace is writing code in it. You can't easily use a normal text editor because you need to be able to input whitespace and still see what you are typing. For example, like Befunge, Whitespace has two input and two output commands:

[tab][space]	read a character to the heap
[tab][tab]	read a number to the heap
[space][space]	output top of the stack as a character
[space][tab]	output top of the stack as a number

However, visualizing which command is which is problematic. Fortunately, Whitespace IDEs do exist; see *https://vii5ard.github.io/whitespace/*. Figure 16-2 shows a typical session with the Whitespace code in the middle (shown in gray in print and in color online) and a text version of the program on the far right.

Figure 16-2: A Whitespace IDE

This slick IDE is the work of Henri Lakk. Do review the main GitHub page at *https://github.com/vii5ard/whitespace/* for more information. The IDE includes an embedded BF interpreter written in Whitespace, which is simply brilliant.

Shakespeare

William Shakespeare (1564–1616) is generally regarded as the best English playwright. Why mention Shakespeare in a book on programming languages? Enter the Shakespeare Programming Language, stage right. Shakespeare, courtesy of Karl Wiberg and Jon Åslund, turns text that reads like a Shakespearean play into executable code.

The main Shakespeare page is at *http://shakespearelang.sourceforge.net/*. From there, download the Shakespeare tarball, *spl-1.2.1.tar.gz*, and install it, ignoring build errors.

```
> tar spl-1.2.1.tar.gz
> cd spl-1.2.1
> make
```

SPL is a compiler from Shakespeare to C. Several examples are included, all of which work nicely except *fibonacci.spl*. To run SPL, follow this pattern:

```
> ./spl2c <examples/hello.spl >hello.c
> gcc hello.c -o hello -I. libspl.a -lm
> ./hello
Hello World!
```

A newer project has created an interpreter in Python. This project aims to make it easier to develop Shakespeare code. The GitHub site is *https://github.com/zmbc/shakespearelang/*, but it's easiest to install with pip.

```
> pip install shakespearelang
```

The result is *shakespeare*, which is able to run the SPL listed examples above.

```
> shakespeare run primes.spl
> 10
2
3
5
7
```

Shakespeare translates text that looks like a play

```
The Infamous Hello World Program.

Romeo, a young man with a remarkable patience.
```

Juliet, a likewise young woman of remarkable grace.

Ophelia, a remarkable woman much in dispute with Hamlet.
Hamlet, the flatterer of Andersen Insulting A/S.

Act I: Hamlet's insults and flattery.
Scene I: The insulting of Romeo.

[Enter Hamlet and Romeo]
Hamlet:
 You lying stupid fatherless big smelly half-witted coward!
 You are as stupid as the difference between a handsome rich brave
 hero and thyself! Speak your mind!
 --snip--

into C code

```
--snip--
romeo = initialize_character("Romeo");
juliet = initialize_character("Juliet");
ophelia = initialize_character("Ophelia");
hamlet = initialize_character("Hamlet");

act_i:                     /* Hamlet ' s insults and flattery */
act_i_scene_i:             /* The insulting of Romeo */
enter_scene(13, hamlet);
enter_scene(13, romeo);

activate_character(30, hamlet);
assign(16, second_person, 2*2*2*2*2*2*(-1));
assign(18, second_person, int_sub(17, 2*2*2*1, value_of(18, second_person)));
char_output(18, second_person);
assign(22, second_person, int_add(20, 2*2*2*2*2*2*2*(-1), 2*2*2*2*2*1));
assign(23, second_person, int_sub(22, int_add(22, 2*2*1, 1), value_of(23, second_person)));
char_output(23, second_person);
assign(26, second_person, int_add(25, value_of(25, second_person), int_sub(26, 2*2*2*1, 1)));
char_output(26, second_person);
char_output(28, second_person);
--snip--
```

This is then compiled to build a standalone executable.

Shakespeare is fun to read, but even more fun to watch: *https://www*
.youtube.com/watch?v=-e8oBF4IrgU. I imagine this is the first time humans
have ever acted out a program, let alone with such wonderful insults.

Whirl

Whirl (and Taxi, detailed in the next section) are two innovative esolangs created by Sean Heber. We'll use Mateusz Chudyk's Python implementation to explore Whirl. Grab it from GitHub.

```
> git clone https://github.com/mateuszchudyk/whirl-interpreter.git
```

The interpreter runs out of the box, but I recommend two simple tweaks to the Python source to make the output look nicer. Do the following, substituting your favorite editor if necessary

```
> cd whirl-interpreter
> vi whirl/commands.py
```

and then change line 194 to read

```
print(int(program_state.get_memory_value()), end="")
```

Likewise, change line 214 to

```
print(chr(program_state.get_memory_value()), end="")
```

These changes prevent output from automatically advancing to the next line. Validate Whirl like so:

```
> python3 whirl-interpreter.py examples/fibonacci.whirl
1,1,2,3,5,8,13,21
```

Yay, Whirl works. But what is it? Whirl has only two instructions: 0 and 1. Seriously, that's it. Whirl consists of two rings with operations and functions on them; imagine actual circular rings with operations and instructions spaced equally along them. The first ring is the "operations ring" that holds 12 control, logic, and I/O operations. The second ring is the "math ring" with 12 math functions. Each ring also holds a single data value. Additionally, there is an "infinite" memory accessed via a memory pointer, much like the tape of a Turing machine.

Whirl's two instructions are:

0 Reverse the direction of the active ring. If the previous instruction was 0, and it did not trigger an execution, then the currently selected command on the currently active ring is executed and the other ring becomes active.

1 Rotate the current ring in the current direction, either clockwise or counterclockwise.

Table 16-1 shows the operation ring commands running clockwise.

Table 16-1: Whirl's Operations Ring

Instruction	Effect
Noop	Do nothing
Exit	Exit
One	Ring value ← 1
Zero	Ring value ← 0
Load	Ring value ← memory value
Store	Ring value → memory value
PAdd	PC ← PC + ring value
DAdd	MP ← MP + ring value
Logic	Ring value ← 0 if memory value 0, else ring value ← ring value & 1
If	If memory not equal 0, add ring value to PC
IntIO	If ring value is 0, memory value ← integer read from stdin; otherwise, print memory value to stdout as an integer
AscIO	If ring value is 0, memory value ← ASCII character read from stdin; otherwise, print memory value to stdout as an ASCII character

For the math ring, the commands are shown, again running clockwise, in Table 16-2.

Table 16-2: Whirl's Math Ring

Instruction	Effect
Noop	Do nothing
Load	Ring value ← memory value
Store	Ring value → memory value
Add	Ring value ← ring value + memory value
Mult	Ring value ← ring value × memory value
Div	Ring value ← ring value ÷ memory value
Zero	Ring value ← 0
<	Ring value ← 1 if ring value < memory value, else 0
>	Ring value ← 1 if ring value > memory value, else 0
=	Ring value ← 1 if ring value = memory value, else 0
Not	Ring value ← 0 if ring value ≠ 0, else 1
Neg	Ring value ← −1 × ring value

When the program starts, both rings are at the Noop position, both ring values are 0, and the operation ring is active. It's the programmer's job to track the current state of the program. There is no way to query ring alignment or which ring is active.

The original Whirl site is gone, but it is accessible via the Wayback Machine: *http://web.archive.org/web/20130116204525/bigzaphod.org/whirl/*. I've taken the liberty of printing this site as a PDF. See *Whirl.pdf* on the book's GitHub page.

Programming in Whirl is not for the faint of heart, but Whirl's no Malbolge, either. For example, this Whirl program from the original website demonstrates again that 1 + 1 = 2:

```
00    run ops.noop, switch to math ring
0     math::ccw
11    rotate to math.not
00    run math.not, switch to ops ring
00    run ops.noop, switch to math ring
0     math::cw
1111  rotate to math.store
00    run math.store, switch to ops ring
00    run ops.noop, switch to math ring
1     rotate to math.add
00    run math.add, switch to ops ring
00    run ops.noop, switch to math ring
0     math::ccw
1     rotate to math.store
00    run math.store, switch to ops ring
11    rotate to ops.one
00    run ops.one, switch to math ring
00    run math.store, switch to ops ring
0     ops::ccw
1111  rotate to ops.IntIO
00    run ops.IntIO, switch to math ring
```

Notice that 00 causes the current command on the current ring to execute, but a single 0 only toggles the direction of the current ring. At all times, 1 rotates the current ring in the current direction without executing a command. These are critical ideas for Whirl programming. Use 1 to set up the proper command on the current ring and then use 00 to execute the command and automatically toggle to the other ring. Lastly, use 0 to toggle the rotation direction for the current ring.

Several other examples gleaned from the original Whirl page are in the *examples* directory. There are additional examples in the *whirl-interpreter* directory as well.

Whirl is clever, and I strongly suspect it's Turing complete because, in the end, it's another imperative programming language, albeit one with a novel twist to it (pun intended). Go ahead, give Whirl a whirl.

Taxi

As if Whirl weren't clever enough, Sean Heber struck again with Taxi, a programming language where the programmer must navigate a taxi with up to three passengers around Townsville while maintaining enough gas and the funds to purchase it.

Like Whirl, the original Taxi site is gone but accessible from the Wayback Machine. For the URL, take a look at the *README.txt* file in the *Taxi* directory of the book's GitHub repository. Taxi is marked as public domain, so I'm including it with the book. I also made a PDF of the archived web page (see *Taxi.pdf*).

Figure 16-3 shows Townsville (*taxi_map.png*).

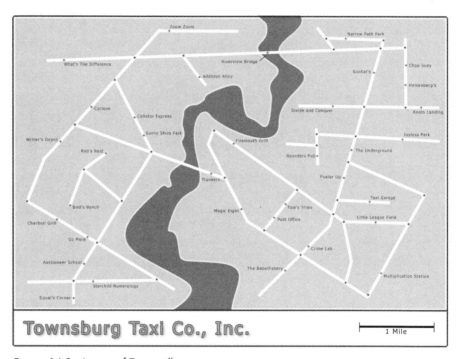

Figure 16-3: A map of Townsville

Every location marked on the map is a possible destination, and each destination performs a different function. Driving the taxi requires fuel, so the programmer must be aware of how far the taxi has traveled and make pit stops when appropriate. Of course, this assumes that the taxi has collected enough in fares to cover the cost of the fuel. Passengers, either a number or a string, pay a flat rate of 0.07 credits per mile, but only pay when they have reached their destination.

Destinations implement the operations of the language. Need to add some values? Take your passengers to Addition Alley. Want a random integer? Pick one up at Heisenberg's, but be prepared for a certain level of indecision on his part.

Some destinations implement data structures. Want a FIFO data structure? Visit Joyless Park or Sunny Skies Park. Prefer LIFO? Then use Narrow Path Park. Running low on gas? Better get to Zoom Zoom for the cheapest gas in town. Avoid Fueler Up if you can. You'll pay too much. The complete list of destinations, and associated operations, is in *Taxi.pdf*. Enjoy the creative names.

Taxi code is verbose, almost plaintext, much like the HyperTalk language used by HyperCard, an old Macintosh programming environment from Apple. For example:

```
"Hello, World!" is waiting at the Writer's Depot.
Go to Writer's Depot: west 1st left, 2nd right, 1st left, 2nd left.
Pickup a passenger going to the Post Office.
Go to the Post Office: north 1st right, 2nd right, 1st left.
Go to the Taxi Garage: north 1st right, 1st left, 1st right.
```

This prints, well, you know what it prints. The program begins with the taxi at the Taxi Garage and ends when the taxi returns to the garage. The first line puts a string at the Writer's Depot, which holds a string constant. To use the string, you must first get to the Writer's Depot from the Taxi Garage. To do that, you need to go west, take the first left, then the second right, then the first left, and, lastly, the second left. Consult *taxi_map.png*, and you'll see that the directions do take you from the Taxi Garage to the Writer's Depot.

The following line, `Pickup a passenger going to the Post Office`, gets the string with the intended destination. So use directions from the current location to get to the Post Office. The Post Office prints passengers to `stdout` (standard output). Pick up a passenger at the Post Office to get input from the user. To end the program, return to the Taxi Garage.

What if you don't return to the garage? The program ends poorly: `The boss couldn't find your taxi in the garage. You're fired!` So return to the garage, or else!

Flow control makes use of labels enclosed in square brackets and the `Switch` statement with references to the labels in quotation marks. For example, the line

```
Switch to plan "loop".
```

is an unconditional branch to [loop], while

```
Switch to plan "end_loop" if no one is waiting.
```

is a conditional branch.

The C++ source code for Taxi is in *taxi.cpp*. I recommend commenting out the startup and exit messages at lines 472, 1267, and 1268. Or not; it's a matter of personal preference.

To use Taxi, first build it with

```
> g++ taxi.cpp -o taxi
```

and then run it:

```
> ./taxi examples/fib.taxi
1.000000 1.000000 2.000000 3.000000 5.000000 8.000000 13.000000 ...
```

Notice that Taxi supports floating-point numbers. Be sure not to miss Nick Turner's RPN calculator in *rpn.taxi*.

Taxi is an excellent example of the esolang community's unbounded creativity. It's possible to imagine using Taxi, or something built from it, to introduce programming concepts. Of interest at a higher level is the fact that operations in Taxi come with a price: literally. Programmers are accustomed to operations having no intrinsic cost other than memory and time. In Taxi, the number of operations, and their relative relationship to each other, introduce another cost on top of the usual memory and time.

Development on Taxi has stalled, but the source code is in the public domain. Perhaps someone will pick it up, refine it, and introduce it again in another form. If targeting younger programmers, I suggest leaving out the travel cost aspect. What about a new metaphor? Perhaps an airplane flying from city to city, or a starship warping from star system to star system?

Dathanna

The original Apple II+ computer from 1979 contained an 8-bit 6502 microprocessor running in a system with a 1 MHz clock, half of which was used to refresh RAM. By modern standards, the Apple II+ crawled along at continental drift speeds. However, modern computers are capable of emulating an Apple II+ at something approaching 100 times its native speed (84 times on my test system). This fact opens up new possibilities for programs written for the Apple II that would be far too slow on a native system but are entirely usable on an emulator running at full speed.

Dathanna, Irish for "colors," is just such a program. Dathanna is an esolang using colored blocks, two stacked one on top of the other, to specify commands. It echoes both Befunge-93 and Piet in how it operates. However, the most important part of Dathanna is that its interpreter is written in Applesoft BASIC and it runs off a disk image meant for Apple II emulators.

You'll find Dathanna, along with all necessary files and documentation, on the book's GitHub site. All I'll present here is a bit of source code to whet your appetite: a program to estimate π using random numbers, much like we did earlier in the book with ABC. See Figure 16-4, which should really be in color. Review the documentation to learn how it works.

Figure 16-4: Dathanna code to estimate π with random numbers

Programming Language Resources

What follows is a prosaic but helpful list of resources to increase your knowledge of programming languages. I selected freely available material presented by the original authors when possible. Naturally, some of these URLs will fail over time, but the internet remembers, for good or ill. If a particular link no longer works, searching for the title will likely locate the resource once more.

Programming languages tend to evolve slowly. If a few of the resources here are a decade or more old, that's okay. The burning need to stay current is less critical in this case.

The following sections divide the resources into three groups. The first is a catch-all on programming languages in general. These resources are similar to what you typically encounter in an undergraduate course on programming languages. The second section covers data structures, which we unfairly neglected in Chapter 2. The third section relates to compilers and interpreters—the methods for actualizing a programming language.

The links are presented as title and URL with minimal comment. I reviewed all the material and found it helpful, though there are definite limits to what you can learn simply by reading. At some point, you have to go further and build something.

Programming Languages

The material here covers programming languages at an undergraduate level. As you read through it, recall the esolangs and other languages we discussed in the book to build connections with the more general concepts.

Concepts of Programming Languages: A Unified Approach by Karl Abrahamson. The first five parts of this book introduce programming language concepts. The later portions of the book dive into functional programming, though there is a chapter on Scheme, which we used in Chapter 8 to implement FRACTRAN. (*http://www.cs.ecu.edu/~karl/ 3675/fall11/book.pdf*)

Advanced Programming Language Design by Raphael Finkel. I read this book in the late 1990s and found it very helpful. Recommended. (*https://www.cs.uky.edu/~raphael/courses/CS655/Advanced_programming _language$_d$esign.pdf*)

Programming Languages and Techniques by Steve Zdancewic and Stephanie Weirich. Use this as a reference and as a review of techniques associated with programming languages. However, the use of OCaml, a functional language, might make direct translation of techniques to other languages a bit more difficult. (*https://www.seas.upenn.edu/~cis120/ archive/20sp/notes/120notes.pdf*)

Programming Languages: Application and Interpretation by Shriram Krishnamurthi. These notes are an alternative introduction to the elements of programming languages using Typed PLAI, a language supported by Racket. Use it in conjunction with the references above. (*http://cs.brown.edu/courses/cs173/2012/book/book.pdf*)

Practical Foundations for Programming Languages by Robert Harper. This book, at nearly 600 pages, dives into the mathematics of programming and is more theoretical than the references above. (*https://thelack thereof.org/docs/library/book.pdf*)

Models of Computation by John E. Savage. This is not a programming language book, but rather an in-depth, highly theoretical exploration of computation, or, as the subtitle says, "exploring the power of computing." Our discussion of Turing machines in Chapter 3 serves as a (simple) introduction to this material. (*http://cs.brown.edu/people/jsavage/book/pdfs/ModelsOfComputation.pdf*)

Data Structures

Data structures are tools used by programming languages to store and manipulate information. The form the structures take is a function of the elements provided by the programming language. The level of difficulty in implementing a particular data structure depends on the language used. Implementing a dictionary in Python is trivial because it's part of the core language. Implementing a stack in Forth is trivial for the same reason. Pascal and C/C++ both provide syntactic support for records and structures. However, doing the same in Forth, at least in simple Forth systems, requires rolling your own data structures and directly managing a space of memory, often at the byte level.

> **A First Course on Data Structures in Python** by Donald R. Sheehy. A basic introduction to data structures using Python. I suggest starting with Chapter 5, if not Chapter 6. (*https://donsheehy.github.io/datastructures/.pdf*)
>
> **Data Structures and Algorithms** by John Bullinaria. This reference is a succinct introduction with pseudocode algorithms and examples in C and Java. If the book above is too much, begin with this one. (*https://www.cs.bham.ac.uk/~jxb/DSA/dsa.pdf*)
>
> **Data Structures and Algorithm Analysis** by Clifford A. Shaffer. This book covers much the same material as the ones above, in Java, but includes analysis of algorithm performance and, in the final chapter, a discussion on the limits of computation. (*https://people.cs.vt.edu/shaffer/Book/Java3e20120102.pdf*)

Compilers and Interpreters

A programming language remains nothing more than a mental construct until an implementation actualizes it. Classically, implementation meant a compiler, as computers were generally too slow to make interpreted programming languages anything more than curiosities. Of course, this is no longer the case, and even simple interpreters are quite fast on modern hardware, to say nothing of the hybrid case of compiling a high-level language to code running on a virtual machine.

In this section, you'll find introductory material to help you learn about the process of building a compiler or interpreter. The latter is more straightforward, of course, but the former is definitely worth the effort, at least to understand the parts we discussed in Chapter 2 at a deeper level.

Crafting Interpreters by Robert Nystrom. This website features an online book about crafting interpreters. Worth a look. (*https://crafting interpreters.com*)

Implementing Programming Languages by Aarne Ranta. Use this book as an introduction. It appears to be incomplete and, given the 2012 date, will likely remain so. However, the early chapters are complete and helpful. (*https://www.cse.chalmers.se/edu/year/2012/course/DAT150/lectures/plt-book.pdf*)

Basics of Compiler Design by Torben Ægidius Mogensen. This book introduces compiler design in much the same vein as the famous Dragon Book referenced in Chapter 2. The treatment is mathematical, so you'll need to know how to read set notation, for instance, but the level isn't that required of a graduate course. (*http://hjemmesider.diku.dk/~torbenm/Basics/basics_lulu2.pdf*)

An Introduction to Compilers by D. Vermeir. Use this book as another reference to the main topics of compiler design. The example code is written in C. (*http://tinf2.vub.ac.be/~dvermeir/courses/compilers/compilers.pdf*)

Introduction to Compilers and Language Design by Douglas Thain. This book serves as an alternative introduction to *Basics of Compiler Design* mentioned above. Take a look. (*https://www3.nd.edu/~dthain/compilerbook/compilerbook.pdf*)

Compiler Construction Using Flex and Bison by Anthony A. Aaby. Flex and Bison are classic compiler generation tools. While there are more current tools, this text includes the full source code for the Simple language. Use it as a case study in compiler design. (*http://www.admb-project.org/tools/flex/compiler.pdf*)

Programming Languages and Their Compilers by John Cocke and J. T. Schwartz. This historical text, from 1970, details compilers as they existed then. Languages discussed include FORTRAN, LISP, and, a favorite of this book, SNOBOL. (*http://www.softwarepreservation.org/projects/FORTRAN/CockeSchwartz_ProgLangCompilers.pdf*)

Postlude

You are still here at the end of the book and I thank you. I hope you had fun and learned things you didn't know before. And I hope you're excited about programming languages, especially the strange, weird, unusual, and esoteric kind.

I encourage you to develop your own programming language, even if you never implement it. There is something deeply satisfying about creating a new way to express thought. I suspect that for every implemented esolang, there are many more existing only as plans, notes, or vague notions. If you do nothing more than write it out on paper, and have fun doing it, then the language is worthwhile solely for the enjoyment its design brought.

However, if you *do* implement it, let me know. I'd love to write some code for it.

Quando omni flunkus moritati.

GENETIC PROGRAMMING WITH FIREFLY

In Chapter 15, we explored the Firefly language with fun animations and music. In this appendix, we'll use Firefly along with *genetic programming* to evolve displays we can then animate.

Introduction to Genetic Programming

Genetic programming became widely known in the early 1990s. Genetic programming uses algorithms to create programs by mimicking biological evolution. Instead of manually writing the code to perform a task, genetic programming generates and runs a population of random programs to see how well they perform. Each program in the population is given a *fitness value*, often called an objective function value, which is used to decide which programs breed to create the next generation of programs. Breeding is accomplished via *crossover* between pairs of programs, which mixes the code of "parent" programs to produce a new "offspring" program. As in biological evolution, there is a small probability a program will undergo a random mutation. Random mutation drives evolution by inserting new "genes" into the population. Biological evolution is driven by other processes, like genetic drift, but we'll keep things simple and rely on crossover between well-performing individuals and random mutation.

How Genetic Programming Works

The general approach to genetic programming is as follows:

1. Create a population of randomly generated programs.

2. Run each program in the population and assign it a fitness value depending on how well it does at solving the desired task.

3. Create the next generation of programs by breeding (crossover) and mutation.

4. Repeat from Step 2 until we either have a program that solves our task to our satisfaction or we give up.

For us, the programs are Firefly code for generating LED displays. We'll specify the display we'd like and let genetic programming evolve a program that creates that display (we hope!).

Typically, using genetic programming is somewhat tricky because generating random computer code that actually runs is difficult. Likewise, mixing two programs to produce a new one is challenging due to syntax issues. However, we are fortunate, as Firefly is extremely simple. *Any* string of characters extracted from the allowed set of Firefly commands is a valid Firefly program, and will thus run without error.

Also, as we are seeking code to generate a particular display, we only need to consider Firefly instructions that manipulate the LEDs. Thus, we can dispense with double buffering, music, and random trails, as they are not reproducible. We only need instructions to move the firefly and set the mode.

We are doing genetic programming, but we'll implement the evolution portion via a *genetic algorithm*, or *GA*. A genetic algorithm is more general than genetic programming, but for our Firefly code, the GA works perfectly to implement genetic programming. We won't dive into how the genetic algorithm code works. Rather, we'll just use the algorithm and see its effects. However, GA isn't all that complicated, so if you read through the code, you'll see what it's doing.

Therefore, to experiment with genetic programming and Firefly, we need the following pieces:

1. Some way to define the display we want to create.
2. A stripped-down version of the Firefly interpreter that only processes move and mode commands.
3. GA code to evolve a population of Firefly programs.
4. Something to package the pieces together, run the search, and output the resulting code.

Let's build what we need, piece by piece. If you want to jump into the Python code now, read through *fly_swarm.py* in the *firefly/GP* directory. Note that the population evolved by genetic programming is sometimes referred to as a *swarm*, even though swarm is most often used in relation to *swarm intelligence* algorithms. We'll use "population" and "swarm" interchangeably.

Defining Displays

The most straightforward part of this exercise is defining the display we want to generate. Firefly's display is a 5×5 grid of LED intensities. Therefore, we'll define target displays using a 5×5 array of numbers stored in a text file. For example, to specify a "ball" located in the upper-left corner of the display, create a text file containing

```
5 5 0 0 0
5 5 0 0 0
0 0 0 0 0
0 0 0 0 0
0 0 0 0 0
```

This puts a medium intensity (square) "ball" in the upper-left corner with all other LEDs off. The text file stores the intensities of the 5×5 array for the genetic programming code to use as a target. The more similar the display generated by a candidate program is to the target, the better.

A Tiny Firefly Interpreter

We need a tiny interpreter supporting only the Firefly move and mode commands to run our programs. We'll make this interpreter a Python class so we can instantiate it easily. The result is Listing A-1.

```python
class Firefly:
    def Move(self, c):
        if self.M == "M":
            pass
        elif self.M == "I":
            self.C[self.I] += 1
            if self.C[self.I] > 9:
                self.C[self.I] =0
        elif self.M == "D":
            if (self.C[self.I] == 0):
                self.C[self.I] = 9
            else:
                self.C[self.I] -= 1
        else:
            self.C[self.I] = int(self.M)
```

```
            i = self.I // 5
            j = self.I % 5

            if c == "N":
                i -= 1
                if i < 0:
                    i = 4
            elif c == "S":
                i += 1
                if i > 4:
                    i = 0
            elif c == "E":
                j += 1
                if j > 4:
                    j = 0
            elif c == "W":
                j -= 1
                if j < 0:
                    j = 4

            self.I = 5*i + j

    def Run(self):
        for c in self.prg:
            if c == "I":
                self.M = "I"
            elif c == "D":
                self.M = "D"
            elif c == "M":
                self.M = "M"
            elif c in self.DIGITS:
                self.M = c
            elif c in self.MOVES:
                self.Move(c)

    def GetDisplay(self):
        return self.C.reshape((5,5))

    def __init__(self, prg=None):
        self.prg = prg
        self.C = np.zeros(25)
        self.I = 12
        self.M = "M"
        self.DIGITS= ["0","1","2","3","4","5","6","7","8","9"]
        self.MOVES = ["N","E","W","S"]
```

Listing A-1: A tiny Firefly interpreter

For each program in the population, we create a `Firefly` instance with the program passed in. Then the `Run` method executes the program and `GetDisplay` returns the resulting display. For example, this code loads the `Firefly` class and runs a program to move north three times:

```
>>> from fly_swarm import Firefly
>>> ff = Firefly("5NNN")
>>> ff.Run()
>>> ff.GetDisplay()
array([[0., 0., 5., 0., 0.],
       [0., 0., 5., 0., 0.],
       [0., 0., 5., 0., 0.],
       [0., 0., 0., 0., 0.],
       [0., 0., 0., 0., 0.]])
```

We'll compare the display returned by `GetDisplay` with our desired target to calculate the program's fitness.

The tiny Firefly interpreter accepts digits, the letters M, I, and D, and the cardinal directions as instructions. The interpreter runs the given program once, without looping, and ends, preserving the resulting display. As we'll see, our GA runs thousands to millions of sample Firefly programs, searching for one that meets our needs. Each run uses an instance of the `Firefly` class.

The Genetic Algorithm

The GA class implements the GA. But we need to define a few things before we can use it. First, we need a mapping between the Firefly code we want and the vector of numbers the GA uses to represent an individual. Second, we need a class to bound the search. Third, we need a class to calculate the fitness value for an individual. A fitness value here is like a golf score: lower is better. If the score is 0, we can stop because we found a program that does exactly what we want.

There are 17 instructions supported by our tiny Firefly interpreter. Thus, we'll restrict the vectors used by the GA to [0, 16] to ensure they contain integers. This lets us map a vector to a Firefly program.

Listing A-2 defines `FlyBounds` as a subclass of `Bounds`.

```
class FlyBounds(Bounds):
    def __init__(self, ndim):
        lower = [0]*ndim
        upper = [len(ALLOWED)-1]*ndim
        super().__init__(lower, upper, enforce="resample")
    def Validate(self, p):
        return np.floor(p+0.5)
```

Listing A-2: A class for bounding the search

Bounds is a framework component used by the GA. What's important for us is that the subclass defines the allowed range of values from 0 to 16 (len(ALLOWED)-1), with ndim being the number of instructions in the program (the dimensionality of the search space). The Validate method takes a member of the population, p, and makes it integer-valued by rounding to the nearest integer.

The last thing we need is a class to measure a program's fitness (see Listing A-3).

```
class FlyObjective:
    def __init__(self, target):
        self.target = target
        self.fcount = 0
    def Evaluate(self, p):
        self.fcount += 1
        prg = PositionToFirefly(p)
        fly = Firefly(prg)
        fly.Run()
        return ((self.target - fly.GetDisplay())**2).mean()

def PositionToFirefly(p):
    prg = ""
    for i in range(len(p)):
        prg += ALLOWED[int(p[i])]
    return prg
```

Listing A-3: A class to measure fitness

Here, target is a 5×5 NumPy array representing the display we're trying to evolve code to generate. The Evaluate method accepts a member of the population, converts it to actual Firefly code with PositionToFirefly, creates a Firefly interpreter, and then runs the code.

The last line calculates the fitness of the program. The output is a 5×5 array, that is, the display. For fitness, we'll use the *mean squared error*, or *MSE*. This is the average value of the squared per-element difference between the program's display and the display we want to generate. The lower this value, the better the program is at creating the desired display. When the MSE is 0, the program has created the target display precisely, so we'll stop searching when (if) that happens.

Using the square of the difference instead of the absolute value of the difference penalizes larger per-element differences more, which is what we want. We want to drive the population toward programs with smaller differences.

PositionToFirefly uses a one-to-one mapping between the integers in p and the characters in ALLOWED to return the program string.

The GA relies on crossover and random mutation. Firefly programs are represented as vectors of numbers. To implement the crossover of two programs, A and B of length N, the GA selects a random index, i, in $[0, N - 1]$. The new offspring vector is $C = A[: i] + B[i :]$, meaning the first i values of

A followed by the last $N - i$ values of B. Mutation is even simpler. A random index, j, is selected, and the value at that index is set to a random number, $[0, 16]$.

We now have what we need to use the GA class and search for Firefly programs. Let's see how to do it.

Putting It All Together

Listing A-4 shows the main function of *fly_swarm.py*.

```
❶ target = np.loadtxt(sys.argv[1])
  npart = int(sys.argv[2])
  ndim = int(sys.argv[3])
  niter = int(sys.argv[4])

❷ b = FlyBounds(ndim)
  i = RandomInitializer(npart, ndim, bounds=b)

❸ obj = FlyObjective(target)

❹ swarm = GA(obj=obj, npart=npart, ndim=ndim, init=i, tol=1e-12, max_iter=niter,
          bounds=b)

  st = time.time()
❺ swarm.Optimize()
  en = time.time()

❻ res = swarm.Results()
  prg = PositionToFirefly(res["gpos"][-1])
  ff = Firefly(prg)
  ff.Run()
  d = ff.GetDisplay()
  x = ff.I // 5
  y = ff.I % 5

  print()
  print("Minimum MSE: %0.8f" % res["gbest"][-1])
  print()
  print("Program: %s" % prg)
  print()
  print("Target display:")
  print(np.array2string(target.astype("uint8")))
  print()
  print("Program display:")
  print(np.array2string(d.astype("uint8")))
  print()
  print("Firefly position (%d,%d)" % (x,y))
```

```
print("(%d particles, %d/%d iterations, %d best updates, %d function evals,
      %0.3f sec)" % (npart, res["iterations"], niter, len(res["gbest"]),
      obj.fcount, en-st))
print()
```

Listing A-4: The main function

The command line is parsed to load the target display, the size of the population (npart), the length of each program (ndim), and the number of generations to evolve (niter) ❶.

Next, we create instances of FlyBounds and RandomInitializer, an object used by the GA to randomly generate the initial population of programs.

An instance of FlyObjective comes next ❸, followed by the GA itself ❹. Executing the search takes one line of code ❺. When Optimize ends, it either has found a program that generates the target display or has run out of generations and abandons the search.

The results of the search are returned as a Python dictionary ❻. The list of successively more fit programs is in res["gpos"], meaning the last element of the list is the best program found. We convert the best position to Firefly code, run the program, and grab the display generated to print it at the console along with the program itself. We also print where the firefly is when the program ends. We'll use this last bit of information in the next section when we piece displays together to make animations.

Evolving Firefly Programs

Let's evolve some code. We'll begin by animating two displays to create a flashing warning sign. Next, we'll animate a radar sweep, complete with a "beep." Lastly, we'll animate a bouncing ball of sorts. For each example, we'll evolve the necessary displays and then piece them together using double buffering to produce the animation.

Warning Sign

The flashing warning sign consists of two displays:

```
5 5 0 3 3        3 3 0 5 5
5 5 0 3 3        3 3 0 5 5
0 0 7 0 0  and   0 0 7 0 0
3 3 0 5 5        5 5 0 3 3
3 3 0 5 5        5 5 0 3 3
```

These displays are stored in *flash0.txt* and *flash1.txt*, respectively.

For the first display, we search with *fly_swarm.py* as follows:

```
> python3 fly_swarm.py flash0.txt 30 60 1000000
```

This means the target display is in *flash0.txt*. We want a population of 30 programs, each with 60 instructions, and we'll stop after 1,000,000 generations, or earlier if a program is found.

My run took about an hour and fifteen minutes to produce

```
Minimum MSE: 0.00000000

Program: 547WMSNMNI9W5NI5EI174D95S415NMN3NW1D3S3WSWES5DI3WN3NND5ESW5W

Target display:
[[5 5 0 3 3]
 [5 5 0 3 3]
 [0 0 7 0 0]
 [3 3 0 5 5]
 [3 3 0 5 5]]

Program display:
[[5 5 0 3 3]
 [5 5 0 3 3]
 [0 0 7 0 0]
 [3 3 0 5 5]
 [3 3 0 5 5]]

Firefly position (4,2)
(30 particles, 939087/1000000 iterations, GA, 49 best updates,
 28172640 function evals, 4445.839 sec)
```

Let's interpret the output. First, we're told the MSE was 0. Excellent! We found a program that produces the exact display we need. Next comes the Firefly code. If you run this program with the console interpreter, perhaps adding H at the end to halt instead of loop, you'll get the target display in *flash0.txt*. We're told the firefly is at location (4,2) when the program ends. We'll use this information to move the firefly back to position (2,2).

The final line of the output tells us about the search itself. Of the 1 million generations we set as the upper limit, 939,087 of them were used to find the program. During that time, 28,172,640 programs were tested, resulting in 49 updates to the best program found. No one ever said evolution was fast!

We now have the code for the first display. Searching for the second display produces

```
Minimum MSE: 0.00000000

Program: 7W2ONE9I3ME5EEN33ESW556633W255NW5WI1MNW788M65NW5S9M55W3NW3SN

Target display:
[[3 3 0 5 5]
 [3 3 0 5 5]
 [0 0 7 0 0]
 [5 5 0 3 3]
 [5 5 0 3 3]]
```

```
Program display:
[[3 3 0 5 5]
 [3 3 0 5 5]
 [0 0 7 0 0]
 [5 5 0 3 3]
 [5 5 0 3 3]]

Firefly position (3,3)
(30 particles, 22431/1000000 iterations, GA, 41 best updates, 672960 function
 evals, 106.111 sec)
```

Again, a program delivering the exact display was found, meaning MSE was 0. However, this run found the program after only 22,431 generations and ran for less than two minutes. Sometimes evolution can be fast after all.

Let's pause briefly to consider what the results above represent. We told GA to search for a program with 60 instructions that results in the display we want. How many possible 60-instruction tiny Firefly programs are there? The interpreter understands 17 instructions. Therefore, there are

$$17^{60} = 67,132,880,600,101,282,948,735,355,994,194,317,620,764,746,$$
$$587,861,166,986,121,564,248,710,884,801$$

$$\approx 6.7 \times 10^{73}$$

possible 60-instruction tiny Firefly programs, which is a number so large it loses meaning. Did GA really find the *one* 60-instruction program that generates the target display? No. There are a vast number of 60-instruction Firefly programs resulting in the same display, and any one of them fits the bill. How many are there? That's a good question—I have no intuition as to the answer or how to calculate it. I expect the number is many orders of magnitude greater than 1, especially if a suitable example was found quickly on the second run.

When developing this example, I noticed that the more complex the display, the longer the searches took—and the more often they failed—even though many were close and only off by one or two intensity values in a few places. This result is reasonable. If you try evolving your own displays, which I highly encourage, make them simpler instead of complicated to increase your chances of finding a suitable program in a reasonable amount of time.

Let's move on now and use the code that cost so very many CPU cycles to find. The "Dance Dance" animation of Chapter 15 presented the code pattern we need to animate displays. We have two here, so we'll show grid B, draw the first display on grid A, flip to show grid A, and draw the second on grid B before looping. To use the display code via cut-and-paste, we'll make use of the firefly location information reported above to move the firefly to (2,2) before starting to draw the next display.

For example, *flash0.txt* ends with the firefly at position (4,2). Therefore, we move it back to (2,2) with MNN. Now we can run the code for *flash1.txt*. Likewise, that code ends with the firefly at (3,3), so we move back to (2,2) with MNW.

Listing A-5 contains the full Firefly code.

```
YA        ! show B, draw A
7W2ONE9I3ME5EEN33ESW556633W255NW5WI1MNW788M65NW5S9M55W3NW3SN
MNW
XB        ! show A, draw B
547WMSNMNI9W5NI5EI174D95S415NMN3NW1D3S3WSWES5DI3WN3NND5ESW5W
MNN
```

Listing A-5: Animating the flash displays

If you run the above code with the console interpreter, it will oscillate at a very high rate; however, you can slow it down by putting PPP after MNW and MNN. For the micro:bit, no pause instructions are needed; see the video on the GitHub site.

Radar Sweep

Our next example is quite a bit simpler in terms of displays. We want to make a radar display, one with a rotating "sweep" and a beep when a "target" is present.

We need eight displays for the sweep:

```
0 0 0 0 0    5 0 0 0 0    0 0 5 0 0    0 5 0 0 5
0 0 0 0 0    0 6 0 0 0    0 0 6 0 0    0 0 0 6 0
5 6 7 0 0    0 0 7 0 0    0 0 7 0 0    0 0 7 0 0
0 0 0 0 0    0 0 0 0 0    0 0 0 0 0    0 0 0 0 0
0 0 0 0 0    0 0 0 0 0    0 0 0 0 0    0 0 0 0 0

0 0 0 0 0    0 0 0 0 0    0 0 0 0 0    0 0 0 0 0
0 0 0 0 0    0 0 0 0 0    0 0 0 0 0    0 0 0 0 0
0 0 7 6 5    0 0 7 0 0    0 0 7 0 0    0 0 7 0 0
0 0 0 0 0    0 0 0 6 0    0 0 6 0 0    0 6 0 0 0
0 0 0 0 0    0 0 0 0 5    0 0 5 0 0    5 0 0 0 0
```

If you look across the displays from left to right and top to bottom, you'll see the sweep make a full revolution. The fourth display has a target at (0,1). We'll add a "beep" for the target when the displays are animated.

The displays themselves are in the *GP/radar* directory as *radar0.txt* through *radar7.txt*. To evolve the displays, execute the *search_radar* shell script using

```
> sh search_radar
```

The script is a collection of individual runs of *fly_swarm* to evolve 40-instruction Firefly programs that produce the eight displays above. Each run uses a population of 30 programs and searches for up to 500,000 generations.

If a display fails, meaning the MSE reported in the results file is not 0, just try that one again manually. I needed to run the *radar3.txt* display twice. The first run did not find a program that included the target at (0,1). The second run did and only needed 18 seconds to find it.

With the display programs located, piecing together the full code is an exercise in following the animation pattern from *flash.fly*, where grid B is shown while the first display, *radar0.txt*, is drawn on grid A and then grid A is shown while *radar1.txt* is drawn on grid B, and so on through *radar7.txt*.

The complete code is in Listing A-6.

```
YVA 5383149W7EE27MEIMEWME4IEM6W74M975W932785 MWW   PPPP
XZB 37N387IM381IMIMW7495N19W645E8M9M4M188ISW MSEE  PPPP
YVA 852MM7W4699793554MNE6791594415NSI6N42961 MSS   PPPP
XZB MI57S49173ME83I613MN7MN6E18125IMN95EME5S MSE   PPPP
YVA 1TJ7TF  ! beep
744299818E488E52I4M66I7M1462I5WW7E122IE1     MWW   PPPP
XZB 7E42943MSM76S6617EM55WI36M9454I57I33M5OW MNN   PPPP
YVA 527S43M2S127778795N8E45MW579233117765277 MNN   PPPP
XZB 697SMW6W99857M662M377242MSI83W35ME2125E1 MNNE  PPPP
```

Listing A-6: The radar sweep animation

Note that your code will undoubtedly look different. Each time you evolve code for the displays, you'll end up with a different program, as there are quite probably thousands to millions of 40-instruction Firefly programs that generate each configuration of the sweep. Don't forget to add code to move the firefly back to (2,2) from its end position before starting the next display.

The beep occurs after *radar3.txt* is drawn and shown but before drawing *radar4.txt*. The beep plays with the firefly at (2,2) by setting the duration to 1 and playing note 7, a B above middle C (1TJ7TF).

Bouncing Ball

Our final example animates a ball moving in a figure-eight pattern. The screens are simple: a 2×2 square of intensity 5 LEDs in different positions to move a "ball" from the upper left to the lower right, then across the bottom of the display, up the lower-left-to-upper-right diagonal, and back across the top to the upper left before repeating—12 displays in all:

```
5 5 0 0 0     0 0 0 0 0     0 0 0 0 0     0 0 0 0 0
5 5 0 0 0     0 5 5 0 0     0 0 0 0 0     0 0 0 0 0
0 0 0 0 0     0 5 5 0 0     0 0 5 5 0     0 0 0 0 0
0 0 0 0 0     0 0 0 0 0     0 0 5 5 0     0 0 0 5 5
0 0 0 0 0     0 0 0 0 0     0 0 0 0 0     0 0 0 5 5

0 0 0 0 0     0 0 0 0 0     0 0 0 0 0     0 0 0 0 0
0 0 0 0 0     0 0 0 0 0     0 0 0 0 0     0 0 0 0 0
0 0 0 0 0     0 0 0 0 0     0 0 0 0 0     0 5 5 0 0
0 0 5 5 0     0 5 5 0 0     5 5 0 0 0     0 5 5 0 0
0 0 5 5 0     0 5 5 0 0     5 5 0 0 0     0 0 0 0 0

0 0 0 0 0     0 0 0 5 5     0 0 5 5 0     0 5 5 0 0
0 0 5 5 0     0 0 0 5 5     0 0 5 5 0     0 5 5 0 0
0 0 5 5 0     0 0 0 0 0     0 0 0 0 0     0 0 0 0 0
0 0 0 0 0     0 0 0 0 0     0 0 0 0 0     0 0 0 0 0
0 0 0 0 0     0 0 0 0 0     0 0 0 0 0     0 0 0 0 0
```

The script *search_balls* in the *GP* directory performs the search for each display. The target displays are in the *ball* directory as *ball0.txt* through *ball11* *.txt*. In this case, we are searching for 30-instruction programs using a population of 30 individuals and up to 500,000 generations. The displays are simple enough that the searches are all successful, requiring an average of 966 generations (minimum 239, maximum 2,010) per display.

Listing A-7 shows the full code including the 30-instruction sequence for each ball position.

```
YVA 9MNW145NM425WSWMSII12D678I97M8 MWW   ! (2,4)
XZB 2I6M5IN9I2499W5989D5E775S5WS45 MNE   ! (3,1)
YVA D83281S355NESW89794M6M92926D47 MN    ! (3,2)
XZB 57M9MEMS78I4M46MS6M95D5E5N25WS MNNW  ! (4,3)
YVA MDIMS5E5S5SMW55NS749I4MD3250W9 MSSE  ! (0,1)
XZB W3540SESWM735MII75N3298525ES5S MSS   ! (0,2)
YVA EWS56MW6DD4D55SIMI115WNS8279ME MENN  ! (4,1)
XZB 89MDM4I972S5WEM57D5N5645WW2I4I MEE   ! (2,0)
YVA 2D764I319D9112615NEI7876SMM5NE MSWW  ! (1,4)
XZB 1835MEN5ENW4S97D46NIS678DDSM68 MW    ! (2,3)
YVA 56647MN5E587795NWNMNNS5I331334 MN    ! (3,2)
XZB 78MNM4WN7E4MI85S94715W6N15S25S ME    ! (2,1)
```

Listing A-7: Animating a moving ball

The comment indicates where the sequence leaves the firefly. The move instructions on that line put the firefly back to (2,2) for the next display. No pause instructions are included to run as quickly as possible on the micro:bit.

For the console interpreter, add PPPP after each move of the firefly back to (2,2) to see the ball move.

Discussion

The examples above demonstrate we can successfully evolve Firefly programs. In this section, we'll take a closer look at just what is happening while the search is active by considering the initial and final populations. What do they look like? Next, we'll take a look at a collection of successful searches. Are the programs found all similar? Lastly, while in general it isn't usually possible to know what the shortest program for a task is for Firefly, we can in simple cases. Can genetic programming find the shortest program as well?

The files discussed in this section are found in the *GP/swarm_convergence* directory.

Population Effects

Genetic programming begins with a population of randomly generated programs. As the search progresses, new programs evolve while the size of the population remains fixed. What happens to the diversity of programs during the search? What does "diversity" even mean in this case?

Let's examine two searches, one for a program of 10 instructions and the other for 60 instructions. In both cases, we are trying to generate the display found in *ball/ball0.txt*, the medium intensity square in the upper left of the display. We'll use a population of 30 programs and only consider a successful search, that is, one with an MSE of 0.

The file *swarm_10.txt* contains the best 10-instruction programs found, followed by the initial population of programs and then the final population. There are 30 programs in the population, so there are 61 lines in *swarm_10.txt*.

```
NW55NWS5E4   ! best program found
3596SW14M5   ! initial population
4N92DNW46D
1EIMIWD6M2
I7WM6I47M8
2467316I63
... 25 more lines ...
NW55NWS6E4   ! final population
NE55NWS6E4
NW55NWS6E4
NW55NWS6E4
NW55NWS6E4
... 25 more lines ...
```

From this listing, it's clear the initial population is quite different from the final population and that the latter is much like the best program found. How can we quantify this difference? One way is to measure the distance between the best program found and each of the initial and final population programs. The average distance should tell us something about the diversity of the programs in each population. What distance metric should we use? We could work with the programs as numeric vectors and calculate the distance for vectors in a 10D space. This is the *Euclidean distance*. However, using the Euclidean distance would require converting the program text to numbers.

Another option is to use the edit distance between the programs. The *edit distance* between two strings is how many letters must be changed to turn one string into the other. For example, the edit distance between "darwin" and "charles" is 5: we need five letters to turn "darwin" into "charles." Similarly, the edit distance between "darwin" and "daniel" is 4, whereas the edit distance between "darwin" and "dorwin" is only 1—change the *a* to an *o*.

We need the editdistance library to calculate edit distances in Python. It's easily installed with pip3:

```
> pip3 install editdistance
```

We can use it like so:

```
>>> import editdistance
>>> editdistance.eval("darwin", "charles")
5
>>> editdistance.eval("darwin", "daniel")
4
>>> editdistance.eval("darwin", "dorwin")
1
```

The closer the two strings are to each other, the shorter their edit distance. Let's use this to calculate the average edit distance between the best program and the initial and final populations for *swarm_10.txt* and *swarm_60.txt*. The code we need is in *swarm_edit_distance.py*. See Listing A-8.

```
import numpy as np
import editdistance

prg = [i[:-1] for i in open("swarm_10.txt")]
best = prg[0]
init = prg[1:31]
final= prg[31:]

i = []
for p in init:
    i.append(editdistance.eval(best, p))
```

```
i = np.array(i) / len(init[0])
f = []
for p in final:
    f.append(editdistance.eval(best, p))
f = np.array(f) / len(final[0])
print("Program length 10: %0.3f initial, %0.3f final" % (i.mean(), f.mean()))

#  Program length 60
prg = [i[:-1] for i in open("swarm_60.txt")]
best = prg[0]
init = prg[1:31]
final= prg[31:]

i = []
for p in init:
    i.append(editdistance.eval(best, p))
i = np.array(i) / len(init[0])
f = []
for p in final:
    f.append(editdistance.eval(best, p))
f = np.array(f) / len(final[0])
print("Program length 60: %0.3f initial, %0.3f final" % (i.mean(), f.mean()))
```

Listing A-8: The average edit distance between initial and final populations

The code loads *swarm_10.txt*, calculates the edit distance between the best program and each initial program, and then does the same with the final population of programs before reporting the average for both. It then repeats using *swarm_60.txt*.

If we run the code in Listing A-8 we get

```
Program length 10: 0.920 initial, 0.103 final
Program length 60: 0.857 initial, 0.066 final
```

Note that we divide the edit distance by the program length, either 10 or 60, to meaningfully compare between the different length programs. The number shown above is then a fraction of the program length regardless of the actual program length.

The initial populations are significantly more diverse than the final populations. For the 10-instruction program, the initial population is on average 92 percent different, meaning the difference between the initial set of programs and the best found is almost every instruction. However, the final population is on average only 10 percent, or one instruction, different from the best program. The population has collapsed, diversity has disappeared, and most programs are virtually identical to the best found. The collapse effect is even more pronounced for the 60-instruction programs.

The results above examine what happens to the population during a single successful search. What if we run the search many times? Will we find the same best program each time? Let's try it and see.

Final Program Diversity

Is the best program found by the search the same each time? To answer this question, let's again search for programs generating the *ball0.txt* display. We'll use 10-instruction and 60-instruction programs, as above.

To do this, we run *fly_swarm.py* 10 times, keeping the best program found in *runs_10.txt* or *runs_60.txt*. Each run looks like this:

```
> python3 fly_swarm.py ball/ball0.txt 30 10 10000
```

The best program found is put in *runs_10.txt*, one per line. Only successful searches, that is, those returning an MSE of 0, are kept. As the display is simple, most runs are successful.

Now that we have the 10 best programs for 10 searches, we'll calculate the average edit distance between the programs. If the search produces the same program each time, the average edit distance will be 0. The higher the average edit distance, the more diverse the programs are, even though each program generates the desired display.

Listing A-9 shows what's in *final_program_distance.py*.

```python
import numpy as np
import editdistance

prg = [i[:-1] for i in open("runs_10.txt")]
dist = []
for i in range(len(prg)):
    for j in range(len(prg)):
        if (i == j):
            continue
        dist.append(editdistance.eval(prg[i],prg[j]))
dist = np.array(dist) / len(prg[0])
print()
print("10-instructions: %0.4f +/- %0.4f" % (dist.mean(), dist.std(ddof=1)/np.sqrt(len(dist))))

prg = [i[:-1] for i in open("runs_60.txt")]
dist = []
for i in range(len(prg)):
    for j in range(len(prg)):
        if (i == j):
            continue
        dist.append(editdistance.eval(prg[i],prg[j]))
dist = np.array(dist) / len(prg[0])
print("60-instructions: %0.4f +/- %0.4f" % (dist.mean(), dist.std(ddof=1)/np.sqrt(len(dist))))
```

Listing A-9: The average distance between pairs of best programs found

This listing calculates the edit distance between each pair of best programs for both 10-instruction and 60-instruction programs. Naturally, the edit distance between a program and itself is 0, so we skip those cases. As above, the edit distance is divided by the program length to make it a fraction to allow meaningful comparison between the two.

Listing A-9 produces

```
10-instructions: 0.6467 +/- 0.0148
60-instructions: 0.8337 +/- 0.0037
```

You'll get slightly different results if you re-create *runs_10.txt* and *runs_60.txt* yourself. The output shows the average edit distance and the *standard error of the mean*, or *SE*. The SE is a measure of uncertainty in a mean or average value. For us, a small SE relative to the average indicates that the average is well known.

Let's interpret the values. For a 10-instruction program, we get an average difference of about 65 percent between the best programs found. Recall that each program is a successful program: each one generates the desired display. So even for short programs, there are multiple solutions, and different search runs find different possible solutions. Which solution is located depends on the population's size, the random initial population, and random factors used in crossover and mutation.

As we might suspect, longer programs have many more possible solutions. I suspect this is mainly because of "junk" code; that is, code that doesn't help or hurt because the rest of the code still generates the desired display. We see this, as the average distance between successful 60-instruction programs is about 83 percent. The programs all solve the problem, but they are very different from each other.

Let's search for 1,000 10-instruction programs to generate *ball0.txt* and see how many of them are unique. The code we'll run is in *ball_search.py*. The code dumps the programs to the file *ball_search_results.txt*.

A bit of processing on the output file tells us how many unique 10-instruction programs were generated:

```
>>> ***d = [i[:-1] for i in open("ball_search_results.txt")]***
>>> ***len(set(d))***
985
```

Note that we turn the list of 10-instruction programs into a set, thereby removing duplicates, before asking for the number of items.

Of the 1,000 successful runs looking for a 10-instruction program to generate *ball0.txt*, 985, or 98.5 percent, of them are unique. In other words, there are virtually no duplicates. This is strong support for our belief that there are many possible solutions to any display we care to generate.

Can Genetic Programming Find the Shortest Program?

We usually don't know what the shortest program is to accomplish a given goal. However, for Firefly displays, at least the simple ones, we can know. Let's continue working with the *ball0.txt* display.

If we look at the display, knowing the firefly starts in move mode at position (2,2), we can easily convince ourselves that the shortest possible program to generate the display has seven instructions. There are multiple seven-instruction programs, but no program with six or fewer instructions can create the display. Can genetic programming find these shortest programs? Let's find out.

A command line like the following searches for a seven-instruction Firefly program generating the *ball0.txt* display.

```
> python3 fly_swarm.py ball/ball0.txt 30 7 16000
```

The search terminates after 16,000 generations if no program leading to the display is found. We'll consider those cases to be failures.

Running 10 searches by hand leads to seven successes and three failures. The seven successful programs, sorted alphabetically, are

```
NW5NWSS
NW5NWSW
NW5WNEE
NW5WNEE
NW5WNEE
WN5WNEN
WN5WNES
```

Notice that the same program, NW5WNEE, shows up three of the seven times.

To answer our first question: yes, genetic programming can find the shortest program to generate the display. We also have a hint that one of the programs might be more likely to show up than the others. However, 10 runs are too few to make any definitive statements about how often a solution appears.

Let's repeat the search we did in the previous section and gather 1,000 successful seven-instruction programs to see how often each solution appears (see *ball_search_7.py*). The space of possible seven-instruction programs is smaller than the space of 10-instruction programs, so we do expect a distribution over a finite set of solutions that we might fully enumerate with even 1,000 trials.

The output of *ball_search_7.py* is in *ball_search_7_results.txt*, which contains the best program found for each of the 1,000 successful searches. If we load the results into Python and pass them to NumPy's np.unique function, we'll get back the list of unique best programs and how many times each one appeared.

```
>>> t = [i[:-1] for i in open("ball_search_7_results.txt")]
>>> prg, counts = np.unique(t, return_counts=True)
>>> prg
array(['NW5NWSE', 'NW5NWSN', 'NW5NWSS', 'NW5NWSW', 'NW5WNEE',
       'NW5WNEN', 'NW5WNES', 'NW5WNEW', 'WN5NWSE', 'WN5NWSN',
```

```
            'WN5NWSS', 'WN5NWSW', 'WN5WNEE', 'WN5WNEN', 'WN5WNES',
            'WN5WNEW'], dtype='<U7')
>>> counts
array([68, 58, 67, 62, 71, 80, 61, 54, 62, 58, 59, 61, 52, 62,
        60, 65])
```

We see that there are 16 possible seven-instruction programs leading to the *ball0.txt* display. Each program begins with either NW5 or WN5. This makes sense, as the program needs to set four positions to intensity 5, and the shortest way to get to the nearest ball position is to go north and then west or west and then north. The final four instructions enumerate the ways to move over the four upper-left display positions.

What about the counts? The results show the counts for each outcome over 1,000 searches. We have no strong reason to expect that any of the possible outcomes is to be favored over any of the others; therefore, we expect the counts to be the same in the long run. The counts are not the same, but they might still be consistent with a distribution where each output program is equally likely. How can we test if this is true?

In statistics, a way to test if a set of frequencies is consistent with each being equally likely is to use a χ^2 (chi-square) test. We want to test the observed frequencies, that is, the counts, against another set of expected frequencies, which is the set where each outcome is equally likely. We could write a bit of code to do this, but fortunately for us, SciPy already has what we need.

```
>>> from scipy.stats import chisquare
>>> chisquare(counts)
Power_divergenceResult(statistic=10.911999999999999,
    pvalue=0.7588072298114652)
```

The return value from chisquare that concerns us is the p-value of 0.76. This number can be interpreted as how consistent the counts are with each outcome being equally likely. If the p-value is low, usually if it's much less than 0.05, we might think that the outcomes are not all equally likely. In this case, the p-value of 0.76 implies there is no reason to believe that any outcome, any best seven-instruction program, is any more likely to be found by genetic programming than the others.

The takeaway from this section is that genetic programming can find the smallest program and will find all possible such programs with enough runs of the search.

Final Thoughts

The examples of this appendix demonstrate the utility of genetic programming for evolving Firefly programs. Genetic programming is not widely discussed these days, but it has shown a slow and steady increase in scholarly publications over time, as Figure A-1 illustrates. The plot shows the number of Google Scholar hits by year, matching the string "genetic programming."

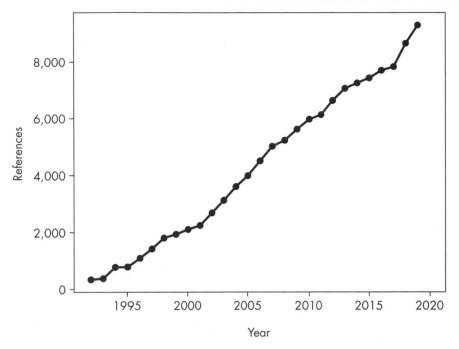

Figure A-1: Number of Google Scholar hits for "genetic programming" by year

We used a GA as the basis for our genetic programming searches; however, there are many other algorithms one might try instead. GA is an evolutionary algorithm, as it simulates evolution to some degree. Another powerful evolutionary algorithm is differential evolution. Beyond evolutionary algorithms are the myriad of swarm intelligence algorithms like particle swarm optimization.

When properly configured, the genetic programming searches above can use these algorithms in place of GA by importing them into *fly_swarm.py* and replacing

```
swarm = GA(obj=obj, npart=npart, ndim=ndim, init=i, tol=1e-12,
        max_iter=niter, bounds=b)
```

with the desired algorithm. For example, to try differential evolution, import *DE.py* and use

```
swarm = DE(obj=obj, npart=npart, ndim=ndim, init=i, tol=1e-12,
        max_iter=niter, bounds=b)
```

Differential evolution and particle swarm optimization are in the *GP* directory. Give them a try, and let me know how it goes. Do the other algorithms work at all? If so, how do they compare to GA?

INDEX

A

ABC, xxix, 47, 195, 428
  definition, 196
  examples
    1337.abc, 198
    dice.abc, 198
    hello.abc, 198
    phone.abc, 198
  implementation, 196
ABC2, 199, 200
  definition, 199
  examples
    add.abc2, 203
    electromechanical
      arithmometer, 210
    hello.abc2, 204
    multiply.abc2, 211
    pi.abc2, 205
  patterns, 215
  Turing completeness, 214
abstract syntax tree, 47
Achelousaurus, 5
Ackermann, Wilhelm, 78
Ada, 19
Adventure (game), 417
Alectrosaurus, 5
ALGOL, 9, 14, 16, 19, 20, 44,
    54, 124
algorithm, 79
Analytical Engine, 7
Anomalocaris, 6
APL, 11, 29, 72
Applesoft, xxv, 13
Applesort, 428
array, 58
array processing, 72
artificial intelligence, 151
assembly (6502), xxvi
Åslund, Jon, 421
AUTOCODE, 9
automata theory, 83

B

Babbage, Charles, 7
Backus, John, 9
BASIC, xxv, 13, 19, 48, 311
BBC micro:bit, xxvi, 373, 412
  configuration, 386
  external speaker, 388
  hardware, 387
Befunge, 297, 420, 428
  commands, 303
  editor, 301
  examples
    befunge.bf, 315
    binary to decimal
      (*bin2dec.bf*), 304
    bridge command (*bridge.bf*), 307
    Brownian motion
      (*brownian.bf*), 310
    calc.bf, 313
    cow.bf, 299
    decimal to hex (*dec2hex.bf*), 311
    dice (*die4.bf*), 308
    die6.bf, 309
    die6_biased.bf, 309
    hello.bf, 302
    line endings (*dos2unix.bf*), 306
    self-modifying code, 312
    zero.bf, 310
  fungeoids, 315
  implementation, 315
  installation, 298
  resources, 315
  Turing completeness, 314
big-endian, 55
Bonacci, Leonardo, 349
Brainfuck, xxix, 162, 268, 271
  definition, 271
  examples
    baby steps, 281
    cat.b, 281
    complement, 283

Brainfuck examples (*continued*)
    countdown0.b, 282
    countdown1.b, 282
    e.b, 293
    factorial2.b, 292
    fib.b, 292
    golden.b, 292
    hanoi.b, 293
    hello.b, 275
    mandelbrot.b, 293
    mult2.b, 291
    mult.b, 290
    multiply, 289
    ones.b, 284
    parity, 286
    parity.b, 288
    prime.b, 293
    random.b, 292
    sierpinski.b, 292
    squares.b, 292
    tictactoe.b, 293
    utm.b, 295
  implementation,
    C, 273
    SNOBOL, 275
  looping, 272
  resources, 292
  Turing completeness, 295
Brodie, Leo, 122
Burgess Shale, 4
bytecode compiler, 46

C

C#, 5, 55
C/C++, xxvii, 5, 19, 28, 44, 54, 55,
    61, 97, 430
Cambrian explosion, 4
Cantor, Georg, 82
cellular automata, 418
chi-square test (χ^2), 452
Chudyk, Mateusz, 423
Church, Alonzo, 78
Church–Turing thesis, 80
CLIPS, xxvii, xxix, 6, 27
  examples
    coin.clp, 170
    factory.clp, 183
    family.clp, 177
    family2.clp, 180
    hello0.clp, 168
    hello1.clp, 168
    irises.clp, 188
    math.clp, 173
    security.clp, 172
    wine.clp, 166
  facts, 169
  installation, 164
  refraction, 168
  rules, 171
  session, 166
COBOL, 9, 14, 124
Collatz conjecture, 236
Collatz, Lothar, 236
Colossal Cave, The (game), 417
Colmerauer, Alain, 21
compiler, 45
  bytecode, 46
  just-in-time, 52
Conway, John, 217
Cooke, Andrew, 416
correlation coefficient, 260
Cristofani, Daniel, 295
Crowther, Will, 417
Curry, Haskell, 38
currying, 38, 70
curve fitting, 344
  least-squares, 344, 365

D

Dahl, Ole-Johan, 16
Dante, 416
data structure, 57
  array, 58
  FIFO, 100
  hash table, 59
  LIFO, 99
  linked list, 58
  tree, 59
data type, 53
Dathanna, 428
  estimate π, 428
De Stijl movement, 261
decision problem, 78
decision tree, 184
  Gini score, 186
declarative language, 21

declarative programming, 70
deep learning, xxvii
differential evolution, 453
Dijkstra, Edsger, 65, 127
disassembler, 53
discriminant, 360
double buffering, 374
duck typing, 28
dynamic scoping, 61
dynamically typed language, 54

E

edit distance, 447
Edmontonia, 5
emulator, 428
Euclidean distance, 153, 447
Eusthenopteron, 6
evolutionary algorithm, 435, 453
expert system, 163
    business rule management
        system, 190
    components, 164, 165
    DROOLS, 190
    forward chaining, 165
    weaknesses, 191

F

Farber, David, 124
Feurzeig, Wally, 15
Fibonacci sequence, 24
Filska, xxviii, xxix, 47, 319
    arithmetic, 327
    arrays, 371
    comparisons, 327
    environment, 322
    examples
        array.filska, 371
        fib.filska, 350
        Fibonacci sequence, 348
        fitting a line (*linfit.filska*), 365
        hello.filska, 343
        hello2.filska, 346
        polynomial roots, 359
        pseudorandom numbers
            (*random.filska*), 352
        roots.filska, 360
        sierpinski.filska, 356
    flow control, 323

idioms, 370
implementation, 331
input/output, 330
mathematical functions, 329
memory, 325
operation, 332
philosophy, 319
syntax, 321
Turing completeness, 371
Firefly, xxviii, xxix, 47, 373
    display, 377
    environment, 374
    examples
        animation, 400, 406
        ball_search_7.py, 451
        ball_search.py, 450
        Beethoven, 402
        building and testing, 392
        bundling, 395
        Dance Dance, 405
        dance.fly, 408
        dance_loop.fly, 409
        dance_music.fly, 409
        final_program_distance.py, 449
        flash.fly, 444
        fly_swarm.py, 439
        fly_time.fly, 398
        hi2.fly, 400
        hi.fly, 393
        ode.fly, 404
        random2.fly, 401
        random.fly, 401
        swarm_edit_distance.py, 447
        tea_timer.fly, 409
        timer, 397
    genetic programming, 434
    implementation, 380
    instructions, 376
    miscellaneous instructions, 379
    movement, 376
    music, 378
    Turing completeness, 412
first-class object, 38, 70
floating-point number, 211
flow control, 44, 64
    repetition, 66
    selection, 65
    structured, 65
    unstructured, 64

Forth, xxvi, xxix, 6, 55, 215, 264, 430
  books, 122
  constant, 113
  dictionary, 97
  input/output, 116
  installation, 98
  memory use, 111, 113
  postfix notation, 98
  sqrt.4th, 119
  stack, 99
  stack-effect comment, 101
  word, 97, 103
FORTRAN, xxvi, 9, 14, 54
forward chaining, 165
fractal, 356
FRACTRAN, xxix, 9, 47, 55, 64, 83, 217, 290
  Collatzian games, 241
  description, 218
  examples
    add2.frac, 224
    add3.frac, 225
    add.frac, 221
    collatz.frac, 237
    copy.frac, 230
    hello.frac, 238
    max.frac, 227
    mult.frac, 232
    polygame.frac, 240
    prime10.frac, 236
    primes.frac, 234
    sub.frac, 226
  implementation
    Python, 220
    Scheme, 219
  importance, 242
  loops, 231
  operation, 224
  POLYGAME, 239
  PRIMEGRAME, 234
  register machine, 222
  registers, 223
  state, 223, 225
  Turing completeness, 239
functional brain imaging, xxvii
functional language, 36

G

Game of Life, 217
GDL, 73
genetic programming, 412, 433
  algorithm, 434
  code, 440
  crossover, 434
  defining displays, 435
  examples
    bouncing ball, 444
    radar sweep, 443
    warning sign, 440
    warning sign animation, 443
  Firefly, 434
  Firefly interpreter, 435
  fitness value, 433, 437, 438
  genetic algorithm, 434, 437
  mutation, 434
  over time, 452
  population, 435
  population effects, 446
  program diversity, 449
  program length, 450
  representing Firefly code, 438
  search space, 442
  search success, 442
  swarm, 435
Glennie, Alick, 9
Go, 4
Gödel, Kurt, 222
Gödel numbering, 222
Goldberg, Adele, 27
golden ratio (ϕ), 349
Goldilocks, 107
Griswold, Ralph, 124

H

Hallucigenia, 4, 6
halting problem, 78, 241
  proof, 79
Harper, Margaret, 9
Harvard architecture, 272, 375
hash table, 59
Heber, Sean, 423, 425
higher-order function, 40, 70
Hilbert, David, 78

histogram, 259
Hopper, Grace, 9
HyperCard, 427
HyperTalk, 427

I

Icon, 162
IDL, 73
imperative programming, 68
incompleteness theorem, 222
Infocom, 417
Ingalls, Dan, 27
INTERCAL, 416
    manual, 419
    operators, 418
    Turing completeness, 417
interpreter, 45
Iverson, Kenneth, 11

J

Jacquard loom, 6
Java, xxvii, 5, 54, 97
Julia, 4
just-in-time compiler, 52

K

Kay, Alan, 27
Kemeny, John, 13
Kilminster, Devin, 236
Kneusel, Paul, 408
Kotlin, 4
Kowalski, Robert, 21
Kurtz, Thomas, 13

L

lambda calculus, 78
lambda functions, 38
lexer, 46
lexical scoping, 60
linked list, 58
Lisp, 9, 164
little-endian, 55
Liu, Q. P., 417
Logo, 15, 27
Lomont, Chris, 230

Lovelace, Ada, 7
Łukasiewicz, Jan, 98
Lyon, James, 416

M

Müller, Urban, 271
machine learning, 151
    accuracy, 153
    classifier, 151
    classifying, 152
    decision tree, 184
    deep learning, 151
    distance, 153
    feature vector, 152
    model, 152
    nearest neighbor, 151
    neural network, 151, 295
Malbolge, 415
    hello example, 416
Matlab, 11, 73
Mauchly, John, 8
McCarthy, John, 9
microcontroller, 49, 55, 121, 375
MicroPython, 381
Minsky, Marvin, 83
model of computation, 79
    finite-state machine, 83
    Minsky register machine, 83
Modula-2, xxvi, 10, 16, 19, 66, 199
Modula-3, 199
Mondrian, Piet, 243
Monte Carlo simulation, 355
Moore, Charles, 98
Morgan-Mar, David, 244

N

network order, 55
neural network, 295
Newton's method, 120
NumPy, 59, 73
Nygaard, Kristen, 16

O

Oberon, 199
Oberon-2, 199

object-oriented programming,
17, 28, 68
  encapsulation, 68
  function overloading, 69
  inheritance, 68, 70
  polymorphism, 68
Olmstead, Ben, 415
Opabinia, 4, 6
operator
  dyadic, 12
  monadic, 12
  unary, 12
Ostracoderm, 6

P

paleontology, 4
Papert, Seymour, 15
parser, 46
particle swarm optimization, 453
Pascal, xxvi, 10, 16, 19, 54, 55, 430
Perl, 29, 63
Perlis, Alan, 295
PICO, 50
Piet, xxix, 243, 300, 428
  codel, 246
  codel chooser, 249
  colors, 245
  Composition II, 261
  direction pointer, 249
  examples
    add.png, 246, 251
    compositionII_pm30.png, 266
    countdown.png, 254
    countdown3.png, 255
    hi.png, 244, 253
    mondrian.png, 265
    npiet-trace.png, 251
    piet_colors.png, 245
    pseudorandom numbers, 257
    random.png, 257
    roll32.png, 248
    taxi_map.png, 426
  flow control, 249
  implementations (other), 267
  installation, 244
  looping, 268
  numbers, 245
  program flow, 250
  resources, 266

  roll, 248
  specifying commands, 247
  Turing completeness, 268
PL/I, 10, 14
Plankalkül, 8, 44, 298
Polonsky, Ivan, 124
Possum Lodge, 432
Pressey, Chris, 298
prime factorization, 222
primitive data type, 55
programming language, 6
  ABC, xxix, 47, 195, 428
  ABC2, 199
  Ada, 19
  ALGOL, 9, 14, 16, 19, 20, 44,
    54, 124
  APL, 11, 29, 72
  Applesoft, xxv, 13
  assembly, 8
  assembly (6502), xxvi
  AUTOCODE, 9
  BASIC, xxv, 13, 19, 48, 311
  Befunge, 297, 420, 428
  Brainfuck, xxix, 162, 268, 271
  C#, 5, 55
  C/C++, xxvii, 5, 19, 28, 44, 54, 55,
    61, 97, 430
  CLIPS, xxvii, xxix, 6, 27
  COBOL, 9, 14, 124
  Dathanna, 428
  definition, 44
  diagram of development, 7
  Filska, xxviii, xxix, 47, 319
  Firefly, xxviii, xxix, 47, 373
  Forth, xxvi, xxix, 6, 55, 215,
    264, 430
  FORTRAN, xxvi, 9, 14, 54
  FRACTRAN, xxix, 9, 47, 55, 64, 83,
    217, 290
  GDL, 73
  generation, 98
  Go, 4
  HyperTalk, 427
  Icon, 162
  IDL, 73
  INTERCAL, 416
  Java, xxvii, 5, 54, 97
  Julia, 4
  Kotlin, 4

Lisp, 9, 164
Logo, 15, 27
Malbolge, 415
Matlab, 11, 73
Modula-2, xxvi, 10, 16, 19, 66, 199
Modula-3, 199
Oberon, 199
Oberon-2, 199
Pascal, xxvi, 10, 16, 19, 54, 55, 430
Perl, 29, 63
PIC0, 50
Piet, xxix, 243, 300, 428
PL/I, 10, 14
Plankalkül, 8, 44, 298
Prolog, 21, 39, 165
Python, xxvii, 5, 11, 29, 61, 97, 125
Scala, 4
Scheme, 55
Shakespeare, 421
Short Code, 8, 44
Simula, 10, 16, 20
Smalltalk, 27, 54
SNOBOL, xxix, 6, 54, 61, 62, 64
Standard ML, 36, 70
Suzy, 315
Swift, 4
Taxi, 425
Visual Basic, 13
Whirl, 423
Whitespace, 419
programming paradigm, 44, 68
    array processing, 72
    declarative, 21, 70
    functional, 36
    imperative, 68
    object-oriented, 17, 28, 68
programs
    1337.abc, 198
    add.abc2, 203
    add2.frac, 224
    add3.frac, 225
    add.frac, 221
    add.png, 246, 251
    alice.sno, 144
    array.filska, 371
    array.sno, 134
    ball_search_7.py, 451
    ball_search.py, 450
    befunge.bf, 315

bin2dec.bf, 304
bridge.bf, 307
brownian.bf, 310
calc.bf, 313
cat.b, 281
classify.sno, 155
coin.clp, 170
collatz.frac, 237
compositionII_pm30.png, 266
copy.frac, 230
copy.sno, 150
countdown0.b, 282
countdown1.b, 282
countdown3.png, 255
countdown.png, 254
cow.bf, 299
dance.fly, 408
dance_loop.fly, 409
dance_music.fly, 409
dates2.sno, 144
dates.sno, 142
dec2hex.bf, 311
dice.abc, 198
die4.bf, 308
die6.bf, 309
die6_biased.bf, 309
dos2unix.bf, 306
e.b, 293
factorial2.b, 292
factory.clp, 183
family.clp, 177
family2.clp, 180
fib.b, 292
fib.filska, 350
final_program_distance.py, 449
flash.fly, 444
fly_swarm.py, 439
fly_time.fly, 398
golden.b, 292
hanoi.b, 293
hello.abc, 198
hello.abc2, 204
hello.b, 275
hello.bf, 302
hello.filska, 343
hello.frac, 238
hello.sno, 125
hello0.clp, 168
hello1.clp, 168

programs (*continued*)
   hello2.filska, 346
   hello2.sno, 126
   hi2.fly, 400
   hi.fly, 393
   hi.png, 244, 253
   indirect.sno, 131
   irises.clp, 188
   linfit.filska, 365
   mandelbrot.b, 293
   math.clp, 173
   max.frac, 227
   menu.sno, 130
   mondrian.png, 265
   mult2.b, 291
   mult.b, 290
   mult.frac, 232
   multiply.abc2, 211
   npiet-trace.png, 251
   ode.fly, 404
   ones.b, 284
   parity.b, 288
   phone.abc, 198
   pi.abc2, 205
   piet_colors.png, 245
   polygame.frac, 240
   poly.sno, 146
   prime10.frac, 236
   prime.b, 293
   primes.frac, 234
   random2.fly, 401
   random.b, 292
   random.filska, 353
   random.fly, 401
   random.png, 257
   roll32.png, 248
   roots.filska, 360
   security.clp, 172
   sierpinski.b, 292
   sierpinski.filska, 357
   squares.b, 292
   sub.frac, 226
   swarm_edit_distance.py, 447
   taxi_map.png, 426
   tea_timer.fly, 409
   temperature.sno, 128
   tictactoe.b, 293
   uppercase.sno, 150
   utm.b, 295

   wine.clp, 166
   zero.bf, 310
Prolog, 21, 39, 44, 165
Python, xxvii, 5, 11, 29, 61, 97, 125

Q

quantum computer, 83

R

record, 55
recursion, 25
register machine, 222
resources, 428
   compilers and intepreters, 430
   data structures, 430
   programming languages, 429
Ridgeway, Richard, 9
Rule 102, 419
Rule 238, 419
Rule 30, 419

S

Sarcopterygii, 6
Scala, 4
Scheme, 55
Schmitt, William, 8
Schoenfelder, Erik, 244
scikit-learn, 184
semantics, 44
Shafto, Michael, 123
Shakespeare, 421
   compiler, 421
   interpreter, 421
   live actor, 422
Shakespeare, William, 421
Shetland Islands, 319
Short Code, 8, 44
Simula, 10, 16, 20
Smalltalk, 27, 54
Smilodon, 5
SNOBOL, xxix, 6, 54, 61, 62, 64
   arrays, 134
   data structures, 125
   examples
      alice.sno, 144
      array.sno, 134
      classify.sno, 155

copy.sno, 150
dates2.sno, 144
dates.sno, 142
hello2.sno, 126
hello.sno, 125
indirect.sno, 131
menu.sno, 130
poly.sno, 146
temperature.sno, 128
uppercase.sno, 150
flow control, 125, 127
functions, 146
indirection, 131
input/output, 149
installation, 124
looping, 127
name, 124
pattern matching, 125
patterns, 139
philosophy, 124
predicates, 128
primitive data types, 128
tables, 134, 137
user-define data types, 133
Solomon, Cynthia, 15
standard error (of the mean), 450
Standard ML, 36, 70
static scoping, 60
statically typed language, 54
strongly typed language, 54
structure, 55
structured language, 65
swarm intelligence, 435, 453
Swift, 4
Swift, Jonathan, 55
syntax, 44
system
    Amiga, 271
    Apple II, xxv, 13, 48, 55, 103,
        121, 428
    Atari 2600, xxv
    BBC micro:bit, xxvi, 373, 386, 412
    BeagleBoard, 122
    ENIAC, 8
    Jupiter ACE, 103
    Macintosh, 427
    Manchester Baby, 8, 375
    Raspberry Pi Zero, 122

TRS-80, xxvi
UNIVAC, 8, 9

T

tail recursion, 27
Taxi, 425
    flow control, 427
    implementation, 427
    RPN calculator, 427
testing pseudorandom number
        generators, 354
Torres y Quevedo, Leonardo, 210
tree, 59
trit (ternary digit), 416
Turing, Alan, 78
Turing complete, xxvi, 83
Turing machine, xxvi, 79, 241, 272
    computable sequence, 82
    description number, 82
    examples, 88
    implementation, 84
    standard description, 81
    universal, 81
Turing tar-pit, 296
Turner, Nick, 427

U

undecidable, 241
unstructured language, 64
untyped language, 55

V

variable scope, 59
    dynamic, 61
    lexical, 60
Visual Basic, 13
von Neumann architecture, 83, 375

W

weakly typed language, 54
Whirl, 423
    1+1 = 2, 425
    Fibonacci, 423
    instructions, 423
    Turing completeness, 425

Whitespace, 419
   IDE, 420
   Turing completeness, 419
Wiberg, Karl, 421
Wirth, Niklaus, 19
WolframAlpha, 239
Woods, Don, 416
write-only programming language, 121

X

xyzzy, 418

Z

Zork (game), 417
Zuse, Konrad, 8, 211

Never before has the world relied so heavily on the Internet to stay connected and informed. That makes the Electronic Frontier Foundation's mission—to ensure that technology supports freedom, justice, and innovation for all people—more urgent than ever.

For over 30 years, EFF has fought for tech users through activism, in the courts, and by developing software to overcome obstacles to your privacy, security, and free expression. This dedication empowers all of us through darkness. With your help we can navigate toward a brighter digital future.

ELECTRONIC FRONTIER FOUNDATION **EFF**

RESOURCES

Visit *https://nostarch.com/strange-code/* for errata and more information.

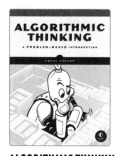